CBC Radio's
Mountaintop
M U S I C

25 Canadian Artists, their favourite music & books

Edited by Michael O'Halloran

Bayeux Arts

Copyright © 2000 Bayeux Arts, Inc.

Published by:
Bayeux Arts, Inc.
Calgary, Alberta, Canada

Designed by Boldface Technologies Inc.
Edmonton, Alberta, Canada

Canadian Cataloguing in Publication Data

ISBN: 1-896209-56-4

1. Musicians–Canada–Interviews. 2. Artists–Canada–Interviews
I. O'Halloran, Michael. II. Title: Mountaintop music (Radio program)
ML205.5,C32 2000   780'.92'271   C00-911221-9

First Printing: October, 2000

Printed in Canada

All rights reserved. No part of this publication may be reproduced, stored in a retrieval system, or transmitted, in any form or by any means, electronic, mechanical, recording, or otherwise, without the prior written permission of the publisher, except in the case of a reviewer, who may quote brief passages in a review to print in a magazine or newspaper, or broadcast on radio or television. In the case of photocopying or other reprographic copying, users must obtain a licence from the Canadian Copyright Licencing Agency.

The Publisher gratefully acknowledges the financial support of the Canada Council for the Arts, the Alberta Foundation for the Arts, and the Government of Canada through the Book Publishing Industry Development Program.

Photo Credits:

page 17–Jeth Weinrich; page 25–Birgit Freybe Bateman; page 37–David Cooper;
page 77–Michael Burke, Northern Pictures; page 107–John Weir;
page 134–Terry Hancey; page 148–David Gray; page 170–Denise Grant;
page 214–Robert Nelson; page 225–Todd Korol; page 242–Andrew MacNaughtan

*To my mom and dad for never discouraging me,
even when it was clear I didn't have a clue.*

ACKNOWLEDGEMENTS

*You do not produce a CBC Radio show for 9 years
without the help of many people.*

*Thanks to les siemieniuk, Joanne Karlsson,
Susan Cardinal, Romie Christie and Pat Fogg.*

*To David, Judy and Andrea, it was my honour
and privilege to have worked with you.
Three distinct styles with one common thread, class.*

CONTENTS

 7 W.O. MITCHELL

 17 JANN ARDEN

 25 ROBERT BATEMAN

 37 EVELYN HART

 48 BOBBY CURTOLA

 60 STEVE SMITH

 68 RITA MacNEIL

 77 PAUL QUARRINGTON

 83 BEN WICKS

 98 TOM JACKSON

 107 DOUGLAS COPELAND

 114 BURTON CUMMINGS

 128 CINDY CHURCH

PETER GZOWSKI 134

OSCAR LOPEZ 148

GORDON PINSEN 159

BUFFY SAINTE-MARIE 170

TIMOTHY FINDLEY 182

TOMMY HUNTER 192

ERNIE COOMBS 203

KAREN KAIN 214

IAN TYSON 225

MORDECAI RICHLER 232

MURRAY McLAUCHLAN 242

FREEMAN PATTERSON 254

FOREWORD

If it wasn't for a tropical storm in Thailand, *Mountaintop Music* may never have been.

In 1989 I left the CBC to travel the world with my wife Donna. We spent some time living as beach bums on the island of Koh Samui. One hot muggy night, as we prepared to go out for dinner, a tropical storm blew in. We decided to wait it out. We always carried a short wave radio with us and as the storm raged I began fiddling with the dial and tuned in the BBC World Service. The show was 'Desert Island Discs', a program that has been running in England for well over 50 years. This particular show featured a knitter, whose name I have since forgotten, who knit extravagant, wildly-expensive sweaters for the likes of Princess Diana and Barbra Streisand. As a radio producer I listened with morbid curiosity. I couldn't imagine an hour-long interview show, with one guest, sustaining itself. Well it did that and more. I was completely engaged. I loved hearing about his rise to the top of the fashion world and the very personal reasons why he chose the Beatles and Bach to take to his desert island. That night I scribbled a note in my travel journal 'if I ever work at the CBC again, this is the kind of show I want to produce.' Seven months later on April 20, 1991, *Mountaintop Music* with host David Gell debuted. To be perfectly honest I thought it would have a short shelf life, yet another radio feature that would eventually lose steam and quietly fade away. How wrong I was.

Mountaintop Music was a show like no other on CBC Radio. Where else could you listen to someone like Karen Kain or W.O. Mitchell tell their life story in their own words and, on top of that, play D.J. by choosing the music that mattered to them most. It was always a surprise to hear that a cowboy like Ian Tyson listens to Miles Davis at the ranch or that Joe Clark throws on a Bob Dylan cd at home. Common industry wisdom has it that any interview that runs over 5 or 6 minutes means you are demanding too much from the audience. With that as a measure *Mountaintop Music* seemed a dicey gamble. A full hour, sometimes two, in conversation with notable Canadians talking about their childhood, loves, tragedies and inspirations.

The premise of the show was simple. We asked the guests to imagine themselves secluded on a mythical mountain peak with only their favourite music and one book for company. They also were asked to choose a location in the world where they would like to spend their final days. Montreal Canadian great Ken Dryden chose the dressing room. Our first guest was 'Crazy Canuck' Ken Read. We never looked back. In 9 years the guests ranged from opera superstar Ben Heppner to CBC journalist Knowlton Nash to Wendy and Trevor McGrath, a couple who travelled the world for 17 years in their Volkswagon van.

In this collection I decided to focus on some of the memorable artists we have interviewed—a wonderful cross section of Canadian singers, authors, dancers, photographers and painters. The most difficult part was deciding who to exclude. Perhaps a follow up book could include Pierre Berton, Maynard Ferguson and Lorna Crozier.

In 18 years I have produced many shows at CBC Radio, national, regional and local. The years on *Mountaintop Music* were by far the most rewarding of all. I think the following pages will explain why.

Michael O'Halloran
September 29, 2000

THE INTERVIEWERS

David Gell has been in the broadcast business for over 60 years. He made his name as a popular host at Radio Luxembourg where he hosted the Sunday night *Top Twenty* program with some ten million listeners. He hosted many television shows in England including *Ready, Steady, Go* and the BBC's *Juke Box Jury*. In those years he interviewed everyone from Nat King Cole to Peters Sellers to A.B.B.A. David moved his family back to Calgary in 1977 where he anchored the *CBC Evening News* and had a long successful radio career including hosting *Saturday Side Up and Sunday Arts*. He was the original host of *Mountaintop Music* from 1991 to 1994.

Judy Hamill has just begun her third season as producer and host of *Daybreak Alberta*, the weekend morning show on CBC radio. Judy has hosted many CBC programs including *The Homestretch, Saturday Side Up, Sunday Arts* and the network show *That Time of the Night*. In 1995 Judy hosted *Mountaintop Music*. Judy's own *Mountaintop Music* would include Harry Nilsson, George Gershwin and Chopin.

Andrea Marantz is a broadcast journalist, documentary-maker, writer and actor. She began her broadcasting career as a producer with the *Radio Show* with Jack Farr. She wrote and hosted nationally broadcast CBC Radio programs for *The Arts Today, Ideas, Open House, Tapestry and the Arts Report*. Andrea was also the voice of *Saturday Side Up* and *Sunday Arts*. Andrea hosted *Mountaintop Music* 1996 to 1999.

W. O. MITCHELL
WITH DAVID GELL, 1993

DG You were born and raised in Weyburn, Saskatchewan, which was I would think a pretty small town to have been in. Your childhood home is still standing, is it?

WO Yes it is. It's a three-storey house on sixth street, about three blocks before the end of the street and the prairie.

DG If I were to take you there today, what feelings would come to you?

WO It's difficult. I had to be in Weyburn for some reason about a year or so ago. We drove by and I saw it, and what happens so often—I think it's universal—something from childhood that you remember so vividly, and you return to it decades later, somebody shrank it! It isn't that big at all. And this really struck me, but I have such memories of it. On the third floor was a billiard room.

DG Were your parents from the prairies?

WO No. No, my father was from Waterdown. My grandfather in 1849 came over from County Down and homesteaded in Waterdown just outside of Hamilton. My father—he was an elocutionist—he put himself through Victoria College at the University of Toronto, in medicine and pharmacy. He ended up a pharmacist. Two ways—one was the Duke of Waterdown, which was a bold Angus bull that I guess was internationally famous and he'd raised it himself and what not. The funds from the Duke of Waterdown and then honoraria from reciting, then he and his brother, Alec, ended up with a drugstore on Queen Street, or King Street in Hamilton. But anyway, I'll cut it short, in 1904 he came west to Weyburn, where he built his drugstore.

DG How did he meet your mother then?

WO My mother, who came from Clinton, Parsons Corners, and mother was an eminent Victorian in that they knew they were upper class, and I mean she had taken music lessons, she was a beautiful contralto, and her friends were people like Aunt Nel—that was Nel Bill, that was the Bill Piano Factory. Anyway, she ended up training as a nurse at the New York General Hospital—McGill wasn't good enough, or Toronto wasn't good enough; it had to be down there. And my Uncle Will and my grandmother and my Auntie Josie came out and homesteaded and built their sod hut just south of Weyburn, so mother came out and visited them. And it coincided with the typhoid epidemic that hit the homesteaders, and mother was called into volunteer service as a nurse, and of course my father, who was the pharmacist, was also doing medical help. That's when they met. Mother went back to New York and three years later she returned and married my dad. The year of the blue snow, the dreadful winter of aught six and aught seven, New Year's day.

DG What a welcoming for her that must have been. How many children did your parents have, then?

WO Four. Four boys. I was the second. My brother Jack was first, I was next, Bob was next, Dickie was next. There are just Jack and I left.

DG Let's go back if we could to those earliest days of growing up with your brothers on the prairies. I get a picture of, you know, gopher shoots, chasing girls, swimming in the river. Is that the kind of life it was?

WO Yeah, yeah it was. It seems cliché, you know, but you see our home, on sixth street, was just two blocks from the edge of town, what was then the outer edge of town. The other important thing to me was July and August were when we would go to our cottage at Carlisle Lake in the Moose Mountains, which were really just skimpy little hills and the trickle down of the Black Hills of the Dakotas. And those summers, July and August at Carlisle Lake—that's the really vivid part for me.

DG Your dad was a druggist. And did that form a sort of focal point for you, personally?

WO Well, it did through my mother. My mother worshipped doctors and she wanted one of her four sons to be a doctor. Now, she never said so, but I think subconsciously she felt she had compromised slightly by marrying a pharmacist instead of a doctor.

DG In fact he died when you were only six years old?

WO Six going on seven.

DG Do you remember him vividly?

WO Yes I do, strangely. Strangely. He died as a result of a continuing and chronic gall bladder problem that wasn't properly taken care of, and made two visits to Mayo Clinic in Rochester after… Anyway, after the first one there was a gap of probably two years at least. He was virtually bedridden—well came to be—and one of my most vivid recollections is of that canary yellow foot of his sticking out of the white sheet in the bed, and I spent a lot of time in bed with him. He taught me to read at the age of four.

DG Really to read?

WO To read out of the *Regina Leader Post*. Then there are other things. He always brought home a present—a balloon, a sucker. What you get are visual flashes. Pink eye—have you ever heard of pink eye? One of my most vivid recollections is in the bathroom on the second floor, and the sting of it as, with my head back, he put drops in my eyes for pink eye. And another one called crossing streams. Have you ever heard of that?

DG No. What's that?

WO It's a ritual. It's a male ritual. When both of ya have to take a leak at the same time you stand at the toilet bowl and you cross streams. Oh yes, my father… Well then, the other thing is that mother intended him to remain with us, so she was always referring to him.

DG The Knox Presbyterian Church was very much the centre of town. Was that because it was the centre of town, a place you liked to go, or did you feel an affiliation anyhow?

WO Well, of course as a child you had to go down to the basement for Sunday school every Sunday. Well you also went to church with your parents and then at a certain point the minister would say, okay, get the kids downstairs to where they belong. So it was an automatic ritual. Actually, the church didn't, and formal religion didn't last all that long with me. I finally quit going to Sunday school when I was 10. I didn't want any more of it.

DG That was your decision.

WO It was too unchallenging and stupid.

DG Really? What did you find challenging if church and Sunday school were not challenging? What did you find challenging at 10?

WO What did I find challenging? Well, with my father dead, going and finding another book in the three walls stacked with his library, and reading, reading, reading, reading—all of Mark Twain, all of Zane Grey, Keats, all of Wordsworth. I mean it didn't matter, and once he started me reading I was addicted. That's what I found challenging.

DG What age were you when, was it tuberculosis, struck you and you had to leave the prairies and go to St. Petersburg, Florida?

WO Yeah. I must have picked it up in raw farm milk from Uncle Jim's, south of Weyburn, probably when I was about 10 years old. Then there was an incubation period I guess, and when I was 12, on the gym ladder, and I was swinging and I fell off and I landed on my wrist, and the next thing I knew it was aching and sore. And then when I held it and squeezed it, it squished, and I was sent in to the Galloway Clinic in Winnipeg and it was diagnosed that I had bone TB. And I lost the use of my right arm; I had to learn to write left-handed. I'm ambidextrous, did you know that? I write as crappy with my left hand as I write with my right one. Then the doctor said, if you get this boy down to a southern climate it might be a good idea. So we went down there and we would be down, but then July and August we'd be back at our cottage at the lake.

DG So you were being schooled as an American?

WO I was a graduate of St. Petersburg Senior High School.

DG Was it a difficult or an easy transition for you?

WO It was very exciting. I mean, come on. The flat, empty billiard table of the prairies—the odd crocus here and there—and then to go down with the brilliance of the tropics, of blow-torching poinsettias, palm trees, and a tide of mint green jelly fish coming in…

DG How long in fact were you in Florida?

WO Four years.

DG And the TB?

WO The TB, by the time I got out and went up and went in—as my mother desired—in to pre-med, I had taken the brace off and I was doing fine until my second year, and it flared up again. And I lost all my labs and had to switch into arts courses.

DG Had you shared your mother's enthusiasm for a medical career?

WO I'd thought I had. Subsequently I realized that… I don't think I'd have made a very good doctor. I think my empathy quality is too strong and powerful; I think it would interfere with an objective assistance to vulnerable people. And it was a beautiful disaster because I then read philosophy.

DG And at that point let's stop for your first choice of music. Now I must ask you about music in your life. Is it important to you, or not?

WO I have to make a public confession. My family knows it. I think I'm tone deaf; however, that does not mean that I am not moved and I do not respond and I do not bond, to music. I think I'm not a bad creative partner to music and, indeed, probably because of my association with my Scottish side of my family—my grandma, Maggie MacMurray—I get a gut thrill feeling of (and this probably argues that I am tone deaf) with the sound of the bag pipes. They really, really get to me.
[MUSIC]

DG You returned to the prairies from Florida right in the middle of the depression. Were you in any way prepared for what you were to see?

WO No. But we had to take it—it happened. And I guess we assumed—we didn't question, most of us—I didn't wonder why everybody was out of work, and on occasion, several times, went as long as three days without food. It did two different things. It did one thing or the other. It turned a number of those old jokers into tight, careful, no risk taking people; or else, I made it through that, I'll gamble again, so what if I blow it—I survived that, I will again. So it either freed you or it enslaved you.

DG What did it do to you?

WO It freed me. It made me. I mean, I've said I'm not a gambler, but I am—If the biggest gamble anybody ever took is anybody who decides to not have a steady job and be on his own and practise an art in a materialist society. Come on, that's the biggest gamble of them all.

DG You started sort of gambling, I suppose, because you moved around. You traveled in Europe, you worked for three years in Seattle, eventually moving to High River. Were you just sort of discovering yourself as you were discovering the world?

WO I don't know, I guess it was just a sort of current of life that you were on… like I finished university. The summer before I had shipped out in a Greek freighter and been in France and Spain, and I was to meet a friend of mine, Connie Benson, in Bellingham, and his uncle was head of McCormick Steamship Lines. And it was both of us wanted to ship out to South America. Unfortunately, the longshoremen's strike hit about that time. That was the end of that. So I was then in Seattle for I guess two years, maybe three.

DG I'm curious about the writing. You sort of referred to doing some writing, was there a point at which it entered your life?

WO The real thing came when the six months I was in—or five months—in Europe, and shipped out. I wrote home every day. I wrote every day—I kept a diary, I was a good boy. And I knew my mother would be worried sick about me. She should have been, too. And when I got back to university a friend of mine had started a literary quarterly, the Tobin—I believe it's still published today—and that was the first place I was ever published. He said to me, Bill, when you were over in Europe did you ever write anything? And I said, oh God, yeah. The result was a four-part serial called *Panacea for Panhandlers*. That was his cute title. And I saw my byline for the first time.

DG How did that make you feel?

WO It was terrific, just terrific.

DG When did you meet your wife, Myrna?

WO 1940.

DG And you've been married now for over fifty years.

WO That's right.

DG Do you think it'll last?

WO I don't know.

DG Sure it will. Now, you entered the publishing world really with a bang, with *Who Has Seen the Wind?*—it came out in 1947. Was it a difficult book to write?

WO They're all difficult. When I ended up in Edmonton, before I married Myrna—it was Myrna who mentioned him to me, Professor Salter. So I gave him my three one-act plays, a novella that I hadn't done anything with, and short stories. And one of the things that I handed in to him was something I didn't think of as writing. I'd never done it before—I just sat down and, with pencil and paper, was remembering those visits out to the cemetery south of Weyburn, at my father's grave, and a gopher that sat up and I was angry because he had dug a hole in my father's grave that wasn't there the previous fall, and then looking up and seeing my mother crying. Well, I ended up with about five pages of this irresponsible, disorderly, chaotic remembrance. Salter was turned on by it. He said, I'd like to know what happened to that boy before and what became of him afterwards, and that turned out to be the genesis of *Who Has Seen the Wind?*

DG The wind is a metaphor you've used again, for example in *The Kite*. ?

WO Well, the wind not so much as the kite was the thing. The idea that it has to be a mortality and that the kite has a limited life depending how smart the person is who's holding the thread. So, yeah, the wind is involved in it. What the hell, if you're raised on the billiard table of southern Saskatchewan you're going to be…

DG Your mother was still alive at the time. She must have been very, very proud of you.

WO She truly was. She forgave me for not becoming a doctor. And not only that, for eight years guess who was glued to her radio set listening to *Jake and the Kid*, every bloody week.

DG Well, let's talk about that after we've had another piece of music. What would you like to choose next?

WO There's a woman singer that I love, Kathleen Battle, and it would be pretty nice to hear Kathleen Battle in a spiritual. [MUSIC]

DG Well now, we've got you on the verge of *Jake and the Kid*. A year after *Who Has Seen the Wind*, you moved from High River to downtown Toronto, you became fiction editor at *Maclean's*—quite a contrast from small town Alberta. Was it a difficult thing again for you to leave the prairies another time, to go to the hustle-bustle of downtown Toronto?

WO Well, it wasn't tough leaving the Saskatchewan prairie at any point in my life; it was great to be a child there, but not after that. But Myrna and I both loved the foothills and we had by this time settled in High River. It was pretty nice. Myrna loved it.

DG Now it was while you were in Toronto working as fiction editor at *Maclean's* that you began to write your weekly scripts for your own CBC radio show, *Jake and the Kid*. How did that come about?

WO While I was down at *Maclean's* on the fiction desk, Harry Boyle spoke to me. And you see I had published by then nine short stories. Harry came up with the suggestion, I think you could do radio playwriting. He didn't know at the time—well he probably guessed—that I had been an actor before I had been a writer. So that was the genesis of that. It got started then.

DG That's an incidental that we haven't had. You were an actor before you started writing?

WO Oh yeah. Well, I'd always been a little ham, reciting and what not. When I went in to school in Winnipeg the first thing I did was get in touch, and then I became friends with—and stay in their apartment on Broadway visits—with John and Irene Craig, who were the founders of Manitoba Theatre Centre. I had always been interested in… My first interest was drama.

DG So when it came to writing a half-hour drama every week, was that a lot of work?

WO Well, not really initially. I already had nine short stories that I had to simply translate into the new mode, and I met Harry—Harry and I used to have a beer at one of the W hotels (I forget which one, on Jarvis)—and Harry, he said I got great news for you; it's taken off like a prairie fire and we're gonna run her right through. Thirty-nine—count 'em—weekly dramas, half-hour, and I have just run off the end of the gangplank with the nine already written short stories. Come on.

DG There was a terrible pressure on you then 'cause you had a weekly deadline. You had to come up with a story each week.

WO Yeah. However, what I used to do was… Well then, you see, what happened was I had promised Erwin that I would be an editor on *Maclean's* for two years and then after that I was going to return to what I should be doing with all my time, was writing. And at the end of the second year Myrna said, well, I think I'll take the boys and go home at the Easter break and stay. You suit yourself whether you want to be here. You see, I'd stayed beyond the two promised years and so I said—I went into Ralph Allen then and said, look , come Easter I'm going back. He said, you lucky selfish bastard. Ralph was a sweetheart. Also he was raised in Ox Bow, Saskatchewan, and also—if he hadn't died of cancer of the throat—would have been a leading novelist. He'd already done two. And so we returned then to High River, and that thing was that you could hang in there as though there weren't a break for the thirteen weeks—thirteen weeks—and do thirteen or more during that time. Build up, and then start in to do number fourteen when number one is done, and on and on, and hope and pray that you'll make it right through to the end. And as it got further and further down the stream, it got tougher and tougher. And there came periods of time when I would—in the interest of their getting early on them—I would send down… I had a set-up with the High River post office—it didn't matter night or day. I could get in touch with them and I could go down there, and they'd take it and they'd ship it out. And I would send maybe two-thirds of a script with the outline of what was going to happen, and then hope and pray that I would get the last third there by Sunday morning. I never missed a deadline.

DG But it was pretty close.

WO Pretty close.

DG Writing is a very lonely profession. Did you feel lonely in writing, or were the characters so much alive that you were just surrounded by a lot of busy personalities?

WO You have put your finger on the fact—on that I am happier playwriting than alone in that 12 x 12 office in the university, with no window. Yeah, it is lonely. It is lonely. And that is why all writers—I know it for a fact—have had supporting partners to dispel that loneliness, to bounce it off against them. And in my case it's my wife Myrna.

DG An interesting thought occurred to me. These years that *Jake and the Kid* was one of the most popular programs in Canada, how did it feel to you having created it when you heard the program on CBC radio?

WO When I heard it? [Sigh] I always listened to it and I always phoned the director afterwards and said, don't get that guy on again. I didn't behave. But it was welcome, it was a partnership.

DG An interesting thing, too—the kid in *Jake and the Kid* was in fact not played by a male, but by a woman.

WO Oh boy. Billy Richards was her byline, Billy Mae Richards was her name. She had, during the eight years of *Jake and the Kid*, three babies by caesarean section. Thank God, because she could say on the Sunday, I'm going to the hospital right after the show—write me out of next Sunday, I'll be back the following Sunday. Which was possible. Indeed a Boston drama academy, a couple of years into the thing, wrote to CBC and said, we have never heard such a fine boy actor and we would like to give him a scholarship at our Boston drama academy. And CBC had to say, sorry, he is having his second child by caesarean section.

DG Let's stop again and have some more music?

WO I'll tell you the composer I really love is Aaron Copland. I met him one time when I was head of the writing division at Banff, just briefly; I would have loved to have spent time with him, but... And I think of Aaron Copland the thing that I love so much is *Appalachian Spring.* [MUSIC]

DG In 1962, your novel, *The Kite,* was released after the collection of short stories of *Jake and the Kid*—a story of the oldest man in the world, Daddy Sharry, and his drive to get the most out of life, a sense of immortality. So that's a question that has always fascinated you, isn't it?

WO It is. I wonder if it's because of my father's early death and those Sundays—morning after morning, spring and fall—out there. Or the loneliness of being taken out of school and being the only kid alive in Weyburn, or Saskatchewan, or Canada, from nine to four, and seeing the cadaver of a lump jaw steer out there. I don't know. I think the emptiness and the space of land and sky gives one a sense of vulnerability.

DG Do you see yourself in Daddy Sharry?

WO Ha! I wrote it when I was in my early forties. I sure as hell could do a better job now, I'll tell ya. No. I knew a lot of old codgers. When we came back after the three years I was on the fiction desk at *Maclean's*, I brought back a trailer and it was my office at the back of my house. And the old retired cowboys and farmers—they couldn't see that I had any visible means of support—so they would drop by my trailer and pass the time of day, and we'd sit outside and... I welcomed them. They didn't know I was plagiarizing them. And that's where I got my Daddy Sharrys and my Jakes and the others. As well, I knew a couple—Senator Riley, the cowboy senator who was in his nineties—and I used to visit him and sit on his porch, I mean. And I chatted with them and they'd fill me in on the olden days. The idea for the oldest man in the world was strange. For six years I spent a month or so every summer at the Saskatchewan Arts Board art school at Qu'appelle, and one summer I was there... Let's see, my daughter Willa is 39, and she was about to—God, it would be 37 years ago—so there was evidently a federal election on and there was a newspaper story about the oldest man living in Canada who had voted. It was a guy named John Hannah. Well, strange coincidence, I received a letter with spidery handwriting on it saying how much he loved *Jake and the Kid* radio shows. So I said to my Auntie Josie Hannah, because I knew that my grandma's name had been Hannah—Maggie Hannah married John MacMurray and spelled the same forwards as backwards she told me. And I said to my Auntie Josie, was there ever a John Hannah in our family? She said, oh yes, that's Uncle John. Winnipeg. Was in the Red River Uprising and then later on the Riel Rebellion—the oldest guy living in Canada at that time. I got, for the next three or four years—he lived over a hundred, maybe a hundred-and-three—I got these Christmas cards with his spidery scrawl on the bottom of them. But that initially gave me the idea, plus the fact that earlier in the *Jake and the Kid* things, John Duraney said, ya know, you ought'a do a character of an old man. And he said, Tommy Tweed can do the funniest old man you ever heard. I said, hell, anybody can do an old... No. No, he said. I don't mean just old, I mean ancient... bleh, bleh, bleh [WO mimicking an ancient man]... And so I listened, talked to Tommy Tweed, and sure enough—and that's the way I first decided on the basis of voice to have an old, old man.

DG Something else you've done which fascinates me. You worked on the Stoney Indian Reserve as a teacher.

WO Well, I was a teacher and an agent.

DG And while you were there you worked on *The Alien,* and as a result of that you reworked it and produced what is probably your most controversial work, *The Vanishing Point.*

WO That's right.

DG Now, this was controversial because it didn't by any means romanticize the native Canadian way of life.

WO It wasn't really controversial. Bob Fulford did a piece in *The Globe* in which he said, Mitchell is either racist or foolhardy, and… because, the guise, it doesn't romanticize and it mentions drinking problems, it mentions—well, Victoria goes in and comes under the spell of an Indian who pimps her and what not. And it isn't, lo, the noble redskin thing. However, Bob Fulford was answered in *The Globe and Mail* by an Ojibiwa woman—a very fine journalist—who wrote and said, when it comes to being racist forget W.O. Mitchell, Bob Fulford has shown himself to be racist with all this crap about lo, the noble redskin, the business of you're not in trouble at all, you're doing just fine—which is the most harmful thing that can be done to vulnerable people. And then there was another one on the radio, *The Native Voice*. Another Indian attacked Fulford's version and then, interestingly enough, about a month or more or so later, we were at dinner at Barbara Frum's—a dear friend—and Bob got me aside and he said, Bill, I gotta tell ya something: I get an awful lot of books to read, and he said, I think I just took a swift run past *The Vanishing Point*. He said, I think it's great, and he said, and I'd like to make up. And I said, yeah… yeah. And he was running on that Ontario special network radio thing, and he had me back two times to talk about *The Vanishing Point*.

DG When you were writing it, what was your motivation? Was it to help these people or was it to let the rest of Canada know there was a real problem?

WO No, I don't think so. This suggests a didactic message, a social comment which is something I have avoided, unlike Shaw or Ibsen or many other writers I've known. I started this with a thematic insight that humans must bridge to other humans. What it started with was not the Indians, but the concept of a vanishing point—the realization there is no such thing as the vanishing point. You and I cannot see to a vanishing point. It's a fiction. And then it hit me that historically the entire human race have been in danger of wipeout, of destruction. And then there have been individual societies and cultures that look as though it's the end of those people. It isn't. There is no vanishing point. So this was the genesis of it. But it wasn't to preach or to persuade sociologically or anything like that.

DG When you're writing something like that do the words come easily, the sentences flow, or do you anguish and is each one giving birth with pain?

WO It varies. Now what happened with *The Vanishing Point*… I'm living out there. I'm in a log building—one half it's the school, the other half is my quarters. And Archie Daniels would drive me in to Longview and Myrna would meet me there and pick me up, and I'd be home for the weekend and then out. Or, when spring came, the little boys and Myrna came out and stayed with me there. Now, while I was there, twice a week up on the hill in the old farm house—they'd cleared it out—they held a dance Thursdays and Saturdays, I think. And I'm the only white there with all the reds. I would go up with them and I would dance, not the ritual dances but the Montana Fox Trot, the Rabbit dance, the Owl dance, just where you're going like this and uh… What the hell did I get off on all of this for.

DG The question was about the writing of the words.

WO Oh, was it difficult? No, the answer is, because I'm immersed in that and I'm teaching every day. But as soon as that's over I'm there. And I'm there at that table and I am working my butt off because so much stuff happened, so much detail, so much this and that, and incidents—that you gotta get 'em down—and it wrote itself because I've never been so immersed in such a stimulating community of people. As a matter of fact, that's the reason I wrote *The Alien* too fast. And then when it went in, John Grey would publish it at *MacMillan's*, but Edward Weeks at *Atlantic Monthly Press,* my other publisher in the States, said it needed a great deal of work to be done. Oh, and it was huge—I think it was about eight hundred pages. And I was arrogant and innocent and even though John was willing to publish, I said, well, if Weeks won't, forget it. Forget it. Took a try at it and put it aside—what, fourteen years later?—came back to it.

DG How do you feel now when you submit your manuscript if an editor or a publisher says, well, I think this should be changed just a little bit now?

WO I haven't had it very much, and my last novel, *For Arts Sake*, again I went in to Douglas Gibson, and he liked it. He said, but Bill, it does lack texture. So guess where I am sittin' on my ass in front of the typewriter for the next six months and doing some of the finest texture bits and findings in the second run. It's not unusual. Mark Twain's finest novel, which I think to be is *The Adventures of Huckleberry Finn*—he abandoned that and came back to it ten years later you know.

DG Let us abandon conversation and listen to music at this point. What's your next choice of music?

WO There's the Corrs—I think they're brothers, I'm not sure. But we were over in England this spring for a month, and my son, who was over there at that time, was speaking about how moved he was at a Scottish soccer tournament when all of a sudden, spontaneously, all the soccer fans began to sing a song, with bag pipes. Well, I guess the rhythm was bag pipe rhythm. There was no music with it, they just simply sung it the way people in baseball do the wave, or those idiots do the Mohawk, or something like that. So my son then got me a recording of The Corrs singing a very moving song that all the Scottish soccer fans sing. [MUSIC]

DG The prairies have always been central to your writing—all the way from *Who Has Seen the Wind?* to *Jake and the Kid*—so, inevitably I suppose, it had to be the case you end up with a tag, in this case the prairie humorist or regional writer. How do you feel about being designated thus?

WO Well, yes, I am a regionalist. Any novelist worth a hoot is a regionalist. It must be unmistakably in some part of the earth's skin, unmistakably at a certain point in time. I can go all kinds of people—Hardy, Conrad, to Steinbeck of course, Faulkner of course, Margaret Lawrence, Alice Munro—I know so many of them. Now, if it is simply… and that's what would be misinterpreted about this term of a regional prairie humorist—if it is assumed that it was written only to celebrate that particular specific region and culture, that's crappy writing. That's major bulls amateur hour. But then it must transcend this region and have universal appeal. My work has done that. That isn't a very modest statement, but the one that truly dramatizes it was a man named Ahmed from Iran, who had the House of Persia—and Myrna and I are nuts about rug art as well as art art. And he had a half-price sale and we went in. And Myrna doesn't like it when, from my depression days, I start wheeling and dealing and argee-barging and whatnot. And in this instance, when we'd made our selection of quite a few rugs that I wanted and needed, and I cleared my throat and I said, alright now Ahmed, I'm paying cash—Myrna just pole-vaulted over the pile of rugs and went right out to the front street and stood out there and waited 'til we were through. Well then, we worked it back and forth. I said, okay Myrna, come on in, Ahmed and I made a deal. And it was lovely. He loved it. He welcomed somebody who wasn't a bloody sucker coming in taking, but would go through the art of bargaining. And Myrna handed him—Myrna handles everything and at the top of the cheque it said W.O. Mitchell Ltd. [W.O. imitating Ahmed]—*W.O. Mitchell! I read your book. I read four times Who Has Seen the Wind. I've got it in my office, I'm learning English from it. You make me cry*. Tell me something. How can this lapsed, continuing Presbyterian make an Arab Moslem cry with a novel about a boy's quest for God on the prairies of the New World? I am **not** a regional humorist.

DG What you are is an ever more active writer. You've got, it seems to me, more prolific in recent years. You've written *Since Daisy Creek, Lady Bug Lady Bug, Roses are Difficult, For Art's Sake*—all of these when most people would be thinking of going off and staying on the beach in the Bahamas or something.

WO Well, there's an explanation for this. It's happened in like the last twenty years, is really what it is. And it's the most marvelous thing and it's why Canadian artists are luckier than any other in the world. The Canada Council, and the artist in residence. Come on, an honorarium? It's probably more than you'll ever earn from writing all during that year. Plus an office, plus a support system. And then, the Canada Council will not let you teach; they've already given the money for the budget for teachers, so you better not use 'em for a teacher. I didn't go with that, I couldn't, in gratitude I would always have wherever I went. I've been in five different universities. Anyway, the long-winded answer to your question—this is the main thing that accounts for it—is that late in my writing life, to be totally free and independent commercially to write books and plays.

DG A lot of people then anticipate, with the history of the writing you've done, that what you're doing now would be potentially a rehash of what you've done before. But you seem to be going off on totally different tangents. How do you keep spontaneity in your work?

WO I don't know. All art is one and indivisible, which Salter said, which is quite true and which is thematically a dimension of *For Art's Sake*. In *For Art's Sake*, as a matter of fact, I used a life model, a very fine painter—Louis Moulstock, a dear friend of years. And Louis has had (as has my fictional character) so many different stages to his art. And as was imputed in *For Art's Sake*, this guy's wife, Art's wife, picks up a piece of metal with rust on it and then he enters into his rust stage.

DG You also have a great partner and motivator, the professor.

WO Oh boy. Yeah, yeah.

DG Tell us about the professor?

WO The professor is a golden retriever. He's just over four years old this June. He's a golden retriever, he was a very smart little puppy and that's why I called him The Professor. It's such a beautiful contradiction in terms. And he talks to me every morning when I come downstairs. He has his toy, which is indestructible, in his mouth, and [W.O. imitating The Professor]… He literally does talk. French is my other language and Myrna and I… We're not doing it lately. I haven't been doing too well to go downstairs and everything and shoot a game of stripes and solids. When I would come home from the office he'd be looking at me and I'd say, professor, veux tu, aller, en bas, l'escalier, eh? Down he'd go, down the stairs and be waiting for me down there, saying move your butt, get down here. Ah, he endeared himself to me.

DG Are you still growing orchids?

WO Yeah, but over the years being away—I was eight years including our year in Windsor—a lot of, several, highly paid professionals ruined a lot of them. I've just got about a dozen left, and if we go to Hawaii or Florida or somewhere I'm going to bring back a barrel of bulbs and get rolling again.

DG How would you like to be remembered?

WO You know, I've been asked that before, and now I'm having trouble thinking of… I'd like to be remembered as being principled and caring. I guess that's it.

DG Let's have more music. What's your next choice of music.

WO Well, a thing I love is *Adagio For Strings* by Samuel Barber.

DG Any particular reason for this.

WO I think because it's such a soft and not sad sadness. I don't know, I just… It gets me. [MUSIC]

DG Well, one of the crucial things about being on your mountain top is you get to take one book with you. What one book would you like to take with you. If you had to be alone in isolation at the top of the mountain, or wherever, what one book would you take?

WO Myrna told me I would get asked this, and for the life of me I couldn't really focus in that closely. And then all of a sudden it hit me. If I'm stranded on a mountain top, and maybe it's my last days in this world, I'm going to have a pencil, I'm going to have a paper, and the book I want to have there is the book I am trying to create right now. How'll that do?

DG That'll do very well. Can you give us a clue what it is?

WO Actually, of my three brothers my dearest was Dickie, who died three years ago, and I went in—he had a stroke and I went in and held his hand. And we talked only by pressures in our hands for three weekends. And then for catharsis, out of my sadness and loss, I decided to recall Dickie and my childhood and youth with him. So I then began to do this freefall—finding, finding, finding, finding—about two hundred pages or so, and in time I will be doing… I think I'm going to call it Brotherhood, True or False? And that's the book I'd be involved with if I were stranded.

DG On our program we, at the end of it, tell our guests they can have one book and they can choose where in the world they would like to be for the end of their days while they're doing this. Now, it doesn't have to be the top of a mountain, it could be an island of the Pacific, it could be anywhere. Where would you choose to be?

WO Where? It'd be the North Okanagan and our lake in the North Okanagan, a place called Mabel Lake. It's pretty lovely.

DG Okay, we've got the location, we've got your final book which you'll be finishing yourself. You have one more choice of music?

WO Well, Aaron Copland has always been a favourite of mine, and the two that really get to me are *Appalachian Spring* and *Rodeo*.

DG Alright, we'll listen to *Rodeo* now. W.O. Mitchell, thank you for talking to us, and a very happy time on your mountain top in the Okanagan.

WO Thank you.

JANN ARDEN
WITH ANDREA MARANTZ, 1997

AM Let's go back to your early days, to your childhood.

JA Oh oh.

AM You grew up in Springbank.

JA Springbank, Alberta. I was in Calgary in a community called Lakeview 'til I was about eight, and then my mom and dad sold their house there for $13,500, which is mind boggling.

AM It's amazing, isn't it.

JA And they bought five acres in Springbank. And they bought five acres and built a house for under $30,000 in, it must have been 1972.

AM One of the most gorgeous areas in the world, too.

JA Oh man, and they just are surrounded now by Calgary Flames and rich doctors.

AM Massive mansions.

JA I mean, when I went to school out there, there was forty kids in my graduating class, Springbank Community High School. My dad said it was every dime that my mom and dad could scrounge together, and they were so worried about the mortgage payments, and uh... boy, it was sure a great investment for them.

AM Yeah, no kidding. So you grew up a country kid, sort of.

JA Basically I had the life of Huckleberry Finn. We built rafts every summer. I had two friends that I ran with for years—Leonard and Dale, they were cousins and they lived up the hill from where we were. And I remember when we first got there my dad built the house pretty much himself—he's been in construction for forty years. They just showed up with nineteen mutt-lookin' dogs in tow and said, do you wanna play—I don't even think I knew their names for about a month. And just, it was really great, you know, oh, catching frogs—literally everything you could imagine. I had a very, very happy childhood.

AM Were you a musical kid?

JA Very much so. I mean, my parents bought me all sorts of musical instruments. My mom said she had no idea why, but I always... I had this organ that ran on air, but unfortunately—I mean it was fun to play, but the air thing, it would go vhooooooo—so only so many notes sounded good with the tone of the air organ. So I had that and I had a little toy piano when I was much younger, but I, you know, I was in band and things like that. There's no musical influence in my family, really. My dad's mother was a big Mormon woman and she played the piano, pounded on it and sang gospel songs, and I remember that and I loved that.

AM So when did you pick up a guitar?

JA I was fourteen. My mom was taking guitar lessons and she'd given it up—just, you know, time and her fingers got just very sore from trying to play. And she had a big orange binder—that she still has—with John Denver songs in it and *Irene, Good Night Irene,* and *On Top of Old Smoky*. Anyways, there was a finger chart in there that told you where to put your fingers and what the chords were. So I haven't really learned much guitar since then, you know, the six chords that I learned in those three months. But I just thought this is something I really like, and I kept it a secret for years.

AM   Did you start writing songs in your bedroom?

JA   Almost immediately.

AM   Teenage angst and all that.

JA   Yeah, yeah. And they were always sad songs. I think the first one I wrote was about my parents dying. And they're not dead at all, they're very much alive.

AM   So you thought you wouldn't play that one for them.

JA   No. I sang at my high school graduation and my mom and dad had no idea that I sang at all. None.

AM   So what did they think?

JA   I think it was upsetting for them, just because, well, they had never seen that side of me. And I was up there, I had borrowed the guitar player's guitar. It was a band called Festival, a Calgary band that we'd hired for grad, and I used the guy's electric guitar and sang this song that I'd written for grad—probably some sad little thing—and I remember my parents just sitting there in utter disbelief.

AM   Did the kids at school know this about you? Did they know that you played and sang?

JA   I don't think so. I mean, I was in school plays and things like that and kind of a… I liked to talk a lot, I was constantly reprimanded for talking too much. Every report card I ever had said, she'd be a really good student, but she just yaps too much.

AM   You were thinking about being a teacher at one time.

JA   Yes. I'll probably always regret it. The only reason that I'd started doing music, really, was just to buy a little bit of time, have a few beers with my friends, and hang out and not go back to school and decide what I was gonna do right away. And, uh, ten years went by.

AM   So you never really changed your mind, it's just life kind of got in the way?

JA   It's a very insignificant group of circumstances that lead one to their destination, and one thing just led to another—literally. And sometimes careers choose you.

AM   Your last name is Richards, and Arden is your middle name. Why did you decide to drop the Richards.

JA   Well, my manager had spoken about it and, you know, Jann Richards/Jann Arden, and he just thought, you know, it was better alphabetical order and it was shorter.

AM   And Keith already had the Richards.

JA   Absolutely. There were enough wacky Richards out there. Yeah, we just thought we would try it. I remember how weird it was the first few times I was Jann Arden—just weird, weird, weird. My parents named me after a cartoon strip called Jan Arden, from the thirties, but my mom didn't like Jan, so she put another 'n' on Jan I'm kinda glad to be Jann Arden 'cause I know when the bills come they come to Jann Richards. I don't open those for awhile.

AM   You were mentioning how the singing career just kind of started happening, but along the way you did other things to support yourself for awhile. You had a job as a golf ball cleaner for awhile.

JA   I drove the tractor and picked up golf balls at Pinebrook Golf and Winter Club just west of Calgary. In fact, I just went and shot a round of golf there about a month ago. And it was funny, everything's so different. The clubhouse looks exactly the same, but all the trees are so big. When I worked there—this is, jeez, twenty-two years ago or something—there was just seedlings. They were little trees. And people used to say, this'll be a really nice course when these trees mature, and they're huge now. We planted fir trees around my mom and dad's driveway when we got there. I remember going with my mom and my grandma with a bucket of water and these little three-inch sprigs, and they're forty feet high now. But my mom had a vision, you know—these will look nice around the driveway in twenty years. I'm thinking twenty years, that's a lifetime.

AM   Yeah. Getting fish in B.C.—that was another…

JA   Worked on a salmon trawler with a guy named Norm.

AM   How did that happen?

JA   Well, I'd been singing in Gastown and got

punched, just knocked out because someone stole my money out of my case.

AM   Busking like?

JA   Yeah, just busking. It was very early in the evening. I mean, it was broad daylight. Anyways, I ended up getting this job, you know. No experience necessary.

AM   Wanting to get off the street kind of thing?

JA   Well, I had to do something, yeah. And a friend of mine, this girl named Janice, had told me about this guy looking for deck hands and that she was thinking about doing it, and so off I went for a month on a fishing boat. You know, just sort of south of the Queen Charlotte Islands.

AM   You were away for a month?

JA   About thirty days. And I remember being at sea for ten of them and I'm figuring, geez, I better tell my folks where the hell I am.

AM   No kidding.

JA   You know, so you're talking on a two-way radio, and the beaches along the British Columbia coast are unbelievable—they're the whitest sand you've ever seen.

AM   So the work wasn't very pleasant?

JA   It was terrible, but I look back to it now and it was a really great experience. I learned how to navigate a boat. Norm was a very old man, I'm sure he's gone now. He was 72 at the time. I mean, he might be with us, but his son had cut a tendon in his toe and that's why he had no one to help him with the last final part of the season. But I think I made two-hundred bucks in thirty days.

AM   Boy.

JA   A deck hand gets one percent of the catch. One percent of the catch.

AM   But once you sign on and you're there, there's no way of quitting, right?

JA   Well, I couldn't go anywhere. I mean, I got to Port Hardy and I actually went out on the highway—I was crying and I was just, I hated it out there—and I got out on the highway and stuck my thumb out and then that scared me even worse. I thought, I can't, you know. What am I… I have no money to get on the ferry, so what do I do once I get to Victoria, or Nanaimo? So I went back and got on the boat. Off we went.

AM   We were talking a little bit about that it wasn't particularly an easy road to get you to where you are right now. You played in a lot of different bands in Alberta and B.C.

JA   Right. Oh, pretty much any variation you can imagine.

AM   So, did you sing anything?

JA   Anything. I sung everything. I sung blues, I sung Led Zeppelin, I sung Nazareth, I sung Tina Turner, I sung Ella Fitzgerald, I sung Billy Holiday, Bob Dylan. You name it, I sung it.

AM   What did you love?

JA   I really like the old, the jazz standards—I mean love singing things like *Moon River* and *My Funny Valentine*, and you know, old Streisand songs. And the blues were great. I sung a lot of blues. I worked with a guy named David Hart for a couple of years and we did a lot of ski hills and things like that, and we did a gig at *Smugglers* on Macleod Trail in Calgary. And my manager had walked in to check the room out for another band, just to see if it was big enough, and there we were sittin' there singing all these old songs. And he decided to stay and watch us and he started following me around.

AM   This was before you knew who he was.

JA   Yeah. I mean, he had worked for record companies before and he kinda looked like a professional wrestler. He's a tall, kind of intimidating looking man with a natural Mohawk and glasses, and you know, a big man. And he finally came up to me, you know, months later—I think I was drunk and singing Christmas songs in June at the Ranchman's or something, something ridiculous—and he said if you're serious about music, call me. He says I called him the next day. I don't think that's how the story goes—it felt to me like a couple of weeks.

AM   Were you serious about music at that point?

JA   Uh, uh. No. Floundering around.

AM   So what was it? What was it that made you call him?

JA   I don't know, there was something about the

way he said it. He just said, I just think you're great and you're kiddin' yourself.

AM   Made it seem possible, did he?

JA   I guess he must have because I did phone him. I took my friend, Karen, with me to meet him 'cause I didn't want to meet him by myself; I thought he could be some crazy person.

AM   This guy who keeps showing up at your gigs all over town.

JA   And he actually broke up a fight during one of those many visits. Some guy came in and wanted to play my guitar and I just said that wasn't a good idea. It was the *Elbow River Inn* where the casino is now, and this guy got very violent and started shoving my partner around. And Neil got up; I remember him getting up and breaking up this fight. It seems like so long ago.

AM   So you thought he couldn't be all bad?

JA   But anyways, it took us… He said, you know, we could get a record deal and he really encouraged me to write. He said, you know, is that your song. And I said, yeah. Do you write much? And I said, well a little bit, but nothing that you'd wanna hear. And he says, well put 'em on tape. And he just thought they were great, thought I was this great songwriter and you should keep writing.

AM   Well, up to that point you'd been writing some songs I read, but you'd never tell the audience they were yours.

JA   No, I usually lied and said this is an old such and such song, or… They always seemed to buy into it.

AM   Did you think they'd take it more seriously if it wasn't yours, or what was the…?

JA   No, I just was ashamed at the content of the songs, I wasn't really comfortable with what I was saying. They were always very personal and I just didn't want anyone to think… and if they were bad, if they didn't like them, I certainly didn't want to take the responsibility for it, so I just thought I'd blame it on Anne Murray, you know—here's an old Anne Murray song.

AM   They still are really personal; have you got more comfortable with that as you've gone along?

JA   Oh yeah. That doesn't bother me at all to talk about things. I find nothing but optimism in my songs. My saddest, most depressing dismal dirge of a song is very optimistic to me, and I take great pleasure in it.

AM   Why is that?

JA   Because I just have an affinity towards somber music and melancholy music. I think melancholy is a perfect state of being. I think it's comfortable. I think it's reflective. I think it's sincere. I think happiness is a form of psychosis—I think it's very dangerous to want to be like that.

AM   Is it hard to maintain? Do you need to be in that place to write?

JA   I would say, yeah. I've never written a line when I'm in a good mood. I wanna be with my friends, and I wanna go to a movie and I wanna have dinner and laugh and go for a run; I don't want to play my guitar. I don't sing around my house. I do very, very little singing recreationally now. I still laugh hysterically. I'll be sittin' on a plane thinking, my God, I'm a singer for God's sake—what is that? I really thought I was gonna do something, you know, important with my life, and uh… I mean, maybe I'm just taking this lightly. I think it is important what I'm doing, but do you know what I mean? I just thought I would be an academic, well-educated person that my parents would be really proud of.

AM   Let's have a piece of music. What would you like to hear?

JA   I would love to hear Karen Carpenter's *Solitaire*. I sung this eight thousand times when I was growing up. [MUSIC]

AM   Do you ever feel like it could all disappear?

JA   Oh, it could disappear. In all reality my own mother says, well, it could go to hell at any minute. But I've really, really tried in the last couple of years to find a balance between artistic integrity and being a very sound business person, and not being ashamed or afraid to feel guilty about making money. Now, I had a guy tell me not so long ago that I was twenty-five pounds away from super-stardom.

AM   Oh my God.

JA   But these are the realities of music. It didn't… you know, I'm thinking to myself as we're driving along, I'm thinking, that was a compliment. And it really was, from his point of view. I mean, I don't really write the kind of music that… I'm a singer-songwriter; it's really quite a miracle that we did the kind of sales that we did on the last one, but I really have Anne Murray to thank for that. I cut a song that I knew full well was a pop hit song. I knew it when I heard it five, seven or eight years ago when I heard it.

AM   That's *Insensitive*.

JA   That's *Insensitive*. And, you know, I made a conscious decision to do that.

AM   Do you remember the first time you heard one of your songs on the radio?

JA   Hmm, hmm. I was driving across Glenmore dam and it was 1993, and it was a song called *Will You Remember Me*. I used to scan, you know, I'd hit to find—well, I didn't have scan, I was driving a bloody 1973 Monte Carlo, I just had buttons. Anyways, lo and behold, there it came on the first few bars, and I just thought I was gonna have a heart attack. But it was very exciting. It's still exciting, but I turn them off now, I switch to another station. I think oh I don't want to hear this.

AM   Does it make you self-conscious, sort of?

JA   Oh, it makes me… My mom says Eddie Fisher used to listen to his own music all the time. Eddie Fisher was a crooner from the fifties, married to—was it Debbie Reynolds?

AM   Debbie Reynolds, yeah, and then left her for Liz Taylor.

JA   Who would have thought. What was he thinking? I hadn't listened to *Time For Mercy* for oh, I bet it was two years, and I put it on in my car and just thought, man!

AM   Did you have a different perspective on it now?

JA   Oh, completely. For one thing I'd forgotten some of the words. When the songs went by I was thinking, man, if I had to sing that in front of somebody I don't even think I'd know what chords to play.

AM   You're biggest hit, I guess, was *Insensitive*, so far. Now, in Italy, The Jean Company used this for an ad.

JA   The Italian rep had gotten a call from this clothing company. She was looking for music. She wanted upbeat, hip things, and so she gave her a stack of records—you know, Boyz to Men or whatever, a stack of all this stuff—and she says, oh, you know, by the way, we haven't put this out in Italy yet, but we just got it, it's an import. And you know, she said to the girl, you'll like this for your house—you know, just take it and give it a listen to. It had nothing to do with the clothing commercial. I guess, like a week later, she gets a call back from this woman. She goes, you know, I didn't really like anything that you gave me, but you know that record that you gave me, that girl from Canada. There's that song. Can we use that song? And the rep is kind of going, uh, geez, I don't even know. We weren't even gonna release it here. So about three months later we started hearing through the grapevine they are now going to rush release this album and start stickering it, and they're going to start selling it in the clothing stores because it's become this massive hit in Italy. Like, thousands of people were phoning when the commercial aired.

AM   Isn't that just the greatest thing.

JA   It's really stupid, isn't it. The greatest marketing plan in the world is foiled by public opinion.

AM   But they wouldn't even know what the lyrics were all about?

JA   No. They would get a sense of it phonetically, obviously—they could kind of sing along that way. But, yeah, just the emotional quality of the song. Plus there was a good looking guy running down the beach half naked. But aside from that… Yeah, it was an interesting thing that happened there; I learned a good lesson that, you know, music really does defy borders, and they heard the same thing in that song that I heard when I heard Anne sing it the first time.

AM   You sang on Letterman. Scary?

JA   Terrible. I sang so bad on that. I just was… Oh, I just was sick about that show.

AM   Really?

JA   Hmm, hmm—I just sung badly. But they made me do a two-minute version of *Insensitive*, which is a verse and a chorus, and I just hadn't really done any TV like that before, and I just... Oh, man, my hair was weird and it was awful. I didn't enjoy that at all.

AM   But you got good reaction to it?

JA   I suppose. I mean, people were so surprised that I was on there, and the fact that David Letterman's people phoned our office—we didn't even solicit the show. He'd heard me sing it. He was on a trip in Jamaica or something and he'd heard it on short-wave radio.

AM   So he liked it?

JA   He liked it, yeah.

AM   What about singing a duet with Jackson Brown?

JA   Well, as much as I'd love to say I was sitting in a room staring into his eyes, I was three thousand miles away when I did it.

AM   But he wanted to do this song, too?

JA   Yes. I mean, we were talking about... When we—when I—said I'd really like to do this as a duet I initially really wanted Lyle Lovett. And that week he'd married Julia Roberts, so you couldn't get within a hundred million miles of him. So that was fate. And I recorded both my records, the first and second one, in Jackson's studio. And from time to time I would see him—he'd poke his head in the door and, [Jann imitating Jackson] I really like you're writing... He's very soft-spoken.

AM   Was he one of your girlhood heroes?

JA   Oh, *Running on Empty* was a record I listened to a billion times. It's a beautiful record, timeless record—you know, an American classic.

AM   Is it hard to keep yourself kind of grounded with all this going on around you?

JA   You know what, not really. And I don't know why. I'm just... I have a really, really great bunch of friends, and my family is so moderate. My mom and dad would be so embarrassed if I ever acted poorly. It's so much easier to be nice to people than to walk around bitter and...

AM   I wanted to ask you about writing one of my very favourite songs, *Good Mother*.

JA   My good friend and work mate—I've known Bob for, you know, at least eleven or twelve years, he's a keyboard player—and every time I went over to his studio to do any demos he'd be playing this beautiful thing. Just a little progression. No melody, just these chords on a big synth. I'd say, what is that Bob, I love that, you always play that. [Jann imitating Bob]—Oh God, I don't know, it's just a thing—do you want me to put it on tape for you? I said, that'd be great, can I try and do something with it? So I took it home and, uh, had **NO** intentions of writing about my parents; and *I've got money in my pocket, I like the colour of my hair*. I wanted to write something that was just... I wanted to write something that was kinda funny. And oh, that turned out funny didn't it?

AM   I cry every time I hear it.

JA   But my parents were just like that. When it started going that way I just thought, boy, this is interesting—you know, *feet on ground, heart in hand, facing forward*—so it's just kind of an anthem. I was very surprised at how many letters I got about that song and, oddly enough, it was played at so many funerals and it was played at a lot of weddings. So I'm thinking, man, that's covering it all, isn't it. And my mom, when she first heard it— you know, I mean, I love my parents very much and always knew how much they loved me. There was never any question in my mind, but we didn't say it a lot. But, when she first heard it, she says, well, I think that's got a really good beat. So, that was our big breakthrough day, but she never made any comment. She knows she doesn't have to. She never says anything about what I write about—never. She'll just tell me that she likes the music. She doesn't want to go near that. You know, she doesn't want to ask me, well, who was that about, or... Never. She's never asked me. And not that my songs are about anyone in particular.

AM   There's a couple on the *Happy?* album that are to someone, though? You don't spell it out.

JA   Yes, there's a couple of dedications. The last track on the album is for my older brother, and that's all I'll say about that. And the *Weeds* song is about... the metaphor behind the song *Weeds* is that it's really hard to stomp them out. You can yank 'em out of the ground and squish 'em with poison and forklift 'em and, God, they're just... And they're a foot tall in, like, four hours. God, if you could grow tomatoes like that we'd really be onto something. They should do… they should blanche those two genes together—splice them.

AM All we need is an attitude adjustment about weeds.

JA Absolutely. And Billy Cowsill, who the song is, you know, loosely based on—alcohol, drugs, struggled for years—after fifteen years of sobriety marches into a bar and orders a double Jack Daniels; I mean for whatever reason—so it's been very day-to-day for him. He shouldn't be alive. He's fifty years old and he shouldn't be alive, he smokes two packs of cigarettes a day. But he's tenacious and determined and sometimes God picks survivors. You're just chosen as a survivor. You don't even want to survive and you do. There's nothing you can do about it.

AM Well, I'm proud of myself. I picked that one, I figured out who that was.

JA Yeah. A lot of people are more familiar with Billy than he thinks. And he really is one of the most beautiful singers I've ever heard in my life. If you close your eyes, it's 1948 and you're sitting in a big Chevrolet and having a milkshake, and you're heart's breaking.

AM Let's have another piece of music. What would you like to hear now?

JA Let's play something by Billy. Let's find something—I can't even name a title—maybe something off one of the Blue Shadows records.

[MUSIC]

AM Well Jann, it's about time to send you off to your mythical mountain top. You can only take one book with you when you go. What book, if you only had one?

JA Well, you know, I'm such a voracious reader this was hard for me to try and decide on a book., but I've picked Steinbeck's *Grapes of Wrath*.

AM Why that one?

JA Well, I've read it a dozen times, you know, since junior high school. First time I read it I was forced to read it—it was part of school, the project of the week. You had to write a review. I didn't get it quite frankly. I thought it was dumb and stupid and the characters were boring and all they ate was potatoes, and, what the hell is this. Get out of the dirt, you know—I had no understanding of hardship. Oh, four or five years ago I read it in Europe, on the road. And, I mean, I'm far away from America, which is where he wrote the book,— you know, about Oklahoma and travelling to California—and I just… It's like I'd never read a word of it. It changes every time you read it. I think the characters are so great, and I think it's kind of funny—there's a lot of humour there in the face of disaster. And I'm interested in food, I love reading about food, and I loved Henry Miller's books for that 'cause he always… much as he talked about his love of women he also talked about his love of wine and food and bread, and you could just picture yourself in Paris on the Park Victor Hugo Avenue, eating a baguette and a big hunk of gorgonzola or something. And Steinbeck in this book spent painstaking time on describing what they ate, and they had very little. But it sounded so good. He wrote lines… You can open any page of that book—I would challenge anyone to read either side and not find a line that is so poignant and clear. And he wasn't one of these… Some of these new writers use more superlatives than a sportscaster.

AM He wasn't a gusher.

JA He was a simple writer. And he said simple things that just… it sounded like he said so much more than that. And I've learned a lot about songwriting from great writers like Steinbeck.

AM So we're going to send you off. Where would it be to, if you could pick any place in the world?

JA There is a lake twenty miles northeast of Wainwright, Alberta. It's called Clear Lake, and my best friend's family have had a cabin out there for forty years. On a summer day it's as nice as Maui; there's cabins all the way around it. There's not a weed in this lake. It's sand. It is so fun to swim in; the last few summers that I've had a chance to go out there we've done… Linda's got four sisters, and kids, nieces, nephews—I mean, the house is full. And we do aqua aerobics out there on the lake. And just having fires at night and sitting there and just talking about it, and the stars are just like…

they're just like you can pick 'em out of the sky. And I thought about all the places I'd like to go, but that's where I felt the happiest. I just felt like crying when I'd drive away. And their whole family, they stand on the end of the pier and they wave. And Linda's dad just passed away a couple of months ago, so it's even, like, more… the last time I saw him was out there.

AM What's your final choice of music.

JA My final choice of music? I don't want anyone to laugh too hysterically, but Shirley Bassey is pretty much—next to Karen Carpenter—one of my all-time favourite singers. For those of you that aren't familiar with Shirley, she was probably mostly known for her renditions of James Bond theme songs, one being my very favourite—which I cut actually as a B side and hopefully it'll appear on a single some time down the road—is *Diamonds are Forever*.

AM Jann, thanks a lot.

JA Thank you.

ROBERT BATEMAN
WITH ANDREA MARANTZ, 1996

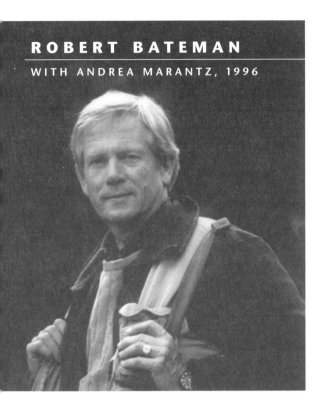

AM Well, let's go back to the beginning. Your love of nature and observing wildlife kind of goes back to your childhood in Toronto. You had a ravine behind your house there on, what was it, Chaplain Crescent?

RB Chaplain Crescent. And ah, it was just such a wonderful world then. The old steam engine went by on the beltline ravine and there was a little stream, and in the stream there were minnows and painted turtles, and of course pollywogs and frogs. And it was a migratory route, it was a branch of the Don (that fed into the Don) and the migrating birds all funneled up—especially in the springtime—funneled up the ravine at our back yard. And we built forts and, ah, of course played in nature the whole time right in the city of Toronto. Now the stream is a storm sewer and the old steam engine line is a jogging track for yuppies, but it's still… I've been back to see what it's like and it still is a very pleasant place. The birds I think, still come through, but birds have got a lot more suburbia now to paddle their way through because they didn't tend to leave the quiet old streams and that sort of thing; as Toronto built up in the fifties, they just kind of bulldozed everything and removed all the trees and started over again with industrial style human habitation.

AM Were your parents as keen on the wildlife?

RB Not especially. They liked it, we went for a drive and a walk every Sunday. But my mum sent me to the Royal Ontario Museum when I was about eight years old, to the Junior Field Naturalists. It was something… You know, other mums sent kids to little league, but I don't have an ounce of jock in me. And it hit a responsive chord and I became almost a groupie of museum people, because they had museum staff helping to teach, and I enjoyed it so much that when it came time to kick me out at the age of 16, I asked if I could come back in and be an instructor. I've always loved teaching, I was a high school teacher for 20 years. But I started teaching at the age of sixteen.

AM Now, your family had a cottage at Haliburton Lake?

RB It was in Haliburton County about 130 miles north of Toronto and we started going there in 1938, the year before the war. And with ration coupons we had enough gas to take us up, mum and my two brothers (the three boys and my grandmother)—coal oil lamps, walking down the road to the farm pump to get our water and carrying the buckets back, and then my dad had enough gas to come up for his two-week holiday. We would go there for a month. And that, and the ravine behind our house I think, really set the kind of guy that I am.

AM Did you start drawing then?

RB Oh, I've been drawing all my life.

AM What kind of animals would you see around your cottage?

RB It was mostly birds. The wolves had long since been driven off. They're actually coming back a little bit more now that farming has gone down; there's actually a lot more forest in Haliburton than there was when I was a kid. I enjoyed those open hills and open pastures and that kind of thing. Of course, there were beavers and raccoons, but there was mainly the birds of course—the loons and the mergansers and that kind of thing, and the birds in our ravine as well.

AM Were you a solitary kind of a kid when you'd go out and look at these things?

RB No, I've never been solitary, although I was an oddball in high school—not being a jock and being a boy bird watcher (if you can imagine a boy bird watcher in the '40's). I had to be a closet bird watcher. It was okay to be an artist and I gained a little bit of, ah, I guess status with my peers, by painting pin-ups on neckties.

AM Really? Closet industry.

RB Yeah, yeah, they had clothes on them. But they were based on Terry & The Pirates characters and they were fairly well endowed forms. So that was okay, and I did posters for the school dances and sets for the school plays and stuff like that. But the bird watching part I had to kind of keep hidden.

AM Tell me about Terrence Short.

RB Well Terrence Short, or Terry Short as we called him, he didn't teach at the Royal Ontario Museum, but he was the artist, the resident artist and illustrator who did all the backdrops for the dioramas and so on—and a wonderful bird man. He was kind of a mentor. So, after the Saturday morning Junior Field Naturalists, a group of us would go up to the back rooms—'cause the staff had to work on Saturday mornings back in those days—and we'd go in the back rooms and just hang out like little groupies with the museum staff. And Terry was always very kind and generous to me and so he was kind of a mentor. He would give me tips as I grew up; I felt he was one of the most sensitive, wonderful people that I knew, and sadly he's passed away now.

AM Did he influence your painting, your approach to the natural world?

RB To be honest, I don't think he did. You know, I sort of hate to say that if any of his relatives are listening, but I guess he was a slight influence when I was younger. But Allen Brooks was a more important influence, he was a much more famous published painter and he was in National Geographic, but he actually was a British Columbian, a transplant from Britain. But I went into a Group of Seven kind of art. People told me—kids who were older than I was who had gone to art college and so on, said, you can't do real art with a little brush. You have to get a big brush to do real art—capital "A" Art. And so I bought that; this was in the late '40's when cubism was just coming in and the Group of Seven were all, you know, in the full glow of their heyday of appreciation, which they weren't of course when they started out. And so I did, I got a big brush and started doing landscape paintings like the Group of Seven, right in the field. I was lucky, I had four different summers in Algonquin Park, so I literally could follow in their canoe paddle steps so to speak.

AM You were working at a camp then.

RB I worked at a wildlife research camp.

AM What was that all about?

RB Well, it was another one of these lucky things that have happened to me all my life. Someone—I was called a junior ranger, I was 17—and someone who was the son of a high-up Ministry (of what they called Lands and Forests in those days) official, they wanted to give him a plum job, but he didn't want to go because he didn't know anybody at this wildlife research camp. So they said, well, pick a friend, and he knew me from—we were in boy scouts together—and so I go in on his coat tails. And immediately I was just like a fish that had been put into water. With him it was a fish that had been taken out of water, he didn't like it at all it was a very important pivotal three years (17, 18, 19) and then I came back again when I was 21 and did fisheries research.

AM What kind of research were you doing there in Algonquin?

RB Well I was just a Joe boy. I dug garbage pits and dried the dishes, the cook wouldn't let me wash the dishes—didn't trust me—and just did all the… filled in the potholes in the road. But I also, because my interests lay in this direction, I ran the trap lines for small mammals, I prepared the specimens, and I was even doing bird census 'cause I knew my bird songs even by then, and this other guy didn't fit in at all. And all these older guys that were graduate students and researchers, I decided they were my kind of species, and growing up in the Forest Hill, north Toronto area, I had never met this kind of species who were rugged, you know, dressed in jeans and plaid shirts, and knew how to dubbin a boot and paddle a canoe and sharpen an axe, and yet they were intellectuals at the same time. They would play, you know, flute duets for fun at lunchtime, and we had lunchtime readings of various authors (James Thurber and Arthur Conan-Doyle), and very interesting discussions. So this combination of the intellect and rough outdoors was a new species that I had never witnessed before, and it hit a real responsive chord.

AM This was in your late teens. Were you kind of going through a now what?—where is this pointing me for a career?

RB Well, I always thought—as I assume all young people do and I also encouraged all the kids that I taught art to for 20 years—a meal ticket is an essential thing. You have to be able to feed yourself and hopefully raise a family, if that's part of your plan, and I did not want art to be my meal ticket. First of all it wasn't, it wasn't really in the cards in those days in the '40's and '50's. As far as I knew, there were only four artists in all of Canada who painted birds, and I was one of them and I was a teenager. And Terry Short was another and he worked at the museum. And none of them, it wasn't their livelihood you know. They had a day job, too. And people did not buy wildlife art and hang it on walls back in those days. This really came in in about the '70's, and it came in along with me sort of maturing as an artist. And so that was never an aspiration, supporting myself with my art. It never occurred to me. And it crept on me, you know, it's not my fault. Other people were the ones that started to sell my things and said, hmmm, you know, I think we could sell this. And I said, oh, and I used to just give them away. So I didn't sell anything 'til I was 35. So I went into teaching, partly because it had holidays I have to admit, and partly because I loved teaching.

AM Let's pause here for your first choice of music.

Was music important to you as you were growing up?

RB Oh yes, I've always loved music. In fact, in those days, in 1947 I learned to play the guitar, and I plateaued in 1948. And so I can play almost anything as long as it's in "D" and if it just has the only Burl Ives… [RB humming]…*Top of Old Smoky*, or whatever it is. Actually, I shouldn't brag like this, but I'm pretty good at a campfire and I can lead songs and go on and on and on with the old campfire songs, and *Frankie & Johnnie*, or whatever it might be. So it's to that level, I've never done it beyond that. But of course I've enjoyed a wide range of music. The only thing I don't like in music is raucous, and that would include Judy Garland or Metallica. I just don't like it big and loud, I like it sort of, you know, with a little bit of delicacy. And I do like guitar music.

AM So what's your first choice?

RB Well, my first choice is Joni Mitchell's *Big Yellow Taxi*. I've been a Joni Mitchell fan from the very beginning and I think this particular song almost sums up… All you need to do is do this song and you've summed up what I'm driving at in all my lectures and the philosophy of things: *don't it always seem to go, you don't know what you've got 'til it's gone; you paved paradise and put up a parking lot.*

[MUSIC]

AM Your painting, we were talking before about how you started with the big brushes doing the Group of Seven thing and were never really comfortable with that, although you did explore that kind of art for awhile.

RB No, I was comfortable and I love… It's fun. Painting with a big brush is fun. Painting with a little brush is okay, too. I use a big brush for most of my paintings now, even though they look quite detailed, and I bring out the little brush toward the end to do whiskers and things. But I really felt, well, is this all there is, you know. I go slop slop slop, and it was quite flashy and it was fun to do—it's kind of self-expression—but it didn't really show what was special about nature, and that is the particularity of every square inch of nature.

AM I read that an Andrew Wyeth exhibit in Buffalo had a major impact on you.

RB That's right. Andrew Wyeth is by far the most famous American painter maybe, next to Norman Rockwell. And he is a realist, and he just paints his own neck of the woods—his own Chadsford, Pennsylvania, and Cushing, Maine, where he would spend the summers—and in a very sympathetic, in-depth way, and doesn't care about anyone else. He never went to art school or anything. Well, from the beginning, from the turn of the century around 1900 until 1962, what was in with the art establishment was basically paint, starting with the impressionists starting to hit their popularity around the turn of the century, and moving right on through Picasso and the cubists and right up to the abstract expressionists. Subject matter was going lower and lower and lower in priority among artists and critics, and simply paint was getting more and more important, 'til finally, in the '50's, the great abstract expressionists—Jackson Pollock and Franz Klein and Ellen Frankenthorn and so on—were doing fabulous great big colour-filled things that had never been done before. I loved looking at those things and I loved kind of splashing around doing similar things, and then all of a sudden in 1962 an avante garde art gallery in Buffalo, had the courage to actually show a realist who cared about the particularity of nature. And I was an abstract painter and I went to see this show at the recommendation of another abstract painter. But I was also a naturalist. And suddenly I saw it was okay, you know, to get a small brush again and look at subject matter and care about subject matter. And it took me about two or three years to evolve out of my abstract snobbery and move into the style I'm in now.

AM Did you have a sense that you'd really sort of come home, found the right place?

RB Yes I did, yeah. And I have no desire to go off in flights of fancy of style any more. All artists worth their salt—I think even Joni Mitchell, maybe—get restless and want to change, change what they're famous for and change their style and that kind of thing. I'm very lucky. Not only did I get it out of my system in my twenties, but because my subject matter is nature it's absolutely a limitless world of visual possibilities. The Group of Seven were kind of restricted. They had to have, you know, certain pine trees going in a certain direction and so on; but when you go into nature in detail, I can paint a mouse or a moose or a colonial garden or a drift net scene, you know, or just a meadow with nothing in it but meadow. One of the things I guess I'm proud of in a way, is that when you flip through my book, unlike any other art book that I can think of—whether it's Jackson Pollock or Karl Rungus—flipping through my book you have no idea what's going to be on the next page. Is it gonna to be an Indian village? Is it gonna to be some puffins? Is it gonna be a sheep? Is it gonna be my house? Is it gonna be a Siberian tiger? And I feel completely liberated as far as my art goes, so I don't need to go flitting around in different styles.

AM Let's have another piece of music now. What would you like to hear?

RB I'd like to hear something by Garnet Rogers. I love all of Garnet Rogers' stuff. I've met him a couple of times and he's from the same home base area in Ontario that I come from. I especially love his instrumentals though, and so just any one of Garnet Rogers instrumental kind of Celtic sounding pieces would be wonderful. [MUSIC]

AM In 1963 you went to Nigeria to teach for two years. What kind of an experience was that?

RB It was a wonderful experience. I love Africa. I just, ah… I saw it first on this trip around the world in 1957, '57-'58, when we went around the world by land rover, when the going was good. You'd get shot if you did the same trip now.

AM When you say around the world, how? Where did you go?

RB We started in England. We picked up the Land Rover—a special one with an ambulance body and beds in the back—and we cooked all our own food and carried our own water and slept in the Land Rover every night, on little paths leading to villages or anywhere we could pull of the road. And we traveled across black Africa, tropical Africa, equatorial Africa—from Ghana right through to well, it was Tanganyika in those days, through the Belgian Congo.

AM So you had gone from England down…

RB Gone by ship, yeah. I didn't want to do… Well, we couldn't do the Sahara Desert. The Sahara Desert is closed because of rain.

AM Because of rain?

RB Because of rain in the summer, you can get flash floods. And now it's closed because you'll get shot by Algerian rebels. And ah, we took an Indian passenger ship to Bombay from Mombasa, travelling third class. We had a hundred-and-fifty people in our state room, mostly Sikhs, and across northern India, up into Nepal, up into Sikkim where we visited with the crowned prince before he met Hope Cook, who was to be his future wife—and we went to the edge of Tibet. The Dalai Lama was still in Tibet; I mean this is all history and much of it you can't do anymore. Then we got a free trip to Burma with a generous Japanese captain, and we drove to Rangoon and we drove out of Burma—with great pulling of strings and difficulty with a British Ambassador—we got permission to drive out of Burma (which nobody did before and nobody… I don't know of anyone who's done since). They're very restricted in Burma.

AM Into Thailand?

RB Into northern Thailand—Changmei. Changmei or Changrei—I get them mixed up. And we were arrested at the border for four days because no one had crossed the border and they had to check into us, and drove the length of Thailand and down to Malaya (as it was then) and Singapore. And then by ship to Australia and across Australia and back home.

AM Oh, spectacular trip.

RB Oh, it was great, yeah. It cost $2000. Including the depreciation on the vehicle.

AM Were you doing any work or were you just soaking up everything?

RB Oh, I was just painting. And we were trapping mice, too—collecting specimens for the Royal Ontario Museum—and just soaking it all up.

AM Maybe that's why you got arrested there. Travelling with all these mice.

RB Right.

AM So you were hungry to get back to Africa.

RB Yeah. So, I wanted to go to East Africa, but I went with the Canadian Government and they sent me to West Africa, where I taught geography. My degree's in geography, not art; I didn't figure I had to take art. I always knew I would be an artist, but I didn't think I had to take courses. And it was a great eye opener and a very enriching experience to be with those Ibo in Nigeria before the Biafra War, which later tried to become Biafra.

AM Were you in the city?

RB No. Well, it was near a village out in the countryside at a government school—it was like a boy's private school, but it was a government school. It had, you know, boys in residence and a house system. And it was a great learning experience for me. I don't know if I helped the kids much. I stepped into the shoes of Mr. Eloji who was… he went upstairs to the Ministry… and he was better in every way that counted, than I was. Here I was coming over a Canadian, with all this experience and an honour degree in geography, and Mr. Eloji, who also had a degree from a British university, was superior for the job than I was.

AM Were you a cocky young thing when you went over there?

RB No, no. I never was a cocky young thing I guess. But the boys, the kids, pointed out to me very clearly—their first question was, "Please sir, may we know your credentials?" And ah, it was very challenging. I've never worked so hard in all my life preparing lessons, and I had to get these… These kids had to be prepared for Oxford/Cambridge exams, set in Oxford and Cambridge and marked in Oxford and Cambridge. I had to prepare them for that. And that made the difference between them going on into the twentieth century or going back to, you know, the subsistence living in their villages. And they had examitis like… I mean, our kids have no concept of what education is like in the third world. They were way, way, way more motivated than any Canadian students.

AM Boy. Now, that would be a whole different natural world that you were exploring there, too.

RB And it was out in the country and I went for hikes every day and did a lot of exploring into the little villages and had a great admiration for the culture. I just have zero… I just have absolute disgust for almost all the African leaders, Nelson Mandela excepted, and particularly in Nigeria. It was quite a good country when we were there and it's gone downhill steadily, since it got money. It's not a question of the economy, it's a question of what you do with the money.

AM   Was Nigeria open to your work, or were people looking at your paintings?

RB   Well, I was an abstract painter. I still was going through my snobbery. I saw Andrew Wyeth in '62. I went over to Nigeria in '63 to '65 and I started doing wildlife art. Actually, my 'Bateman, the wildlife artist' career started as a whim, a calendar competition for East African Esso. We went to East Africa on a holiday. I arrived there, got my kids ready for the exam, and then I had a two-month holiday. I mean, it was shockingly generous what happened to me in Nigeria. And so I went over to East Africa to join my buddy, Bristol Foster, who I'd gone around the world with, who was just arriving, and I saw this flyer for East African Esso calendar competition. I said, oh, I can do that, so I painted a pair of starlings and a Thompson gazelle. I didn't win the contest, but my paintings were the most popular. They had a show there. And so people started to say to one of the dealers, the big dealer in Nairobi at the best art gallery there said, who is this guy anyway? And oh, he's a high school teacher in Nigeria. And she started selling everything I could paint, and so I had a wafer thin fame all around the world in Germany and America and Britain—people visiting East Africa. And here I was a high school teacher in Nigeria and Burlington, Ontario.

AM   So what kind of things were you painting for her?

RB   Well, I was painting wildlife, mostly African wildlife.

AM   So Allen was born there?

RB   He was born there. I'm an inveterate planner. Everyone said, it's a great place to have babies. And we had free hospitalization, it was a good hospital run by Irish Presbyterian people—a mission hospital. And I said, well, I want to take the long way home when I go home, what age is it best for babies to be when you're travelling with them? And they said, well, if you're breast feeding, five months is a good age. So, okay, we put them right on target and conceived Allen to be born five months before we started home. And we traveled home through Egypt and Greece and Crete and Rome and Spain, Toledo, and finally… Poor little guy had I guess twenty-six landings and take-offs, and he saw the world, you know, when he was five months old.

AM   With his eyes barely open. Let's have another piece of music. What shall we play now?

RB   Some Bach cello suite, it doesn't matter which.

AM   Now why do you like this.

RB   Well, I like slender kind of music. I prefer this to Bach's mass in D minor for example, although it has some nice little passages in it as well. And with the cello you can really pick out tunes—it wears very, very well. You can listen to it over and over, and then the more you listen to it actually, the better it gets, unlike some music. And it also reminds me of a wonderful afternoon in Bavaria. We went to live in Bavaria for a year, my wife and our two boys and I, so that they could learn to speak German before they were 12, which was a little deal they had with their grandfather. So we put them in a Waldorf School in a charming town and we lived in a 200-year-old farmhouse. And one of the teacher's in the school's wife was a cellist, and I did a sketch of her at one of her concerts. It's such a civilized area there. Every little village has string quartets and, oh, the countryside had hardly changed since the days of Mozart, and yet they had, you know, fax machines and Mercedes and I could go on and on and on about there's some pretty civilized parts of the world that I think we could learn from. But ah, to repay us, to repay me for my little drawing that I did of her, she said the gift I can give you is, you know, will you come to our apartment in this old farmhouse and I'll play you some Bach cello suites. So we went with our kids and our whole family and sat there and got a little personal concert of some of these cello suites.
[MUSIC]

AM   Now, you didn't start being a full-time professional artist 'til you were in your forties?

RB   That's right. I was a full-time high school teacher 'til 46, and I took a… I was selling, I was having sell-out shows during these holidays; I was working away, and every day after school. I moved out of teaching geography into art full-time so I wouldn't have to mark papers, and so I could paint. And then I… My dealer in Nairobi was sold to the Trion Gallery in London, England. And in a fit of foolishness I had signed a contract, which I've never done since—I don't have any contract, I don't have any agent or any contracts with any art dealers. I have a contract with my print publisher, but that's it. But anyway, I had signed this contract, so this English dealer at the Trion Gallery—the best wildlife dealer in the world at the time—had to buy me like buying a hockey player. And so I was inherited by the Trion Gallery.

AM   So, up to that point you were still dealing with this Nairobi gallery?

RB   Yes, And they had moved a branch down into Nairobi, and so… But then they wanted me to have a one-man show in London, so I took a semester off teaching and I let it be an omen. If the show sold well—I knew I could sell locally in Burlington and Hamilton and Toronto—but if the show sold well overseas, on an international scale, it would be an omen that I should leave teaching. And of course the show sold out, so that was it, the writing was on the wall and I put in my resignation.

AM   You were just forced right into it.

RB   That's right, that's right. And I didn't leave teaching 'cause I didn't like it; I thought, I couldn't believe why they paid me all that money to go down and have fun with teenagers every day. It was really a joy to teach, but it interfered with the painting.

AM   I wanted to talk a little bit about your technique as an artist—the detail and the motion that you get into your paintings. How do you do that? Is it just that you've got a really good eye?

RB   Okay, the detail and the motion are two totally different things, conceptually and artistically. The detail doesn't matter. It's mickey-mouse as far as I'm concerned. People often come and ask me, or say to me, I love your work, it's so detailed. That to me is not a compliment. It's not an insult either, it's like saying, I love your sweater, it has so many stitches in it. That does not mean it's a great sweater, it's got nothing to do with quality. And I think I'm primarily an impressionist anyway, who then goes on and tickles up certain little selective parts to give the illusion of—well, I want to actually capture the texture, but I don't do every single detail, hair or blade of grass. But the motion is… that's a totally different thing, and that's what I'm after. It's the static motion—if that's not an oxymoron—as well as the dynamic motion. The static motion is more interesting to me. It would be like the motion in an A. Y. Jackson. And since I was a Group of Seven kind of painter, what I'm after is a feeling of rhythm and form and a dynamic composition, so that you have sweeps moving through the… It may be a very still, very tranquil composition, but I want the big passages—almost like the cello maybe in a string quartet—so that you can feel there's an underlying [RB humming]… you know, a big underlying form and theme. And that's kind of the main abstract thrust to the paintings. And I work on that right at the beginning with a big brush and slapping the paint on quite loosely, and standing up while I paint and going back and looking in a mirror behind me to see the painting in reverse, and I can sometimes see the big themes that way. Then I start cutting it up—you know, cutting it up finer and finer and finer like, I don't know, preparing coleslaw or whatever, and toward the end I do the detail and the particularity. But at the very end I may get the big brush out again and reintroduce the themes—the highlights and the pale passages and the dark passages. Working in acrylic I can do this with thin washes, which dry fairly quickly.

AM   So it's the motion of everything, of subject and light and everything else that goes through the painting?

RB   That's right. With things… I'm not sure if you're original question was more restricted, like actual dynamic motion like a flying bird, that's hard to sketch. I'm a fast sketcher. I can even sketch while I'm driving the car. I've got some sketches in my sketch book that I've drawn with my right hand while I steer with my left hand. A bird flies across the road and I can capture the essence of the movement.

AM And you haven't driven into the ditch very often?

RB No, no. Well, I don't need to look. Actually, although I took geography at university, I took life drawing every Thursday night with Carl Schaefer. Some of your listeners might know, he was a generation after the Group of Seven and was a semi-famous Canadian artist, and there we had to draw an entire model in something like 10 seconds. And you don't have time to look at your drawing, you just look at the model the whole time, and you immerse yourself. This is the whole essence in a sense of the way I work and the way I observe. I look deeply at my subject, whether it's in real life or a photograph, and then my hand just goes ahead and does it. But you have to really understand what you're seeing, you have to really see. And so, ah, I do these fast sketches, and then I do models. I make models based on these sketches of the flying birds, say.

AM You've also been known to collect dead birds, things that have smashed into windows.

RB Yup. Or, ah, maybe I picked it up along the road. If they're ones I want, then I prop them up in life-like poses—especially flying poses 'cause they're the tough ones—and freeze them in the freezer. And then I can take them out and work on them until they sort of slump. I guess about a quarter of our freezer was full of propped up birds until my wife, Birgit, insisted we get a his and hers freezer.

AM I don't blame her. It would be a bit of a shock to your house guests I bet. Now, one of the things that your work is noted for is this sort of an intimate look at the ordinary, sights that people will have seen and not noticed. Like you were mentioning before, a meadow with nothing in it but a meadow. What is it about that that appeals to you?

RB Well it's pretty obvious to the human psyche to love a sunset, or love a rainbow, or love Mount Rundle with the sun on it or whatever, the beauty of the Rockies. And ah, in a sense it doesn't need… it's kind of gilding the lily to paint it. It doesn't need to be reworked. There are a lot of artists out there that that's their milieu and they… oh, I shouldn't say, but they crank out these pieces showing the glory. But, you know, Niagara Falls and Fuji and all that are glorious enough, and what I think is more important is just the world at our, you know, at our doorstep, the world at our feet as we go walking through a local park or a bit of pasture or something like that. There are all kinds of living things in there and there are all kinds of exciting possibilities, visual possibilities in that world, and I think this is what an artist responds to. Or a poet, writer and so on—the kind of writers and poets that talk about the particular and evoke, you know, those little moments of things that you've seen but haven't noticed. That's the kind of thing I respond to.

AM It's interesting hearing you say that. This is the sort of thing you hear prairie people say, that, you know, the beauty is there, you can't just drive past, you have to get out of your car get on your hands and knees and go look at something small.

RB Exactly. The world in a grain of sand is what Whitman said.

AM Now, the two places that you've spent a great deal of your life, southern Ontario and the west coast, you've produced a lot of work from those two.

RB Far more from southern Ontario of course, because that's where I grew up and, let's see, in 1985 how old was I? I was 55, that's right, so I did the first 55 years—I'm hopeless at anything with numbers in it—first 55 years I was an Ontario boy, and now I'm a B.C. boy. So most of my work is, of course, based in the Ontario area. But it's increasingly… B.C.'s kind of creeping up on me.

AM Well it's not hard to have it creep up on you.

RB That's right, although it is a bit glorious at times.

AM I wanted to ask you about the otters. You have a family of otters that lives near you?

RB Near us? They live under us. Our house is the otter house. They vary. They're kind of itinerant, but up to 12 otters we've counted coming out from underneath our living room. And we're built on kind of a rocky slope overlooking the sea, and they fish in the sea although they're river otters. And that's great, except they've torn out half the insulation and (I guess three-quarters of the insulation now) and they're starting on the wiring.

AM Are they insulating their own place?

RB Well, they like to roll in it and they make little dams out of it mixed with otter poo, and it's backing up water underneath the house and rotting the beams. I'd think it would be very unhealthy for them. But anyway, I've built an alternative otter house near… As I say, I can't see them when they're under the house, I can't enjoy their antics—sometimes we see them coming and going—so I built an otter house out in front where I can see from the bedroom and from the studio, and they totally ignored it. It's a very expensive otter house I think, but my wife promised not to tell me how much, and they still keep getting under our kitchen and having babies. But it's an honour having otters, even though they are ruining our house.

AM Let's have another piece of music. What shall we play now?

RB Any Mozart piano concerto would please me very much. I have a complete set that happen to be by Murray Perahia, and music lovers would be absolutely horrified if they knew what I did. I've taped only the second movements because I'm an adagio kind of guy. I mean, I'm just sort of a… I'm a quiet, laid-back guy. I don't like rowdy stuff and so I've got second movement after second movement after second movement. Other people might find it really snorey, but I find it wonderful and emotional and delicate and romantic. [MUSIC]

AM Your exhibit at the Smithsonian in 1987 was very important to you.

RB The Smithsonian show was the—the Smithsonian Museum of Natural History may I point out—was the pinnacle of my career as far as art display goes. There will never be anything like it again. There never was before and there never will again, because there won't be budgets any more. It was in the '80's, and the '80's were very special in the history of the planet—in some positive ways and in a lot of negative ways. And it was huge. They redid all the architecture of the Evans Gallery, they had even special lighting—they lit my paintings with the philosophy of the painting. The one I did for Princess Grace—I am in Princess Grace's in the Palace of Monaco. And Prince Charles has the one that Canada gave him for a wedding gift. Too bad about that, but anyway. They lit the Princess Grace one with a large soft spot on the rhododendron and a little tiny spot on the golden crowned Kinglet, etc. A thousand people at the reception, including Lorne Greene, who came… he came because he's a fellow Canadian. And he gave quite a touching speech at the opening and he said how much, you know, how wonderful he thought I was. We had met earlier at the Canadian Embassy, but just the night before, and then he said, ah… I remember he was getting a little bit older and he's passed away now—a wonderful man—but he said, surely Robert Bateman is a legend in his own mind. And everybody looked at each other [RB laughing]—this wonderful, deep voice, so profound—and they didn't know whether to snicker or what. But he was in all seriousness, and I hope he just got his nouns a little switched.

AM Just got his words mixed up.

RB That's right. Yeah, they said that it outdrew the air and space museum one day, which the naturalist museum had never done. It had the record-breaking crowd, so it was a great feather in my cap. I even got reviewed by the Washington Post art critic. Art critic, not outdoor critic.

AM And…?

RB And ah, I got panned. But it was an honour to be panned by the Washington Post art critic, and it was a good… I've been panned by a lot of art critics, especially Canadian ones, 'cause they, I guess, if you stick your head up they like to hammer you down. I don't know what the reason is. But he said it was a glorious show. He said it was too glorious, that was the problem.

AM You don't want glorious?

RB It's not in right now. And he said I was very talented—he had many nice things to say—but he said, where is the dark underbelly of nature? And he was absolutely right. And he described an experience he'd had in England where he watched a stoat, which is like a weasel, kill a hare, and it took a long time and the hare suffered a lot and it screamed, and there was twisting and writhing. And he says, where's the foul weather, where's the dark underbelly of nature. And that is a problem with a lot of wildlife art—it's all kind of sweet and nice and da da da da. You know, birds in gilded cages so to speak. However, the curator of the show, who won't be listening I assume, was a botanist. And I have done some blood and guts. I've done miserable looking birds in the rain and penguin chicks with krill, barf and penguin poo all over the whale bones and so on, and a vulture with a wildebeest skull. He curated them all out of the show, and so it was an intelligent criticism and a justifiable criticism and it was a great honour to be even criticized by him. A lot of my so-called fans were outraged, but I thought it was an honour.

AM Is it true that you don't seek out that part of nature, though? I mean, you have action, you have painted those kind of action scenes, but it's not what people think of first when they think of your work.

RB Well, if you just take a look through some of my books—again, I sometimes have to fight to get some tooth and claw into the books, and there's no place for them really in prints, because the reproduction print market is a business, and there's no use doing a print if nobody's going to buy it. It's wasting paper, I would disapprove of doing a print just to show you've got guts.

AM I would say that the dark part that you paint, you've painted some fairly political scenes—the giant sitka and the tree cutter. I mean, those are dark sides of nature as far as I'm concerned.

RB Oh yeah, and the drift net and the dolphin, sure. And you know, overall I'm a cheerful guy and I celebrate nature; but I'm—not only with my own eyes and my own voice do I draw attention to the dark side of nature and the threats to nature—but I do put it in paint.

AM Now, we've sort of talked around it a little bit, this idea that your work has sort of been a flash point for artists and art critics; they take a great deal of perverse pleasure I guess in poking holes at it. How do you deal with that?

RB I used to find it a little, well first of all, puzzling, 'cause… everybody likes to be liked by everybody, and then when you suddenly—you know, you think you're a nice guy and you're trying your best—and you find there's a whole element out there that know about you and don't like you. I've been told I've set Canadian art back 20 years. I got, you know, just a dreadful hatchet job in Canadian art during my last book tour, but it was so… it was facetious, it was so totally stupid. Comments like, Bateman admits that he did not see the moose in the landscape for his winter sunset moose painting, which by the way was done on the Banff highway just a kilometre to this side of Banff on highway 1. Oh yeah, so Michelangelo admits that he didn't see God come down from a cloud and touch Adam. I mean, since when… It's kind of fun, you know. It's a bit amusing to me and a bit of fun and a bit of a challenge. I don't get upset over it. And actually I feel sorry for the priesthood, as I call them now, because modernism is over, and this banner that they still seem to think has any meaning that it's never been done before, it's over. Andy Warhol's prediction has come true—everybody's famous for fifteen minutes. And there really has been nothing interesting happen in the so-called cutting edge of the art snob kind of a priesthood type of art since the beginning of the seventies. And so we're now in a delta, and you know, good art is good art, whether it's—abstract is here to stay and realism is here to stay and, you know, all forms of art are here to stay—and we should just celebrate creativity instead of… But I feel, they're kind of like the Politburo, the old—remember them up there in the May Day parade, sitting up there with their manifestoes, saying, it says here and this is what art is—in the meantime the world is, just like communism, the world has just gone around them and is totally ignoring them.

AM Let's have another piece of music.

RB *Mood Indigo*. I don't know, I don't have any great philosophical reason for doing it. I just love this kind of quiet, moody sort of music. And *Mood Indigo* is one of my favourites. [MUSIC]

AM Tell me about meeting Prince Philip.

RB Oh golly. I've met him a number of times, and the last time was the most rewarding. The first time was a bit frustrating. He's not a wooden post (like he seems to be on television) in person; he's absolutely totally unpretentious. He's brash, he is rude if he wants to be—he does not suffer fools gladly. He's been a great chairman for World Wildlife Fund (for WWF)—he's a roll up your sleeve, let's get the agenda going chairman. Oh, he has an eye for the ladies. He has to have techniques—which I hope I never have to go quite that far, because my life on this book tour is just a little sample of what his entire life is like—with meeting the public and being 'on' all the time. So he has these techniques of having quickie little kind of superficial conversations, and then moving away and spreading himself thin over the crowd. Like, my first conversation with him I was looking forward to some profound, in-depth chat, and all he wanted to talk about was how these North American drinks—he had a cocktail—had a swizzle stick, and when you tip the drink the swizzle stick swings around and pokes you up the nose. And then he said, excuse me, and he was off to somebody else. So that was my first conversation with Prince Philip. I've had others more in-depth later; I was on a fundraising birdathon bird-watching thing with him in Vancouver a year or so ago, and that was kind of fun.

AM   How about Princess Grace?

RB   That was a magic moment. It was the year before she died, and I had done this painting especially for her. I had done research into Grace Kelly, who grew up in Pennsylvania of course, and I knew she loved flowers, and so I used a bird that's found both in Europe and in Pennsylvania—it was the golden crowed kinglet (and of course it's found here, too)—and put the rhododendron in it, and she shoe-horned us into her schedule very graciously. She had a really busy time. And so my wife and I had this wonderful meeting in the palace. First, we had a great chat with her lady in waiting, a wonderful middle-aged Englishwoman who was a very witty person. Then Princess Grace walked in the room; she was wearing an ultra-suede suit just the colour of the rhododendrons, and I told her how my mum had problems with the painting, she couldn't quite understand—she thought the water was the sky, etc., etc.—and we had a nice little chat there. And of course it was terrible to hear of the car crash that killed her. But we still get a Christmas card from Albert from her son. I've been with Albert also on a wood bison project here in Canada in the prairies, and so we still exchange cards with the palace at Monaco, and I hope the painting's still there.

AM   Well, before we send you off to your mythical mountain top, you get to take one book with you. What book would you choose?

RB   Well, I wracked my brain because I love books, I love reading—I've just finished reading Vladimir Nabokov's *Speak Memory*, his memories of his childhood, a fascinating period at the end of the nineteenth/early twentieth century. But I think my favourite, and the one that sprung to mind, my first one that sprung to mind, was one called *Cider With Rosie*, by a British poet called Laurie Lee. He's a man and he's an older guy, even older than I am, and he grew up in the Cotswolds area in a cottage with his mother and a whole passel of sisters. This is the story of life in a British village before World War I, when it was a kinder, gentler life in many ways. It was a harder life, it was more of a struggle, but traditional man and traditional agriculture are very… they have a nice, pleasant interface with nature, and he is just such a rich writer. And we actually read this when we go on camping trips and kayaking trips with our kids. We sit around the campfire and read excerpts from *Cider With Rosie* by Laurie Lee. And any passage from it anywhere, it's just wonderful rich reading.

AM   Now where would you go, if you had to be sort of isolated for the rest of your days and you could choose any spot in the entire world?

RB   Oh golly, you tossed in the word isolated. I've never been isolated, and my first thought when I was thinking about this originally is that I always want to be where I am. Like there's no place I'd rather be than right here right now, believe it or not. But I am on… we are on Salt Spring Island because we researched it, and that's where we want to be for the rest of our days, 'cause I want to be near the sea. And it's not on a mountain top, but we're below (well you wouldn't call it a mountain in Alberta) an 800 foot hill. We do have a little island just off the coast, it's about a 15-minute boat ride from where we are, that has no electricity or no phone—so that would take in the isolated thing. And we do have a little cabin on it. I would love to be able to spend a week every time—winter, spring, summer, fall, every season. I have yet to spend more than two nights, just because of my crazy agenda. But I guess somewhere in that neighbourhood is where I would want to be.

AM   And what would be your final choice of music today?

RB   Oh, it would be Neil Young's *After the Gold Rush*. And once again, I can't explain this. I like everything Neil Young has done. I like his poetry, and *After the Gold Rush*, which has a bit too many… I guess a little bit too much connection to that kind of hippie era, which I didn't really participate in; however, the sensitivity and the poetry of it, and I love the line in the first verse: *Look at mother nature on the run in the 1970's*. Well, look at mother nature really on the run in the 1990's. It's continuing.

AM   It's been a real pleasure meeting you. Thank you so much for doing this.

RB   Great. Thank you so much.

EVELYN HART
WITH ANDREA MARANTZ, 1996

AM You were born and raised in Southern Ontario. So what can you tell me about your childhood hometown?

EH I was born in Toronto actually, in St. Michael's Hospital, and spent the first five years of my life in Port Credit. And I have very vivid memories of that.... well not that little house...but that house in the church in Port Credit. But my main memories are for Peterborough Ontario. And the house at 480 Thompson Avenue.

AM What was that like?

EH Well, it was interesting because it was, the three girls were in rooms upstairs and we had a rock garden out behind. And it was a fairly modest, simple house, but it was the first place where I began to be interested in dancing. And the main memories are being in the living room and putting on an old tutu from the woman across the street that hung down to my knees. And dancing around the living room to a Beethoven Symphony.

AM So how did you get the tutu. Did she know that little Evelyn just loved it, or...

EH She was actually and ex-ballet teacher. And it was only at about age eleven that I became interested in dancing when I had seen Veronica Tenant dancing Romeo and Juliet on television. And then my mother had taken me to a lecture demonstration in a church basement by the National Ballet School and I began to realise, oh, they didn't actually wait till they grew up to become this gorgeous creature that I had seen on television. And my initial desire had been to be a Bride or a Princess, then a scientist and then I thought maybe an actress. So somehow, dancing seemed to fill all of those needs, you know, you often....yeah, it's very scientific what I'm getting into in my technique, technical things. So, she sort of began to see that I had this interest and it seemed to combine my love on music as well.

AM Now, did these loves come from your mom and dad?

EH I think basically, the main one of music came from my father. And my mother was part of the musical clan, but we all took instruments and all studied instruments piano, violin and trombone and trumpet.

AM What did you play?

EH Violin and Clarinet and Oboe. A little bit of each. I wouldn't say I'm proficient in any of them. But it certainly gave me an appreciation for music.

AM So when did you get to take ballet lessons?

EH I had a few lessons when I was about eleven at the YWCA and it was an ex-student for the National Ballet School. And then we moved away to Dorchester, actually, just outside of London and I'd actually gone to a summer school, the National Ballet School, because a girl that lived down the street, two houses down, was a student of the school, so I knew about it then, and I went to audition and I was accepted for the summer school. And I went and the teacher there happened to be Victoria Carter. And I recognised her picture and the boy in my class, who's picture was in the newspaper when we were visiting my grandparents, and realized they were from London Ontario, so they moved to London Ontario, pestered and pestered my parents. We went in I had a little; kind of, audition, and they said, yes we'll take her and we'll teach her. It's a little bit risky, little bit dangerous, she's fourteen already.

AM That is late, isn't it?

EH Very. But I think what it's done is its always kept me interested and kept me on the cutting edge so to speak, because I never take anything for granted. I feel as though I'm always learning and I've never lost interest, I've never been bored.

AM So did they see your potential right away, in London?

EH I think so. I remember her looking and saying boy she sure has the physic for it. So, that's all they really told me, they were very careful for fear that I would get complacent, so they never really gave out praise too easily. But I always was grateful for that because I think it gave me a realistic work aesthetic, you know.

AM Now that school, was that an academic as well as ballet school?

EH No. She's more of a general school, in the sense that she taught general level children as well. And it wasn't really a professional school at all but, the training and the standards and the lessons that you learned were much more than just ballet, you know. I was very lucky to come in touch with those two people.

AM And did it absorb all your energy right from the start?

EH Well, yeah. Yeah. Once I began it, I realised that there was just nothing else in my life. I quite frightened my parents. Because I became, as most people know, quite obsessive about it. Being a perfectionist, it was like all of a sudden I found the thing that gave me my identity. And they were, to the exclusion of everything else, and I didn't really spend time with school chums. Course it also correlated to the move that we had made from Peterborough. And I was never a real social creature from day one, just because I had my twin sister and she was my best friend and I didn't need any other friends, you know. And I actually spent most of my life in a fantasy world. I would go up with my books and my music, and I remember being fascinated by classical music, I could listen to classical music and hear amazing things in it from day one. My favorite thing would be just to sit there and listen to music and dream. And that's still my favorite thing, to this day.

AM Evelyn, tell me about going to Winnipeg to study at the Royal Winnipeg Ballet. That was 1973, you weren't through school yet, were you?

EH Well, I had finished grade twelve. And it was all they could do to keep me in school, because by the time I had the ballet bug I just really wanted to dance and do nothing else. And I'd had a brief time at the National Ballet School but didn't really deal with that very well emotionally and so was sent home, and that was the beginning of the experience with anorexia. And so they felt it was best that I go back to a more stable home environment but there couldn't have been anything worse, as far as I was concerned, because I just really wanted to dance.

AM Was that the main problem at the National Ballet School?

EH I think so, I realise now that I was quite homesick for my family. And I was quite aware that it was not a choice and it was not something that my parents were happy about. I think, deep down underneath it all there was a difficulty there, and I think it's taken me a long time to come to terms with that. But I finally have. Finally.

AM That you were making choices that your parents couldn't support.

EH Well, that they really didn't approve of, totally. I think it wasn't so much that they didn't approve of it, I think that's the way I perceived it.

AM What were they worried about?

EH Well, I think it was the general perception of the kind of life of a dancer. Of coming from a very religious background, of perhaps becoming a very loose life, and the alcohol, and the party life and they really had no experience with any kind of artistic life and the only experience they had was the stories that you hear, you know. The obsessive kind of life and I think they were just were quite terrified by it. And also the fact that they had heard that it was a difficult life, and that you didn't earn much money and chance with success within that career, it was a path completely unknown to them. And I think it was understandable, although, the artist in my Father was a little bit more supportive, in the sense that he had, at one point, wanted to study the organ and he had been given an audition with Sir Kenneth McMillan, and he chickened out at the last minute and he didn't go. And so I think that part of him understood the artistic soul in me and though, "whatever makes you happy is most important". But it was hard for my family because it was very close knit family and it also means that I had to go away. And that was hard for them. Hard on me too.

AM So, did you just sort of hop on the train and off to Winnipeg?

EH No. My mother came out with me on the plane. And I thought I had been accepted by the school because I'd had and audition, and we arrived and we discovered that I had to go through two more weeks of auditions, and of course I was terrified that I was going to come all this way, have my hopes dashed again. As it turned out, I was very lucky because I was taken into the school.

AM What brought you to Winnipeg?

EH Well, because my teachers had stepped in at that point. And they felt after the National Ballet School that it was really important for me to dance. And they didn't want to give up, they felt that knowing who I was, that if I didn't dance my soul would be broken. And so they were looking for different schools, and they actually took me in the summertime to New York, just to show me that the National Ballet wasn't the only place that I could dance.

AM These were still your teachers from London?

EH Yes. And I stayed with them in the Waldorf-Astoria and they took me around to different classes and I auditioned.

AM That must have been a super adventure for a young girl.

EH It was amazing. I still remember, I came off, I was a lifeguard that summer, and I came off dressed in this really ridiculous little outfit that I thought was very chic, but they just about died. They said I looked about 10. With this floppy hat, thinking I was going to get dressed up for the big city. And I was totally tanned. My hair was bleached blonde from the sun. So it was quite funny. And I still remember, you know, the hotel room and being in New York, it was just such an experience. Going up all those steep stair cases into the old studios for ABT. I was quite lucky, I was accepted to every school that I auditioned for. But, of course, for my parents, between that and Winnipeg, Winnipeg was a lot safer, they were just not going to let me go to New York City.

AM Tell me what does that do for your confidence level, and your ego as a young girl, to be accepted at all these places that must have been sort of, dream places for you.

EH You know, interestingly, it kind of gave me this feeling inside that yes, I could become this ballerina that I dreamed of. But, to another degree, it didn't change the fact that I didn't see what I had special, and I just felt inferior.

AM You still didn't, at that point.

EH Oh no. I still don't. I come to a point of sometimes being more satisfied with my work, but if you put me into a group of twelve ballerinas I'm convinced I'm the worst one. Always. But that's okay, that's just me.

AM And then you were off to Winnipeg, and you did get through those two weeks.

EH I did, painfully. Apparently, David Moroni nicknamed me "The Wild One". I just emoted and I was just dancing away with lots of emotion. Schmultz galore. And he just took a look at this person with back that bent over backwards just a tremendous raw talent, but just this emotion. I remember him coming up to me and saying, "What's your name again"? and I said "Evelyn Hart" and he said "You know, that's a very good name for you because you dance from the heart". And I remember being shocked by that.

AM Well this would be a good time to play your first choice of music. What should we play first?

EH Well, I think one of the things that still is one of my childhood memories, is, I used to love to go to my father's weddings when I was a child, and of course, hence, that's when I wanted to be a bride, and I had my whole wedding planned out, you know. Of course, I'm never going to get there now, but you know it was the dress and everything. My favorite thing was, he would always have played when the bride had gone away to sign the register and come back, he would always have played in this booming organ, "Praise my soul, the King of heaven". And somehow, the older I get when I hear those words, and the magnitude of those words of love, and joy, and this great sense of God is a creator, whether you believe in God or not, but this great sense of something greater than ourselves. And I'll never forget always seeing these brides faces coming down the aisle, just glowing, with such a luminescence. And so I think that would be one thing that I would like to hear. [MUSIC]

AM Praise my soul. The choir of Paisley Abbey. That was the choice of my guest on Mountaintop Music, Prima Ballerina, Evelyn Hart.

Now you moved up remarkably quickly from the time you arrived at the Royal Winnipeg Ballet in 1973 and were the little wild one, to a principle dancer by 1979.

EH I had joined the company in '76 and then two years later was promoted to soloist and then the next year was promoted to principle. And I think it was, of course, in one sense, I think I suffered, because it was, of course much too early, I think, in one sense. I think it was a product really much more that the company needed a classical ballet dancer at that point. Some other dancers, their ballerinas had left and they really needed someone to step into it. And I think, had I had a few more years, to kind of develop into it, and gain confidence, I would have perhaps not suffered quite to much, a little bit later down the line. But then of course, there's also that, that ignorance is bliss when you're young, that you just go out and you do things anyway on shear raw talent. So perhaps it wouldn't have been any easier had I taken longer.

AM So what do you think, Evelyn, that you weren't emotionally ready but that you were physically and artistically ready, or both.

EH I think it's just a combination of everything. I think that, and I keep saying this to very talented people, that the biggest problem is when you're young is that you have a vision, and this is what your talent is, is that you have a vision of what perfection you are trying to achieve. And even to this day, sometimes, a lot of times, I'll have a great insecurity because other people will look at my work and say "But it's fine, it's beautiful". And yet you know that there's something else there, that there is something else that you want to achieve with it, that it can be smoother, it can be higher, it can be better. And it's really frustrated because your think that everybody looks at this big gap that you feel. You understand. You have this big gap between what you dream of being able to do and what you actually are doing. And when I was young, this is what it was, is that people were just, I think, infatuated with the actual natural talent and this ability to express emotion, and that's what was important to them. But for me, I was very aware of the fact that this wasn't it, honey. It wasn't all there. I thought, no this can't be, this can't be what I see in other ballerinas. I just had this sense that I wasn't at the level that I needed to be or wanted to be.

AM Did you see that in other people that you'd watched too? Were you

critical of other ballerinas and see the same kind of gap that you could feel in yourself?

EH You know, I was always critical of other ballerinas, I think I was from day one. I would look at a dance and immediately say to myself, "I'd do it this way". And so to me it's not really a matter of criticizing. It's a matter of being aware from day one that I hear music differently, so I would never really say that it's a criticism, I would say it's more of looking at someone else, and just learning from them, and saying, you know I like that, I don't like this. Or looking at them and saying that could be so much more. Or, if they did it two counts more over here it would be more effective. And yet there is other things that I look at other ballerinas and I know immediately I could never begin to do. And I admire them for that. So, I hesitate to say, and yet other people would look and if I make a comment like that, they say "Oh, that's very critical" but it's not meant in that way at all.

AM It's searching more.

EH Yeah, definitely.

AM Karen Kain once told us that she could count on one hand the number of times she's been completely happy with her performance. Do you have that many?

EH Actually, probably, yes. Because I find that it's the older I'm getting, it's now becoming much more a thing of the soul, and much less a thing of the technique and the more that one comes to terms with what your technical abilities are.... I'm just so grateful now if I get through the performance, and it's not so much important whether or not I accomplish a perfect technical performance, but whether I've had enough technical confidence to be able to get into the soul of it.

AM To sort of accept that part of it.

EH Exactly. For example I did a performance just now in Munich and I was a little bit devastated because certain things technically didn't work. But I felt that my soul was just rejoicing in every minute on stage.

AM And that's satisfying

EH Even though there were a few moments where I was just terrified, I thought, I'm not even going to make it through. And somehow I just let myself go through it, even if there were mistakes or whatever, I just said, just finish it, just do, just don't think. And by the end of it I realised that I just... it was paradise. And so I realised my satisfaction is now a different quantity. I don't measure it now at all in the same way that I used to.

AM And it's taken all your career, I suppose, to get to this level of acceptance of yourself.

EH Absolutely. And it's probably going to take longer to really be able to understand it and deal with it.

AM Well, what would happen before. Would you almost be having a fight with yourself onstage as you were dancing. I mean, not that the audience would be aware of it at all.

EH The actual performance I think is a natural instinct in me as a performer that just keeps going no matter what. I mean, I would never ever, ever, given up on a performance even if it's going badly. Never thrown a temper tantrum on stage, so to speak. But for example, I remember my very first *pas de deux*, not my first one but one of my very first *pas de deuxs*, when I was a soloist and I went out on stage and I was supposed to do twenty fouettes and I did twelve. And I had eight more counts, and I remember being so shocked that I didn't finish these steps that I started doing Temps Leve in a circle. Temps Leve and Temps Leve and Temps Leve… and I was so devastated that I ran from the stage, I tore off my costume, I tore off my make-up, I put my jeans on and I ran from the concert hall to my home which was about a mile, in about eight minutes. I had so much adrenalin. I was so devastated and embarrassed and just horrified that this happened to me over eight fouettes. And now I would come off and I would be disappointed and I would be upset and maybe sometimes if I was really upset I would throw a point shoe or something. And maybe let out a little bit of a four-letter word. But, you know, it all depends on the preparation, now I realise, before the performance. If you prepare yourself for a mistake, and prepare yourself not to be perfect, then if you aren't perfect you don't react quite as disastrously. Now I would never run a mile in eight minutes ever again, I think my body is just too sore for that.

AM Evelyn, let's have another piece of music now. What should we play?

EH Well, I don't know if you can get a hold of this, but one of the other things I was going to say is just anything sung by Brent Carver. Because, I went to see his one man show in the summer last year. And I think, of course this is why I went to see it because I had seen him in Kiss of the Spider woman and he sung also for the Dances for Life Gala: And I had not come across a performer that touched me and moved my soul so much as this man. And I just think that almost everything he does, it's just amazing, he brings life, he opens the sky for you.

AM And that was Brent Carver from 1974 with the Lullaby from the musical Jubliade. The choice of my guest on Mountaintop Music, ballerina, Evelyn Hart. Now, Evelyn, you've been called "Little Miss Leningrad", what does that nick name mean?

EH Oh, that was Arnold Spohr. It was because, you know, the Russians were known for their emotion in their dance. And so, when he first saw me and I was full of this kind of grand movement and Port de bras and lush kind of way of feeling the music, over emotion to die for. You know how the Russians are just emotion galore. And he just looked at me and that's what he called me. He said, "oh, it's little Miss Leningrad". So, it's been great. And it was wonderful because for the longest time I had a real affinity to the whole concept. When I was first eleven years old and my mother got me books from the library, I got books from Ulanova and Plisetskaya and all the great Russian ballerinas. And was only in my mind that that was the only kind of ballerina to be, I had no idea that you could be less than world class. And so Ulanova was really the example, I read about her. And about how she was unique in the sense that she could move people with her dancing and that people, when they would see her would be totally involved. And I think that's what was so special, for me, about experiencing Brent Carver on stage, because that was the first time that I really felt, for a long time anyway. I mean, I felt that way with someone like Veronica Tenant, but, felt totally drawn in to the performance. And, this is what I read about with Ulanova, and so, when he called me little Miss Leningrad I considered it a great compliment.

AM How pivotal to you career was winning that gold medal at the International Ballet Competition in Bulgaria, 1980?

EH I think at the time, it was of course a terribly exciting event. And wonderful for me because it confirmed in my mind that I had talent.

AM You finally believed it.

EH Yeah, I always believed that I had talent, I just didn't know that I had the talent to become a ballerina: The flip side of that was that it was a bit disastrous, because I was all of a sudden thrown into a lime light, to be this guest artist, and this person that I knew, that yes, I was special, because of my artistry, but I knew I didn't have the technique to stand up in those situations. And this created quite a bit of stress, until I was about twenty-eight, actually. When I think back about it now, I mean, I was put into positions where, I was very lucky, and yet it was terribly difficult, I had to learn my first Swan Lake in six days and go on. I had to learn my first....

AM And where was that?

EH In Cambridge. In a big tent. Oh, that was a great experience. My first performance was, I didn't even have a run through, I hadn't seen the version. And there had been a rain storm in the tent, and they struck just before my performance of course, and I was thinking "Oh, yes, please strike, so I don't have to dance the show tonight, it will give me two more days", and of course because the cellists were complaining, because their chairs were sinking in the mud, and their cellos were going down in the mud. And they had to outline with tape over the stage, puddles. And I thought this is taking Swan Lake a little too realistically.

AM Sloshing through the snow.

EH Not only did I have to worry about the steps that I barely knew, but I had to worry about, you know, singing in the rain, kind of thing. Or dancing in the rain. And then they would say to me, things like, it's okay, don't worry just follow Jennifer. And I thought, "Great, Jennifer's got red hair". So I was standing in the wings and I got there and I realised that they all had black cloth over their hair. Which one in Jennifer? I had no idea. And things like the sets would come down. And I was in the fourth act, you know, emoting like crazy and tripping every time I'd hit the wings. Because I'd tripping over the wings. Those kinds of things, you know. And then on top of it, I had this huge head cold. And then I'd put my hair over my ears and I'd put the Swan's fins, I could not hear the music to save his life. It was a deaf Swan. But I made it.

AM Evelyn, let's have another piece of music. What should we play?

EH Prokofiev's Romeo and Juliet. Anything from that. The full score, although there's a moment in the third act that is just heaven. It's right after I've gone to fire Lawrence. And I've gotten the potion. Even talking about it, I'm breaking into tears. It's just beautiful. [MUSIC]

AM The Montreal Symphony under Charles Dutoit, with part of act three, from Prokofiev's Romeo and Juliet.

AM   Now, ballet's pretty hard on the body after awhile; do you still have to work out every day?

EH   Every day. Well, I mean we have a few days off per month, and it just depends on how tired you are. You have to kind of really go day by day; it's one of those things that it's never the same. It's the wonderful thing about the human body. And just when you think you've got something under your belt and then you wake up the next day and it's elusive; so that's the real challenge.

AM   Some days just stretching, or how does the regime go?

EH   Well, I mean basically bar in class and rehearsal. I mean every day if you could. I mean I try to do, every say two weeks, take one day completely free, so I just would sleep in and…

AM   And eat chocolate.

EH   Eat chocolate and ice cream, that's right. And pasta. Absolutely. White chocolate preferably.

AM   White chocolate, this is your favourite?

EH   Yeah. So that, you know, if anyone listening out there would like to send me white chocolate, feel free.

AM   All presents will be gratefully accepted.

EH   That's right, and will be gratefully consumed.

AM   Do you just suffer guilt over it though, Evelyn?

EH   None. None.

AM   Oh good, I'm so glad to hear it, you know.

EH   Not a bit. I figure I work hard enough. I deserve my treats.

AM   So, how about dancing in pain—you must have had to do this through your career?

EH   I'm doing that right now. I have a soft corn in between my fourth and fifth toes, and it's the kind of pain that you think your foot is broken. And it was infected. And it's just… it's like it goes through to the back of your eyeballs, and each step you take you're kind of ooh, ooh, ooh, ooh… it's quite painful.

AM   So how do you get into the emotion of the part when your foot's hurting?

EH   Well hopefully it's a dramatic part. But, you know, there are wonderful little things that they're invented now, like gel pads and second skin, and it's amazing the technology that's out there to help you. And then you, you know, take what I call, you know, Canada's food guide for dancers—three servings of vegetables, three servings of fruit, three servings of pasta or carbohydrates and three servings of Advil a day. And that gets you through.

AM   Now, I read an article about you being very hard on yourself about your looks, your appearance. Have you got past that?

EH   No, I think it's again another one of these things of coming to accept it. There's one place in Giselle where Albrecht takes me, and I'm looking down, and he picks me up by my chin and looks at me and says, oh, I just have to marry you. And every time I'm just so embarrassed. Inside, I just go, oh, no no really, you don't have to say that, it's okay, it's quite okay. So I just… it's… now it's more of a joke for me, it's not so important.

AM   Well that's good. But you agonized over it when you were a kid.

EH   Oh yeah. I thought I was a blob.

AM   You're the tiniest little blob I've ever seen.

EH   But you know, because it's… I mean, you know, you take a look around you, and especially in the ballet, there are a lot of really very beautiful ballerinas, beautiful women. And you come to realize it. But I'm learning now that, you know, it's one thing to also have a soul and a spirit to compensate. And it helps to have a sense of humour.

AM   So tell me about your shoes. All ballerinas are obsessed by their shoes, aren't they?

EH   Do you really want to hear this 'cause this is really… I have a friend who looks and says, I don't want to hear any more about your shoes. Yes, my shoes are the bane of my existence. They're a blessing and a curse at the same time, because basically they are your final contact with your technique and the floor, and they are the instrument—it would be in the sense of the wheel of the car—that if there was something wrong with the wheel, it doesn't matter how fine the motor is running, or how comfortable the seats are; if those wheels aren't right you're not gonna drive very far. And this is really what the biggest problem is with the point shoe because each day your foot, your musculature is different, it's more tired, it's stronger, it's weaker, it doesn't fit in the shoe the same because each shoe is hand made. And of course if the shoe—it's like the princess and the pea—if it isn't mechanically working quite right with your foot, you're having to fight and compensate through the back of your mind in every step you take, and it will put a different stress on a certain part of your foot. And sometimes you can actually, if the shoe is really wrong and you've danced a ballet on it, injure a part of your foot. And so of course to make the shoes just right, because I like them quiet and malleable and soft, and because I have a very high instep (which is the shape of my foot—the arch is very highly… it bends quite highly) that it's much more difficult to get the exact position of the shoe to give me the support that I need to be able to be free enough on point. But when you finally do get it, it's a joy to dance on point. It's just… it's magical; you think to yourself there's nothing strange about being up there.

AM How long does a pair of shoes last?

EH It really depends on what you're dancing and how well they fit. If they fit well they will dance—they will dance, isn't that a Freudian slip—they will dance, they will dance… you know, sometimes I can go through with one pair of point shoes for a whole Swan Lake, and sometimes I will have done the whole Swan Lake first and then wear them still for the whole ballet. So it's remarkable. It just depends on… because I don't really need so much of the shoe, I just need the support in the right place. And that's really where the science comes into it.

AM And then you just work and work and work to find who makes a pair that works really well, and then get modifications for you?

EH You can do that. I find that sometimes the more I ask for modifications from someone making the shoes, the worse they become, and the best thing is for you to try to do the modifications yourself. So sometimes it can take… that can really spend… you can spend a lot of time. I remember one time I was dating a man who just could not understand why I would spend so many hours sewing my point shoes (couldn't you pay somebody to do it for you). And I said, no, this is a rather personal thing. Because there's something about that fact that you have to have hands-on to your point shoes to sew them and to be in the right way. It's… really, it's part of it, you know. It's like putting… One of my favourite things is putting on my makeup just before the show. It's almost like a rite, it's a ritual.

AM Do you have rituals, little superstitions—other kinds that aren't so sensible?

EH No, not really. I mean there's all sorts of things. Like they say you should never put your shoes on the floor, you should never get yellow roses on stage, those kinds of things; and I don't really think much about them. I'm not really too superstitious. I find that just… if you've done your hard work, that's your best—your best confidence builder.

AM Contemporary ballet has been a large part of your life, as well as all these classical ballets. How do those two worlds meet for you?

EH Oh, it's fascinating because I find that the one feeds the other and the other enhances the other. You know, it's a kind of… I mean, contemporary ballet for me is never as fulfilling of course as the classical ballet, as far as my perspective is, in the sense that—except for one choreographer perhaps, which is Henny Jurriens. He manages to capture emotion in such a way that you move with your whole body and yet you are just as fulfilled as if you've done a full-length ballet. It's quite phenomenal. In seven minutes you get as much fulfillment as you do in three hours. But classical ballet is such a tremendous challenge in its esthetics and in its mastery. You know, you really are working at a craft and you are… it's the whole total sense of the tradition and the breathing and the dramatic interpretation—it brings everything together. Whereas a lot of contemporary ballet—not all—but a lot of contemporary ballet is much more abstract and it's dealing with emotion and more visceral movement, you know, much more of a free movement, and so it lends a joy in itself that you are doing something that there are no set rules to go by. So you find an expression of every muscle and fibre in your body, and what I enjoy so much is that when you move that way and you discover those things you can bring them back to classical ballet and sneak 'em in here and there, and therefore find a way of making…

AM   What kind of things?

EH   Well just certain things. For example, in a ballet I'll use a contraction or I'll, you know, bend an elbow here or I'll bend my knees, or I won't be afraid to turn in here—it's just a matter of you discover a language of using your whole body; whereas if you take a look at someone who has been trained only with the classics, it's much more difficult for them to create circular movement within the classics. You know, it's very up and down and it's very… the whole concept of how you move is from one position to the next position, whereas in contemporary ballet you more often are dealing with very different transitions from movement to movement. And then you can bring this into classical ballet. You can say, oh, well, I don't have to just go to this pose here, it's how I can move from this pose to this pose, which becomes different and therefore more expressive.

AM   Let's have another piece of music.

EH   Okay. I think what I was going to say was anything by Brahms, but one of my favourite things is Brahm's *Piano Concerto No. 2*, I think it's no. 2, the second movement. It's absolutely beautiful.

AM   Why is this one important to you, Evelyn?

EH   Two reasons. One is because it was the piece of music that Henny, who is my great mentor, was listening to just the week before he died, and he handed me a tape and gave it to me and let me listen to it, and so it was in my mind right after he had died. And secondly, because Brahms was one of my father's favourite composers. I danced a solo by Frederick Ashton to five Brahms waltzes, and after I've done four of these five dances I pick up a whole bunch of rose petals and I walk to the back very quietly, and one day in performance, out of the blue—I don't know why—I had a vision of my father's funeral. And I got to the back and I felt that my father was so close to me with the beginning strains of this music, and every performance since I have the feeling that he's right there. [MUSIC]

AM   The second movement of Brahm's *Piano Concerto No. 2*, the choice of our guest on Mountaintop Music ballerina Evelyn Hart.

How important was Henny Jurriens, former artistic director of the Royal Winnipeg Ballet, in your life?

EH   Probably **the** most significant person in my life. I met him in 1981 when I went over to Dutch National Ballet to guest with them, and he was my partner in Four Last Songs, and that's also probably going to be my next selection of music. And to meet him was amazing, and I still remember that very first meeting. He came in, wearing this long, navy blue woolen legwarmer, and I was standing on the side. And he came up to me and just, before he did anything, just grabbed hold of me, gave me this big hug and said, you must be Evelyn. And I looked at him and I said, who are you? [laughing]. And you know, it kind of shocked me because I wasn't used to that at all. And from the very first minute he gave me his soul in a sense; he just believed in my art tremendously and he taught me about life as I've never been taught before, in the sense of how to accept myself, how to understand myself, how to understand others, how to appreciate life, how to… And he just looked at me once and he said, you know, Evvy, I just—one day when he was quite exasperated with me and my insecurities—he said, I just wish with all my heart that one day you feel as good in your skin as I feel in mine. And then he kind of pinched his arm and he said, you know, I wake up and I'm so happy in my skin. And one other thing he used to always do was he would look at his arms whenever something would move him, and it was anything during the day—it was remarkable how full of love and passion he was for everything and everyone. And he would always roll up his sleeve and you could see that his hairs were standing on end, and he'd look at you and say, goose bumps. And I still, I find myself doing it, three or four times a day now. I mean it's just part of my life. Because somehow, just the way he saw the world, was in vivid colour.

AM   And great acceptance.

EH   Total acceptance. And therefore he was… acceptance of flaws, too. This was what was so amazing. Total acceptance of all the flaws and he rejoiced in the flaws as well as the perfection. It was just that someone who touched people so greatly— it was really tremendous. And to be able to work with him that closely and to have someone actually take the time to try to get to understand me. See, a lot of times I think in my career I've run into that problem that people, especially when you're talented or you're in a position of privilege in a way, they don't really want to know what makes you tick and they don't really want to deal with you, 'cause you're just a frustration. And he was quite avidly involved with trying to understand what made me tick so he could help me understand myself. It was quite wonderful. But he would do that with everybody, not just me. He would often times say now, you know, I sit back and think how can I help this person come to understand what they need to do.

AM He wasn't at the Royal Winnipeg Ballet long.

EH He was actually with the company for two years before he took over, but he was only director for eight months.

AM And then he was killed in a car accident.

EH Hm hm, with his wife. But what was phenomenal was the day before he left, I'll never forget him looking at me. He said, Evvy, he says, I want you to be able to do this on your own. And he said, besides, I have to go. And those were the last words he spoke to me.

So it's quite profound. And interestingly enough, he died on exactly nine years to the day of our premiere, Four Last Songs, which was the connecting point to us. Isn't that interesting?

Funny how life really…

AM Goes in circles and interweaves…

EH Totally.

AM Have you ever been interested in trying your hand at choreography?

EH Never. I'm good at fixing things, you know, because I think that when I see something I know how I feel and I know how it would have to come through my soul and the choices that I would have to make in order to make it be expressive. But as far as creating something from scratch, like to watch someone like James Kudelka… I just don't know how he does it, how he has these images and ideas that just come out of the blue. And I could take an image that I'm given already and sculpt it for my own body, but to actually… It would be like taking a clothes designer, you know, the actual designer that comes up with the actual first garment. I'd be able to look at it and say, oh, well if I added a brooch here or a scarf here, or if I made it shorter or I tuck it in the waist it would look better on me, and feel more comfortable. But to actually make the first garment, I don't think I've got that talent.

AM I want to ask you about how different countries approach ballet. For example, there are big differences between Russian ballet and American ballet?

EH Definitely. I mean, really one of the things is you take a look at all the great companies and the great schools in the world—there's the Paris Opera, there's the Royal Danish Ballet, there's the Royal Ballet in England, there's the New York City Ballet, and of course the two Russian companies—and basically each company is so distinct and so different, and yet you see similarities in technique. But, for example, I would say that the French are known for their footwork and their incredible physicality, and in a sense elegance and breeding; and the Russians, at the moment I would say, are much more known for their expressiveness and their schooling, their style. And the Americans are known really for their incredible legs and incredible technique and speed, and the British are known much more for their phrasing and musicality.

AM How about us Canadians?

EH Us Canadians, I'd say we fall somewhere right in the middle.

AM Of all of that?

EH I would say that, really, you know… yeah, I would say we're kind of a good balance between both. You know, in a way I'd say our style is still technically very strong, but nothing about us Canadians I think is extreme. In other words, we've got good technique, we've got good expression and we have an ability to be versatile, but our style is less—how would I say it—less stamped, you know.

AM Is there anything recognizable about a Canadian company, though?

EH I would say one thing is the fact that still there… In Canada there's a marked, noticeable quality in the performances that is lacking in a lot of the other big companies. That in other words the Canadian companies still, I think, take time to work on the details and the level of the partnering and the level of the point work, and there's distinctly, still to me, rather than just going for sheer physicality—see how high you can lift your leg, see how many turns you can do, see how many jumps you can do—it's much more still integrated of you use the technique to express the story, or whatever it is, or the music, whatever it is you're doing. And I'm very proud of that because I think that's quite wonderful.

AM Let's have another piece of music.

EH Richard Strauss, *Four Last Songs*, the fourth song. It's one of my favourite pieces to do. [MUSIC]

AM That was the last song from *Four Last Songs* by Richard Strauss, the choice of my guest on Mountaintop Music, ballerina Evelyn Hart.

Evelyn, just before we send you off to your mountain top, we let our guests take one book with them. What book would you take?

EH I was thinking about this a lot. I think the book that I would want to take would be actually a blank book, one that I had put in several quotations from different people, such as Joseph Campbell, or Aristotle—just different people, different… some sonnets from Shakespeare. And then I would want definitely to have many, many blank pages so that I could write what I feel, what I experience, what I think, that I could write letters even if they wouldn't go anywhere. But the most important thing for me is the ability to be able to express and put words on a page. And I think that's one of the things that I love so much about Shakespeare is that, especially coming back to Shakespeare after having been away from him since high school in a way, and re-falling in love with him again and reading those words, and the wisdom behind those words. But also the poetry in the language and the music in the language, it just… you just feel as though your soul is going to burst, and I find such a great pleasure in taking a pen in my hand and being able to write. If, for example, you see the moon or a sunset, or if you've been touched by an event in your life, or you've heard a piece of music, or you just, you're feeling melancholy, or you're feeling extraordinarily joyful, or you're totally frustrated—that you can somehow put down things of the soul in front of you. And there's so many ways to do it and it's just such a creative, beautiful thing.

AM Words?

EH Language. The ability to communicate with other human beings.

AM Now, you can also choose where in the world that you'll be cast away. It doesn't have to be the top of a mountain, it could be, oh I don't know, one of the beaches near Winnipeg or cottage country in Ontario. Where would you go.

EH Oh, good heavens, that's hard. Um, you know, I think it would definitely… wherever it was it would have to be near water. So I think probably the West Coast. Two friends of mine live in Lyons Bay, and I think the combination, or somewhere maybe on Vancouver Island, where you have this combination of these incredible huge pine trees, woods and rugged rocks with waterfalls, and then the crashing of the sea and huge mountains. I think there's just nothing more beautiful than there.

And it's also my beloved winter, because I think that there's nothing more beautiful than our Canadian winters. And so I wouldn't really want to be stuck somewhere where I couldn't experience the snow and that quiet white.

AM Evelyn, just before we say good-bye, what's your final choice of music.

EH Actually, anything by Barbra Streisand. I think she's another person who I just adore—her voice—because she somehow stirs something inside of my soul, and one of my particular favourites was something then very funny, like for example, *I am the walking illustration of our love…*

AM From Funny Girl.

EH *You've gotta have a swan, or you're out of luck; 'cause a chicken wouldn't do he'd only cluck…* So there's both sides.

AM Barbra Streisand as Fanny Bryce doing Swan Lake.

AM Evelyn, it's been a real pleasure talking to you.

EH My pleasure, totally.

AM Thank you.

DG One of the very first questions somebody in the office wanted to ask—is Bobby Curtola your real name?

BC It sure is. And that's a funny story because my grandmother was Italian. Sicilian Italian. My grandmother, because of her heritage and being the boss of the family, when my mother came home with Robert on my birth certificate, she sent her back to the priest to put Bobby on it, because they used to call me Bobbito—Bobbuto, Bobbito—something like that.

DG How many b's?

BC Oh God, that's a good story. You heard about that one?

DG Tell us.

BC I started off as B-o-b-b-y, and in the seventies, when the groups were so very popular and it was difficult for a single artist to find a spot, I moved into the clubs and I got married and had a family, and I actually got tired of everybody trying to compare me to 1962. So, because Engelbert had such a great idea with his name, I dropped a "b" in my name. It was Bob with a "y"—'cause I wasn't a Robert, I wasn't a Bob—so it was Bob with a "y", still pronounced it Boby. But what it did was, when I got in front of the deejays it was controversial—Boby, Baby, Booby, Boby—I mean, they called me all these crazy names, and what was interesting was,· it ended up them asking me why I did it. So I had a chance to tell them that things had changed for me, that I was doing the Las Vegas thing…

DG Today and not yesterday.

BC Yeah, today and yesterday, and that family was important, that all the things I thought I'd missed in the sixties I was getting a chance to do.

DG And in fact your home town changed its name, too. You were born and raised in Port Arthur, but of course we call it Thunder Bay today.

BC That's right. A great place. I always say that if you make a friend in Thunder Bay, it's forever. And one of the reasons why we ended up moving to Alberta was because of the same kind of feeling here. It's truly the west and people care, and they're of the earth. They—you know what I mean, the farming community—is so important and the

BOBBY CURTOLA
WITH DAVID GELL, 1994

heritage is so important. And I kid everybody. I say, you know, when we were on tour I was living in Las Vegas, at the time in Toronto, and I came to Calgary and Mayor Ralph said, well Bobby, why don't you move to the suburbs?—and I got on no. 2 highway and it ended up in Edmonton. So I kept driving. At least he's up there now.

DG Tell me, your dad ran a garage.

BC That's right, a service station.

DG Did you work in it?

BC I sure did.

DG Did you think this was going to be your life?

BC You know, I always loved to sing. They used to kid me because my dad, he was associated with the dealership for awhile, I was ahead of the cleanup crew. I mean, where do you start when you're a kid. And of course, when you're the boss's son, everybody sat around and said, well if we don't do it Boby's gonna get you know what for it anyway. So,

I ended up learning to work very hard in my life, and I used to buy the cars that they never wanted. I'm still car crazy. And I'd fix them up and sell them and, while I was cleaning up the floor in the back end, the salesman would come in to show the used cars and say, Bobby, turn the radio down, we're tryin' to sell a car. Can you keep quiet. And years later they laughed because I ended up getting paid for just the very thing I was doing in the back, singing along with the radio.

DG Was there music in the family?

BC My mother always loved to sing and we used to sing some of the songs she recorded. She used to keep my brother and I from wrestling by getting us to sing at home. I mean two boys, you know, a couple of years apart—whaddaya do?

DG What were you singing? Rossini?

BC Actually, we were singing some of the songs she wrote—things like, [singing] *Gina, tu se mi amore, Gina, you're the one I adore. There's a little town in southern Italy, where a pretty little maid, she said she'd wait for me…* Somethin' like that—I mean, she had some great songs.

And the school of the year program we used to go to; my brother and I used to sing together with a couple of guys down the street 'cause we got in for free. We used to get the free popcorn, and it was the days of the Lyceum Theatre and, in my high school years—the girls that remembered me singing at the skating rink, the last skate at the rink shack before they would shut the rink shack down at nine o'clock, we'd have that last skate before we went home. And I used to listen to the radio all the time and the girls, they used to ask me, come on Bobby, sing that new song on the hit parade; so we'd do a big chain and we'd skate around the rink—hand-in-hand all of us—and I'd sing the latest song on the radio and they'd sing along with me.

It was fun. I was always singing. My neighbour used to say, "Mary"—my mother's name was Mary— "Listen, here comes Bobby." I'd be comin' down the alley, 'cause it was like a reverb echo chamber, and I'd be singing all these songs and I sang a little in the church choir, but I went to—because of where we lived—we went to a Protestant school. I was raised Catholic, so it was difficult for me to get over to the other side of the city. So mostly the high school choir. And it was good for me because I got to understand the differences of, you know, of religion—that all rivers lead to the same place; you just need to find your way to say thank you.

DG How did you find your way to Bobby and the Bobcats?

BC Unbelievable accident. I was the backup singer. The girl that remembered me singing at the skating rink was president of our high school—it was a brand new high school and there was no real seniority, if you were in grade 12 or 13. In Ontario we have 13. So, the grade nines had just as much seniority as the older guys, ya know what I mean. So, when it came our turn to put our little assembly on she remembered me singing, and there was a couple of guys who played in the band, so I was one of the backup singers. And I sang a couple of songs and the girls started to scream. So my buddies in the band said, you better sing some more songs. So what happened, I sang a couple more songs and we ended up with two bands that were really the same band. It was Brian Merrit and his Band, and then it was Bobby and the Bobcats when I was singing lead. So it was the same guys, but we just, we sort of changed the package a little bit.

DG Were those guys involved in *Hand In Hand With You*—because it was not long after you recorded that song.

BC Actually, what a strange coincidence. And I often wondered about this 'cause my biggest record was a song called *Fortune Teller*, and: [quoting lyrics] *Fortune teller, can you see what my future's gonna be; can you see at all in your crystal ball; have you got a dream for me?* Well, I used to dream about this. I mean, I used to go to bed wishing to be a singer and to have a chance to do some of these things in my life, and the moral of the story is, if you wish hard enough and you reach for the stars, every once in awhile ya get one. What happened was that they were in the process of forming their own record company and recording some of their music, that they had been writing for years as a hobby with their relatives—their sons and daughters as singers, called The Dawn Trio, and a local night club band called The Buddy Edwards Trio. And they were in the process of doing all this while I was getting all this notoriety at high school. And one of their sons, Butch Hurden was in grade thirteen—told his dad about this kid that everybody liked. At the noon sock-hop we had all the other schools comin' to our high school to hear our band play. And, as luck would have it, they said let's try this guy out. So, to make a long story short, there I did—I walked into that situation that they were already in the process of making this record, and I ended up the lead singer with The Dawns as my backup group instead of the lead singers. And it worked, because of a brave deejay named Doug Burroughs in Winnipeg, Manitoba, who said he'd play this crazy record. And actually the only people that outsold us, in England, was the Beatles. It was number one for months. And my first professional appearance was on the *Bob Hope Show*—I was scared to death.

DG We're gonna' come to that later 'cause that's really something to talk about. What did your family think when you actually were there on a record?

BC They were in awe. But, being Italian—I mean, my managers, who were also songwriters and owned the record company, were very well respected people in my home town of Port Arthur/Fort William. The Hurden brothers used to run Manpower, and one of the slogans they came up with if you remember—I don't know if you go back this far, but, [singing] *Don't wait for spring, do it now; when there are men who know how.* You know, for the home improvement stuff during the winter was one of their things they did, and had a couple of hits in the swing era. And Basil, who was a resident engineer for Saskatchewan Wheat Pool elevators. They were very well respected people and my parents trusted them. And, as luck would have it, who thought that the record would sell. All I always say is, thank God for large Italian families.

DG Every member of the family bought.

BC Yeah. They were very kind to me, God bless them, they always supported me. And my home town was wonderful that way; they always supported me. And through all those years of high school, my high school chums would put my record on in the juke box—it was like Happy Days. We'd go to the local restaurant, which was Farrels Restaurant in Port Arthur, and, you know, they had the juke box and they'd play my latest song and they'd say, Bobby, that's not as good as *Hitchhiker*—they used to razz me, but never, ever belittled me. They were always so supportive; it was a great, great youth I had. I'd get on an airplane on the weekend, on Trans Canada Airlines, and I'd fly away to all these exotic places I used to read about, and then I'd be back in school on a Monday tryin' to concentrate, you know. It was, like, it was wild.

DG We've gotta listen to some music right now. What would you like us to play now?

BC Well, you know, the thing that we were talking about—*Hand in Hand With You*—one of my all-time favourite songs because it was the song that changed my life. I was a kid going to high school, dreaming about, you know, another life; dreaming about making records like all these other guys were doin', and with that crazy song—thanks to those unforgettable disc jockeys across this country—I got a chance to live a dream. So simple, but it worked. Thank you. Thank all of you out there.

DG In fact, that song was turned down by all the major Canadian labels, wasn't it?

BC That's right, yeah. And it was funny how it went, actually. When we first released our first song, they said, oh, it's just a lucky break. But it worked. I mean, it worked in every major market—started off in February, late January release; by February it was number one in Winnipeg, and slowly it went across the country and then back to the east and, in June, number one in Toronto. So it took us awhile…

DG That must have just felt sensational. How old were you at this point?

BC I was what—sixteen, seventeen? Sixteen.

DG Now, we've talked about it being released, but what about the record label? I mean, if the big guys didn't take it, did they create their own label?

BC They created their own label and I was an artist on it, and after it started to work so well they made me a partner, which was wonderful. I mean, they were straight-up guys.

DG It was very courageous on their part, wasn't it? I mean, they must have sunk some dollars in that.

BC Yeah, they did. They took that gamble and the industry said, no, it would never happen. And it was because of our trip to England in the sixties—our fifth record started to work for us, and then *Fortune Teller* hit and a guy named Bunny Lewis brought us to England. We were starting to have some success in Canada and America—in the U.S. with *Fortune Teller*—and while we were in England… England had a content law, and they had that twenty percent foreign music content law. And I brought that idea back to Canada, and the results of it were that we ended up with our content law. But they screwed it up here. I mean, I don't know how they did it, but they screwed it up. If they would have just left it the way England did it, it would have been perfect. But they had to change it. And I don't know how they did it, but they somehow figured out a way to get all of us Canadians fighting over our twenty-five percent, and they left seventy percent open for the rest of the world, so. But England did it right. They had a content law where only twenty percent of the foreign music was allowed in the country per month, and what it did was it let the English artists cover the songs that weren't released. And it didn't prevent the foreign music from being released, but it gave them the jump—not unlike what happens in Quebec when they cover English tunes and convert them to French. And what happens is that the artist, when you end up copying a Picasso enough times, you end up painting one. So, if you end up cloning some real great music, you end up writing it after awhile. And the English explosion is history, but that was one of the fundamental things that happened over there that helped those first artists make enough money. And you know what happens with an artist; if he sells a picture he goes and buys more canvas. So it wasn't a complicated deal.

DG Well okay, Bobby, let's get back to the record you've chosen, one that truly changed your life, as played by those very same deejays—Boby Curtola's first hit, *Hand In Hand With You*. [MUSIC]

DG When you started your recording career, and working—'cause this relationship between the performer and the songwriter has got to be a very crucial one—there must have been occasions when they said, here's a song we'd like you to do, we think this is good; and you looked at it and you thought, no, I don't like this. Or did that ever happen?

BC Well, yeah. I mean, there's a lot of times you're not sure. In fact, the songs you never think are gonna work usually do. In fact, there's the story on *Fortune Teller*. That song—this is funny—it was the last tune in a batch of tunes that we'd recorded in Nashville, 'cause we tried—we went to all of the places in Canada that we could go, and we ended up in Nashville, to be able to compete with the U.S. product. And Nashville, I couldn't believe, there was Floyd Kramer, Grady Martin, and Chet Atkins playing on our sessions. And the Anita Kerr Singers and the Jordanaires—no wonder those records sold. And this kid, Bobby Curtola from Canada, how lucky can he get. But what happened was that we tried all those other places to record, and Nashville gave us the best product. It was something there that worked. It was the last tune in a series of tunes we'd recorded in Nashville, and what had happened was they were afraid to release it 'cause it didn't sound like anything else, it didn't seem to fit on the hit parade. And what happened there was, I mean, they were just forced into it because we had nothing else to come out with. So we ended up releasing *Fortune Teller* and, in Canada, it only went up to the top twenty—it never broke in to the top ten. And thanks to a guy named Red Robinson in Vancouver, who sent it to a friend of his in Seattle, who sent it to a friend in Hawaii, soon as it hit number one in Hawaii—and we were sending records from Canada—all of a sudden the Canadian radio stations got back on the record. As soon as it hit in Hawaii.

DG When you were working with the brothers Dyer and Basil Hurden, was your interpretation of their songs what they had in mind, or did they sort of come around to your way of thinking?

DG I think what happens, and it's not unlike, [singing] *Do you know the way to San Jose?*—Dionne Warwick and Burt Bacharach, when they were writing together—there's a magic in combinations.

And what happens is that you end up expressing yourself through each other, and there's some synergy that happens there and I think that we found it together. I was able to give some life to the things that they were trying to say and express, and they were able to capture my expression in their music. Like, we just sort of came together. It's a hard one to put into words, but it's like E.S.P. in a way. You know, everybody has a different way of saying the word 'love' for instance. And sometimes you have a different way of singing it, to give it real meaning. The difference, like myself or Ray Charles singing the same lyrical line would be different—to make it believable. I would have to express it another way, the same line, and I think that we came together, not unlike Dionne Warwick and her writing crew in those early years. And it took her a long time to find the next step, and that's sort of what happened to me in the seventies. It was hard to replace that incredible thing that happened when we were all together.

DG   When you were this youngster—sixteen, seventeen, eighteen—and so much was happening to you, especially when finally *Fortune Teller* did take off, were you in sort of a haze; did everything just happen around you and you wondered, gosh what's going on?

BC   No. You know what, it's funny. When you're a fan of music, which I was—I was a fan of music who ended up singing and being a part of the *Photoplay* magazine that I was reading, you know. But they used to wonder about it. I mean, number one, I come from an Italian family, and there is no place for an ego in an Italian family. I mean, you know, they say the males sort of strut around—and that might be true in some ways—but when it comes to that other part of it, no. My father, my parents—nobody would put up with that, nobody around me. But what happened was that when things started to work, if you were in that situation and things started to work for you, the comparison factor was what the reactions were for the other successful artists. So when we started to get the results that other successful artists were getting, it was business. We only assumed that that's—we had no measuring stick, so we figured, well when you're successful they scream and tear your clothes off, and if they don't you're not successful. It's got nothing to be with being egotistical; it's got to do with being in the ball game.

DG   Well, let's break off and have another choice of music. What's next?

BC   Well, here we go. You were asking some of my favourite songs; well I can't believe what's happened to country music. And the guy who's really changed it, who's taken it across the line, is a fella by the name of Garth Brooks, and I really like what he's doin'. And I love this song because everybody loves to sing it—*I Got Friends In Low Places*. [MUSIC]

DG   Bobby, at one point there were something like 350 fan clubs. It depends who you quote—250,000 members, 500,000 members—you were the biggest thing this country had ever, ever seen. Did that kind of adulation take any kind of toll on you? You know, lack of privacy and not knowing who your real friends were, and so on?

BC   Why, it wasn't the real friends, actually; it was responsibility. You know, I was the guy next door, and all of a sudden it worked. And the interesting part of that history is that, because it was so new and we were the first, there was no way of recording all of this stuff. It was like this little mini army would go and capture this hill, and then it would move on to the next one, and we never had anybody to leave there with the flag. So it was really hard to document all of this stuff 'cause it's goin' so fast. But, what happened was that, with the write-ups and the way I was raised, and all of a sudden being thrust into this situation where, you know, the recognition from a lot of parts of the country and a lot of people—there was a responsibility as a teenager to live up those things that they thought I was, and which I really was. So I had to be twice as careful about all of the other things. The room for error was eliminated; I had to be responsible. It was tough for me all those years in a lot of ways, but you know, I can appreciate how some of those other guys felt because you had to play it right, and you had to do the things right, and a little bit of error—the consequences were incredible. So I managed to do it. I mean, I managed to keep my nose clean and stick to my rules and do the things I believed in.

And specializing all those years as a young teenager being in business, with all of that responsibility, was incredible. As the things changed for me in the seventies and I ended up in the night clubs, you know, and I fell in love and ended up with a wonderful wife, Ava, and two great kids—all of the things I thought I'd missed, I ended up having a chance to do.

DG When you were sixteen-seventeen, you were graduating from high school age, maybe go on to university type possibility…

BC Yeah, I had a scholarship waiting for me, actually at the University of Detroit.

DG So that was a door that had to be kept shut because you had other things that took your time?

BC It was unique what happened to me. There I was, specializing in a field where there was no matrix, there was no college course for it, and I was successful on records making money and learning a lot about the entertainment business. And we had a little meeting—the family and the principal and the record people—and what we had decided was that, who else would have a better shot at something than a guy like me that had it already working, and that, you know, there was always another opportunity around the corner if I decided to go back to school. But somehow I managed to be an honour student and I graduated, and I often wonder what would have happened, you know, if I would have followed that road; but I'm not so wealthy that I can't handle it, and I'm not so poor that I can't survive, so.

DG You mentioned earlier the mob scenes, and clothes being ripped off you. How did it feel the first time this happened to you?

BC Are you kidding? It was the most exciting thing that ever happened to me in my life; I couldn't believe it. It was an absolute thrill. But you see most people don't realize that it was the second row that wanted to be the front row, that were pushing and screaming and grabbing. The people in the front were just pleased to be there to talk to ya, but it was the second and third row that were out of arms reach, if you know what I mean. And that's how all of that happened. But when they ended up there, they were normal, they were just wantin' to talk to ya. But it was an incredible thrill—I mean, it was just an incredible thrill.

DG You were probably one of the first Canadian pop acts able to make a name for yourself internationally without leaving the country—you remained Canadian. Is being Canadian important to you?

BC Well, it was because it was the way we started, you know. We would have actually loved to have gone to America right away with that opportunity for success, and I have to salute those other great Canadians. I mean, Paul Anka opened the door for all of us to say that you could be Canadian and do this. But the difference for us was that we couldn't get a record release with a major label, and because we were home town boys so to speak, the records were in the trunk of the car. So we had to travel to the local radio station and do the local show. And it was, I guess, the only door open to us, and by doing that, by going to Winnipeg and doing the local show, and then going to Regina and then to Edmonton and then to Toronto, our little record company ended up with distributors in all those little towns, and it was the only way open to us. And because of that we ended up with that grassroots support, and the deejays liked us because the kids liked us. They'd bring us in for shows and we were accessible, whereas the Americans and the other famous people were really hard to get to come in and they cost a heck of a lot more than us at the time.

DG Let's move on to something else, too. You dabbled in acting when you played the lead in the CBC drama, *Charlie Love from Liverpool*.

BC How did you get that information?

DG 1964.

DG Did you see yourself, when you got that, moving into a whole new world as a thespian?

BC Well, you know, I was such a shy guy—even then, I was a nervous wreck. I was trying to figure out what this little guy out of Thunder Bay/Port Arthur-Fort William, was doing in the middle of Toronto in a movie. And I was tryin' to figure out what I was doing in the middle of that recording session at The Little Studio with Bill Porter, who used to record Elvis—who I met by the way, going in to a session after we were coming out for the first time, in Nashville. I was scared to death.

DG I think we should say at this point that this is not the first time you and I have worked together, because I was the host of *Ready, Steady Go*, one of the first rock shows on BBC—on 'British' Television, it wasn't BBC, it was the other…

BC On British Television. And that's where… I'm a little excited even being here, David.

DG And you came on the program.

BC Yes, that's right. We met for the first time then, on my trip to England. And it was right in the middle of the British explosion, before the rest of the world was aware of it. In fact, I brought a record back, David—you'll laugh—it was called *From Me to You*, that the Beatles had recorded. And no one in North America had heard of them by then. And actually, I've got a session… We recorded it, actually. It's somewhere in those piles of tapes that I have in my basement somewhere. But I brought it back and, my manager said, you know Bobby, it's really gonna be hard to sell that stuff in North America. He said, I don't think they're gonna make it in North America. Boy did he eat those words. But it was incredible what was happening in England; it was just, there was a feeling over that—and we talked about this—that you can't put into words. It was normal to go down to the local club and see an incredible band making incredible music. And they'd get off stage and another group of people would get on stage and do the same thing. It was… everywhere you looked and went it was normal to be in the middle of that environment. There was no pressure and everybody was having fun. Incredible—you can't explain it. It wasn't prefabricated, it was normal. And what a time to be there. I was in awe—I just was in awe.

DG Were you tempted to stay?

BC I wanted to. In fact, one of my big regrets was that I did not stay. We were on another program that we had talked about, *Thank Your Lucky Stars*, and I was on singing my *Fortune Teller* over there. And all the fans outside of the studio were waiting to see who they were waiting for—Tommy Tune was on the show, and a lot of the famous English artists. So, there my manager and I are waiting to see who they're waiting for. The last guy leaves—they were waiting for us.

I couldn't believe it; we were so excited. So now we're tryin' to get to the limo—this beautiful limousine. Like, you know, remember the cartoon Ritchie Rich, with the chauffeur and the open—it was a Bentley with the first part open and the back part covered?

Well, it was this incredible classic car that he gave us for our tour. And the chauffeur would drive us everywhere and we'd go see all the deejays, so now we're tryin' to get from the studio to the car. The guy drives it around the corner, we're cutting across the back lot—it was like the three stooges, but the two stooges, Basil, my manager, and myself. We peak out of the fence with the security guard the car's across the street, no fans. We start. Soon as he lets us out the gate, by the time we hit the sidewalk they were everywhere. Now he's got me by the back, he's dragging me through the crowd and I'm laughin' and gigglin' 'cause they're tearin' at a little of it… He ended up into the back of this Bentley with a crowd of girls, and half of his suit was ripped off; I had lost my shirt, I lost my jacket—I had my drawers on, that was it. And they're all gigglin' and laughin' and we couldn't believe it. I mean…

DG There was no malice in this at all, was there?

BC No, no. People don't realize, it wasn't vengeful or… it was just, they were gigglin', they were laughin'.

DG Okay, well let's have another piece of music. And this is something from the same period, isn't it?

BC The Beatles, it has to be because of the impact that they had on the whole world with their music. And it was a thrill for me to even be there at that time, you know, when they first started. And being in England, the record I bought of theirs and brought back to Canada—the first one, *From Me to You*, The Beatles—why not? [MUSIC]

DG Television's been good to you and, as you mentioned earlier, one of your very first television appearances was with Bob Hope, and that was in

Winnipeg.

BC   In Winnipeg. Actually, that's what started me off-I was on the Bob Hope Show, and there we were with our one record. Of course Patrice Wymore, who was a very famous actress, was on the show in the *Rifleman* with Johnny Crawford, and we never had time to rehearse. So there we are with the Jack Shapiro orchestra in the dressing room with a sax player going over the song, looking at the music, and there I am when Bob calls me out and I run out on stage and of course the Dawn Trio are with me, and the Jack Shapiro Orchestra. Ronnie, the older son, said, I'll grab the mike at the end of the stage and bring it to the centre and we'll sing behind you Bobby. The mike at the corner of the stage is nailed down. He does a little loop-the-loop, he's red as a beet, everybody laughs and they're all relaxed—so now the group sets up over on the end and I'm in the centre by myself. I'm a nervous wreck, but you know we got a great round of applause; it was as though we had staged it. I mean it was perfect 'cause it broke the ice. So there we go, the band starts and it's all quiet. And of course on a big stage like that—my first real professional appearance—you can't see anybody and it's quiet. I'm scared to death. Never mind the vibrato in my voice was fast then anyways; now I'm really dying. I'm saying, oh… this is it, I'm in trouble. At the end of the song they go crazy, they give us a standing ovation. Now, do you believe this? Outside of our dressing room on the intermission we have more people outside our dressing room door than Bob Hope. He comes over, he says, "I gotta meet this guy." So that's when Bob was an incredible experience for me. He was always nice to me a lot of years. I've appeared with him a few times and what a launch into the entertainment business—to meet a superstar like that who is actually nice to you, because not all of them are. He had no ego, he was very, very kind.

DG   We were talking about Louis Armstrong awhile ago. Well, we'll talk about him later on, but that was another example of…

BC   I've got a story for you there, too.

DG   Okay, well we'll get to that in a minute. Now, 1967—an important year for Canada, 100 years old—but you had toured until '67 and then you moved into the night club scene. So, why didn't you continue recording? Why go to that night club scene?

BC   Actually, we were a phenomenon. In those days we were like a cross between the Elvis Presley thing, the Frankie Avalon thing; we were a combination of a lot of that. We were getting the fans from those different artists for us, and we lasted a long time. Most artists never… I mean, seven years—a strong seven years in this country was unheard of in those days—and we were filling the arenas. I used to tour Canada twice a year, coast to coast. We wore out a lot of Cadillacs I'll tell you. But they were still showing up for us even though the British thing had hit so strong in '65. By '67 we were still filling arenas but we had to pick our spots. And my managers figured that Bobby, you better be like Rocky Marciano and hang your gloves up while the arenas are still full. So, in '69 we made that transition into the night clubs and my first professional appearance was with Louis Sachmo Armstrong; I was opening for him. It was difficult. To answer your question about radio play, there was really no room on the charts for us as a single artist unless we had gone into being a group. The door that was open for life was the nightclubs, to go with the audience that had remembered you and that was growing up with you. And the record business seemed to take a left turn at that time. If you weren't a group it was really hard to get the air play. And you know, in retrospect, my reaction then was thank you; I didn't feel bad about that. I mean, I was so thankful for what had happened to me for that period of time. The record business was never meant to be owned by anybody, I've said this before. I mean, you're so lucky to have the world focus on you for that moment. And Roy Orbison and I talked about this. I mean, look at all the great entertainers and singers there are out there. The difference for us was those hit records. Without those hit records, I mean, it really humbled me many times to sing with so many other people that had so much talent but for whatever reason had not put the other pieces together. And I don't know what that is, I don't know what makes the difference. It's not about money, it's about the right people coming together at the right time that are due to make a step. And what simply happens is you step off of a curb, and by accident—or is in an accident—you step with your left foot first, you lift your head up to brush your hair with your right hand.

DG As you saw your fans growing older, too, and you had to look in the mirror and think, hmmm, I'm not sixteen anymore.

BC No, that's right.

DG Did you sit at home some time and then sort of take stock of yourself and your career?

BC It was hard—you know, nobody's ever asked me that question before, David. That's an interesting question because, you know, you meet the same people going up as you do on the way down, and that's true. So if you do it right and you're not a complete jerk, he'll help you. But if you're you know what, you know, you have to face it. You always end up facing it, and we tried; I mean, we didn't do everything right, but we tried. And, while I was going through that I did do a lot of soul searching. I'm a spiritual kind of guy anyways because I always felt there was something else that happened that made this happen for me, and I don't consider myself any different than anybody else. But I do consider myself a lucky guy 'cause I was at the right place at the right time with what I had to bring, and I genuinely gave it, and in going through this process again, because of the responsibility and the effort, it was tough for me to decide whether I should just hang my guns up and go back to university, or continue. I already had the car, the house, and you know all the rest of that stuff. What else was I trying to achieve here? And it was a major decision to actually go on, to go into the nightclubs and continue with the entertaining.

DG It must have been around what, 1970 that you first went to Las Vegas to perform?

BC That's right.

DG And as you indicated before, that turned into a major career move.

BC Incredible.

DG You were one of the first to be signed to a long-term contract. How did that come about?

BC Same think as the record success when we started—the right place at the right time and we didn't try to do a tough deal. But we were spotted in Canada and we were asked to go down to America, to the Hughes hotel. And my good friend, Hymie Gershwin, who was a junket operator out of Calgary, managed to set up a meeting for us down there. And, this is a funny story. It took three days. We waited in the lobby of this gentleman who was running the Hughes Hotels for Howard Hughes—his name was Walter Caine—and we waited three days in his office 'cause he was talking to Frank Sinatra on the phone, or Sammy, or Robert Goulet. I mean it was endless, 'cause he was booking all these hotels and Walter Caine probably taught me more about the entertainment business than anybody in my life. He was absolutely a genius. He used to run some pictures for Howard Hughes, and discovered people like Lana Turner. And it's endless, it goes on and on and on; but our first meeting with Walter we waited three days. On the fourth day we end up getting into his office for this meeting. During the three days the secretaries all think well, this guy's not a bad guy—he's sort of cute, he's a nice guy—so I ended up making friends with everybody in the lobby. And Eleanor Gosse, who was the number one secretary there and who was his assistant, after we got into the meeting and they're talking about me like a hunk of meat, ya know—blah blah blah blah—and that I'm the talent but it doesn't matter, and Walter's saying, well no, we want Bobby to audition. My manager's saying, look at his records, Bobby doesn't audition. You want him you hire him; if you don't want him we'll go back to Canada, there's lots for us to do. But if you want him you hire him; he's not auditioning. So they're going through this, da da da da and all this stuff, and Eleanor winks at me. She goes behind them, lifts up the top of the vestibule there and puts the record on the record-player. This is like a Donald O'Connor movie now—Walter in the big chair, the cigar, the whole thing—and us over there trying to sell our act. The record goes on and I think this is humorous; these guys are talking about me like… She's looking at me, we're laughing 'cause this is funny 'cause these guys are tryin' to do business; so I stand up and I start to sing to the song that's on, and it happened to be a cover of R*ose Garden*. So there I am, I got my nice suit on and I stand up—[singing] *I beg your pardon, I never promised you a rose garden; along with the sunshine*—and I'm singing along to this song. All of a sudden they shut up. All of a sudden their body of secretaries, ten of them that are outside of this office, the typewriters stop. Everybody's looking in this room and I'm doing my little thing, and I do a little pirouette and I sing. He goes back in his chair, he says you got the job—and they're all applauding—you got the job. So he gave us a two-week booking, and from the two-week booking I got a standing ovation for every show. Every show they just… I guess they had never seen what I did, and it was the audience participation and it was incredible who used to hang around the Sands Hotel in those days. I mean that's where Frank Sinatra was, and I mean all the movie stars. Desi Arnez came up one night. I asked him, I said, Mr. Arnez, would you mind singing *Babalu* for us? He says, I can't do it, no no, I can't do it. You need a conga drum and I'll do it. He didn't think I'd have one. By accident I had one in storage around the corner. So I bring this conga drum out and there we… I mean, we were doing these crazy things, a conga line through the whole club. Joey bishop brought his whole show in. He was having so much fun, he says, wait—he goes back and gets everybody from the main show. This is before the main show and they're doing some stand-up comedy. It was incredible because of the stars that were hanging round. And I didn't know any better; I used to ask them 'cause this is how our shows used to go.

DG And your two-week venture lasted five years.

BC Well, they gave me a five-year open-ended contract; I was the first guy to ever sign a million dollar deal in a lounge, for a lounge performer, in the history of Las Vegas.

DG What did the other artists who'd been doing short-term contracts think about that?

BC They looked at me sideways, they weren't too happy with me.

DG We'll talk about that after we've heard another record. What's next?

BC Well, you really want to know what I like, huh. This gal I think says it all—Whitney Houston and *I Will Always Love You*. I saw the movie and that song, the way she sings it, just goes right through me. It's so well done, it's so well said. [MUSIC]

DG The Sixties seem to be making a comeback?

BC If anybody would have told me that in 1993 the sixties would be as popular as it is—now this really makes me laugh—all these experts decided that radio should program itself, you know, in all dimensions, like country… not country. They did all of these things and then when the economy went for a you know what they said to the radio broadcasters who were losing their buns 'cause of lack of ratings and the lack of advertising dollars—they said, okay you guys, no we're not going to program what you play, play what you can sell. Where did they go? They went to the solid gold format, musically. And I'm not talking about talk radio. They went to the solid gold format in country. Now, if anybody would have told me that in 1993 the solid gold format would be selling like it is, people would be listening to the music buying all those collector's products, I would have told them they were crazy. I never in a million years expected this to happen. In fact, I'm looking over my shoulder today saying, this is incredible that I'm even talking to you on the radio and people think it's important. I mean I'm thrilled they do, but I never ever imagined that this would happen for me.

DG You do a lot of charity work—telephones and television—what does that give you?

BC It's a wonderful reminder that after you read the newspaper there still are people out there who care that the world is such a rotten place, and that after looking at the news on television there really is some joy and happiness out there, because you get in front of a camera and you talk to that camera about things that count. And the phone rings—somebody's watching, somebody cares—and you don't get that feeling in your everyday life anymore. People are so busy we don't have time for each other. And what the telethons and the charity work does for me is it's a reminder that, God forbid, anything traumatic should happen to me in my life, somebody'd be there to help me. And we have to be there for each other. So for me it's a healer for my soul.

DH .You divide your life between Edmonton and Las Vegas. What's it like living in Sin City?

BC Well, I get to hang out with my peers, which I really like. I get to see Rich Little a lot, he's a good friend. And I make the rounds to my show business people that I know, and what I love about Las Vegas is that the people move and we don't have to. So us artists get to stay there a little bit and get to socializing with each other.

DG Is there a real community in Las Vegas?

BC Oh sure there is. And actually, you know, you get off the strip and it's normal. I mean it's normal family life and it's ended up the largest retirement community in North America, too. So it's an interesting base for an economy because the retirees really don't need manufacturing; they don't need to be part of the workforce. So it's interesting. You know, the value of living in Las Vegas is those special discounts on the food and the shows that are very economical, and if you can afford to stay there it's not expensive, if you know what I mean.

DG How about the kids then? Do the boys have any aspirations to follow in dad's footsteps?

BC You're no different than I am that way, David. I don't think any of us are. You want your children to be the best they can be and you want them to have a choice of what it is, and if they decide to get into the entertainment business I'll support them every way I can. The older boy has taken some drum lessons and music lessons, and the young fella too, and they do a part in their school plays and they've had some bands. But whatever they want to do. I think it's too early to tell, and I don't push them. Whatever they love—I mean, they like sports more than anything. I mean, to them Wayne Gretzky and you name it, Dan Kepley they're the stars in their lives and I'm the dad, which is sort of nice..

DG Let's get back to records. What's your next choice.?

BC Well, here we go, you asked and I'm going to tell you now. Elvis of course. I mean, this guy was so nice—always. He was very nice to us, I mean in those early years when we were recording he was such a gentleman. He didn't ever want a lot of people around, and in Las Vegas he used to come in a couple of times to see me at the Desert Inn, in disguise. You'd never know it was him I'll tell ya. But you could always tell by the security guys.

DG Presley in disguise?

BC Oh yeah. It's the only way he'd go out—when he went out.

DG What did he look like?

BC Completely opposite to what he looked. Red hair, padded suit—you'd never think it was him. And he always had two gorgeous ladies so that nobody could sit beside him. And when he came into the club where we were ,nobody would know he was there. He'd go to certain security people and the zone would be cleared, the waitress would be taken off the floor. There would be no service, so nobody could come anywhere close to him. And in those days they had these small walkie-talkies that looked like a little cassette deck—the technology they used was incredible. So they could talk to each other.

DG How did you rate him?

BC An original. How can you rate somebody that's an original? I mean, he lived in another dimension as far as I'm concerned because he had done it all. He was the pioneer of all of it and, if it wasn't for Elvis, none of this would have happened for so many of us. But Buddy Knox and I used to talk about all of it, because Buddy was back there with him when they first started, and this thing they called rock 'n roll. 'Cause they were all doing rockabilly back in those days and Buddy used to tell me that, you know, it was after meeting Elvis that he really got after it. And they added a drum to their session, which was a cardboard box, for *Party Doll*. The drum you hear is a cardboard box that they're playing. So, Elvis was the basis of all of it, and because of Elvis I got to meet people like Brenda Lee and Roy Orbison, who was a good friend of mine. But none of the rock 'n roll music would have ever happened for any of us if it wasn't for the King of Rock 'n Roll. And one of the songs that he's recorded that has transcended the element of time—because everybody in the world has recorded it—is *Can't Help Falling In Love With You*. So I picked that one, because it's back on the hit parade but by somebody else. Again. And I hope he's still alive. [MUSIC]

DG   Bobby, before we send you to your mountain top we let you take one book with you. Which book would you like to take with you and why.

BC   Well, that's a hard one, because I... That's a real tough one. I got two favourite books: *The Prophet*, by Kahlil Gibran, because of the philosophy of it, but I guess out of it all you got to take the greatest book of it all, and that's the Bible, because you need to feed your mind and your soul, and you have to be able to evolve from what you are for where we are in this space and time. And I think it's all there in the Bible. I think that's the only real book that would last you that long up on that mountain.

DG   You do have one final decision to make, and that is where your period and place of isolation is to be. It doesn't have to be the top of a mountain, it could be anywhere in the world. Where would you choose, what's your favourite place?

BC   You know my favourite hangout, out of all of the places in the world—and I've seen so many of them—and I mean I love the Caribbean. But what's so great about Las Vegas is that it's as though you took a little fence around this little town, even though it's in the middle of the United States. It's like a country, because people from all over the world come there. And I've gotten to meet so many interesting people from all over the world in Las Vegas, that I normally never would ever get to say hello to, that that's probably my favourite spot to hang out. It really is. I really enjoy myself there.

DG   Well, you're the first person to have suggested Las Vegas, I must say this. You're number one.

BC   Well, if you're not happy you're running away from what's your reality.

DG   Okay. You have one final choice to take with you with your record collection.

BC   Oh boy. Well, this is really a very sentimental song for me because this was in the period of it sort of being over. Like the concerts were over, and I still had the recognition, I was still filling those arenas, but it was just a matter of time. Bobby, what were you gonna do next; and my first night club appearance in this transition—and I did a lot of soul searching and it was funny, I was trying to help a friend of mine in the entertainment business at the time, it was an opera singer out of New York, and in my trying to help her I was really helping myself understand whether I should go on or not. And I accepted this night club engagement and I was opening for Louis Sachmo Armstrong, and in the middle of this fear I had of being so close to an audience, and this fear of whether I could do this again—like, was it over or was there another spot for me, or should I just say thank you and try to do something else—going on that first show I'll never forget because he knew. Louis knew I was a nervous wreck and he complimented me on the things that I was able to achieve in this country, with my records and the rest of it, and I'll never forget it... going on stage he'd come out of his dressing room and he'd come to see me open, and he hit me on the cheeks and he says, "Kid, get out there and just be yourself." That's all I needed. So I went out there and, standing ovation, the reviews were great, and it was him that actually turned it around for me because I really wasn't sure whether I was doing the right thing, whether I should just say thanks and get at something else, or go with this thing again. And that was the beginning of my night club run.

DG   And what by Louis Armstrong would you like to hear?

BC   Well, the song that sort of says it all—*What A Wonderful World.* There's a lot to say thank you for.

DG   Bobby Curtola, we thank you.

BC   Thank you David. I've had a marvelous time and you've gotten me to talk about some things that I've never talked about before. It's been a great experience. Thanks.

AM Right off the top, in real life are you a handy guy?

SS You know, I used to be. But then we got a nicer house and I'm not allowed to do anything.

AM Don't touch it, you might break it?

SS Exactly, you know. And I've been married a long time, so she's seen all my efforts and she's basically given up on me, so… And I think that's a very wise decision.

AM Let's go back to your days growing up in Toronto. Were you a bit of a class clown?

SS Yeah, I was. I was an unusual class clown, though; I would just say things. I never did practical jokes, I never did a prank or anything, but I would make comments and I'd make them out loud. And from about grade six to grade eight I had the same teacher every year—it was kind of an experimental thing they did in Toronto—and, ah, the teacher said no one can speak out in class except him. I was allowed to say things 'cause she found that what I said was funny, but it didn't disrupt the class and it didn't take it off on another tangent. So, it was a great message for me because it really encouraged me to pursue that.

AM That that was a positive thing?

SS Yeah, and saying what I thought didn't always alienate people, you know.

AM How did your family react to your humour?

SS I'd say my grandmother was the biggest supporter. She lived with us and she just had a great sense of humour. Her initial reaction was to laugh at everything. My mother laughed at most things and my father would come in third in that contest.

AM And you went to Streetsville High School in Mississauga? That's where you met your wife?

SS Right. Yeah.

AM High school sweethearts—holy mackerel.

SS Actually, this is really, really sickening—on her sixteenth birthday she invited me out. So she actually asked me out the first time. It's just so bad—it's you know, it's like Frankie and Annette. So I'm so sorry about that. And we got married, and we've been married, well, it was thirty years last year.

STEVE SMITH
WITH ANDREA MARANTZ, 1997

AM Did you marry young or did you just go out for a long time?

SS No, we married really young. I mean, the odds were totally against us. We were public school teachers, and in Ontario at that time, after high school you'd go to teachers college for one year and then you were teaching. So you'd be nineteen teaching fourteen-year-olds, you know.

AM How long did you teach?

SS I taught for two years.

AM Did you like it?

SS I really liked the first year and I really hated the second year—I had some problems. I have problems with bureaucracy, that is a recurring theme. So I was having problems with the whole way that the school system was set up, and I wanted taller audiences. So I left. Like I say, we got married really young and then, after a couple of years of teaching, left that to be in a rock band. I mean, let's make it as hard as we can, you know— walk away from a secure job where you get your summers off. And at that time, I mean, teaching had nothing but a rosy future; it wasn't going through the difficulties that it is now.

AM   Hmm, hmm. But you were so young. I mean, you'd be what?—twenty, twenty-one at that point?

SS   Twenty. And our parents never tried to talk us out of any of that stuff. So I give them a lot of credit for that.

AM   How was the band?

SS   The band was called Jason and it was a kind of a show band—we did cover tunes. So we would do, you know, Beatles songs and Beach Boys and all that stuff. And we did a lot of American college work, and it was a really defining moment in the band, uh, about two years into it. We were doing really well. I mean, not hugely well, but better than anybody expected us to do, including ourselves. And we played a concert at Cornell University in Ithaca, New York, and the manager of a group called Deep Purple came out to see us. And, you know, I mean usually when somebody comes to see you—I'm sure you've experienced this—you just have your worst possible… everything goes wrong and ya stink and it's all over. And this was one of those magical nights—everything went right. I think we had six encores in front of this packed college crowd. Anyway, I couldn't wait to meet the guy. So, you know, later on he comes in the dressing room and I said, well, what did you think of that? He said, well, it was interesting. I said, interesting?—we had six encores—man—you know. He says, yeah, he says, but you know, you did the Beatles, the Beach Boys, the Four Seasons, the Mamas and Papas. He says, I know all those groups and you know what? They do what they do better than you do what they do. What do *you* do? And it was such a wham. And at that moment I decided to create whatever it was that I was gonna be doing from that point forward, and take the heat for that, too. And no one in the band would go along with that plan. And my wife was in the group and obviously she and I concurred, but the rest—it was just too comfortable a life. So we left the band within a few months and started *Smith and Smith*, where I was writing all of the material, and man, I'll tell ya, for the first eighteen months we were selling stuff so that we could pay the rent. And this is from, you know, years of—well, the teaching was always a solid income, and the band had always been a solid income, and we had never really looked down the barrel of the gun before. And we got to the point where we were just about ready to pack it in. I came home to tell my wife that that was gonna be it, and she wasn't there and she'd come home from the doctor and found out that she was expecting our first child.

AM   Oh boy.

SS   And, you know, the fact that we were really happy about that—I think back about that now and I think, why would I ever worry again, you know. If that doesn't, you know… if you have some sort of raw faith it'll work out, you know. And it did.

AM   At that point you were *Smith & Smith*—where had you been performing?

SS   Well, we started just doing small local taverns and stuff that really needed—what they wanted was a cheap band. And that's not what we were doing at all. I remember a guy coming out representing the Holiday Inn. He auditioned us in our own dining room—we did about a half-hour—and he said, you know, I don't think you're suitable for Holiday Inns. And I knew we were on the right track. So we worked very sporadically 'cause we were doing all original material, and then…

AM   Folk stuff at that point?

SS   Yeah, I guess it was folk based—it was me playing the guitar and us singing things. And like, our background had been music and I thought that I had some ability in comedy, but I wasn't comfortable to get away from music, so I put the comedy into the music. We got an offer from a promoter to be an opening act for Al Martino, who was like, an Italian crooner—so we did maybe seven concerts across Canada. It was terrific work, it was like, the National Arts Centre; we played the Jubilee Auditorium in Calgary. That would have been '76, somethin' like that. My wife, well we really felt we belonged on television, so we were talking to the local television station. I couldn't get a meeting with the guy, so that was going nowhere. So she started harping at me to keep bugging this guy. Well, you can only call so many times. So I said, look, if you're so smart, you call. So she called and got right through. Like, you know, this is the seventies, you know, and I gotta tell ya—when a woman phones to speak to the general manager, the receptionist has no idea what's the origin of this call, and she better hedge her bet and let it go through. So, uh, she got the meeting and we ended up getting a go-ahead to do a pilot. He had been in the audience. He had been in the audience when we opened for Al Martino in Hamilton at Hamilton Place, and thought we were just terrific and felt that we should be on television, blah, blah, blah, blah, blah… But, the interesting thing is, he didn't call us. And we weren't hard to find, you know, so there's somethin' in that, ya know. You gotta go out and sometimes go after those things, even though the person's very motivated to help you, but you've gotta at least meet them half-way.

AM You and Morag did that show all yourself?

SS Yeah. The budget for our pilot was seven hundred dollars, and that was to pay the band. You know. We're very compatible, we get along very well, and it makes us a little bit invulnerable. And we were always prepared—and are today—for it all to come to a crashing halt. We'll be fine, we'll find something to do, you know. We like each other, we get along, and there's a real strength in that.

AM I think there is. Because there's not a note of panic in anything that you ask from anyone else, because there's not your whole life riding on it—whether this person says yes or not.

SS No.

AM And people pick up on that

SS Yeah. And, you know, you're not crushed by things going badly, and you're not way over the top by things… Like right now, I'm having a lot of fun with Red Green. It's very successful, in my terms, and people who know the whole story see it as a miracle, which is what it is. But, you know, it's just… it's not something… I don't strut around or anything, you know. They can take it away. It's the fans. As the fans give it to me I accept it as graciously as I can, and when they stop giving and take it away or something, then I just will appreciate the number of years I had out of it, you know. I can tell you for nine years on *Smith & Smith,* the negotiation was, I would go in and sit down with this man who I liked a lot, and I'd talk about what I wanted to do, he'd talk about what he could afford to do, and half an hour later we'd shake hands—there was never a contract and neither one of us would ever consider breaking our word. And now a contract's not enough, you know. I mean, it's sad really.

AM You gotta have the agents and really nail it down.

SS Oh, absolutely. Absolutely. I mean, I've had situations where somebody with a signed contract says to me that they're not going to honour the contract. I mean, this is—it's unbelievable. Now, they will do that out of expediency, but in fact the whole industry suffers when those kinds of steps are taken, because our society—of all humans, I think—is based on trust, and as soon as we start eroding that we get into… We see a lot of that south of the border. Once you take trust out of a society, boy, you're into dangerous water.

AM You spent those years learning an awful lot about TV.

SS Well, that's another thing I… You know, no one wanted to do it, and there was no one there to do it, so I wanted to do it—it was a terrific opportunity. That's the trick, you know. If you can take something that other people see as a disadvantage and turn it into an advantage for yourself. I mean, I've learned how to produce, how to direct, how to edit, how to do sound recording—I mean, just the whole gamut.

AM On your feet, as you were doing it.

SS Yeah. And every area I wanted to expand in to, there was no resistance, they welcomed it.

AM Now, it was on *Smith & Smith* that Red Green first appeared?

SS Yeah. Actually, you know, that show was like, a bunch of skits and stuff. And I was making fun of Red Fisher—it was a fishing show.

AM Of course.

SS 'Cause I used to watch that.

AM I watched that when I was a kid.

SS Like it seemed to me that, you know, he had the attitude that nothing would bore you. You know? I mean like, he'd fill a half-hour—you had to make it interesting. I couldn't believe it; they'd have a half-hour fishing trip, they didn't catch anything.

AM [laughing] I know.

SS And they didn't go re-shoot another one or just say, well, we'll just eat that one—no, no, we're puttin' her on boys. I mean I just, like, I make fun of it; but you know, it's with great affection because that takes a certain kind of attitude, which I actually admire. Again, it's an invulnerability. So anyway, I started the character making fun of him, and that was like, 1980, so the character's been around a long time. And actually, the station offered me a series for that character in about '82. They were running the hockey games and they never knew when the hockey game was gonna finish—it might finish at 10:40—and they need something to take them up to the hour. But all they wanted me to do was sit on a picnic table and talk. And I thought, oh man, that'll kill it for me, and the audience not far behind, or maybe they'll even beat me to it. So then, in 1990, my wife didn't want to do TV anymore, so she said, you go—and this is what I'm talkin' about freedom—she said, you go do whatever you want and we'll live with the consequences. Well, I mean, you know, if I had a hundred million dollars I wouldn't have that kind of freedom, you know. So I decided, I don't know what I want to do, but I've always enjoyed Red Green, and so why don't we start there. And it was really, honestly, supposed to be a summer job in 1990, and that would be the end of it. So my friend Rick Green, who had been writing with me for about ten years, we created the show together and put it on, and the critics picked up on it right away.

AM Let's have your first piece of music. What should we listen to first from this list?

SS Well, let's listen to the first one. I mean, this is a very defining song for me by Neil Young, who I love. This is called *Long May You Run*.

AM Why is this one important to you?

SS I'm not going to give you any clues about that. I work in comedy, you know. You don't ever explain the jokes. And you don't ever explain the other stuff. [MUSIC]

AM Considering this huge international success that the *Red Green Show* has become, it almost never made it—it was cancelled.

SS Oh yeah. Actually, my show, my *Red Green Show*, was cancelled half-way through its second season. The viewers *Red Green Show* is the one that has gone on to success, because it was the overwhelming response of the viewers when the show was cancelled. And you know, for a Canadian show it's not unprecedented. I mean, I think Don Messer, you know, had a great outcry too. But for me it was a complete shock. And unbelievably heartfelt letters, petitions…

AM Now what then—when it was cancelled—what was its reach, where was it playing?

SS One station—Hamilton; the same station in Hamilton, Ontario, but different management. And, you know, a lot of… I know that we have to, you know, smart size and down size—we have to get our act together, okay—but we cannot let computers make decisions. We're not getting to that point. I know one just beat… I know Big Blue beat the guy at chess, but…

AM Which proves they can play chess, that's about all.

SS Yeah, right. That's right. But, you know, there's so much temptation for computers to take over 'cause rational thought and instincts are tough, and it scares people to make creative decisions. But the decision by that station at that time was to discontinue all production—you know, everything they were doing, including the *Red Green Show*. They did it, and in fact I'm not bitter 'cause that was the beginning for me. If they hadn't done that, I wouldn't be where I am now because it enabled me, actually, to buy all of my stuff back; because they were my financial partner, too.

AM The ones that had already been produced?

SS Yeah. But the support—I mean, petitions from high schools. You know, when I was in high school, to try to get me to sign a petition for a television show—or a Canadian television show in particular… So that was really, that was huge to me—to me personally. I'll never forget that. I went south of the border, but I went down with a different attitude. I went down with the attitude of, I think the support for this show is at the grassroots level and not at the twenty-third floor level. So, if you want to go grassroots in the American marketplace on television, where do you go? I figured PBS. Because you can have a small audience, and if they're willing to pledge for the show they can keep it on the air.

AM   So you took a hockey bag full of stuff and…

SS   I had a hockey bag full of that very mail I described that came in to keep the show on the air. I mean, I could've taken ten hockey bags—I think we got thirty thousand letters. So I would take this thing down and I'd put it on a guy's desk and I said, you know, you're a distributor, or you're a broadcaster—whatever he was—I'm a producer. Here's some mail from the people who aren't guessing, you know. And I never claimed big audiences, but I did always say we will get a devoted audience—I'm not saying how big it will be. And then the PBS thing started. Detroit was the first station to pick it up, and they were respected, and in fact the *Red Green Show* was the first Canadian show to go on in prime time in the States. And they ran it at 8:30 Thursday night at that time. And then we picked up a few—we had five stations in the fall of '93—and we were just ecstatic. It was not enough money to make any difference, but it was just the breaking in—the first one's the toughest, you know. And then I would go and pledge support, where you'd stand there and say, if you like the show send in some money and keep in on the air; and I'd say, and if you don't like it send a lot of money, they can buy something better. Like, I would do it with the same attitude—I'd do it as Red Green and I'd have that attitude, and people thought it disarming. So they were getting a lot of money and they were getting money from people who don't ordinarily pledge. The people are there—I mean, they're leading me. I mean, I'm really not being facetious here. My show was cancelled, I did my big ego trip

and they looked at it and said, I don't think so. And now I'm sort of doing their show. From that point forward, when those letters came in and the thing got back on its feet, I made a huge change. I insisted on doing the show in front of a live audience—because it's their show, I want to know how they feel. And we go out now and do a sketch in front of a live audience. They tell me when the scene's over, not the script. In fact, when we finish the scene I'll go back stage and I'll mark on my script when that ended, and then when I go to edit it I obey what the audience said, whenever I can. Sometimes I—I end up with a show that's only seven minutes long.

AM   Do the characters develop according to mail and things like that? Do people suggest things?

SS   You know, yes and no. I mean, the odd thing is that people want to help you and they want to make suggestions, but the truth of the matter is that this is not what they've chosen to do for a career—they're just nice people who enjoy the program and wanna help you. Most of the ideas you get are things—they don't even realize—but they're things they've seen before, so they're not original. And if I get consistent mail that people don't like something, then I will take it out, I'll remove it. But generally, the way it works is, we stick our necks out 'cause we always had to be doing new things, or we get stale. So we do a new thing and then we watch the reaction. If the reaction's good we keep it, if the reaction's not good then we just let it slide.

AM   I mean, the program is definitely a Canadian show. Was there any pressure from the Americans to change it a little bit, to make it more American in any way?

SS   There may have been. But I send out these vibes—it's like, don't go there, you know.

AM   Dangerous, dangerous.

SS   Yeah. So the only thing I've done with it is, I honestly—I don't steer away from Canadian references in the show, but I don't drive towards them either. Like, you know, I don't want to be talking about Chretien or Ottawa or any of that stuff to try to tap into some source of a quick, easy laugh—for a couple of reasons. First of all, it's not the kind of humour that I do, and there's a lot of Canadian funny people doing that kind of stuff. But, every close-up of a possum van, those are Ontario plates on there.

AM   Tell me about the audiences, the live audiences. Who comes to see the taping?

SS   Oh, it's just… Well, you know, we have one of the biggest fan clubs in the world. We have over eighty thousand members. Most of them now are American, and when we tape the show, most of the people in the audience are American, even though we tape it in Hamilton. I mean, one night we had seven families from Colorado and none of them knew the others were coming. I mean, that's a commitment. And people take their holidays based on when we're taping.

AM   More guys than women?

SS   You know, it's funny, there are a lot of women fans—which surprised us. One lady I think explained it. She wrote me a letter—she said, I sit in the living room, I watch with my husband. He thinks I'm laughing at the show.

AM   That's exactly what I was thinking, exactly what I was thinking.

SS   Oh yeah. Or they'll say to me, you know, you're so much like my dad, or my uncle, or my brother.

AM   Let's have another piece of music.

SS   Okay. This is one of my favourites, and for a whole lot of reasons. Bryan Adams, *The Summer of '69*.

AM   Give me a couple of those reasons.

SS   Well that would be when we left teaching and went into the entertainment business. We got a lot of memories of that year. [MUSIC]

AM   You know, Canada has a lot of really funny people, people that have made it in all different aspects of the comedy business—from, you know, stand-up to writers, all different kinds of things—and yet we have this legacy of being bad at sitcoms, at comedy television. Is it true? Is it a perception? What's the deal about, you know, Canadians can't do comedy TV?

SS   Well no, I think we can do comedy TV, but, you know, if you're talking about sitcoms—situation comedy—you know, it's a question of resources. You know, the American system has unlimited resources. They will do a program and they'll have fifteen writers, they'll have access to the best actors to perform your writing, they have a huge promotional machine behind it. You know, if you and I were going out to each buy a car and I have a thousand dollars and you have a hundred thousand dollars, you can make a heck of a mistake and still get a better car than me, you know. But having said that, the part where we're equal is in the writing. Writing has no budget, you know. And we can write funny stuff and we can write sitcom; we just don't have the process here—it hasn't been brought in. It can be brought in; all it would take is for somebody to make the commitment to comedy that they make every day to documentary and drama and sports.

AM   *The Red Green Show* has gone to other countries. It's being played outside of North America, too?

SS   Yes. Yes, we're in Australia and New Zealand, Trinidad, Turkey, Denmark.

AM   I don't know. How would it play in, like, Turkey and Trinidad?

SS   Well, in Trinidad it plays really well. They find it exotic. Because of, you know, the snow and the types of trees and, you know, just an—it's an odd show for them. And, you know, it's a male dominant society, and the same thing with Turkey. And there are not many programs that can make fun of men in a male dominant society and get away with it, and we can. And I think it's because of that sort of gentility of spirit you talked about, you know. Some guy, I think it was the *Globe and Mail*, said this show manages to send up, and celebrate—at the same time—what it is to be a man, you know. So, I think that we can… And even in Australia, and Australia to me is still, you know—with all apologies to Helen Reddy—a male-dominant society. Though you can't really hear them roar that much down there.

AM   Do they dub it, in like Turkey?

SS   No, they run subtitles.

AM   Subtitles?

SS   Yeah. And a lot of the… like Denmark, a lot of

people speak English.

AM Any thoughts of making a movie?

SS Yeah.

AM Oh really?

SS Absolutely. Yeah, we've already started the ball rolling on that.

AM A full-length feature?

SS Yeah. Like, I'm saying a TV movie, they're saying theatrical release. But realistically, you know, I've been lied to by the best and, like, I can kind of smell it now. You know, I mean really, what are our chances of getting a theatrical release, you know. I always say, plan for ground zero and adapt to good news. You know, so let's do a TV movie but we'll shoot it thirty-five ml—that it could play in the theatres—and we'll work like hell trying to get a theatrical release, and if we do, great. And if we don't, well, that was never in our plan anyway.

AM Perfect. Great. Are you working on a script?

SS Yeah, I've got a treatment in. It's complex, but it's basically… the story is the lodge is in financial difficulty—wow. And Minneapolis, which is the head office of 3-M, is having this huge international duct tape contest, so we—the guys at the lodge—decide to go in that so we create a replica of the Wawa goose, all in duct tape, and I tow it behind the possum van. And of course as we're going we keep having problems that we have to solve with duct tape, and the only source is the goose.

AM [laughing] Oh no, so there's nothing left of it?

SS Well, it's not a goose by the time it gets there. It's more like a goose at Christmas in Germany, you know.

AM So where did the duct tape schtick come from?

SS Well, you know, it came out of the handyman corner segment being—again, we always think limited resources, you know, because the person that we're representing can't just go and buy that special tool, or can't even go and buy the part, you know. So what do we all do?—we use duct tape, you know. So it just started, and it just clicked—it was one of those touch stones that, oh my God, that's what Al does, you know. Hey Al, here's your duct tape guy. Now everywhere I go people have me sign roles of duct tape. I have signed Red Green more than I've signed Steve Smith, and Steve Smith had a forty-five year head start.

AM Now, before we send you to your mythical mountain you can take one book with you. What's your book?

SS *The Fountainhead.* Unbelievable.

AM Ayn Rand. Why *The Fountainhead?*

SS It just, when I read it I read it late in life—I didn't read it when everybody else read it—it just, ah, I just thought, okay, now I know why I think the way I think. And it really gave me a lot of courage to keep hammering. You know, I pretended that it wasn't fiction, and therefore it would happen, and uh, I can vouch for it. I'm not that pure, but my life has shown me that it does come around, and if you go away from what you honestly, truly believe, you're lost anyway. No matter what level you're lost at, it's not as good as knowing where you are—anywhere—even at the bottom. I'd rather know where I am at the bottom than to be lost at the top. And I really think ultimately those are the life choices that I've made, and one of the key lines in the book was, —one character had done something terrible to another character, to the lead character, and they met later and the first character who had done the bad deed said, "Whatever must you think of me?" And the lead character says, "I don't think of you." You know? And that's what happened to me in an interview. Somebody said to me, you know, "With your show in the States, what do you think Americans will think of Canadians?" They don't think of Canadians, you know. We're just entertaining people.

AM You also get to choose where in the world you'd be cast away to. Now, if you were going to spend the rest of your days in one spot, where would that spot be?

SS Oh boy. First of all, it would be in the far distant future. I would probably say Bermuda. I mean, that's just… I'll tell ya, that I have a mind that it's like—I guess I could've been a real problem. My mind is always going, there's always a movie running inside my head. I can be anywhere and be inside myself—it's a terrible problem. I am the worst person, like at a social gathering I have to keep reminding myself that I'm there, there's people around me, talk to these people and everything. And it's not that I'm not interested—I like people very much—but it's like I have this internal problem, something's connected wrong. So it's scary, but I honestly think that I could sort of be almost anywhere and I could be okay.

AM What's your final piece of music today?

SS Well, this is a song of seduction and watch out for it: *American Woman* by The Guess Who.

AM Steve, thanks so much for coming in today.

SS My pleasure.

AM Have you brought along your little Yorkshire terriers on this trip?

RM Oh, I wish I did have them, I miss them terribly. But they're home with the sitters right now—friends that are kind enough to take the little darlings in. But that's not a problem because they're both so adorable.

AM Bonnie and Didi.

RM Yes. They're hard not to love, they're beautiful little dogs.

AM And a great name—I have a dog named Bonnie.

RM Oh, well there you go, great names for sure.

AM They're terrific little dogs. And you take them with you whenever you can?

RM Ninety percent of the time they travel in the airplane. They sit right under the seat and they travel together in one little bag, and all told they probably weigh together a total of nine pounds, and they're four years old and they're spoiled rotten and they're dearly cared for.

I got them from a breeder in Ontario. And I always wanted a little dog, and when I got one I couldn't leave it alone it was so attached, so I got another one, and I'd have ten more if I was retired. But it's too much on the road, it's too confusing.

AM Let's go back to your early days in Big Pond. You come from a family of eight children. What was it like growing up in a big family?

RM Well, it had its moments. See, the thing with my family, we all lived at home at different stages because sort of three families in one really, because some of us moved away and then the younger ones were left, and when I was young the older ones were… but it was very interesting and everybody cared for each other very much and worried what the other was doing. They're still pretty much that way. When you come from big families that's what tends to happen.

AM Where do you fit in in the eight?

RM I'm about the fifth one.

AM Now, the MacNeil family goes back a long way in Big Pond; you have deep roots there, to the nineteenth century?

RM Yes, yes, we go back a long, long way.

RITA MacNEIL
WITH ANDREA MARANTZ, 1998

AM What brought your family to Cape Breton?

RM If I can speak about my parents, as long as I can remember there's just, you know, always this talk of our ancestors coming from Scotland and different reasons why people left, and my experience with the whole Scottish heritage was the chance to go to Scotland on one of my tours and to actually go to the Isle of Barra And I met some relatives there, which I couldn't believe. I stayed at this… I think they have one little hotel there, and they put on a ceilidh for me one night and one of the women that was singing had remembered the MacNeils from (and had been to) Cape Breton and had remembered going to the area where I'm from. So it was quite a wonderful, wonderful thing, and I really didn't appreciate it as much as I do today. I wish I'd have had more time, but it was sort of on one of those tours where you're just into performing, you don't get a chance to really, you know, sit down and take in all the good things that are happening. But that was a highlight to meet some of the…

AM The family several times removed.

RM Exactly. It was very exciting.

AM Family that's been separated for three hundred years or so?

RM That's right, that's right. And I got to walk on the hills of Bara and it was very emotional.

AM Describe the countryside around Big Pond for those of us who've never been to Cape Breton.

RM Well, it's best to describe… well actually, summer or winter it's quite beautiful. It's right on the Burdora Lakes and you have that massive inland lake to look at summer or winter. A lot of people ice fish on certain parts of the lake. There's just such an array of beautiful trees and rolling hills, it's very lush. In the summer it's extraordinarily beautiful when it's in full bloom, and it's one of those little villages that's sort of picture perfect—you could picture it on a postcard. I think everything is set so nicely with the church on the hill, and when you're looking out at the water or back towards the land you have this sense of long ago, you have this great sense that you know you're not the first one on this land. It has a wonderful spiritual sense about it. It's a very special little village.

AM A lot of people talk about how the landscape that you come from creates who you are. Do you feel that about your hometown?

RM I certainly think it helps shape you in some ways. I know when I lived away from that landscape, that particular part of the world, I could never settle. It was always this incredible pull to go back, and although I only got to go back during the vacation time for a few years, it was like that's all you worked for all year, and you had this vision and you just couldn't get it out of your mind or your heart. The pull is extraordinary. So I couldn't see myself living anywhere else.

I was in Toronto recently and I had lived there for a number of years, and I thought, well, could I ever live here again. And as much fun as the city is and it's great to visit and certainly wonderful to fun around shopping and all that—that was good—but oh, I couldn't see myself in that place any more, you know. I just feel much more grounded at home.

AM Absolutely. Now, your book, as the title implies, *On a Personal Note*, is a very intimate portrait of your life. Was it difficult to open up in that way?

RM It was very difficult. I, of course, have written songs over the years and some of them pertain to my life, but the book was much different and certainly more in-depth, and it's once again a sharing of feelings. But I guess I felt safe doing that because I think sometimes when you talk… when you let people glimpse into your life you find out that other people have had similar experiences; it's quite amazing the people that just so far have come up to me and talked to me about that very thing. And, you know, they say that they felt it was inspiring, and I think that's the one thing I like people to come away with is, you know, that there were so many people in my life that have been inspirational to me that a lot of times that certainly is what got me through. But yes, it was hard to write the book and why do we write these kinds of books? I don't know if there's any one answer. For me it was, I had a block of time to do it, it was something I always knew that I would do and I do write about feelings so it wasn't a far… you know, a far reach to put the book out. And there it is.

AM And in following your music we get glimpses of these things that have happened in your life.

RM You certainly do, and people come up to me with all kinds of questions and write me about all kinds of things, so this book in many ways will answer a lot of questions, maybe certainly more than they've asked for. But hey, that can be good.

AM Was music important to you when you were growing up?

RM Oh, very important. From the time I was six years old I had this love of listening to melodies and always humming, and music always to me was a healing… a very wonderful expression. And I would daydream, I would rock—sit on my rocker and rock for hours—and I would daydream about being, you know, singing and uh… I knew from a very young age that's what I wanted to do, and I stayed with that dream. It was probably the one thing that really… it was really, um… I didn't think of anything else. Like, I didn't think, well I'd like to be this or I'd like to do that or try this. It was always music. So I'm glad that it worked out the way that it has and that I'm able to still be doing what I love.

AM Yet you were so shy as a child, the only person you'd sing for was your mother.

RM Hmhm.

AM She made time for it though.

RM Oh, she made more than time. She was great, she was a great audience and of course she thought I was—you know mothers—she thought I was just so wonderful and this and that, and she had great expectations.

AM But that obviously soaked inside you, that you know, that sense of someone thinks I'm wonderful.

RM That belief in what I do, and as you say, I was very shy, so I had a lot of things to work through before I was able to perform, you know, in front of an audience.

AM You tell a story about having to sing for gorgeous George, the wrestler.

RM Oh, I didn't know who he was, but my father certainly knew and they were so excited he stopped by the store, and ah, I remember they stood me up on a stool and, ah, I sang. You know, my father got... they were always proud and always wanted to let people hear me sing. So it wasn't an uncommon thing to walk in the store and hear me singing.

AM What did you sing for him?

RM I can't remember what I sang for him. It might have been Mollie Bonn—that was my father's favourite song or Danny Boy. So they were on overplay for most of my young life, like, one more version of Danny Boy…

AM You had a rough childhood in many ways with the several operations you had to go through to cure your cleft palate.

RM Yes. Well, I was very lucky because my cleft lip was not as severe as some that I have seen. The split didn't go right through, it only went a partial part of the way, so the operations I'm sure in those early days were… I don't know if they were up on all the new—well of course they weren't up on all the technology and the new things they can do now, so I did have some operations when I was young, but I also had a series of operations when I was older when I was in my, of course, adult years. But they're doing marvelous things today with the Cleft Palate Association, and certainly with the beautiful babies that are born now with this affliction they're able to do so much more, and that's wonderful. Of course, when I was born in '44 it'd be terrifying to the parents, particularly to the mom of the little one, because they would never have seen that and would not be aware of what it was.

AM But it all worked out.

RM It all worked out.

AM Let's have your first piece of music. What would you like to hear?

RM Well, I love John Prine, he's one of my favourite performers. So anything by John would be just a delight to hear.

AM Well let's pick one. What do you think, what would you like?

RM Oh, I'd like something off, if you have anything off his earlier albums, like *Common Sense*, that would be great.

AM Have you ever met him?

RM Oh no. That was my… My dream was to meet John Prine. I went to a concert once and I took my son, and I was so upset because my son got to meet him, I near bat him out of the way—no, no, I want to meet him—but he got his autograph on a record and I had to live with a second-hand glimpse of that. [MUSIC]

AM So you went to school in a one-room schoolhouse for a bit?

RM Yes, I did.

AM Is that a good way to learn, with different kids?

RM I don't know if I learned very much. I was a bit of a day-dreamer, loved to look out the window at the falling snow, and I'm not sure what we learned. I don't remember any of it so it didn't have a profound impact. But that school is still there, you know, in Big Pond, and I was trying to get it to redo it, but it's gone to rack and ruin so it's too far… because my father built it of course, and I was lovin' to restore it, but I had this vision in my mind of getting this wonderful little one-room schoolhouse and just fixing it up, and when I walked into it it was just like, oh, a horror—it was just a shambles.

AM Too far gone?

RM The amazing thing was the blackboard was still there and the wonderful ceiling that he had put in, and I'd always remembered the big windows that I looked out, and I thought, well, if nothing else I'll be able to take the windows. But even they were gone. All you could see was the print of where they were. So it's funny how in your dreams things are much different in reality; but it's still there in Big Pond and they don't use it for anything.

AM Just sort of slowly crumbling down.

RM It's going, yes. We're losing it.

AM At 17 you left Cape Breton for Toronto. What made you want to go there?

RM Well I think, you know, work was one of the motivations. There wasn't a lot of employment around home, and of course I think I just wanted to get away and I wanted to see what I could do about this career I was going after, and Toronto seemed to be the place where all Cape Bretoners at that time were going. We certainly experienced a grand time of people leaving the island, so I was one of the islanders that left for awhile.

AM Bit of a culture shock arriving in Toronto?

RM Oh, I want to tell you I couldn't believe it. I didn't know what—I was terrified, absolutely terrified. The first thing that struck me were the lights, you know, at night. I just thought it was amazing. And I was really too shy to be there because I went with a friend and I literally walked behind her, or hid behind her should be more like the truth, and I knew I had to get a job—I didn't know what I was gonna do I was so scared. And I didn't have a lot of courage to push myself forward, so it was a big step for me, it was amazing.

AM And you were young. I mean, 17 is still a little girl in lots of ways.

RM I was, in a lot of ways.

AM You put a lot of energy into singing at women's rallies and that sort of thing. Why did you pick that?

RM Well that happened in the '70s, and I had no intention of going to any rallies, or meetings—I wasn't into that—but a friend had asked me to go and so I went, and it was certainly an amazing time of my life and certainly a chapter I can't leave out because it was a time of great awareness. I became very aware of the world around me and certainly politically aware. I became certainly more involved in what was happening and certainly, too, believing in equality for men and women and all those things that came out of those '70s for me were things that helped me in my later years. And I wrote a lot of songs during that period of time because I wanted to express myself in the meetings, but I was unable to do that because I was too shy, but I found that if I sang what I was feeling that it was much easier for me—to put it forth in a song. And they allowed me to do that. And that was the early years of my writing, that was the beginning when I started writing when I was involved in the women's movement in the '70s.

AM And how were they received? How did your audience accept it?

RM Well they enjoyed them very much and were very, of course, once again encouraging. And I wrote a number of songs pertaining to that time and the particular things we were going through, but I realized too that I was writing other songs as well, which was, you know, the start of the whole thing. I was writing about being away from Cape Breton, I was writing about people I was meeting; so all these things were coming out and I found that the expression, the feelings I had inside were coming out a lot easier through music than any other way.

AM You had some tough years in Ottawa—a single mom and young children, doing some house cleaning, even a time on welfare. What got you through those rough times?

RM Well, I think you just, at the end of the day you have to push yourself through because you are there, you do have two children, and you have to keep going. Not that you don't get down, but ah, I guess I come from a family that, you know, probably instilled that—that you just keep going no matter what. And you know, talking about the hard times, if I didn't live through them—and I did, which was good—I don't know if I'd be the person I am. I think I learned a lot about caring for others, compassion. And I think that was my path, you know. I had to go through all these things and I'm glad that, you know, I came out on the other side not doing too bad.

AM   And all that came into your writing as well.

RM   Yes, I've… You know, I've shared a song with people, *Southeast Wind*, it speaks about the marriage, the divorce; and I've written a song about my daughter called *City Child*. There's just so much of my life in my music, that's true. There's a great deal of it.

AM   But you don't read or write music?

RM   No, not technically I don't, but I certainly feel it and experience it in a very fulfilling way.

AM   I read that when you're on the road you sometimes call your answering machine and hum a little tune to it.

RM   I know. They bought me this little machine that I'm supposed to be using when I write a song, but I forget it or the batteries or dead or something, and I learned that if I don't get it on to the answering machine—'cause I write so many songs at one block of time I might lose it—so I phone home and sing so I can keep at least the first two lines, and then I'm fine.

AM   Let's have another piece of music. What should we play now?

RM   Well, I've been introduced to the music of, what have I got, Oscar Lopez—yes—anything by him. Now I don't know which album or whatever you have, so…

AM   We have them all.

RM   Well just play any one, it'll be just fine 'cause he's fabulous.

AM   How did you come across Oscar's music? He's a Calgarian so we're all very possessive of him.

RM   Oh, well let me tell you how I came across his music. My son said, you have to hear this album, and ever since he played it for me he hasn't got the album back. I've leant it out, we've taped it, we've bought more, and I've got other people at home—it's wonderful, it's just absolutely brilliant. [MUSIC]

AM   For a number of years you played small folk clubs and those sorts of venues, before you had your really big break at Expo '86 in Vancouver. What was it about Expo that turned the tide?

RM   Well, when I was first asked to perform at Expo, I can remember I was very (of course, once again) nervous to do so, because I wasn't sure, you know, were they going to have me outside singing? Would I be on a corner? Where would I be? I wasn't… I just was very unaware of what was going to happen, but when I got there my schedule was unbelievable. I was there for six weeks; I believe I did four or six shows a day, I'm not sure—probably four, six is probably exaggerating a bit—and I…

AM   Just gruelling.

RM   It was. And I was at the Folk Life Centre, I was at the Xerox Theatre, I was at the Canadian Pavilion; it was the most amazing time I'll ever remember. And I think the music got out to so many people because of course it's an Expo, a world Expo. And the press was very kind—the Vancouver press. And I think it opened a lot of doors for me as far as my career goes, and after Expo I released *Flying On Your Own*, and that was another step, and ah, from there…

AM   So you'd kind of developed that base audience from Expo and they were people that were ready to hear you?

RM   Well that's true, very true. But, prior to Expo I had worked for many, many years building a grassroots following for sure, and at the folk festivals and so many clubs, so many nights in pubs and clubs, and that was a great place to begin. Although I could never see myself going back there to a smoky bar, I certainly appreciated the time I spent there and the people that came because they were just amazing, supportive, and I could always try out my new songs at the club or the pub and it was just great. And so I don't regret any of it. It was all a lot of hard work, but it was good work and I loved doing it. And then Expo is just another stop on the way.

AM   And when you're doing four shows a day and rushing from stage to stage, you couldn't have any time left for stage fright?

RM I don't know, you know, stage fright is a funny thing. It's with you, it's not something you like to talk about because the problem with it, it really doesn't go away. And you know, you think, well my God woman, you've been performing so long now by the time you get rid of stage fright it'll be over anyway. But that's how it is, I don't know what to say about it—it's there and I still get it.

AM I've heard some people talk about it as a kind of energy, that sometimes that stage fright just kind of boosts your energy level a little bit and maybe that helps your performance. What do you think about that?

RM I think if you can control it, it could be helpful, but if it gets out of hand it can also put you under.

AM Tighten up your throat?

RM Yes. So you have to kind of really… But it's the audience that puts you at ease, which is strange in itself. Once you're out there and you get your sea legs as I say, then I think you're pretty well alright.

AM But the first walk across the stage…

RM Oh, it's just… and you say, am I crazy, why am I putting myself through this. And how can you love something that terrifies you so much. But you're right, you do get a rush and you do get excited, and it's a matter of keeping it all… You get terrified. I mean you can't believe it and you think you gotta' be nuts to do this.

AM Let's have another piece of music, Rita. What would you like to hear?

RM Oh, the wonderful voice of Trisha Yearwood would just be fine.

AM What do you like about her?

RM I just love the natural way about her and just the way she comes on to a song, she just delivers it with great passion. [MUSIC]

AM You mentioned the real breakthrough hit, *Flying On Your Own*. Did you have a sense that was going to be the one?

RM No, I wasn't sure, but I was very excited that it was the one because that song means a lot to me. So you never know in this business… And you can't do your music that way, thinking it's, well maybe it'll…

I don't write from that perspective. I write from, you know, just if the song is there I'm gonna' put it out. But I'm glad that *Flying* did so well and…

AM It's a very autobiographical song, it's a personal song.

RM I think so, yes, it is. And it's a song that a lot of people can relate to. Doing something by yourself you know can be a frightening thing, and when you're flying on your own, you know, you're out there, that's for sure.

AM Was that the first time you'd heard yourself on the radio?

RM Oh no. I'd had an album out prior to that, *Part of the Mystery*—I'd heard that, you know.

AM Is it odd to hear yourself on the radio?

RM Well, when you hear yourself on the radio it's wonderful, it's exciting, you know. You kind of, oh my God. It's nice. But if I'm in a place and they have my music on I'm kind of, oh, turn it down a bit. It's nice that they cared enough to put your song there. And that's what music is about—it's about sharing, you know, and listening to music—and when you hear your song you think, wow, that's great, maybe somebody's listening to my song like I listen to others. It's great.

AM How do you go about composing a song? Is it work? Do you sit down and say, okay, I gotta write a song now?

RM No I don't. I've only done that with one song, and that's *Reach the Sky*—I wrote that for a particular reason. But for most of my music it's driven through an emotion that I'll be feeling about someone I've met, or a situation. And the music—the melody and the lyrics come together and then I just let it happen and I don't really use pen or paper. And as you say, I use the answering machine, and I'll sing the song to the band and then we work it out together.

AM And does it change several times as you…

RM No, no. I go with…

AM No. It comes in a piece?

RM It comes in a piece. I never mess with my first instinct and my first lyric; I keep it.

AM Great. I guess your greatest public exposure

must have been the TV show, *Rita and Friends*. It was very successful. Hugely successful CBC show, all full of Canadian talent. What did you take away from that experience?

RM Oh, it was a crazy time. It was so busy and it was so wonderful. I think what I took away from that was, for me, my own personal self, was the fact that I was able to meet so many performers that I'd admired. And also I was able to introduce so many young performers that are up and coming, and you know, I felt I was a part of something that was special; you know, supporting Canadian talent. And I was proud of that fact, that we had so many new people on the show, as well as the seasoned performers, and also that we had such a mixed bag of music.

AM That was a really outstanding feature of that show, that it was a completely mixed bag of music.

RM Well I think that was part of its great success, because I personally, that's why I was excited about the show, because it was all different types of music. In my own life listening to music over the years I've listened to all kinds—blues, rock, love rock… you know, folk, instrumental, classical—I love it all. So I was really excited that on this show you didn't know what you were gonna hear, and it was great. And I found that the guests, they were very excited to be on the show. There was always a good buzz around the studio. There was always an excitement, everybody was so into it. That was great for me to experience. It never got to be a ho-hum experience for anybody, and I think, you know, people were treated very well. I know I was treated wonderfully well; but the guests themselves, and everyone had their special little moment, and I just thought well, that was great.

AM Are you really positive about the music scene in Canada now?

RM Oh, I'm positive for the most part. think it's doing very well and, you know, there's some great performers here and they're doing great and they're doing great world-wide and they're getting support, and hopefully that will continue, you know. It can only get better.

AM Well, tell us a little bit about your famous Tea Room in Big Pond. Is that a building you once lived at?

RM I lived there with my two children for a time. I bought it when it was converted into a house, a small house, and it is an authentic… it was an authentic school room and it's tucked into the landscape. It was very small when I opened it up as Rita's Tea Room. I started out with—my two sisters were working with me and some local people as well—and we started on a shoestring budget and our inventory was very sparse, and I didn't have any teacups at the time so we put the word out around the neighbourhood that we needed some china to pour the tea out. So everybody went into their cupboards, and you know those cups you get sometimes for weddings or anniversaries, well everybody came forward with this incredible collection of teacups that were just outstanding, and I used to hate to serve tea out of some of them because they were so beautiful, and the risk of breakage was very high because everything was being done by hand in this tiny little kitchen. But people came by the droves, and the baking was done right there and it was just this congested area of happiness that just had this warm, wonderful feeling. And nothing fancy, but just very warm and exciting; and there'd be times when I'd go there—not that often in the early days—and It'd be so crowded inside that people would be panicking. So I'd stand out on the deck and I'd sing a song, and that way people would get out so they could do the dishes. Little did the people know; they thought I was singing for them—listen, I was singing so the dishes would get washed. It would get you out of there.My daughter runs the tea room now. It's gone through changes. The tea room now looks nothing like the old tea room. Of course, like everything else, change comes. It's expanded. Because of the numbers we've had to expand the building and it's pretty… I think it's pretty grandiose, but it's still a warm place and it's still kept the main part of the structure and, to me, I love to go there. I'm not there a lot, but I do love to go there 'cause I still get that sense of just being grounded, and it's a nice place.

AM And it's provided some good employment for Big Pond.

RM It does. It provides a good employment for quite a few people and, you know, it's just amazing because it's set in this little village out of the way, and people take the time to go through and come to the tea room. We've been very fortunate, it's certainly held its own over the years.

AM Well, it's a good spot to have another piece of music. What would you like to hear?

RM Well, I'm a fan of Amanda Marshall and I love *Dark Horse.*

She was on the show, but I didn't get close to her because she was performing when I was in back interviewing somebody, talking to someone; but I just can't say enough about her talent. [MUSIC]

AM You must have a real flare for business because you've also launched this line of clothing. Why was that important to do?

RM Well, I got together with the designer from *Rita and Friends,* who designed a lot of my clothes…

AM Oh, you wore some beautiful things.

RM He made some beautiful things and we got along famously, so we got involved in the Rita clothing line. Now it hasn't, how do I say this—it hasn't taken off the way I had hoped, into the sunset, but we haven't given up. It's very hard in Canada to get the retailers, to get their attention; but we're working on it. So it's in its infancy stage and it's going to surface I know, because we believe in it, and of course I got into it because of the plus size market which I feel is certainly not being met here in Canada. I've done a lot of shopping in the U.S., but let's face it, I don't want to go there all the time I want some clothes. And to find something affordable and something that, you know, will last awhile and you can get in the larger size, I think is important. So that's why we're sticking with it and, you know, we're going to prevail.

AM Now, I heard that you have quite a bit of say in terms of the design and styles of the clothes, that you're quite involved with that?

RM Oh yes, I have a say because, working with Lee who is the designer, he's well aware of problems that the larger size person can encounter, and I think, you know, maybe it's not just a matter of taking a size 10 and making it a size 20—I think there's other things to consider. And he's very tuned in to all of this, so there's a lot.

M: You have such an incredibly devoted fan base; I mean your audience really, really adores you. They feel very, very connected to you. What does that kind of support do to you, both as a performer and just as a person?

RM Well, you realize when you have that kind of support, you're not flying on your own, you're pretty well lifted… well, you know, with the spirits of other people and the encouragement and, ah, I feel like I have friends everywhere. And people that wish me well here, you know, in Calgary—hello, how are ya' doin', why are ya' here—I think it's just great when you hear those kind of comments and people that wish you well. You know, that just spurs you on and keeps you involved.

AM And there's that security in knowing that people are… I mean, I think it's a rare thing for a performer. Many performers have audiences that watch them, waiting for them to fail. Your audience watches you, encouraging you to succeed. They're with you.

RM Yes they are, they're very protective. They don't take kindly when things aren't said in my favour, which has been very touching to me, and they, you know—yes, you're right—they're there to see that all goes well and that's what they want. And I don't think you could ask for anything more. You know, to have that kind of feeling inside you for someone—wow, that's pretty special.

AM Why do you think this is?

RM Well, I think if you followed the music you'd have to get to know me a bit, and if you followed the music you must have… if you feel that way towards me you must have heard something in the music that touched you. So I think it's that kind of support, you know, that you've connected. And when you connect with someone you want to make sure they're alright, you want to make sure they're doing well.

AM Let's have another piece of music.

RM Well, one of my groups I'm listening to now—this was my favourite tape all summer—the Philosopher Kings.

AM How did you get interested in their music?

RM Well, of course after hearing them I thought the singer was remarkable, I loved the sound. And this is the one song I think—*It Hurts To Love You*—I played that song over and over, and seeing them perform on television was so exciting to me, and when I tune in to something like that I really get hooked on it, so I enjoy them. [MUSIC]

AM Well, before we send you off to your mythical mountain top we'll let you take one book with you. If you only had one book for the rest of your life, what would it be.

RM Oh my goodness. Well, the books that I've read, one of my favourites was—I don't know if I'd take it for the rest of my life, but certainly I'd take it for a few more years—was *Aztec* by Gary Jennings. I loved that book and I remember I read it in Big Pond, and it took me quite awhile to read it, but it kept me up all night and deeply moved me, and I can't tell you anything more about it. I'll just say that was my favourite book and I still have it.

AM And if you could choose anywhere in the entire world, any place at all to go to live out your days, where would that be?

RM Well, in one of my songs I have a line of *when the sun goes down on this patch of ground, that's where I'll leave my soul*. And of course I'm singing about Big Pond, so that's where I'd like to be.

AM And for your final choice of music, Rita?

RM Well, Iris Dement. I love her voice, it's quite unusual, um… she's wonderful to listen to, does a beautiful production on the albums, and I… you know, I like her very much.

AM Which song?

RM I think it's called *The Way I Should*. I hope it is—if not, whoops.

AM Rita, thank you so much, it's been such a pleasure visiting with you.

RM Thank you.

PAUL QUARRINGTON
WITH ANDREA MARANTZ, 1996

AM Do you still lift weights?

PQ Well, occasionally. I'm more—swimming is my thing these days. I'm a mad keen swimmer, but I occasionally lift weights because I tell myself I'm developing certain swimming muscles.

AM Swimming muscles. And you have to balance them all out, right?

PQ You have to balance them. I was lifting weights the other day, I forgot about that part and I threw my arms up in the air and then screamed, and I haven't done it since then. That was a couple of weeks ago.

AM Now, your parents were both psychologists?

PQ Yes.

AM Did you ever entertain the idea of making that your career?

PQ When I was in university, actually, I did quite like psychology, and I spoke to my father and mentioned off-hand I was considering it, and he was quick to talk me out of it.

AM Oh yeah?

PQ Yeah. I mean, I don't know, I don't want to get my father in trouble with other psychologists, but he figured, for the amount of time you spent in university you might as well become a doctor, you know. So he was a little, uh… he talked me out of that.

AM Well, you've written a lot about sports—about hockey, fishing, all kinds of sports—but when you were growing up you weren't really a super athletic kid?

PQ I was not athletic, I was anti-athletic. I was the anti-athlete, and I was widely regarded for my inability to do anything. But what happened was… I mean, all those books—it's true they're about sports—but I think they're mostly a fan's books. You know, there's kind of, um, from the outside looking in. Also, because I sort of had nothing to do with them—I certainly hardly ever played hockey, although they sometimes would install me in net because I was a nice wide kid and, you know, I could just stand there and block about seventy-five percent of the shots. And baseball, I remember playing on one occasion and I believe I got hit in the head with a ball. But anyway, because I was not involved at all in the sports, I had an opportunity to look at them, and so I always connected sports in my mind with monomania, or passion, you know. It's a good arena to see some passion, same as fishing is to a certain degree. So I think that's the connection, not that I was that keen a participant.

AM And one of your neighbours when you were growing up was Dan Hill—singer Dan Hill?

PQ Yes.

AM Was he an earnest young man when he was a kid?

PQ Oh, he was fairly earnest. Our fathers knew each other. His father, Dr. Hill, is a… I guess studied sociology, and my father was actually one of his professors, which is something—whenever I'd see Dr. Hill he'd say, "How's your father?—he was one of my teachers." So, my brother and I had this little group—you know, we were musicians, and he played bass and I played guitar—and Dr. Hill came over once and brought Danny with him, and we sort of let him audition for the band. And we were like, ten and nine, that kind of age—and Danny did kind of a Sinatra thing, you know. He had the mike and he would pop his fingers and, I don't think we thought he was good enough, so…

AM No. Kicked him out of the band?

PQ Kicked him out of the band, yeah.

AM Well, music's always been a pretty important part of your life then?

PQ Well, you know I come from a long line of,—my family is either musicians or teachers or, in my father's case, both. He was a trumpet player and his father was a violinist, and my father's uncles were… Like, there's Rance Quarrington was a singer and an organist—he was quite popular on the radio in the twenties and thirties, and you know, all, just all musicians all throughout the family. So it was a bit like me like it is for my brother's kids. Now my brother is the principal bassist for the Toronto Symphony, and he has two kids and they're like fifteen and thirteen now, but when they were like, four and five and five and six, they had no idea that there were people who didn't play a musical instrument. I mean, the only people they knew were musicians. So I was a little like that, too. So it was just a fairly natural thing to do.

AM And then you spent a long time with *Joe Hall and the Continental Drift*.

PQ Yeah.

AM How did you hook up with those guys?

PQ Well, my brother was playing with them—my brother Tony, my elder brother—and they played at this place called The Black Bull in Toronto that had draught that cost a quarter. So my friend Marty and I, we were trying to be a folk duo then—Quarrington-Worthy, that was his last name. No, his last name was Worthy, my last name was Quarrington. So we would go down there, because it only cost a quarter, to have a beer and, over time, it became clear they needed a rhythm section. So Marty could play the drums, so I decided to learn to play the bass. So we did that and then we got to play with them and, just went from there.

AM How old were you then?

PQ Oh, I don't know—in my twenties somewhere. Maybe I was twenty-six.

AM Oh, so well out of school and all that?

PQ Oh yeah, yeah.

AM So you even had a number one hit with that band?

PQ Well, actually the thing we did that did best in the records was something Marty and I did—a Quarrington-Worthy single called *Baby and the Blues*. I think that was in '78… It was number one on the middle of the road, you know, adult oriented—the play list that means that people who are listening are too weak to get up to turn the dial is what it meant. So we were number one—for one week, one week only.

AM Well that's good!

PQ And then Kenny Rogers or somebody came and bumped us off.

AM Oh, boy… When you were playing bass with Joe Hall and the Continental Drift, you played with them for ten years—were you writing during that same time?

PQ Oh yeah, I mean, I think being a musician is a great job for an aspiring writer because, for one thing, you're usually in cities where you don't know anyone or have anything else to do anyway. Your actual work hours are nine to one.

AM Nine p.m. to one a.m.

PQ Nine p.m. to one a.m.—so you got a lot of the days free. So it was a great opportunity to get a lot of work done. Now the down side was that the Joe Hall band played in a lot of places, or stayed in a lot of hotels, that didn't actually have desks in the room. So that made it a bit hard to write. But I would take the top drawer out of the chest of drawers and turn it upside down, and rig a desk and that's how I managed to get some writing done.

AM You were also moonlighting as a security guard at that time?

PQ Well, when the band wouldn't get work, you know, I would work in security. I worked for a great company—Cavalier Security—I thought that was the best name.

AM   Very cavalier.

PQ   And this is another great job for a writer, you know, they say. Especially, what Cavalier Security did was a lot of conventions, and they'd set up the displays and then they'd want security there; so they'd stick you in a room essentially, and lock it, and you know, eight hours later they'd come and let you out. And you'd been security. So it was good. There would be interesting things like, oh, a big fast food convention—that was one of my favourites. And I'd do odd things. I had to sleep in cars because, you know, when they'd have a car in a shopping mall someone has to look after that car, so I'd climb in there and fall asleep, but uh, But you could get some writing done, too.

AM   Intellectually demanding job!

PQ   Well you could read and write, you know.

AM   And that became the background to your first novel, right?

PQ   I do allude to the security business. The what is it in *Home Game*—well actually, it's a little hard to say what my first novel was 'cause I wrote one called *The Service*.

AM   That's the one I was thinking of.

PQ   Well, *The Service* grew out of another odd job I did, which was, um—these people would help people find places to live. You know, that is to say, they wanted to rent something and people would give them their specifications and a sum of money, and we would find them—that was our stated goal, you know—the perfect place. But, you know, the problem was people would say, well, you know, I want essentially a mansion and I have seven hundred cats and two hundred and fifty dollars a month. And you'd say, fine; if such a place exists we will find it. But anyway, so someone—a co-worker—once mentioned these people think because they give us a certain amount of money—you know, here's twenty-five bucks—we're gonna solve all their problems. So I had this idea, well suppose someone did offer that service—in this case fifty dollars, solve all your problems—so that was the premise for that.

AM   Well, let's have your first choice of music now.

PQ   Well, I actually allude to this in my book, *Fishing With My Old Guy*, 'cause I find this the most, ah... Well, what I'm talking about is Beethoven's *Seventh Symphony*, and especially the finale, although I love the whole thing. But I'm starting a campaign to... You know, someone—a critic—when they premiered the symphony, said that Beethoven must have surely been drunk when he wrote it. And this was meant as condemnation. But I think, of course, it's high praise; so I'm starting a campaign to have the symphony sort of nick-named along the lines of the choral or the pastoral—this is the drunken symphony. So my first choice would be Beethoven's 'drunken symphony'. [MUSIC]

AM   You also helped write the screenplay for *Whale Music,* which won you a Governor General's award in 1990. What was that process like? How different from writing the original book?

PQ   Oh, well, I think it's a chance to maybe do some things differently that you hadn't, you know, thought of. You know, the director and I co-wrote the screenplay, and we decided to take a certain tack. You know, I think what people don't realize—especially people involved in the movindustry I think—is that movies are a much smaller vessel, much smaller container than a book is; and so, they're really quite limited in scope in terms of what you can do well. So we had to get rid of quite a bit of the book and, you know, I had no objective way of saying this is important or this isn't important—'cause they were all very important to me. At the same time, I had no objective way of clamouring for something's inclusion. But, I think it's ultimately a pretty satisfying experience.

AM   Well, and you'd been a playwright before that; so are those things connected?

PQ   Well, no, not actually. I mean, I think playwrights are kind of frowned upon in the movie biz because they tend to be a bit gabby, you know. I mean, that's what I love about writing plays, is that, you know, people do talk; but movies, they don't necessarily want people talking. They like to keep on saying and drilling into your head that it's a visual medium. I actually think they should encourage poets to become screen playwrights as I say, 'cause they're used to thinking in terms of those concise visual images.

AM   Right. And paring down all the time.

PQ   And paring down all the time. But they tend to go for novelists, who have this kind of megalomania and aren't used to having anyone else offering any suggestions whatsoever; and they don't deal well with the movie industry.

AM   I'm sure. I'm sure. It's gotta be kind of difficult—after you've poured all these hours into a chapter—to say, oh, that's irrelevant.

PQ   Oh yeah, and I mean everyone in the movie industry—everyone—has notes or, you know, wants to offer their opinion on what should happen. And I often say the difference is like it would be if I'd written a novel and I go in to the publisher, and as soon as I enter the building the receptionist is telling me to change chapter four, and, you know, everyone in the hallway has their idea. It would be quite maddening.

AM   Well, and, if it's true that you've got these sort of reclusive tendencies, being in something that communal as film making is a real change.

PQ   Yeah, yeah. Well, that's true. That's actually one of the good things about it, of course, is that it gets you out of the house. And I like actors. You know, I think actors are kind of fun.

AM   You're pleased with the film?

PQ   Yeah, yeah. Absolutely.

AM   It sure has done well.

PQ   Yeah. Well, it's, you know, it's done better some places than others; so I never study numbers or anything like that. I only have one way of judging whether or not I think something is a good movie, and that is this: that I've seen *Whale Music* maybe five or six times all the way through, and my experience is always the same—when I start watching it 'til the time it's over, I never worry once about having to go to the washroom. Now that's how I judge a movie.

AM   There you go. It's a good flick. These different disciplines that you write in—like the novel and then for stage and screen—do they influence each other? Like, after you've done a screen play, when you next approach a novel, are you writing differently?

PQ   Well, I'll tell you one thing. I wrote these screen plays and for awhile—after *Whale Music* and before my last novel, *Civilization*—there was a space of about five years where I didn't write a novel, and part of it was kind of a mini burnout situation, I was also very involved with screen plays. So, when it came time to writing a novel again, I realized I'd acquired this kind of screen writer's mentality and I had this, it was like a gorilla commando and my attitude was, you know, get in, do the work, get out. And I thought, this doesn't really help, you know. Novels, you get the impression that it's much more time and it's more leisurely; but then I thought, no, it's probably still a good idea—even in a novel—get in, do the work, get out. So then I could start writing again. So I don't know that they influence each other, but I think you learn things from them all and then you can apply it to them all. I mean, I think my grappling in the movie industry has ultimately given me a kind of, ah, sense—dramatic sense—that, you know, I can apply to novels and stuff; so I think they all eventually help you be a better writer.

AM   Do you know where your characters are going when you start writing?

PQ   Not really. I think that one of the differences is, when you're writing a movie you have to have it kind of all plotted out, you know; but when you're writing a novel you create them and let them go about their business, and half the fun is watching—see what's gonna happen.

AM   Let's have another choice of music.

PQ   Well, there's a fella named Mickey Newbury—he's a songwriter—and has written a lot of great songs: *She Even Woke Me Up to Say Goodbye*. He lives around Nashville, and he wrote this, called *The American Trilogy*, which is really just a stringing together of three American folk songs, you know, that kind of reflect what was happening in the Civil War. Elvis Presley used to do it. It was Elvis Presley's big tune in the later stages of his career. But, the other thing about Mickey Newbury is I think he's got just the best set of pipes I ever heard on a guy. So this is some beautiful singing. [MUSIC]

AM   Paul, tell me about your time as writer in residence at the library in Orillia.

PQ Well, this is a program that they had in Ontario, and I take it they still do in some places in Canada (when they can find the money from all the rapidly dwindling money); but I would go to the Orillia Public Library, I think three mornings a week, and then anyone in the community who was interested in writing would come in and show me their stuff and we'd discuss it. So it was great, and there were a lot of fine writers there—no, there's people there who are very under the influence of Stephen Leacock, you know; so I got quite a few would-be Leacocks, which, you know, I'm not that fond of Leacock, let alone would-be Leacocks. But be that as it may, it was great—some of the kids, you know. And the best writer I had there was like, a ten-year-old girl—I thought she was a great writer. But the other thing is, you know, in these small communities, if you have odd thoughts your temptation is to write them down rather than speak them aloud, which is likely to get you into trouble, so you write down your odd thoughts and then you're a writer, and then you hear that there's someone at the library who's gonna have to read it and talk to you about it. So you do get some of these, you know, quite odd—channeling, er… And then some of them aren't odd, they're just kind of ill-advised. Like, there was this one guy I quite liked who wrote all of his stuff like they were thriller novels, and he wrote them all in capital letters. And I said, you know, why are you doing this? And he said, well, he was stationed up in the Arctic, and this is how they communicated on the Telex, in capital letters. I said that was not a good reason.

My friend, Guy Vanderhage, he did it, writer-in-residence, in Ottawa. He's done it a couple of times, but he was telling me he had one, uh—one guy submitted like a four hundred page novelization of Mork and Mindy, which it ended up with Mindy strapped to this table and these guys were about to commit heinous…

AM Unspeakable acts.

PQ Unspeakable acts. Mork was powerless, and this hero entered, who happened to have the same name as the fellow writing the book, and saved Mindy. But I never got anything like that.

AM Gee, too bad for you, eh?

PQ I did get one. There was one woman who sent in a manuscript that was—it was a bit odd. You know, she was into channeling and, there was this creature she communicated with—Frodo or something, who was from another dimension and had taught her the philosophy of… his philosophy—and she would say Descartes was wrong when he said this because this Fromo, or whatever his name was… And she came in and was quite a sedate woman and we spoke for about half an hour, and she said, fine, and left. And I said, well that was painless; but the next day I got a letter and she said that Fromo had contacted her in the night and said that I was to be her collaborator and between the two of us we could probably rule the world, if I would only set her words down

AM And then what do you do?

PQ Well, you know, we're working on it.

AM You'll be ruling the world soon.

PQ Yeah.

AM You have a long history as a playwright; you started writing plays in high school, was it?

PQ Well, I did write plays in high school, yeah. Now, when I started writing I wrote plays, like when I was, you know, twenty-two or something, I wrote plays and novels kind of alternately. Or, you know, I mean I thought they were both great; so plays I certainly started with early, but I haven't been, for whatever reason, as successful with them as with novels. So I tend to have gone over more to novelization. But just recently a friend and I were trying to develop a sitcom for CBC TV. We both worked in a bookstore, and—it was years in development with CBC—and they finally killed it; so my revenge was to write a play about two guys working on a sitcom for the CBC. Well, if the play doesn't work I'm writing a novel about a guy writing a play about the two guys working… We'll see how it goes.

AM Do you sit in an audience when your plays are being performed and sometimes listen…?

PQ Well, I sit in an audience and cringe.

AM It must be tough?

PQ It's very tough, yeah; and movies the same way. And my wife won't go to movies, or actually plays, to the same extent with me because when I'm not cringing I tend to be laughing—in what she considers an unseemly way—at my own jokes. But I keep on saying, no, it's not the jokes, it's the delivery, you know. These actors are brilliant, but she just feels it looks bad.

AM Well, here's probably the toughest question for you. Okay, we're sending you up the mythical mountain top and you only get to take one book with you. What's it gonna be?

PQ Oh, right. Now I thought this was very interesting, the way you've set this up, because, you know, a writer can have, you know, several favourite pieces of music and only one favourite book; but it's more likely that you're gonna have, you know, one favourite piece of music and a lot of favourite books. But, there's an American writer, now deceased, named John Gardner. There is a John Gardner who continues to write James Bond novels, but he's not the one I'm fond of. This is John Gardner, who died about twelve years ago now, and just a wonderful writer and has written a lot of wonderful books; but the one I chose of his is called *The Sunlight Dialogues*, just because it, uh… I've read it, you know, three or four times I guess in the course of my life, but the first time I read it I was working I think at that job, you know, that I was kind of being circumspect about—and I was not the happiest guy in the world—and this book, it's one of those great thick books; it's a whole other world you can kind of get into, and peopled with fascinating people. It's a great big fat juicy novel, and I admire it very much. I always remember it 'cause some day I want to write a big fat juicy novel so I can make one of these alternate worlds for young men and women who are dissatisfied with their crummy jobs.

AM Now, we don't have to send you to a mountain top; you can pick any place that you'd like to go. If you were going to be isolated for the rest of your days, where would you go?

PQ Well, I think I'd probably go fishing somewhere—maybe in the Himalayas or something.

AM Are you drawn to the mountains?

PQ Well, no, just the streams. They just happen to actually—they start coming down from there. And I actually did—without meaning to sound morbid—I told someone in the past that, you know, if I ever died on a fishing trip that they should be happy because it would mean, by necessity, that I'd died happy. But when your question was originally put to me, you know—if this was your last day on earth where would you like to be?—my initial response would be, I would be hiding from whoever decided it was my last day on earth.

AM But hopefully hiding on some trout stream.

PQ Yeah, a trout stream would be good.

AM Okay, well let's have your final choice of music.

PQ Now this, just in terms of sheer beauty, is my favourite thing. The middle section, which is probably called an *Adagio*, from Brahm's *First Piano Concerto*, and I think this is great. I actually want this to be played at my, uh—if I should happen to die, ever! But this is one of my favourite, most beautiful things ever.

AM Great. And thank you so much for coming in today; it's been a real pleasure.

PQ Well thank you.

BEN WICKS

WITH DAVID GELL, 1992

DG Now, you grew up in the shadow of London Bridge, a poor neighbourhood (Southwark) and also a pretty tough part of town.

BW Yeah. It was a tough part of town. I was a twin actually, something I found out years later. The reason I mention that so early is that there was a saying or a belief that the twin was always… the surviving twin would get everything else that the both of them should have got through their lives. So at a very young age I started to get all these diseases, I mean that children get—measles, scarlet fever—I seemed to go through the gamut. So consequently I was away from school a lot. And yes it was a tough neighbourhood and I seemed to get picked on a lot. I think this is partly because I was the sort of weaker one of the crowd that was going around.

DG In fact, that's where Charles Dickens grew up, wasn't it?

BW That's right, it was very Dickensian. In fact, everything was named after Dickens. The school I went to was Charles Dickens School, and the tenement building where I lived, which was five floors, in front of that the little alley was Little Dorritt's playground. He was actually there. The reason he lived there… he lived there as a child with his mother because his father was in the Debtors' prison, so they were waiting for dad to come out, and that's the reason he lived in the area.

DG Because of what you were living in and the atmosphere and the fact that everybody else was the same as you, did it occur to you that there was poverty around you? Or was that just life?

BW No, I think it was just life, you knew nothing else. What you did know was that you shared the toilet with three other families and it was your turn every three days to clean it. I always felt this was unfair since Sebastians next door, they also lived in three rooms and they had ten kids. And I felt sure having to clean every three days and they had ten of 'em using it was sort of out of whack. I had very loving parents, I had terrific parents—mum and dad and two sisters. Dad was the shyest man I ever knew. In fact, he was so shy he never came to our wedding. My mother was a complete opposite, she was the antipathy of gregariousness. At the drop of a hat she would do a *Knees Up Mother Brown*—didn't matter who were there. I can remember to this day dad, at five o'clock, always coming up the alley (we would see him) and mum puttin' the kettle on. In fact, he was so shy that it was forty years, I'd be forty years of age before I found out that I was a twin in fact. He'd never told me. This would happen… I'm sorry to jump ahead, but it takes us back to the beginning. We were at a small family reunion. I'd come over from Canada with the kids—and dad was sat there and mum and all of us, my sisters. Dad had had a few beers and my sister said, ask dad about your twin brother. And I said, what twin brother? And she said, ask your dad, he looks like he's in the mood to tell you. He told me the following story: He said, when you were born, he said, I went to Guy's Hospital, which was at the foot of London Bridge and just up the street. He said, and there were two baskets either side of your mother. You were in one of them and the other one was empty. And I said to the doctor, where's the bloke that should be in this one. And he said, I'm afraid I've got bad news Mr. Wicks, I'm afraid he died in the night. And since he was more than three days old, the responsibility for his burial is yours. Dad said to him, well I've been out of work for three years, I haven't got any money for a burial or anything. And he said, well that's not our concern. So dad went off, found he got refused any help from the Welfare or whatever it was down the street, and he then went to the most remarkable man that I ever knew, ever. He was our local undertaker. He was someone we saw almost every day because of the kind of area it was, and he used the pub a lot. Alf was a big drinker—his name was Alf Smith—and he was stood in the bar this day and dad went to him, hunted him out and told Alf his problem. And Alf said to my dad, he said, well you're in luck, he said, we had a fire in the basket factory last night. He said, I've got one laid out in the front room, hardly a mark on her—he said, she didn't get any flames, she just got a bit of smoke. Providing you don't wanna know who she is or where she's going, I'll pick the boy up from the hospital, put him between her feet and put the lid down, and he'd get a Christian burial. And that was how my twin brother went. So it's very much… I'm sure it's the same everywhere, in every ghetto, slum or whatever it is—there's one person that will pull everyone through, and for us it was Alf Smith, the undertaker. It's bringing back all these incredible memories. Well, we would see him almost every day, swaying as he tried to lead his little procession of a horse pulling the coffin along, with his top hat, dressed all in black, doing the whole bit, you know. And all of us would immediately turn our eyes to the floor as he passed. This was not out of respect, this was because it was a well-known fact that if Alf looked you in the eyes and took off his top hat at the same time, you were the next to go.

DG And you believed that, you knew that to be true.

BW Listen, I believe it to this day. If Alf was to pass here today, in no way would I look at him.

DG I think a lot of our listeners of course will know much of your childhood already from your bestselling book in 1985, *No Time to Wave Goodbye* a book that told the story of the thousands, millions of children who were evacuated from London. How many children in fact were evacuated?

BW Well, there were 3.5 million children who were evacuated from the inner cities of Britain. They chose the cities that obviously they felt would be likely to be bombed, and in fact started the evacuation two days before the actual war. You know, it was interesting how I came about to write this book. I was being interviewed by TV Ontario, who'd decided to do a series with Adrian Clarkson, myself, and the great Margaret Laurence, and the idea being that they would track through our youth and gradually go through a three half-hour program thing—you know, for television. And so of course it was Adrian growing up in Hong Kong, Margaret growing up in a small western town, and me in the east end of London. The camera crew came around the office; the producer was wonderful—he said, I should tell you that this has been incredibly well researched, a tremendous amount of time has been spent on this, and there are times when it could be quite painful for you. And of course me in my old flip way, you know, oh well, not to worry about this—you know, the old experienced interviewee or whatever. So they set up the cameras and they set it up in a very interesting way. For one thing, the interviewer stood behind the camera. Consequently, for those listeners who wouldn't understand what that meant, it meant you had nothing to hold on to, there was no one who you could share the camera with. Not only did that isolate you from him and give you a sense of being cut off, but the next thing was even more devastating in the way of an interview. When the interviewer asked a question, the producer said, what I'd like you to do is I'd like you to repeat the question, in as casual a way as you can, because we intend to take the interviewer out of the series and keep cutting backwards and forwards to you, Margaret and Adrian. And so consequently, if he would say, *where were you born?*—instead of saying, London, you'd say, I was born in London, so that they got the full message. Anyway, we started this and what happened, we got to the period of 1939 when I was evacuated, and the interviewer asked me… He said, now in 1939 the war was about to start. Tell me about you, what happened to you? Do you remember that first day of September? And I said it started on September 1st, I went to school. And boy, I got halfway through this story and the biggest lump in my throat, and before I knew where I was the tears welled up in my eyes, they started to come out on my cheeks. I'm sure the cameraman pulled in for a tight shot, they always do. But of course I stopped, I couldn't speak. I felt very embarrassed. The lighting men were all looking at their feet, shuffling their feet. Everyone was really embarrassed, but they were very kind. The producer said, don't worry about it, that's fine, he said, we had the same thing with Margaret, you know. He said, so this is to be expected. But when I left the office, I decided something had hit me that I'd locked up inside that I had not spoken about. And I decided, I thought, boy, what a fantastic book.

DG You, yourself, and it's interesting you should have chosen that title *No time to Wave Goodbye* because you had no idea that you were going to be evacuated?

BW No no no, that's right. I mean, up to that time… And the astonishing thing was (the first thing they found out that really stopped us dead in our tracks) that this had been planned in 1924, and in fact the researchers managed to get a hold of copies of the original documents during that meeting (between all men, 10 men) who met for three for four days, deciding that the next war was going to be an air war. 1924 this was, and deciding what they were going to do, and… They never mentioned an enemy, the word used was a 'belligerent.' And a very interesting thing came out of those documents: 1) their concern was panic in the streets, and they felt this was going to come from two sources. The panic was going to come from the poor and the Jews—interesting, eh?—which showed the underlying antisemitism that was there, you know. And of course it turned out, when it came, they were the last ones, the ones who were leaving were the ones who had cars—you know, who were rich enough to have a car and were speeding out of the cities. So no, I went to school on that Friday morning, September 1st. The headmaster got us together.

DG You were how old at the time?

BW I was eleven. Yeah, I was eleven years of age going on twelve. And the kits had already started, we'd been warned about it and told about it. Posters had been put everywhere. A huge propaganda campaign had started by the British Government, which suggested to mothers in particular, that if you were not willing to hand over your children you were playing into the hands of Hitler, which of course would prompt the rest of the street to say, well she can't think much of her kids if she's not sending them. The schools were about to be closed. So consequently, tremendous pressure. And you have to understand—and I think listeners will feel this, particularly when I tell them the ages. The ages started at five years of age, five to 14. So if anyone listening has a five-year-old or above, imagine handing that child over that morning, September 1st. Anyway, I went to school. He got us all together, the headmaster, and said, *I* want you to go home, pack a bag, and be back in two hours. I went home. We didn't pack a bag, we never had a bag, we never went anywhere. So my mother threw stuff into a pillow case—some socks and whatever and a shirt and stuff. And back I went. And after we went to the nearest of the eight railway stations that were chosen in London. But you have to understand, this was happening all over Britain. And at the same time, at 4:30 that morning German troops had rolled their way into Poland, they'd crossed the border. So at the identical time the Germans were rolling into Poland, kids were heading for the railway stations in Britain.

DG Let's have your first choice of music now.

BW Oh yeah, this is gonna' be very fancy stuff, unlike what most people expect of me, I'm sure. But I'm a great lover of music. *Pomp and Circumstance* is something that's performed at what they call the Sir Henry Wood Concert. Sir Henry Wood was a very famous British conductor, and they began an incredibly popular series every year, and it was called the Sir Henry Wood Promenade Concert, and the last night of the proms continues to this day. You would have something like, oh I don't know, eight to ten thousand requests for tickets, and of course you could only take a couple of thousand. So it was almost like a lottery to get one of these tickets. And I remember getting a ticket for one of these. And what you do is you stand, I mean everyone—there are those that are in seats—but you're standing right up against the orchestra, and there it is on the stage, a full orchestra with a choir. So it's an incredible ensemble of musicians and singers. And part way through they play this wonderful *Land of Hope and Glory*, and of course the old Brits love this—they figure this is them, the master race, you know, the chosen ones. And halfway through the conductor, and in this case I think one of the best recordings of it—Colin Davis—Colin Davis turned, faces the audience, lifts his baton and everyone sings and cries. I mean, it's one of those magic moments, it's one of those silly things. I'm sure the Germans did it with Hitler, but we did it also. [MUSIC]

DG What stikes me from looking at all those old news reels is how happy the young evacuees look?

BW Oh their laughing and giggling, 1) it's a Friday, they're not going to school; 2) many of them are going on a train into the countryside for the first time. And in fact they would later find that many of the children would refuse to drink milk once they saw where it was coming from. So they were that strange to the countryside. So it was a sort of happy band of little ones that set off.

DG They probably all thought they were coming back on Monday anyhow, didn't they?

BW That was it you see. I mean, everyone thought, there was no way this war was going to last. Britain was going to kick the hell out of Hitler and it would all be over in a few days. So off they went. But it was still a heart rendering thing for mothers. I mean, we had letters of the most incredibly moving things. A mother said… A woman wrote to me to say, she still cannot walk past Waterloo Station because she can still see her mother's face pushed between the railings with the tears rolling down her face. And she cannot walk past Waterloo Station today, more than fifty years later. So you had this. You had the terrible thing of—and once again I'm voicing the letters—someone wrote in saying, I remember my mother saying, whatever you do, don't let go of Billy's hand. Who she was speaking to was an eight-year old daughter who had a five-year-old brother to hold onto. Imagine the responsibility. And of course at the other end there was a very good chance she would be split. And in fact there was a horror of it. Every evacuee remembers what they call the cattle call. You see, once we got on the trains, no one knew where they were going, let alone who they were going to end up with. Now when the train shunted off, and as I remind you, four thousand trains were used, they got off at the various villages in the countryside. Then the other children get off the train, as I did, and we were immediately taken to the village square or the small school, and you were lined up. And there you stood with your labels hanging from you, and the villagers stood there and they picked who they wanted. So it would be, I'll have him, I'll have her, give me two of those, give me one of those. And here you'd have the case of where the young girl, the eight-year-old and her five-year-old, could very well be torn apart, and someone would say, well I want him but I don't want her. And this happened. So you had this nightmarish scene of kids being torn apart. You had remarkable stories. Of course, this gave the advantage of those who were of a mind to perform these sex abuse acts, and of course this is what came out of the book—that no one had realized—and this is what they were writing to me about. They'd been sexually abused, they'd been physically abused, and of course the others that wrote were writing to say they'd had a wonderful time. One man wrote to say, I remember getting off the train with my class, and we got onto a flat-back truck, all stood there. The truck slowly made its way to the village, and by now word had got out that we were about to be picked. He said all of us felt very sorry for a little boy called Teddy Cook. He said, Teddy Cook had these dreadful steel-rimmed glasses that were prevalent at that time, and buck teeth, and as he described him a very unattractive little boy. He said, we all felt there's no way anyone's going to pick Teddy Cook when they see him. He said the truck stopped in the village, the villagers circled the truck rather than wait for the kids to get down, and to everyone's surprise a woman pointed to Teddy Cook and said,

I'll take him. Teddy all excited, around eight years of age, dropped his pillow case down to the floor, scrambles down, and no sooner had his feet touched the floor than she said, oh, I've changed my mind—she probably got a close look at him—I'll take the twins, you see. Poor Teddy climbs back on the truck. The wonderful ending to the letter was this: the twins that she took turned out to be absolute sods, and in fact the very next day set fire to her haystack. Teddy Cook ended up in the most wonderful home where he was treated like a son. I'd ended up in Eastbourne. Our train shunted off to Eastbourne, a seaside resort on the south coast of England. And I remember being picked by the grocer, which was terrific for me. For one thing, he had a car—I'd never driven in a car before. So we went to the grocery and he was quite successful, they had rooms over the top of the grocery. They had one child, a son, and of course they had electric lights, something I'd never seen or never experienced, which was wonderful to me. They had an electric train set, and within a few weeks we'd got into a fight for something or other, I don't know what it was, but the mother had found us and was very unhappy about this. And of course there was a quick gathering of the family and the decision was made that one of us had to leave the house—either the son or me—so it didn't take long for a unanimous vote, and I found myself back with the billeting officer, who then took me to a woman who had a boarding house, being that this was a seaside resort. A lovely little roly-poly woman—I remember her vividly—took me in. She had two other evacuees. I thought, boy, I've really landed on my feet—she was a lovely warm, friendly person, and there we were all day. And that night her husband came home. Well, he was an absolute disaster. I mean, having come from a loving home I suddenly found myself ending up in the house of a drunk. He threw all his food up against the wall, our food—I mean all the food went all over the place that she'd cooked. And we lived in this house for months with this horror getting drunk every night. Came the time of course when the Germans made this massive breakthrough, and the news quickly spread that if they ever took France there's no question that the children that were evacuated onto the south coast would be closer to the enemy than anyone else, so they'd have to get rid of them, they'd have to move on. And I might add, with no hesitation at all, that the children in that house along with me, I think we were the only ones that were actually rooting for the Germans. We couldn't wait for France to fall fast enough to get out of that house. So of course when it did fall we were back on the trains and we shunted off to Wales, to South Wales, and of course lined up again. And a miner and his wife took me in (a little tiny, tiny village) Cross Hands it was called—one mine, and of course the big slag heap dominated everything, this mountain of slag, and of course everyone a miner. The young miner who took me in, and his wife, had no children of their own, and after two weeks decided what a wonderful idea it had been, their original idea to have no children, and so I was back with the billeting officer again. And the village smithy took me in. By now I was probably almost 13, so this was just the kind of labourer he wanted, someone who was strong enough to work in the forge pumping the bellows, and could also go to school. And of course although Mr. Roberts took me in as that, he was fantastic. He and Mrs. Roberts were a second mother and father to me and I loved them dearly. They had this tiny little farmhouse by the school where they had a couple of pigs and lots of chickens, and of course me going to the forge, and I remember him… To this day I remember when I'd go to bed, as I'd go to bed Mr. Roberts would sit by the table there in the kitchen with his cap on—I never saw him take his cap off—short, stocky man counting all the change. He had all the money set out all in little rows. The only drawback was they didn't speak English, they spoke Welsh. So I had to learn to speak Welsh. I can still, when I've had a few drinks, sing the Welsh national anthem in Welsh. And in fact we went back years and years later. My wife came from Bristol, so Doreen and I, we (with the kids) went back to Cross Hands in order to try and hunt it out, and we found this small village, we found the house by the school. And I said to my wife, well you wait in the car with the children and I'll go up this little path. And I knocked on the door and this woman came to the door. And I said, I know this sounds silly, I said, but, I said, my name's Alfie Wicks ('cause Alfie, we'll come to that why it's Alfie) and I lived in this house as an evacuee during the war. She threw herself into my arms—it was his daughter and we'd been playmates as kids. I'd forgotten. She said, oh, come on in, come on in. And I figured, well mum and dad would have long been gone, you know. And she said, mum and dad are gonna love to see ya. I said, mum and dad are still alive? In their nineties, she said. They're in the kitchen. I said, well I've gotta get my wife and children. Well, she made such a fuss. We all go in there. Now, I don't think they remembered me frankly. They were in their nineties, he still had his cap on. And so it was a wonderful reunion. He did something that was really… set the old lump going in my throat as I left. As I left—it's a habit of the Welsh that when a stranger passes the doorstep with children, the child cannot leave without silver passing the palm of the hand. And as we left he gave each of my children a silver coin. And my boy was 14 years of age, my son, at exactly the same age I was when I left, and when I came back and told my mum, she said, well, we still have the horseshoe that he gave you, and she pulled it out from under the bed in amongst a load of stuff. And I have that horseshoe to this day. So he'd pressed it in my hand at exactly the same age as my son.

DG Ben, we've got you bounced around as a youngster. Finally, the Roberts take you in and you are happy. What about your own parents? Tell us about the reunion, I mean when you came back, what period of time was that after you left?

BW It seems awful; this is 1941-42 and I don't remember it. I don't remember coming back. It's sad. It's the craziest thing. I had a woman contact me who said she came back with me. She told me there were 30 of us on a train and I don't remember a thing about it. It was just awful. I sort of got back home and just picked up where I left off. I was now 14 and of course had left school, had to leave at 14, and got a job in the fruit market, in East Street fruit market, and that's where I went to work as a barrow boy.

DG In the next years you were a bit of a Jack of all trades. When the war ended, you were a commercial artist, a window cleaner, a professional musician. What instrument were you playing?

BW Well, I played clarinet and saxophone after a fashion. I was a professional for nine years.

DG How did you pick that up?

BW I went back to London, and in that very poor area Cambridge University had a wonderful idea. They decided that they would open up a small club (the university itself) for the poor in that area, for somewhere for the youth to go. I probably went 'round there with a couple of buddies to break the windows, and then when I got inside there signed up. And it was wonderful, it was fantastic. We had the usual thing, cards and drafts and whatever, but it was a house, somewhere to go. So we quickly made friends. We had a soccer team that never won a game. But there was a group of us, five of us got together, and we made strong buddies and we decided we'd like to form a band. And when everyone had decided on their instrument, I was left. And they said, well you can play the clarinet, and I said, alright, and I went out and so for five dollars—it would have been I suppose about five dollars—I bought a clarinet, an old clarinet. And every Monday night we would play at Sammy Vericho's house while his poor mum and dad would have to suffer this—we would play Doc Pound Struthers Ball , or our version of it. We never knew another tune. Now the others slowly got fed up with this, but I really enjoyed it, and I thought, boy, I'm gonna take lessons. I went… answered an ad in the paper—it was a saxophone club—professional saxophone player and clarinet player. He said, you know, if you want to be a professional, your fastest instrument is saxophone. And he said, depending on how much you want to practise, is how fast you'll turn professional. I'm a pretty disciplined person, and this once again points out my mother and father, what remarkable people they were. Living in the tenement buildings like this, obviously the walls are like paper. I mean, you knew everyone's business. So consequently, for someone to arrive with a saxophone who's going to practise every night, I mean the rest of the building had better know what was gonna happen. My dad decided on a wonderful idea. We had a large dresser, you know, that you hung your clothes in, I don't know what you call it. Anyway, this large dresser, and he would open the two doors, and because we were under gaslight, you know, and no electric, he would hang a torch in there from the rail that hung the clothes. Now he would set up the music stand for me with all my scales on it, I would sit with the chair—the two legs at the front of the chair half into the dresser, and the two legs half out. I would then get into this chair, right. Now I'm facing the back of the dresser, the two doors are either side of me. My dad would then drape blankets over me and cover this all in blankets. I would sit in there for a couple of hours practicing scales. I worked like crazy at that.

DG And no complaint from the neighbours?

BW No, no complaint. I had a wonderful compliment after a couple of months. Mrs. Leigh downstairs said to me, oh, she said, Alfie, that trumpet is coming along lovely. And I never, to this day, I don't know whether it was a compliment or not. But anyway… And there was a place in Britain called Archer Street. Every musician went to Archer Street on a Monday afternoon. All musicians. And what you did, you went there to meet your buddies or you went there to get a job. And I was told that there was an agent looking for musicians on the continent to join various groups entertaining the American troops. I got this job, off I went, I ended up in Frankfurt with my saxophone and clarinet. That evening decided to go out for a drink and I ran into another group. And this guy was an American musician and he said to me, where are you going? And I said, well I've joined this group and we're heading to Vienna. And this guy said, I've never been to Vienna, how would you like to go to Berlin? And I said, well I don't care where I go, you know. So he said, why don't we switch jobs. Tomorrow morning, he said, is our first rehearsal with the group. They haven't seen us yet; you show up for my job, I'll show up for yours. I said okay. God, it was a sneak. He was a real sneak, because when I turned up next morning to this place, there they were: nine American showgirls, a pianist (who's a wonderful friend, turned out to be a wonderful friend—Wayne) and, as I say, these nine gorgeous American showgirls. And I thought, my God, this is going to be fantastic, I'm going to travel through Europe with this group. It was called the Gypsy Markov Show. Gypsy Markov finally arrived after half an hour. She was an absolute horror. She was a brilliant accordionist who played classical accordion. And the first thing she did, she sort of nodded, half spoke to me, walked past Wayne, and she unfolded an orchestral piece of *Hungarian Rhapsody* that had been put together for her by the Brooklyn Navy Dock Band or something. But it was an 18-piece thing and there was two of us. And she started by stomping her little foot, you know, while she did this incredible thing as she started… [BW mimicing accordion sound] all over the accordion, before we came in. Then it was a case of us trying to catch up, you know, because it was ridiculous. I think I finished, as I remember, three bars in front of Wayne. So I sort of won that contest. But she was absolutely livid. She stood there, stomped her feet, told us that we were absolutely the most useless musicians she'd ever seen. And we kept together for six months. Gypsy never changed. We ended up in England, where she met her match. We came into a (she cursed everyone)… we got to our first British hotel in Oxford, and we sat there waiting for our rooms because Gypsy had to have her room first. She stomps in, tells the guy she wanted to be led to her room. So she breezes up the stairs, she comes down, shouting and screaming like crazy because her room hadn't got a heater, right (the guy as calm as you like). She demands to see the manager. The manager comes out and in this very cultured English voice said, yes Madam, can I help you. She is literally screaming and stomping her feet. He said, oh, I'm terribly sorry, well I'm sure there's something we can do about this Madam. So he writes on a scrap of paper and he says to her, there you are, there's the phone number of the hotel down the street. She stood there absolutely astonished. And he threw her out. She could not believe it, she'd had months of this domineering everyone. Anyway, life went on and I went back to Archer Street, and a guy said to me, well, I play on the ships. I said, what ship? He said, I play on the Queen Elizabeth (which at that time was the biggest liner in the world—84,000 tons) backwards and forwards to New York from Southampton. I said, it sounds a fantastic job. He said, it is, but you get bored with it. He said, now, if you want the job, I'm quitting next time. So I said, fantastic, terrific, who do I get in touch with? He said, you get in touch with a guy called Barber. Now, I've never forgotten his name because it was one of the most remarkable things that ever happened to me. It's now Monday afternoon. So he says to me, he said, I take it you play, you read the notes, you know. And I said, yes, I play with music. He said, can you play without music? I said, well yeah, after a fashion, you know. So he said, okay, Barber's going to ask you this question because of the requests that the passengers would give on the boat. He's 'gonna ask you, can you play without music? And you say to him, I'll play anything you'd like to mention. And he said the wonderful thing is, Barber (it was his mother who had the contract for auditioning the groups) but he himself is not only tone deaf, but he only knows two tunes. And I looked at this guy and I said, I can't believe… is this a put-on? I don't know anyone who only knows two tunes. He said, it's an absolute fact, he only knows two tunes. He said, he's going to ask you, can you play?… You say, I'll play anything you'd like to mention. And he's going to say, okay, let's hear *Lady Is A Tramp* in 'C', or *Night And Day* in 'E' flat. They're the only two tunes he knows, he said, and he doesn't know what it means when he says C and E flat. Well, I practised for a week, don't I. I ring Barber, Barber says, I've got enough people. And I have to persuade him on the phone to listen to me. He says, okay. So we end up… Anyway, to cut a story short, I'm facing Barber. So he gets out a piece of music—and I remember it to this day—it's *Swedish Rhapsody*. And he said to me, okay, let's hear this, right. And I began to play this. Well, this thing looked like a pigeon had run all over it, you know, and I squeak and the sound's… And he walks around the desk and I figure, well that's it, it's all over. And he said, listen Wicks, he said, before you get on the boat, make sure that clarinet is clean. So *Swedish Rhapsody*, if we could hear that. Is it possible to hear that?

DG Yes, let's do it right now.

BW People will have some idea of how difficult it was for me… [MUSIC]

DG Ben, you met and married your wife, Doreen, in England. Can you remember in fact when you first set eyes on her?

BW Yes I can, I can remember that very well. As I mentioned before, I'd become a professional musician and had this wonderful seaside job. And of course, for four months of the year I would play in Cornwall, and then the rest of the time take various jobs on board ships or whatever. And I was back for another season, I think it was the third season, and what we would do—I mean, in this period when we're aware of sexism, you know, this is gonna sound very sexist, this particular remark—but the fact is, being musicians, and young musicians at that, was a wonderful thing, because those going on holiday, the young girls, were going there for one week only, you see. So consequently they'd come to the only dance hall in town, which was ours. So Saturday night it was a matter of looking over your music and seeing who was new coming into town, and when you were seeing them off at the railway on Saturday afternoon, watching to see who was new coming into town that week. So consequently you could look out in the dance hall and see who appealed to you, and this was it. I remember seeing Doreen, very attractive—she's still attractive to this day—a very attractive blonde dancing around the dance hall. And of course, I was trying to get her eye, and I tried to make my way to her as soon as the intermission came, tried to get to her before the rest of the band, you know, because everyone kept it very quiet as to who they had their eye on. But I couldn't get near her, I mean, she had so many admirers around her. So next day was a Sunday, and I was on the beach and I was walking along the beach, and lo and behold, there was Doreen sat with her sister, who she was on holiday with. So I walk over—bronzed Ben with his wonderful muscles rippling—walk over and say, hi, you know, and hello, whatever. And now this is where Doreen takes over because I'm sure hers is closer to the truth. She tells everyone: then this strange little man sits down beside us and starts talking to us and proceeds to eat our toffees (we had a bag of toffees she said). And by the time he stood up and left, not only had all her toffees gone, but he'd borrowed a quid off me. Now that's Doreen's story. My story I hope is a little more balanced. I said to her, well I saw you in the dance hall last night. And she said, oh, did you? So I said, oh, you didn't see me? And she said, no, I don't remember seeing you. And I said, with real bravado, but I'm a member of the band. And she answers, I never look at the band, which was really devastating to me when I was expecting somebody to be falling all over my feet and kissing my feet. Anyway, I wandered off and persisted that week, and saw her home every night (her and her sister). And I must confess, at that time I was near 29, I'd already joined a bachelor's club—we vowed to stay single for evermore. Mind you, the club collapsed after a month when the president got married, but other than that, up to that time I was still a member. And of course when Doreen left, I vowed to write every day, and I did. I wrote every day and remained true to her. She really hit me. She was 19… I think she was 18, and a young nurse. All manner of things… she hits me the same way today I think, because of her manner, her honesty. And of course I met up with her in London. Although she was from Bristol, she was at the hospital in London, and within months I proposed to her at Trafalgar Square by the fountain. Doreen was my other. She was coming 'round the various dance halls, I was now on the Mecca circuit, where you had this bandstand turned around, so you had Ted Heath on one side, and a small quartet like myself (playing clarinet) and three rhythm, on the other side. So that when we were on show everyone would go to the bar, and as the Ted Heath Band would start to play and we'd start turning around, everybody would come out of the bar. So nobody knew you were there. But we decided to go to Canada, and what decided on Canada was the fact we decided to go somewhere in the world, and the only person I knew anywhere in the world was a trombone player, called Bill Coates, who lived in Calgary. If he had lived in Melbourne, we would have gone to Melbourne.

DG   Now, something I've got to ask you. Well, two things I want to ask you: one is, you were Alfie?

BW   Yes. Oh, I'm sorry…

DG   …and we've never found out how you've become Ben, so let's find out, I mean before we get you in print.

BW   I became Ben because the first job I had with this first band, The Roy Kenton Band, the guy changed his name to call himself Roy Kenton 'cause he thought Kenton was really big, and this was a rub-off on him. And as soon as I joined the band… At that time in 1954-55, they had the habit of putting the first name of the musician on the bandstand, and since I was the lead alto player right in the centre of the band it meant that my name would have to be 'Alfie' (in the middle of the band). And the leader said, in no way am I having the name 'Alfie' on the front of my band stand, he said, so from here on in you're going to be called Ben. Benny.

DG   And to this day you're Ben.

BW   …out of Benny Goodman, but I think it was out of sarcasm more than anything, the way I played the clarinet. And to this day then, everyone I met after becoming a musician, I was known as Ben. No one knew me as Alf. You know, my dad once wrote to me and said, dear Ben. And I wrote to dad and said, don't ever do that again, I'm really proud of the fact that I'm Alf to you, and that's how I'll always be.

DG   What's it all about Alfie?

BW   Well, this is it, you see. And Michael Caine I knew. He lived in the area of course where I grew up.

DG   I was going to say, he was an evacuee, too, wasn't he?

BW   He was an evacuee too, and when we spoke to Michael—and of course he wrote the intro to the book, *No Time to Wave Goodbye* because of that. But in fact, when Michael made the movie that gave him this fame, *Alfie*, the guy he picked to model on (lived in our building, St. George's building) was Michael's best friend. And if you can believe it, to this day this guy got all the best looking girls. And when Michael did the film, *Alfie*, he remembered this guy and figured that that was the manner of this guy.

91

DG Now, the other thing we've got to find out is, so far you've given no indication of either being able to sketch or being able to write. Did these come into your life earlier?

BW They did. I'd always sketched and I'd always drawn because I was hopeless at school. I was absolutely useless at everything. And the only class I enjoyed was the art class, and that was because it was taken by the maths teacher, who knew absolutely nothing about art, so consequently I was able to go in there and get no criticism at all. I went out and I bought a book on cartooning. And it had two pages in there of magazines that bought cartoons, starting at the very top with the *Saturday Evening Post*, which was the most important magazine at that time, and secondly The *New Yorker*, and it worked its way down. It said that you should submit six cartoons with your name on the back and the address and a stamped addressed envelope. So I did this and I set up a little filing system, and I thought of it as fun. As they'd send the cartoons back I'd send it to the next magazine down and whatever. And I did these six cartoons and I sent them off to the *Saturday Evening Post*, and five weeks later I was coming down the street and Doreen's waving this letter in the air, and she said, it's the most incredible thing. She said, the *Saturday Evening Post* have just written to you. They want to buy your work, but since they don't know who you are, they want three letters of reference. So I wrote… I sat down and I wrote the three letters of reference, and I drew for them for two-and-a-half years, three years. So it really launched my cartooning career because very quickly other magazines wrote. With the *Saturday Evening Post* the interesting thing was, something happened in Calgary City Council that really bothered me. I forget what it was now. I went to the *Albertan*, the morning paper at that time. I said to the editor, I'd like to do an editorial cartoon on this. And he said, well we have an editorial cartoonist. And I said, well why don't I draw a little cartoon, a pocket cartoon. And he said, I've never heard of them. And it was a fact; they were very big in Britain these pocket cartoons.

DG Like Osbert Lancaster?

BW Yes, Osbert Lancaster. Not well known here, but a very popular pocket cartoonist. And he said, that sounds a good idea, how much would you charge us? And I said, well, I'll charge you five dollars. And I did the cartoon on this remark that had been made in city council, and the very next morning when it appeared in the paper, the city councilman who it was aimed at stood up and said, is there anything that can be done about a cartoon that is maligning the intelligence of the city council. I remember that line. Eric Watt (bless him), the editor, rang me immediately and said, could you do this every day? And I tried it and before I knew where I was, we had a dozen newspapers phoning to ask where it was from. To move on, *The Toronto Telegram* offered me a contract, I went to Toronto with Doreen and the kids, and of course then *The Chicago Tribune* wrote to ask if it could be done on American politics. Before I knew where I was, the *Los Angeles Times* had offered a contract, and I was quickly drawing for a couple of hundred newspapers.

DG Where did *The Outcasts* come from?

BW I was drawing, and in fact was in the middle of a very busy period doing television, and *The New York Daily News* and *Chicago Tribute* syndicates contacted me and said that there was an incredibly popular strip in the States that had just taken off—a thing called *Doonsbury*—that was on politics, and they'd been hunting around (since it was in the house of another syndicate) for a cartoonist who could rival this. They'd tried various American cartoonists and it hadn't come off. And my name had been mentioned and would I be interested in doing this political strip. I said, for one thing I'd never looked at *Doonsbury*, so if they'd give me a week to look at it. So I did, I took a week and I rang them back. I said, I'm incredibly busy, but I don't understand it. I said, but I'll have to do a cartoon of my own if you want me to do it. So I did a very, very rough idea, couple of ideas of *The Outcasts*. This was a group on an island that was run by, at that time, Gerald Ford. And of course he was constantly promising them he was going to get them off the island, and it never happened, so… I thought it was brilliant [laughing]… I'm tryin' to think of the right word. That is a good word, I thought it was brilliant. They also agreed, so I flew down to New York and we had one of these wonderful meetings where they tell you that you're going to earn millions and we're going to make billions of dollars all of us, and everyone's mentioning all these huge figures. And when they'd finished around this table with all the chiefs, I said, so how much am I getting? They said, well you're gonna make millions. I said, well I know what I'm going to make, but how much am I gonna get now when I do this six weeks' work. And they quickly told me that no cartoonist ever gets paid for the six weeks samples because these are in effect samples, but reminded me that there would be millions down the road. And I said, well, I'm so busy I haven't got time unless I'm gonna get paid. Anyway, I demanded that they pay me ten thousand dollars, and between their lawyers and mine it went on for months, and finally a $10,000 cheque arrived and I sat down and did the cartoons for them. I did the six weeks cartoons which I'd been paid for, and then they found they couldn't find one newspaper that wanted to buy it. In the meantime I'd done the Canadian version and it had taken off. So there it was in Canada, it appeared in *Time Magazine* and God knows what, and it took off here, but it never did make it in the States.

DG In any week, how many people would have seen your cartoon?

BW *Time Magazine* I think was sort of overdoing it, but they claimed I probably had an audience of 50 million readers, which was really astonishing. Even I was astonished when I read the figure, so I don't know where they got it from, but that is what they estimated. I think they were looking at the circulation of the various newspapers.

DG You could have asked for more money on the basis of that.

BW Well, I was getting pretty well-paid as it was. I was getting 50 percent of what everyone paid for it.

DG Let's have some more music.

BW Well, I think you know, one of the things that I mentioned earlier when I went for an audition on the boats, was one of the tunes Barber knew—he only knew two tunes as you remember, *Lady is a Tramp* in 'C', and *Night and Day* in 'E' flat. And when he said to me, can you play without music?, I said, anything you'd like to mention, as I'd been told to say. He said, okay, well let's hear *Lady is a Tramp* in 'C'. So I played this, I was astonished. Anyway, his second tune, which should have been *Night and Day* in 'E' flat, I was ready for. So I was now with the clarinet, he said, okay, let's hear you on the clarinet, can you play anything on the clarinet? I said, anything you'd like to mention. Now I'm ready for *Night and Day* in 'E' flat, the only other tune he knew. I picked a day when he only knew one tune. He could not for the life of him remember *Night and Day* in 'E' flat. He said, well let's hear… gee, let's hear… And I thought, should I say *Night and Day* in 'E' flat, but it's a bit suspicious. And he suddenly said, oh to hell with it, let's hear the middle bit of *Lady is a Tramp* in 'C'. So here we have *Lady is a Tramp* performed by one of the all time great performers, Lena Horne, and it's been a favourite of mine ever since that time.

DG And it includes the middle eight.

BW And it includes the middle eight. [MUSIC]

DG Okay, now the editors told you that you should draw in a more sophisticated style. Do you have a distinctive style?

BW Somebody calls it primitive, which is said as a compliment. I have difficulty drawing. I mean, as everyone says, you know, hands are difficult to draw and feet are difficult to draw, and in fact they are. There was a time when I had everyone's hands in their pocket (I figured that was the quickest way out of it) and sat them behind the desk.

DG The slouch cartoon.

BW Yeah, the slouch cartoon. But no, it is, it's a very simple style and, frankly, I'm fortunate. Because knowing my limitations it means (and I think this is important) is knowing when to stop. That's the real secret of fine art, is knowing when you've done enough.

DG When the cartoon is finished you mean.

BW When the cartoon is finished, or any art form. Picasso said it, and I think it's right: the single line form of art is probably the purest form of art. And

Picasso certainly proved that with his wonderful single line simple things. But once again, it's extremely difficult to do, because you really feel, well maybe I should draw laces in the guy's shoes, now I should draw a tie, now I... And before you know where you are you're into braces and a full suit, you know.

DG What is the most difficult thing about doing a sketch, doing a strip?

BW My kind of work, I think because we're one of the few that do it now (my son draws the strip now) is anticipating the news. And I think that's the most difficult. We draw six weeks ahead, and for a comic page that's fine—of course it appears on the comic pages in many cases—but with a political cartoon it's extremely difficult. You find yourself trying to anticipate what the news will be in six weeks time. What I found was that a good 50 percent of the news it is possible to predict.

DG Apart from all the jobs you've had, it was in journalism that some of your most memorable work came. You covered the war in Biafra for *The Los Angeles Time*, and that was in the sixties. Was that a situation where you were trying to alert the world to a horrific tragedy?

BW Well, very quickly that came quite by accident. I was not a journalist at that time and, of course, as a cartoonist and being widely syndicated, working for John Basset at *The Toronto Telegram*. And a large church group got in touch with Basset and said, if we could get Wicks to go there, and Worthington (Peter Worthington, the famous Canadian foreign journalist) and we could get a report that would make people aware of Biafra, the horrors of it. I think what was to happen, was of course the most horrific experience for me, was Ethiopia when that came. By now Doreen, my wife, had got involved deeply in the third world. My daughter, my eldest daughter, Susan, had dropped out of school. And what had happened, Sue was one of these incredible students who worked so hard (one, two o'clock in the morning) and always got 49 instead of 50, and that was never recognized, as it never is in our system. And so she was frustrated to the point that when I did a story on Haiti for *The Globe and Mail*—I'd been at Haiti—I wrote about a Sister Joan, who was an 84-year-old American nun working there in Port of France, in the slums of Port of France, finding children who were disabled. And she had two hundred children in this old home. So I stayed with her for a week and wrote this story. Anyway, when I finished the story and it appeared, my daughter read this and was so taken with this—for her it was an escape—so she insisted she wanted to work with Sister Joan. So she went to Haiti, and during the period of working there (Doreen, of course, was on the phone every night). And in the end, Doreen said, I've got to go and see her to see how she is. So Doreen left her nursing job at Sunnybrook Hospital and went to Haiti. Susan took her around the slums of Haiti and of course Doreen quickly began to examine the children. She saw a woman who gave birth and cut her own cord with a machete that had been smeared with cow dung to keep away the evil spirits. The result of this was, of course, a large number of babies with tetanus because they'd gone through the same thing. Doreen, although she'd nursed since she was 17, had never seen tetanus, let alone in a baby. So she saw horrors she'd never seen. She came back to Toronto, and I'll never forget it, she just could not sleep. She said, I cannot get it out of my mind, those children. So by the time the weekend was over she said, I've made a decision. I'm quitting my job and I'm devoting the rest of my life to children and mothers in the third world. And that was the start. And out of that grew this incredible organization of hers, GEMS (Global Ed-Med Supplies), and of course, during the course of this, having started eleven years ago, soon after the Ethiopian crisis happened in '84, and out of this, this horror. And we suddenly got a call from a priest who said, I have two men that I want you to meet who are from Eritrea. Now, few people had heard of Eritrea at that time, but Africa was experiencing its longest war in Ethiopia—26 years it had been going on. So on a Sunday morning we met these two Eritreans, two wonderful men. And the first thing I asked them, I asked them where they were from and what they were part of. And as they described it I said, are you part of a rebel force? And they said, yes, we're two members of the EPLF (rebel army). And I'd said to Doreen, you know, this is going to get very political, you should be careful. And she said to them—and she made the right answer—she said, do you have women and children that are starving and suffering and in need of medicine? They said, by the hundreds of thousands and nothing is getting into there because it's in the war zone in the north. So Doreen said, I don't want to hear anymore then, that's it. She then turned to me and said, will you take the medicines in for us to make sure it gets to the right place. So Doreen was very generous in handing out her jobs. Doreen flies into these areas and sets them up. For instance, we've just opened our first shelter in Brazil for the street children. We are now involved deeply in Uganda with the children, the orphans of the AIDS victims. But they're all put together by the people themselves, it belongs to the people themselves. Doreen helps them and, of course, out of that she's become remarkable now—she has the Order of Canada and B'nai Brith Woman of the Year, and all these awards. You know at the turn of the century, it was a well-known scene that we would see, was the English explorer going through the elephant grass, followed along behind by the bearers carrying these large bundles on their heads. In 1992 it's my wife, Doreen, going through the elephant grass followed by her husband carrying two suitcases, and both of them are hers.

DG Do you ever get a feeling of hopelessness, that you've done so much it's like a bottomless pit—no matter how much you do it's never enough?

BW Doreen answered it in a wonderful way. She was asked this a month ago. She just got back from somewhere, I think it was Uganda, and a reporter asked her, do you ever throw your arms up and say, you know, what's the point? She said, yes, I do throw up my arms, she said, when I get to Canada, when I get back to Canada and I get off the plane and I throw my arms up and say to myself, what the hell are they arguing about? Here they have this remarkable country and they're bickering and saying silly things amongst each other. And I think that's worth repeating. Yes, that is the frustration I get. I get frustrated about this country, that they themselves are so inward looking. And yet we have a country that is incredibly caring, and we have to start looking outwards and realizing how fortunate we are.

DG The stories you're telling, you've been through such horror, and at the end of it all you're laughing. Is humor a vital part of this?

BW Oh, absolutely. Humor and tragedy run side by side. I mean, Chaplin is the best example of that: you know, the blind man… the blind girl and the tramp. No, humor in tragedy has to play a part. I mean they run side by side, and if either crosses the line—that's the interesting thing about that—they each negate the other. You can go in the most horrific situation… I remember in Biafra, in a small school and the floor was covered with dead and dying, young kids of 14 in army uniform who had been wounded. And as we stepped over this horror (Peter Worthington and I) with this old Irish priest—he could see we were really shocked by this—and to ease it, he suddenly pointed to a guy in the corner. He said, do you see that one over there? And we looked and we saw this young man lying there. He said, I've given him the last rites three times, if he doesn't go soon I'm going to go over there and kick him up there. It was just the kind of remark that was needed to break the tension, you see. And that was it, that's humor and tragedy.

DG Let's break off for some more music.

BW Oh, Frank Sinatra, it has to be Frank Sinatra. I'm a tremendous Frank Sinatra fan. I've never seen him and there's no other reason for having it played other than I really love Frank Sinatra. How about something cheery like *Come Fly with Me*. [MUSIC]

DG Your latest book is called *Promise You Will Take Care of my Daughter,* which looks at the British war brides, and of course during World War II, romance, despite the war going on… The fact is that they came over here in large numbers and what happened was, because of the war, news on the generals and so on, people didn't really realize what was going on.

BW Well, the astonishing thing is that there are 48,000 of them, 48.000. Basically from Europe, this army of women came to Canada. I think the thing that really interested me in the story was that it's really the story of Canada, you know. This is what our country is. In this particular case it happened to be an army of white, basically white women. But every minute of every day we have people from all over the world—black, yellow, blue, green, whatever— this is our country's strength. So that once I started with the war brides I realized that that's part of what I was writing about. The story itself is a fascinating one. You know, you have to look, as I said, about my kind of nationalism, where being asked are you willing to die for your country, and saying no—you have to understand why a person goes into the services. In many cases, the majority of cases, they're 17, 18, they're fed up with their jobs, they live in Moose Jaw, Medicine Hat, wherever. And they meet with the boys and they say, let's join the services, or I'm going into the services—with a bit of luck we'll end up in Paris. And of course what a lot of Canadian soldiers did was ended up, in fact, in almost as good… They ended up in Britain in the early part of the war. Now the Americans had yet to arrive, so there you have this wonderful fortunate group who have it to themselves. The men are all gone, they're in North Africa and in France, and they have a country full of women.

DG And they've got cigarettes and they've got chewing gum and…

BW That's right, and they've got more money. And of course the women in turn are listening to this accent that they figure is the Hollywood accent. I mean, this is the American accent. It's North America, it's friendly, it's warm, it's everything… They only have one major problem—the father. Because the father of these women had served in the First World War, and he knew very well what these Canadian soldiers were after, and in no way were they going to get it from his daughter. So that was the first problem. And of course these barriers broke down eventually, I think partly because they were hoping that someone was treating their sons and daughters overseas as well as what they wanted to treat the Canadians. So they opened their doors. And of course what came was this wonderful union of European women coming to Canada to live. You see, we often hear the saying, the boys went away boys and they came back men. What was much more dramatic was they left girls behind, but they came back to women with a great sense of confidence in their own ability. Women at that time had survived without men for four years, five years, six years. Now this guy was coming back and saying, okay, move aside. And the women were saying, why? I've done it, I don't need you. You see, I remember speaking to a welder, a woman who'd been a welder during the war. She said, we'd been told, oh, to be a welder, you know, would take years, you know, of training. She said, in three weeks I was in the Brooklyn dockyards sending down a liberty ship every day, you know. One of the tragedies that we don't recognize in the Second World War was the tragedy of those who were born when the fathers then went off to war. They were born after the father was gone, so they did not know their fathers for four and five years. What I was amazed at was at the number of letters I got saying that I could not communicate with my father when he came back. And they never did. One woman wrote to say, for 35 years I could not communicate with my father. Then he had a stroke and he couldn't speak; now we can communicate. Another woman wrote and said, that when I went with my mother to pick up my father I was five. She said, we sat in the back of the car, my dad and I—this man I'd only seen as a photograph—he put one arm 'round me and he handed me a silver coin. And I said to him, I'm sorry sir, I'm not allowed to take money from strangers. And he answered, I'm not a stranger, I'm your daddy. But look at the gulf to be bridged. So for me that book was satisfying, if just for the fact that those women wrote to me and said, now at last I can overcome it. I had one three weeks ago. I was at a small library outside of London, Ontario, a place called Taverstock. There were fifty people packed in that room. Half way through talking the way we are, there was a woman sat near the front row began to cry. She came up to me afterwards, she said, I've been under a psychiatrist for years because I've blamed myself. I always said to myself, what did I do to my dad to make him like this? We never really talked. He never took me onto his lap. Now they all say the same—funny, eh?—never picked me up and put me on his lap. She said, now, she said it all comes home. She said, you have no idea what you've done. She wrote to me last week, a three-page letter saying what a burden it had taken off; she realizes that the problem was not her, but of course the absence of the father at that time.

DG Now, before we let you go to your recluse, wherever it is (and we'll come to that in a moment) you are allowed to take one book with you. What book would that be?

BW One book! Oh God… Well, that's easy for me. What a shame it isn't two. It would be a choice between *Autobiography of a Super Tramp* by W. H. Davis, the Welsh poet, or it would be *Wars* by Timothy Findley, that I absolutely love. So I think what I'll do is I'll tear the cover off *The Wars* 'cause it's a smaller book, and I'll put the whole of the *Autobiography of a Super Tramp* in between the middle covers, so that everyone will think it's one book and in fact it'll be two, and then I'll tromp up the mountain with that and sit down and be happy ever after.

DG You're devious. All right. You've got your single book containing two stories. Then you can take your music with you, an unlimited supply of solar batteries so your music will go on forever. Where in the world would you be able to be happiest in isolation? It doesn't have to be the top of a mountain, it could be if you wished an English seaside or the lush hills of Uganda. Where would you choose?

BW This is going to be so disappointing to most people. I'm really happy where I am, living in Toronto down on the water. I'm happy surrounded by my family, and that's where I am at the moment, so I'd be quite happy to continue on living there. I'm living a very contented life. And understand this, that I'm the kid from the centre of London, so for me… As one woman who was living in the centre of London was once asked, after going to the countryside for the first time, what she thought of it. She said, well it's okay, but it's just a lot of scenery out there. And maybe for me that's it, it's just a lot of scenery out there. I'm happy living in the big city.

DG One final choice of music.

BW Mozart's *Clarinet Concerto*, purely for the simple reason that whoever is playing it on record always plays it much better than I ever could, and I love the piece.

DG Ben Wicks, thank you very much.

BW Thank you.

TOM JACKSON
WITH JUDY HAMILL, 1995

JH   Let's go back I guess to the beginning. You were born on the One Arrow Reserve by Batoche, is that correct? In Saskatchewan? And then when you were a kid your parents moved everybody to Winnipeg. That must have been a huge adjustment for you.

TJ   We drove to Winnipeg in a 1953 Chevy, and my dad, not being heavy in the foot department, drove all the way from Edmonton to Winnipeg at 45 miles per hour, with me and my sister in the back and my mom in the front. That was a long ride. We got to Winnipeg and I had never seen so much snow in my whole life. I remember going down Portage Avenue and it was the 17th of December, and I remember driving down Portage Avenue entering the city—and I guess that'd just plowed the streets—and there were probably snow banks on the side about, I'd say eight feet, nine feet high from the plows. And I couldn't see the buildings from the car. I went, holy mackerel! Me and my sister, the first thing we did, is we went running up the snow bank onto the top of a bank—an actual bank, and it might have been Toronto Dominion or Bank of Montreal or one of those things—and we ran off the roof and jumped into a snow bank and got stuck.

JH   And then you left home when you were what, fifteen?

TJ   Yeah.

JH   By choice, and still loving and having a good relationship with your parents. But you hit the streets at the age of fifteen.

TJ   Where do you get this information?

JH   Oh, here and there.

TJ   Hey, I should do an interview with you.

JH   Did you sit down one day and just say, okay, I'm just going to strike out on my own and see what's out there. Is that how it happened?

TJ   Well let me just say that my hair is turning grey, and with each hair that goes grey goes the memory. When you ask me to think back to when I was fifteen and I left home, as to why I left home, I'm not quite sure. But I can tell you that my fondest memories of growing up were, in fact, those memories of being on the street. It was just… I mean, if you can imagine—and I guess I have to in some ways as I mentioned my memory not being that clear at the time, or of the time—a kid who was fifteen, from the country, on the street, eyes as big as saucers and going through a formative period with a group of friends who were adventurous and reckless and rogues and thieves and, you know, it was like a gang of pirates or something. And I just remember having nothing but glory days, you know.

JH   The freedom.

TJ   Yeah, absolutely.

JH   How did your poor parents feel about this? Did they worry?

TJ   Uh, I think they kept one eye open, you know. And I think if I'd have had a serious trip and fall that they would have been there sooner than… or, you know, they just would have showed up and I wouldn't have even known why, and it was probably just 'cause they had an eye on me. My parents were very loving, I loved them very much. My mother's past on, but they were the joys of my life, they were just the best parents anybody could ever have.

JH   Well, who did you get your height from—6′5″? Is your dad a very tall man?

TJ   No. He's about 5′9″… yeah, 5′9″. And my mother was about the same. Well, not the same—she was about 5′7″. My uncles on my mother's side—all her brothers—were very tall. I think the shortest would be 6′6″, 6′5″, and she had about… I think there were six brothers. The tallest was 6′8″.

JH   You could have played basketball, Tom, if you'd stayed in school.

TJ   Well, I think that was part of my reason for dropping out, 'cause I actually played basketball for the first time when I got to Winnipeg, and I enjoyed it so much. But my studies suffered and I remember the coach coming to me on a given day and he told me that if I didn't get my studies together I was gonna have to quit the team. And I knew I wasn't gonna get my studies together, so I decided I better quit school 'cause I couldn't play basketball anymore. What a cop-out, eh? Geez, what a guy.

JH   It worked out though, didn't it?

TJ   It did. I eventually got to play basketball. There was a group called Youth Opportunities Unlimited, which in a lot of ways changed my life. It was a drop-in centre that was sponsored by the Mennonite Church. I sort of felt like I was playing basketball, or was being handed a basketball in one hand and a bible in the other. And I'm not particularly a religious man, but I'm not a man without religion. It was sort of a made-for-television movie type basketball team; we were sort of a pretty hard-core group. I remember, there was a guy by the name of Roger Greening, who's still a friend of mine to this day, who came out to be the coach of this team, and he got knocked out by one of the players on the first day because we were scrimmaging, and he blew the whistle and he told this guy that he had to get off the floor and let another guy play, and he didn't want to get off the floor and Rogers said, you gotta get off the floor, and the guy hit Roger. Poor old Rog went down and there he was knocked out. We eventually became a championship team.

JH   What about the musical ability, Tom. Where do you think that comes from in your family?

TJ   My mother's side of the family was pretty musical. I remember my uncles coming over on occasion with stand-up bass and guitars and fiddles, and they used to sing Ernest Tubb songs and that sort of thing, and I used to sit on the stairway after it was time for bed. I'd sneak down the stairwell, sit around the corner and listen to them play. My father, unknown to me… oh, I guess I might have been twenty-five or somewhere around there—I went over to my parents' place with a friend of mine, who is now passed on, Frank Crocket—hi Frank, hope you're listening—went over to my parents' place with Frank and a friend of his who was a banjo player, and myself, and we went over to mom's place and we were sitting around playing. Now Dave Kramer was playing harmonica in front of me, and all of a sudden I heard this other harmonica. I went, who the heck's playing harmonica? I figured it might have been Frank or somebody, but it wasn't. I turned around and it was my dad. My dad was playing a chromatic harmonica and he was good. I mean, there he was playing; I was twenty-five, twenty-six years old, and I didn't know my father was a musician. I had no clue. So maybe there's this hidden seed in my system that comes from my father.

JH   Here's another circle in your life, too. Graham Jones, one of the Wild Colonial Boys; was he the first person that said, why don't you get up and sing a song, why don't you become a musician, or got you started along that path, at any rate?

TJ   He got me focused. I had always, as long as I can remember, had a guitar. And at the period of time when I was living on the street and having this wonderful life that I so aptly described, Graham Jones, who was the director of social activities at the Indian and Metis Friendship Centre in Winnipeg, came up to me and basically put his hand on the scruff of my neck and suggested that I do something other than what I was doing with my life. And he at the time played in a folk group, and they were great and I was a great admirer of his and the group. I asked him, well what do you suggest I do? And he didn't have any great suggestions and I said, well, why don't you show me how to play guitar. And he showed me some basic things and I went out and learned some songs—I think my entire repertoire of three. One day he asked me, when he and his group were playing—they had to go out and play at this school—he asked me if I wanted to come along and asked me if I wanted to play. So I sang my full repertoire of three songs. One of the songs was *Homeward Bound*, and there's this line in *Homeward Bound* that goes… [singing] *homeward bound, I wish I was…* so there was this line that dropped down, and I, in his opinion, had picked the wrong key in any event, so when I hit this low note he sort of went, hmmm, that was interesting. I sort of went, oh, that was interesting based on the reaction of the people who were listening, and I was sort of hooked after that.

JH   What was the reaction?

TJ   They clapped—and I'm not sure that it was because I sang the song particularly well; it's because I sang it low.

JH   Here's this kid with an amazing voice.

TJ   Yeah, I don't hit any high notes. But I do remember, there was this guitar in a place called Hammerton's and it was a Martin D18; and I got offered a job—and it was $375—I got offered a job to record a song called, *White Man Listen*. I didn't even want to record it, but they offered me $375. And this was an omen to me. So I decided that I was going to record this song, which I did. They gave me my $375, I went to Ray Hammerton's and bought this D18 Martin, which was made in 1945, and it was a masterpiece of a guitar. And I think, had I not done that—again, one of those cornerstones of my life, had I not done that, I would not have that guitar and I never would have become any kind of a musician.

JH   I think we should start into some music, of your choices that you can take to your mountain top. What would you like to start with, Tom?

TJ   Well, one of my absolute all-time favourite writers is Kris Kristofferson. Now here's a guy who has the same range of singing as I do, and I think maybe that's why I homed in on him, but he has an album that was just absolutely brilliantly written,

and this is the title cut off that album, and it's called *The Silver Tongued Devil and I*. [MUSIC]

JH   Who's songs did you pick up to sing? Did you start writing your own at that point, because, you know, three songs isn't going to keep the crowd happy?

TJ   I didn't start writing until, I think, I was in Montreal, and I did this gig with Ian Tyson. And he of course will never remember this, and I don't blame him; but I had another friend of mine—and I have to backtrack a bit—I have another friend of mine who is a singer-songwriter by the name of Rick Neufeldt. His claim to fame at the time would have been a song called *Moody Manitoba Morning*. He came from Boissevain, Manitoba, and he had this record out and he was a very good friend of mine. Anyway, he called me over to his farm one time and he said, listen, I got this song I think you should learn. I think it's a great song, it's just perfect for you. And it was a song called *The Renegade*, which was written by Ian Tyson. And he was right; I loved the song so I learnt it. When I was in Montreal playing this gig and Ian Tyson was on the show, it was one of the few songs—and I was never a great one for learning a lot of songs so my repertoire was somewhat limited—and it was an appropriate time to sing the song and I was embarrassed to have to go up to Ian and say, listen, I hope you're not going to sing *The Renegade* tonight because it's one of the songs in my repertoire and I wanted to play it. And I thought that was pretty ducky of a guy to go up to the writer and say, excuse me, but don't sing that song. So when I got home from Montreal on that trip I decided, I guess if I don't want that occasion to happen again I should start writing. So I started writing—that's what inspired me to write songs.

JH   What did you write about—the first early songs?

TJ   I think my inspirations at the time were very much motivated by the activity on the native front, as it were. In the United States there was, during the civil rights movement, there was a thing called the Black Power movement. The Canadian equivalent was called the Native Movement. And I said to my brother, Bernie—I said, Bernie, what the heck is this Native Movement thing? And we were a little lost in the who we were and what we were gonna do in our life, and we actually traveled—and this was 1971—and we hitchhiked across the country and ended up sleeping under a 4 x 6 sheet of plywood in a ditch in Banff to keep the frost off. And we hitchhiked to Vancouver to find out what this Native Movement thing was—because we actually saw there was a newspaper called The Native Movement—and we went out and found out that this was a spin-off of what the Black Power Movement was and which would eventually become the American Indian Movement, which became a very militant force and, of course, peaked with the occupation of Wounded Knee in South Dakota. And my brother and I went down, during the occupation at Wounded Knee, to a place called Rosebud. We in fact were shot at by sentries and snipers and what not, you know. And I don't think it's anything that I wave any flags about except that I could hear the bullets going through the leaves, you know, in the middle of the night. It's a pretty scary thought.

JH   You were spotted and recognized and taken for native Indians, and it was just shoot now ask questions later type of thing?

TJ   Yeah. In any event, when we came back from that experience we sort of looked at each other and said, okay, so we understand who we are, what we are—we've proved that to ourselves. We would in fact lay our lives on the line for the fact that we were natives, but we decided that there had to be a better way to create change, or to do this fight, rather than have people shooting, you shooting back maybe, you know. And for myself, I decided that I wanted to write songs and sing songs, and that I could. My romantic belief was that I could change the world by doing so. Now I'm not totally sure that I ever fulfilled that dream, but I do know that I believe that choice was right. That inspired me in any event to write, and I wrote at the time a lot of songs about the strife of native people, you know, things that were fresh on my mind.

JH   Would you say they were protest songs?

TJ   Some of them were, yeah, some of them were. Some of them were just simple descriptions, you know, of what life was like. And a lot of it, you know, some of it was funny and some of it was about love. It's... you know, even today, I talk about how people very often live their lives in the we/they syndrome. You know, *North of 60* is a grand example of how that can change. I think *North of 60* is a program that's a window into the life of native people that makes the viewer go, oh, we have problems like them. You know, it's a we world—it's not we and they—it's a we world. And I discovered that through the process of writing of songs I was learning as much as I was attempting to teach—that in fact there was a whole lot more of we out there than I actually had anticipated.

JH   Yeah. Have you always kept the songs you've written, 'cause you've written a lot of songs?

TJ   No. Most of the songs that I'd written I keep in my head, because I'd quit school so early I was pretty much illiterate, and somewhat dyslexic to boot. So, to actually write stuff down I had to scribble... I mean, it's not like I can't write and it's not like I didn't, but for the most part I kept it just in my memory.

JH   We're going to make quite a quantum jump here to 1981, your first acting role in *Ecstasy of Rita Joe*, in George Riga's play. Was that the very first time you stood up on stage and acted?

TJ   Well, in my opinion it's the first time I did theatre. But I had considered, when I look back in retrospect, as to how it was I could just get up on stage without doing any of the traditional training that people should do when they become actors or, you know, if they want to get into that area of the field they should take some training—was because, in fact, I had been playing on stage live music for years and years and years and years. And I thought to myself—and I say this again in retrospect—I look at it and I go, I guess maybe I was just acting through that period of time, too. You know, 'cause you had to react to the audience and it was real time, and so the transition to actually do theatre didn't seem that foreign to me, I wasn't so intimidated by the fact that I was up there performing.

JH   How did it go for you? Was it okay, I've tried that, that's all right, I can do that?

TJ   I got, um, panned by one of the local critics in my first show, but I had… I was so moved, and I think it had to do with the piece as well—the story of Rita Joe is a story about a native girl who comes to the city and it's about her experiences, tragic as they may be—I related to the story in a lot of ways. I knew the Jamie Paul's, which was her boyfriend in the story, and I knew the David Joe's, which was her grandfather, which in fact was the role that I played the first go-around.

JH   Which is the role that Dan George of course had played before.

TJ   And made very famous. And the show was very successful and it ended up going on tour. It ended up in New York City. So I, with that first experience, went from Prairie Theatre Exchange small theatre stage to goin' to New York. I dare say that the excitement that created really did keep my interest in the acting field.

JH   No kidding. I feel like another song, how about you?

TJ   Oh, why not.

JH   What shall we hear now?

TJ   Well, I think this writer—as much as I mentioned Kris Kristofferson this is my other favourite writer—I think that if you were to listen to lyrics that say a lot, and I'm not saying this is his most brilliant piece of work, but it is a fun song and if I were stranded on a mountain, or on an island, I'd trust that one of the reasons that I might be there was because I was trying one of the *Fifty Ways To Leave Your Lover* [MUSIC]

JH   That's Paul Simon, of course—music chosen by my guest on Mountaintop Music, the star of CBC television's *North of 60*, and singer and producer and director and you name it, he does it—Tom Jackson

TJ   So did you know that the drummer on *Fifty Ways To Leave Your Lover* was a guy by the name of Steve Gatt. Steve Gatt introduced a style of drumming on that particular song, which was taking two sticks in each hand as opposed to one, and that's how he got that interesting sound that you hear.

JH   Yeah, it sounded like the sound that the little snare drummers play as they march along, you know, in a parade. Okay, let me ask you this question. It's a long way from playing David Joe In *The Ecstasy of Rita Joe*, your first acting role, to playing LaKanta—I think I've got that right—LaKanta in *Star Trek: The Next Generation*?

TJ   It is a long way, it's light years away.

JH   An invitation that someone like Whoopi Goldberg said she would have just died for, and got. How did you come to get a role in Star Trek?

TJ   I believe it was destiny.

JH   It must have been.

TJ   I was sitting on the porch of my friend, you might be familiar with Graham Greene; he and I—and I love name dropping, particularly his—he and I were sitting on his porch watching these geese. He has geese in his backyard, and he's got a fox and a skunk and he's got a pond that doesn't have fish even though he sits out there and pretends he's fishing. We were sitting on his back porch one day and it was probably, I would suggest, a month maybe prior to me getting this call, and we were looking at each other saying, I wonder what would be really interesting to do. And we both came up with the conclusion that we would like to do a role on Star Trek. And a month later I get a phone call from Los Angeles from Paramount Pictures, and they said we have this role in Star Trek and we'd like very much if you would send us a tape, we'd like to see your stuff. And my agent sent the stuff down and they phoned back a day later and I tell you, it was the most exciting moment of my entire career, I believe, when she phoned me and said… they called and said, okay, if you've got the time get on a plane and get down here.

JH   Tell me what it was like?

TJ   It was just… To be in the business and to be on the Paramount lot and see buildings that were named after Lucille Ball and Desi Arnez—you know, the Lucille Ball building and the Desi Arnez building—it was sort of like walking on hallowed ground, you know. But actually being on the deck of the starship was something that everybody in the world should do. Unfortunately, last year was the last season so you can't go down there, but it was in fact like being in space, and everything you could imagine.

JH   Wow. You mean you got beamed up to the Enterprise?

TJ   You didn't actually see me get beamed up, but I got beamed up. I was there.

JH   Well, you're gonna live in rerun heaven forever?

TJ   I know… I know. I remember when I was watching Captain Kirk… Did you watch Captain Kirk? Were you a Trekkie?

JH   Yes, I sure did.

TJ   When I was watching the old Star Trek it was like it was a religion. And I mean I guess it is—I mean I guess that there's a lot of people out there who are Trekkies who… who with, in fact, it is some kind of a religion—but I remember feeling, you know, that if I missed an episode of Star Trek I was gonna… something in my life was gonna change. So I grew up being a Trekkie, so to have that opportunity to go down there and be actually on the deck was quite an experience, even for a guy my age.

JH   Now what did Graham Greene—to get back to you sitting at his empty fish pond—what did Graham Greene have to say when you had the experience you were sort of just fantasizing about?

TJ   You know, I saw Graham just a couple of weeks ago and I was wearing my Star Trek jacket, and he looked at me and he said, I could've had one of those. But you didn't, Grae. I got it—I got the jacket.

JH   Back to earth now, Your role as Peter Kennedy on *North of 60*—is it still fun? Is it a challenge, is it something that you're still growing in to?

TJ   Every day that I go to work on the set of *North of 60* is exciting. The location where we work is exciting; I mean, I believe that out of all the jobs that I've had—the actual going to work and doing the work—this project is the most enjoyable that I've ever had. But it's not just the work, it's partially the fact that we work outside a lot, that we work where a river flows and we work on the side of a mountain and the fresh air and the trees and, you know, the wildlife we can hear. We can hear wildlife in the bush all the time. That's the real common denominator of all the pleasures that I'm sure that we all have. And I hope I speak for everybody else on the crew because it's a very congenial cast and crew and production people that we work with. And I think if you were an outsider coming into that and just observing—coming into the town of Lynx River—you'd think that these people were Moonies. Why are these people all so happy? You know, it's true. I mean, even in the tensest moments… I mean, sure, we have small problems on the set, but it's because there's a hundred and fifty people or whatever it is that live in this community on a daily basis, working under high pressure demands and in a creative world. So there are, as you will have in a family, small little problems here and there. But…

JH   Do you get letters? Could you figure out why people have latched on to it so strongly?

TJ   We get a lot of mail, but I'm not totally sure that I've been able to figure out by reading the mail as to why people have embraced this show. My guess would be on two-fold, one of them that in fact, as I mentioned earlier, that it's a window into a community and a way of life that allows people to see things they have not seen before; that's number one. And number two, because the characters in this show are so easy to identify with that, that the problems you see and how they deal with those problems in a lot of ways are exactly the way you and I would deal with problems. I include you with I as that we and they syndrome that I was talking about earlier. Um, we have the same problems. And it's easy to identify with people who have the same kinds of problems that you have.

JH   How about some more music, Tom.

TJ   Sure. I had for years played in a lounge called The Teepee, and one of the favourite songs in that lounge was, *Mama, Don't Let Your Babies Grow Up to be Cowboys.* [MUSIC]

JH   Tell me about playing "Billy Two Feathers" in *Shining Time Station*?

TJ   I took on the role of Billy Two Feathers in *Shining Time* because I believed it was important, which is the same reason I do *North of 60*. And I think it probably is my most important work. I get reactions from England, I get reactions from New Mexico, reactions from the North. I get letters from young children who have identified with Billy Two Feathers, who in fact is an adult character in a children's world; and whenever there's a problem the children can go to Billy and ask him, you know, the solution, and he always has the answers. And I think that it's probably one of—if not the only—native character on network television that is a positive reinforcement. There are a lot of shows that deal with native issues, deal with history, that in fact they're not negative in the sense that I think they don't have a place. And they're not negative in the sense that I don't think that they're good shows. But they have, as history itself is in a lot of ways and in how it relates to native people, is a very sad statement on life itself, you know. Even though native people have been able to hold their head up and we've been able to maintain a contact spiritually, I think history—and I think everybody knows this, how we have been moved around and what's happened to our people over three hundred, four hundred years—is a well-known fact. But it's not a pretty story. Billy Two Feathers on *Shining Time Station* is positive reinforcement, and I think that that's probably why I consider it to be my most important work, because I think that it's very useful to have positive reinforcement where you are in fact looking at native people. I think that's as important as recognizing the history. Children relate to him, you know, and I'm very proud of the letters and pictures and love notes, if you will, that I get from all over the world as a result of my work on that show.

JH   Do you get little folk tugging on your pant legs at about knee height in the malls, or whenever you're out in public?

TJ   Absolutely. I have a wide variety of people who give me the recognition, and I'm very flattered by it all. I have little guys and I have big guys, and it's great, just great for me.

JH   I see a profile sort of building in my analytical mind here, of you as a risk taker. Is that would you say true?

TJ   I do if in fact there's a good challenge. I had, in fact, resigned myself to not doing acting at some point; I'd done it for awhile and I went okay, been there done that, and I took the time off to do other things. And I got a call from the same director that had called me to do *The Ecstasy of Rita-Joe*, and his name is Gordon McCall, and he's a very close friend of mine and has been over the years. He gave me a call and he said, I want to do a production of *Othello* and I would like you to play Othello. Well that to me is… that's bizarre, I mean, first of all I can't read and even if I could read I couldn't understand it—Shakespeare that is. I went that's nuts, no, hung up the phone, gave it some thought, thought about it. And it was the challenge that made me do it, it was actually the challenge. And I phoned him back and I said, sure, yeah, I'd love to do this; carried on and learnt Shakespeare and became—what I consider as a result of taking that small risk—I became an actor. By the time I was finished the production I considered that that was the one sole thing that taught me how to act. Prior to that I was a hacker, but once I was finished with this show I believed I knew something about the art.

JH   Were you happy with your role? Were you happy with your performance as Othello?

TJ   Very much, and I'd like to do it again.

JH   Let's take a break for another piece of music, Tom. What would you like to hear next?

TJ   The next tune on this list is a song that was inspired by a girl by the name of Theresa. I remember when I was I'd say nine years old. The snow was fallin' and there was these big flakes and I could see them goin' past the street light, and I was pulling this sleigh and on the sleigh was a girl who I had a crush on, and her name was Theresa. And we were, you know, going across this long field and we were singing *Silent Night*, which I had learned from at the time, Bing Crosby. [MUSIC]

JH   All right. Let's get to a subject that I know is really near and dear to your heart, Tom—The *Huron Carol* series of concerts. Is this another circle as I've been describing it? Is this paying back a little for the time you spent on the street, and helping some other young kids maybe?

TJ   What it has to do with is the fact that I was handed down a globe from my mother's shoulders. I watched my mother watch newscasts and come to tears, and I watched my mother pick people up off the street, and I watched my father do the same. And I always wondered why my mother had this responsibility to carry the world around on her shoulders and I was always frustrated, you know, because I didn't understand this. I thought, why are you doing that, why do you do that, you know. And as I got older—and my mother as I mentioned earlier has passed on—but as I got older I began to understand that what you do in life, and how you do it, is reflected by everybody you know. So if you want to change the world, and I decided at the point when I picked up my guitar and decided not to pick up a gun, that I wanted to change the world, that I wanted to make a difference. And the way to do it was by example. I think that the people who have changed my life are nameless and faceless, you know—people—I don't know them. I was in a city once, and I won't mention the name, but I was in this city once where I watched a guy be passed over, walked over, walked around—people did not want to touch this man. And he was laying down at a bus stop, and I stopped and looked at him and his eyes were open and he didn't look like he was out of place other than the fact that he was dressed maybe a little spiffier than the area dictated. And I thought maybe he'd been, you know, knocked himself out or something—who knows. But his eyes were wide open and I said, are you okay? And he didn't say anything, and he just looked at me, and there was sort of this look of terror and I found out that he had fallen down because he had a cardiac—a heart attack—and he had broken his collar bone. I once, when I was younger, shot a moose. And the moose didn't die right away. He dropped to the ground, but he didn't die, and I walked up to him and he was heaving, you know. You could see his breath, these big breaths, and you could see his antlers, his grand antlers, going up and down as he was heaving. I looked at this man and he right dead on reminded me of this moose that was dying. I couldn't figure out why people had walked by him, and I imagined myself lying there, knowing I was dying, and watching people walk by me. And I thought to myself that it had to be because they thought that they were going to catch something. If they touched this man they were going to get a virus that was going to make them be like what they didn't want to be. Who knows what this person was, what he did for a living. He didn't die, he was fine. And some people might say, well isn't that neat, you save somebody's life. It wasn't me, it was him that saved my life because I decided at that time that if I wasn't gonna to do something for myself, then I was gonna do something for somebody else. And from that point on my recognition of people who are in the trenches, just trying to get out, has been so clear to me—that those are human beings. Those are warm, breathing human beings, and without our help those warm human beings are gonna turn to stone. They're gonna be cold and they're gonna be laying under the ground, and if you don't help them that's what's gonna happen. And I don't have the answers as to what put people in situations, I mean homeless people in particular. I don't have those answers. History tells you that homeless people are always around, they've always been there. Since the beginning of time there have been homeless people. So that problem, if it's a problem, is never gonna go away. I don't have the solution, but I know that if I don't do something then somebody's gonna die, and I don't want that to happen.

JH With all that you do, do you still think of yourself as a singer at heart?

TJ What seems to be all my life, I've enjoyed singing; that was my first love, my way out of doing things that I wouldn't necessarily want to be doing today. So I've always enjoyed singing and it's my first love, and to have the opportunity to do it again because of the success—I've no regrets thanks to Gilles Paquin and PEG Records and the record company that took a chance on this project—has given me and my singing a whole new life, you know. And it's absolutely wonderful for me. I'm very humbled by it all.

JH Let's have another piece of music. Okay, let's get down that list. What's next?

TJ Well, I remember years ago sitting with my friend, Marvin Kwan, and we were talking about classical music, and we had a mutual friend—her name was Giselle—and Giselle told us this story about an African tribe who had a rite of spring. The elderly men of this tribe would circle this tree, sit in a circle, and the youngest girl, who had been groomed from birth, would in fact—from the community—would in fact dance around this tree until she died. And I couldn't believe that that had actually taken place. And then they played me Igor Stravinsky's *Rite of Spring*, and I closed my eyes and I could actually see this girl dancing, and it's my favourite, favourite classical piece. Well, it's not really classical, but if I were on a deserted island I'd want to take this with me. [MUSIC]

JH   Okay, Tom, before you head off to your mountain top or wherever you want to go, we let you pick one book to take along with you. What would it be?

TJ   Well, I think I'd choose one of the *Far Side* books. Why? Because I don't have to read a lot to get a lot. I think you can open up a page and every page is a double take, you know—what the heck did he mean by that? Oh, I get it. And it stimulates the brain and, you know, you could open up one *Far Side* and take the whole day to think about it and you wouldn't necessarily have to sit there and read it.

JH   A Gary Larson fan. Okay, so you've got your *Far Side* tucked under your arm, where will you spend the rest of your days? Lake Winnipeg? Bragg Creek, where you filmed *North of 60*? Where would you go?

TJ   I think I'd probably spend them on Molokai. Molokai is the smallest of the Hawaiian Islands, that hardly anybody goes to. And it's a wonderful, wonderful, serene little place where it never seems to rain and you can get up in the morning and watch the sand crabs scurrying across the beach. And you can walk out into the ocean for about a half a mile before the water actually reaches your waist, and that's probably where I'd like to be. You know, I heard this story once about this guy who was stranded on an island and had been there for, oh, let's say fifteen years. And all of a sudden, like a vision, came out of the water this woman who had just walked off the cover of Sports Illustrated, and she was wearing a wetsuit and she asked this guy—like a Genie might ask somebody—so, what would you like after fifteen years on this island? And he said, you know, I haven't had a taste of scotch for fifteen years. And she reached inside the wetsuit and she pulled out this twelve-year-old scotch and said, here you go; what else would you like? He said, boy, I'd sure like a cigar. She reached inside this wetsuit, gave him a cigar, and she looked at him—she sort of started to undo the zipper of this wetsuit—and she said, you wanna play around? And he said, don't tell me you got a set of golf clubs in there.

JH   You pulled back just in time; this is a family show. So there you are in Molokai. Well, we'll have to get the music started then. What's your choice of music, Tom, as you head off to your island.

TJ   Well, I know that I've always wanted to play the drums. Every musician that I know of, if he was a drummer he wanted to be a guitar player, every guitar player in the world wanted to be a drummer. And it's probably going to take me a lifetime to figure out how to play this solo, so I figured I should probably take it with me to my island. This is called *Wipeout*.

JH   Oh, this is so appropriate. And before we hit our surfboards I have to say good bye and wish you bon voyage. Thank you, Tom, for spending this time. I've enjoyed it so much.

TJ   It has been a pleasure.

DOUGLAS COPELAND
WITH ANDREA MARANTZ, 1998

AM Now, you grew up in Vancouver with three brothers. Tell me about your childhood, what was that like?

DC I've heard this theory once that your childhood should never be so good that you spend the rest of your life trying to recapture it, nor so bad that you spend the rest of your life trying to overcome it. And on that scale my childhood was almost inert. Certainly it was neither too good or too bad, it was just there. My two older brothers, they're real hell raisers, jocks, and they loved shootin' critters. I mean, we were up in the mountain suburbs of Vancouver, which might as well have been in Prince George or something, they're so remote from the city. And, you know, police officers would show up with, you know, half a cat in each hand and say…

AM Oh no…

DC …your children have just shot the Jones's Fluffy. It's like…

AM So you were an angel by comparison, anyway.

DC Not a problem. I think my parents were just so relieved, it's just… we'll just let, you know, young Douglas do whatever he wants to do. I mean, we have a sort of guns and ammo family, one of those 'moose strapped to the hood of the Fairlane' families. We were looking at home movies the other night, and to look at the super-8—my dad loves super-8—you'd think I was born on a dock with a fishing rod in my hand. And we'd go on these hunting trips into the interior and up the coast and… But I think they knew even from a young age that I'm happy to come along on the trips, but… It's strange, no one ever gave me a gun because they just knew that I wasn't gonna fire it. And I was down at Twentieth Century Fox ,in Los Angeles, and I was doing some work with some people down there, and we went on this tour as sort of a lark, and this woman who was doing the tour (who must have done the tour a million times) hands me this fake gun and says, now you get to shoot and kill me. And I said, I can't.

AM No.

DC So, I mean I think I'm number three, by the time it got to me, mom's womb was so cleared out from manufacturing jocks that this sort of ectomorphic brainiac came out instead.

AM So what were you interested in when you were a kid?

DC I've always been divided equally between hard core science and art. I was in the High School Physics Olympics—a little known fact. Writing was something that turned up quite by accident in the late eighties, and I was writing about art. It certainly never entered anyone's head, let alone mine, to write in any form, let alone for a living.

AM Your dad is a doctor, and your mum was a theology grad. So what kind of influences…?

DC My dad is a real type A doer—he can't sit in a chair, and if he has an idea he just executes the idea, and I think I get that from him. If I have an idea, I just do it, whereas, you know, mum is not an initiator… she loves change, but she won't make it herself. So they complement each other that way.

AM Some of your philosophical questioning, would that come from your mum?

DC Mum listens. And dad's not a talker that way. But one thing I will say is that I was always left alone to think my own thoughts. Mum's grandfather and my great-grandfather, as well as great-grandfather on my dad's side, Presbyterian ministers of the fire and brimstone type. And actually, Great-grandfather Campbell is down in High River. I think both my parents—and I don't even think this is something they even consciously thought of—were both reacting against an overly religious, or overly moralistic or overly something, some sort of creator realm that they didn't want to be a part of. And so they moved to Vancouver, where in Canada ,when you want to get as far away from something as you can that's where you go, it's the end of the line. But of course the kids got everything osmotically, so now, especially as I'm, you know, at 33 now, I find myself unbelievably attracted to issues more eternal than temporary.

AM So even though grandpa was a minister you didn't grow up doing the Sunday school thing?

DC No, we've never been to church in our life and we were never allowed to discuss religion.

AM Never allowed to discuss it?

DC No. It was like it was just not brought up, and if it was brought up it was stopped. And I think this suppression… it wasn't suppression, it was just, that's not something we talk about.

AM Your parents didn't like it, so then…

DC No, they wanted us raised without it.

AM Deliberately?

DC Yeah, very deliberately, and that creates its own needs in me and my brothers as well. And it's sort of strange now, I guess. No matter what you do, I mean human beings want something transcendent.

AM Was there music in your house? Did your family listen to music?

DC No. [laughing] Oh no. But I will say to my parents credit that I did love playing the piano, and I'd stay at school and drive the teachers crazy until Dr. Sampson, the principal at Glenmore Elementary, phoned up my mum and said (not quite in as many words), but if you don't get your kid a piano we're going to have to throw him out of school—he's just driving us nuts. And so, oh, I had even no idea he cared about the piano. And so they got one. They were, like, quite baffled by it.

AM Well, let's talk about the first piece of music that you've chosen today. It's Catherine MacKinnon.

DC I wasn't even quite sure the name of the song, that's how far back it goes, the first piece of music I ever remember, aaaah!—music has this incredible power to take you wherever it was at, and to me it just evokes a certain… You know, in Canada we're not a flag-waving, cigar chomping bunch of patriots, but there are certain more gentle things that bring out that sort of lump in the throat, or make you feel like you're from somewhere. I guess this is one of them. [MUSIC]

AM *Farewell to Nova Scotia*, the first choice of my guest on Mountaintop Music, Douglas Copeland. Doug, after you graduated from high school you went to study art in Vancouver. How did you end up at the Emily Carr?

DC Well, there was actually one interim year spent studying particle physics at McGill, and there was a big housing shortage at the time and I ended up living at the Presbyterian College at the corner of Milton and University, and that was a thousand times more interesting than what was going on in the labs, and all these wonderful discussions between, you know, the students there and…

AM Was it a mixed group of students?

DC There is a diocese in college, which is Anglican. They were next door and so there's, you know, I mean it's like Tide arguing with Oxydol, they're so close. But, it was just so much more, you know, that part of your brain that actually feels alive was much more stimulated, and I realized I couldn't go on with science. And I was back in Vancouver, I was going away to work in the summer, and the day before I was going to go away I bumped into my old high school art teacher at a drugstore. And she said, oh hi, and I said, hi. Oh, they've just finished building the new campus down on Granville Island in Vancouver, and ah, why as a matter of fact I think they're taking applications today. And it's just sort of as if, you know, your head's been held under water for twenty years and suddenly you're allowed to breathe, and you know, just racing to the surface and the bubbles… And I borrowed a friend's car and drove down and applied and was accepted and came home—this is the day before I go away for the summer. I said, well guess what? In the fall I'm not going back to McGill, I'm going to art school. Of course dad was mortified.

AM Was he?

DC This is fifteen years later and he's still tryin to get me to med school. You know, doctors love their kids to be doctors. "You know, they love mature students, they bring a certain added value to the…" Dad, I'm not going to be a doctor.

AM Give it up.

DC And mom was, of course… Mom remembers, you know, the phone call about the piano, so she wasn't surprised. It was also the early eighties, too. I mean in Vancouver it was still an extremely expensive place to live, and art school was like $1.95 to attend, so it was very cheap and easy and wonderful, and a place and time to be, and I've never once regretted for a millisecond, going there.

AM What was important that you learned at art school?

DC I have this ongoing argument with Brian Eno. He says, nobody should go to art school, and I think everybody should go to art school. I think art school in conjunction with some design study, too, and typography, it allows me to look at any object—for instance in this studio the colour of that plastic telephone, the foam on this mike, the shape of that foam, the tissue box right here. I can look at anything, I can place the materials, why it is that colour, its historical antecedent. Nothing about the world overpowers or intimidates, or if does that means it's something new or resonating there, and it just makes you feel completely alive and a part of the three-dimensional world, and aware of detail. And one thing I've noticed that, you know… it's not you pop out of school feeling this way, it's a trickle-down thing inside your brain, it takes about five years and it just kicks in and you realize that, oh, the world's much more understandable. Maybe it's a bit longer than that. That's when I started writing I think.

AM At art school, or once you were out of art school?

DC Years after. But suddenly, it's like jello—it's liquid and then suddenly, boing! it's jello.

AM Let's go to the next piece of music.

DC Let me put on my radio voice.

AM Okay.

DC Next, we're going to be listening to *Begin the Begin*, by REM, from *Life's Rich Pageant*, possibly the best rock 'n roll album ever made.

AM Why?

DC They're great, they're the band that encapsulates from '85 to now, for me. And I guess, you know, they're all the same age and everything as me, and so, you know, they just sort of think alike. But, they're great musicians and…

AM And the lyrics, too?

DC Well, part of the thing I like about the lyrics is that they're indecipherable [laughing]. Peter Buck was interviewed once and he said, well, we kind of like that 'cause people can make them whatever they want to be—it's a bit more poetic that way.

AM So what about this song in particular? Is it the music? Is it the lyric? What's the strength?

DC Ah… I mean, certainly it's not their best known song by any stretch of the imagination; it just seems to be the REM-iest. [MUSIC]

AM One of your first jobs after you got out of art school was designing baby cribs. How did that happen?

DC Oh, that's right. I had won this big glitzy scholarship to study design in Milan, and there was all these, oh, good-bye Doug, we'll never see you again parties. And I got to the school and it was just this bogus, horrifying, useless school. And I won't mention the name. Anyhow, I came back to Vancouver and was just unbelievably depressed, and after having been on my own for years it was that whole, you know, back in the guest room thing, and it was, like, it was a genuine clinical depression. And finally, after two months, mum (bless her) came storming into my bedroom and said, we love you, but you're driving us nuts. And she had the yellow pages there and she says, now, there's this company out in Richmond and they make cribs, and you like working with shapes and colour and I think you'd be very good to work there, so you call them up. And I called them up, and when you're depressed, of course, you can barely function. You're like, [DC mimicking depressed voice] hello, you don't want to talk to me, I'm a loser. They're like, no, no, come out for a visit. They had never once had anyone express interest in their product before. It was so sad almost. And so they hired me on the spot. And they were doing cribs; oh my God, they were just like something like, you know, before the war, they were so outdated looking. So I basically came in and, you know, revamped the line, sort of made them GAP cribs. And gosh, they're for sale all over the world. They still haven't changed the design since, you know… It's like another part of my life, it's like another incarnation. But I'll be in a JC Penny's in Honolulu buying some socks or something, and there's my crib, or you know, I'll be walking by a window front in Philadelphia and there's my crib. I got a lot of satisfaction from that.

AM Through this time you were still creating your own art, you were doing sculpture? Because a few years later you had this one-man show.

DC Yeah, yeah… Good research I must say [laughing].

AM So, were you working at home sort of, keeping involved in things?

DC No, no. I mean, as soon as I could I got out. I decided what it was I wanted to do, and… In life, I think, once you know what you want to do, everything else just falls into place. And so for me it's always a matter of figuring out what it is I want to do. And I began doing this show with Willard Holmes, who (I think he's from Alberta originally, then he went to Vancouver, and then now he's one of the curators at the Whitney Museum in New York) you know, gave me my chance, my big art break, to have a show at the Vancouver Art Gallery, which I did over a period of two years. And in order to meet my bills, around the same time the girl down the hall, Allison, was moving back to Halifax, and she sort of knocks on the door and says, I got

to leave tomorrow and everything in my apartment's going for sale cheap. So I bought her answering machine, first one, for like, five bucks or something, hooked it up, went down to Guenther's Deli, came back and like, my first message ever, the blinking red light. And it was Mac Perry, who was editor of Vancouver Magazine, saying, Copeland, get down here, we want you to write a story for us.

AM How did that happen?

DC Well, life is so random, also in the eighties I got a degree in Japanese Business Science in Honolulu and Tokyo—that was another scholarship. I sent a postcard from Japan, which someone had put up on their fridge, which Mac Perry had seen at a party. Then, "oh, a writer, you know a writer". And, "Doug? Doug's not a writer, he went to art school, I don't think he's ever written a thing in his life". Which was true. And, "oh no, he's a writer".

AM Because of the postcard?

DC Yeah.

AM A few lines on a postcard?

DC Yeah. And he called up and he said, well look, you know, it's your money, and I promise you nothing. And so three days later I was down in Los Angeles writing this story about a Vancouver guy who was involved in art swindles involving Andy Warhol paintings.

AM Oh yeah, I remember that big scandal.

DC Yeah, yeah. And they'd had trouble finding someone to write it because you had to know about art, as well as know the story. So I just wrote it, I didn't even think twice about it, handed it in. Great. What are you going to do for us next month? And it just became this wonderful…

AM There you were, a writer. Now, is it true that they sent you to cover the inaugural Reform Party meeting?

DC I was there. That was my second story. So I went there, and I was worried about the people, 'cause that's all I… I'm more interested in people than anything else. So I wrote about that, and it turns out it's the only coverage that exists of the entire… 'Cause at the time no one thought it would ever lead to anything, that it was just some sort of joke at the time, and um, yeah, I guess I was there.

AM So did you start thinking of yourself as a writer at that point?

DC No no no—writing was always just a bill-paying device. Everything I've ever written, it just went straight to press, they ran a spell check and that was that. Living in Toronto, and I was working… you know, I was just krill on the food chain of this business magazine.

AM That was *Vista*?

DC Yeah. 'Cause I wanted to be part of the Toronto art scene, which is the centre of the Canadian art scene, and I just had to get to Toronto.

AM Now art, visual art? You're still thinking visual art?

DC Visual art, yeah, the visual art scene. And Toronto back then, it was just… it was the peak of the eighties and everything cost four times what it does today, and so I had this job and that was my entry into the art world. I remember standing outside of the entrance to the Davisville subway station on Yonge Street, and it was sunset, and I just remember feeling profoundly disgusted with the entire media art system and how there was just something implicitly bad about it, and how I couldn't be a part of it anymore, and how I just had to… So I went and quit, and I decided I had to write… If I was going to be a writer I had to write fiction, that I couldn't write nonfiction, which is not perhaps the smartest decision considering I'd never done it before. But then, you know, again, life is deciding what you want and then doing it. And I managed to get, it was $22,500, which wasn't much then and it wasn't much now, but it was enough to get me out of—as an advance—for *Generation X*, which was then, had no title, but it was just supposed to be some sort of nonfiction handbook. And I was just, yeah, yeah, yeah, yeah, just get me out of here.

AM Yeah, give me some money to escape.

DC Yeah. And I figured, you know, if they didn't like it then I could just treat it like a student loan or something and…

AM Right. Well, let's talk about *Generation X* after we hear another piece of music. What shall we play this time?

DC The live version of *Suffragette City* by David Bowie. Why it? Because it, probably more than any other one song, just sums up every part of my life from about 14 to 21. [MUSIC]

AM David Bowie in *Suffragette City*, choice of my guest today on Mountaintop Music, Douglas Copeland. So, *Generation X* started off as a nonfiction idea?

DC That was basically, you know, an amoral artistic thing. Basically I had no dough and I had to get the money to write. And New York back then, there was just so much money flying around on so many other big books, that a little drop in the bucket like this they just ignored completely, to my pleasure. So, while I was writing it, I think they phoned up once to see I was alive, that was it, and I handed it in.

AM And it was totally different than what they expected?

DC Oh, they were horrified. Yeah, no, they were just mortified. And they were originally gonna print 15,000 copies and then they cut the print run in half, and they cut the publicity budget to zero and they just put it out as a loss. Oh, no, it was originally gonna be published by a Canadian publisher, then they read it and said, no way. And so they sold it to another publisher in the States, and then McClelland & Stewart was the distributor in Canada and they wouldn't distribute it, and so I felt like such a fraud being back in Vancouver now at this point, saying I wrote a book, it's been published. And everyone's like, [sarcastic laughing], right.

AM Yeah. Did you lose faith in it?

DC No. I mean, I'd never done a book so I didn't know what to expect. I mean, I just, you know… I guess that's what happens when you do a book, you know. And then it sold out very quickly and they grudgingly decided to do another press run, and I think it's up to 16 runs now. And I don't talk to the publisher very much 'cause there's really nothing to talk about, but they always publish it with the idea that it's gonna die any second. They can't believe—you know, it's in 23 languages now—that it has any longevity to it. That's just the way publishers are, they just sometimes don't get the point. And ah, there was never like, some big, magic moment when a limousine pulled up to my house and Winona Ryder…

AM   Ed McMahon jumped out and…

DC   …hopped out and said, hey, come on in and party, you know.

AM   It doesn't happen like that?

DC   No, it was incremental, it's always been incremental, which I think is best… and with a publisher who is always waiting for your book to die, and who chose not to publish my second book. And so I moved on to Simon & Schuster from there. And then a lot of people wanted to believe… I mean, I think all this time later, I think people finally recognize the fact that I am a writer and that's what I do. But I think a lot of people wanted me to be sort of disposable, bad, just add water, and that's over now and I'm glad that that's over now.

AM   But they're a different look, a different kind of book than people are used to, than publishers print, you know.

DC   Hmm. I think that was just 'cause of the art school influence.

AM   Well, I was interested in that when you were talking about how you approach the world visually. Your books have a very strong visual element to them.

DC   Yeah, I like every book to look and feel different, and for the first two books I got away with that because nobody cared. I mean, really, things were just so, you know, small.

AM   There's freedom in that anonymity I guess.

DC   There's freedom in that anonymity. And then later books I got to experiment because they were actually interested in experimenting, and you know, I think there are some writers who develop a formula and they stick with it and it works very well for them. But that's the last thing I think I'd possibly want, is a formula. You know, there's a part of me that's always out there smashing particles together.

AM   But you did become… I mean, even if you consciously reject being asked to speak for a generation, being asked to sort of have these pronouncements, people did come to you for opinions on things.

DC   Oh God, did they ever.

AM   Well, what's that kind of fame like? I mean, it's got to turn your world upside down a bit?

DC   Well, as long as you say no, it's nothing.

AM   But then you do opinion editorial stuff for The New York Times and things like that?

DC   Oh yeah, no, I'm always… That's the magazine part of my background. Magazines are my laboratories; that's where a lot of new ideas sort of— you can try something and it's also… The thing with books is you write them and they don't even hit the stores until more than a year later, which is an ice age. And so…

AM   While your head's moved on.

DC   Oh, your head's always somewhere else. And magazines at least give you a bit more fast feedback, and as a writer, I mean, you know, I guess you just need that. I need that, and a lot of wonderful ideas and things have come out of magazine work, and I think it's something I'll always be doing.

AM   Do you hang out with writers?

DC   The only writer I know really is Bill Gibson out in Vancouver.

AM   Do you deliberately avoid them?

DC   I don't know where they are. I don't know…

AM   But you don't sort of have that community of writers thing?

DC   No, I don't. Maybe in New York, where there's a higher concentration that exists or something. But no. I know a lot of people in magazine. *Wired* for example. But *Wired* is sort of more an idea first, a magazine second. And they're just idea people who actually have people who sort of stick the ideas down on paper for them, but ah, no. Well, you must interview a lot of writers here. Do writers hang out with writers?

AM   Some of them do.

DC   Do they? What do they talk about? Like, my pen ran out of ink yesterday?

AM   Nobody uses pens anymore.

DC Really? I always write everything longhand first, and then input second.

AM Is that right? That's interesting.

DC Yeah. I think 'cause it's an economy of ideas.

AM Well, it's just about getting to be time that we're to send you off to the top of this mountain. So, if you were being sent away to live the rest of your life in splendid isolation, where would you want to be sent?

DC Where I grew up. I mean, where I am now, which is Vancouver. Up in the mountains. I consider myself a mountain person more than anything else. I'm not happy unless I'm surrounded completely by trees.

AM And if you were going to take one book—we just let you take one book with you—what book would it be?

DC Oh, it would be… It's actually two books, but they're so closely linked they might as well be the same book. It's *The Pursuit of Love* and *Love in a Cold Climate*, by Nancy Mitford. And it sounds like they're Harlequin romances, but they're not, they're just wonderfully, beautifully written. I actually… I reread them like four times a year. I'm reading it right now at the hotel. Just an incredible… Nancy Mitford, I think, was a lonely, unhappy woman who came from probably one of the most eccentric families in British history. But she wrote just wonderfully, endlessly engaging, charming, funny books. I just love these two, which I call one.

AM Well, thank you very much for coming in. And just before you go, what's our last piece of music?

DC Oh, gosh, that's a song by *Nirvana*, from the "Unplugged" album. I was there for the taping. I was at Sony studios up in New York. I was a doing a series of things with MTV back then and I was—if you look in the video, I'm there, just row three almost directly in front of Kurt—and ah, it was really… it was… You know, I'm not psychic, but I was there with two friends and we all knew it was kind of the end for Kurt. It was just… we looked at each other, it was like, you know, "the end." And then it was also (these are two friends who I'd known since kindergarten and they were sort of married) and then that was the last good night we ever had and then they got divorced. It was like, sort of the last of so many things, and it's just… To me, it just sort of… it's the last song of the first half of the nineties. So it's just like farewell to so much, that everything that led up to my, you know, being whatever I consider myself in my head now—a writer or whatever—it's just like an Apollo rocket shedding the last stage or something behind it.

AM Thanks very much for coming in.

DC It's a pleasure to be here. Thank you.

BURTON CUMMINGS

WITH ANDREA MARANTZ, 1998

AM Now, I'm at a decided advantage since you don't know me and I've known you since I was about twelve years old.

BC My goodness gracious.

AM You want to know? The first 45 I ever bought? *No Time*.

BC You're kidding.

AM The first present I ever bought for a boy for no apparent reason, *American Woman*.

BC My goodness. Bless your heart. We need more folks like this girl in the world, you know.

AM So you're the original thing. You're the true baby-boomer. You were born on New Year's eve.

BC New Year's Eve of '47. Yeah, so I qualify right down the line.

AM No debate there. Now take me back to your childhood, what was it like?

BC I came from a broken parentship actually. My dad left when I was about a year I guess, so my mother grabbed me and moved back in with her parents, and then my grandmother kind of became my mother and my mother kind of became my father. She went out to work to support me, and there was always music, always, in the house. From the time I was crawling around, before I can even remember being able to walk, the radio was always on and my mother had a collection of 78s. So I was being force-fed music from a very early age. Way before kindergarten I learned how to climb up on the chair and crank up our old wind-em-up Victrola, put my mother's 78s on, and she had things by Perry Como, Eddie Fisher, Theresa Brewer, Bing Crosby, Frankie Carl and his honky-tonk piano, Doris Day—you know, the music du jour at the time. Early fifties.

AM How about instruments? Did anybody play?

BC Well, there was always a piano. There was always a piano in the house and my mother had had lessons and so had her two sisters, my aunt Pat and aunt Molly. So they all played. My grandmother even played a little bit of piano. Every once in a while I recall she'd walk over and plunk out a tune with one or two fingers, you know, so there was always music in the house. And I do remember…

I'm old enough to remember the days before television. We didn't get a television set 'til I was about six I think. So that early, early childhood age was music, you know, was a big, big part, 'cause the radio was always on and the 78s. And my mother, before she would go to work in the morning, would play these 78s for me and I always was fascinated by that. And I learned about the concept of freezing time very, very early in life. I learned, even before kindergarten I realized that if I play this record by Guy Mitchell, and I want to hear it again when it's over, I just lift the needle back, put it to the beginning and I can hear it all over again. If I still want to hear it again I lift the needle and put it back. And that was really due to my mother's love of music, you know, so even before she kind of forced me to take piano lessons she was already laying the ground work for a life in show business—even unbeknownst to her. But I think she knew I had a proclivity toward music very early, because I would sing along and tap along—even as a baby I remember that. So it was a house full of music. Christmastime was great because my uncle George or my mom would play the piano and everybody would sing carols. And you know, St. Patrick's Day they'd haul out the Ruby Murray records and, I mean, it was just like most of the special events of the year had their own genre of music to accompany them. So I was blessed, like from a very early age. We weren't an affluent family, but certainly the music and the love was always there. So I wanted for nothing, even though I didn't have a dad, you know, and in some strange ways I think it may have even led me to show business even more. 'Cause I was an only child, and my grandmother—bless her soul—by that time she was pretty old so she wasn't about to get down on the floor and roll around with me, like, so I spent a lot of time introspectively, playing in my own head.

AM So you started taking piano lessons, quite young.

BC I was about six I think, maybe even five.

AM Did your mom have to make you practise and all that stuff?

BC Oh, she certainly did. I wanted nothing to do with it. When I was a kid I suppose, the same as any other kid in the prairies of Canada in the early fifties, I wanted to play in the NHL. That was my goal, to make it to the NHL. And my heroes were Rocket Richard and Doug Harvey in the early, early Montreal Canadians, and George Armstrong from the Maple Leafs—you know, from the golden age of hockey when there were only six teams. I really wanted to be a hockey player. My mother had to fight like hell to get me to practise, up until I was about ten.

AM What changed?

BC My teacher was very straight and square and she thought nothing was any good unless it was played from sheet music; and Beethoven and Chopin were the gods and pop music was drivel. You know. When I was about ten I discovered C, A minor, F and G—the staple chords of pop music—and suddenly I could play *Diana*, by Paul Anka, and *Poor Little Fool* by Ricky Nelson, and some of the Elvis stuff, and well, that was it, you know.

AM Were you playing by ear what you heard on the radio?

BC Yes, and then the light clicked on in my head. And then after that my mother couldn't drag me away from the piano. And then I learned bumble boogie and then I played it at school for the kids, and it gave me some status at school, and I became special at school because I could play *Runaway* by Dell Shannon, and stuff like that, and it just all snowballed. There was, you know, it was like a volcano erupting and I never looked back from that. I knew that's what I wanted to do. You know—and more fortunately than most—it became a reality for me as opposed to an infantile dream. By the time I was twelve, I think—well around the time of my thirteenth birthday, I weaseled my way into the Devrons, and…

AM You also picked up a saxophone.

BC Yes. I had always been a huge fan of Fats Domino, and he had those great saxophone players on his records, you know, and I picked up a saxophone for twenty bucks—which I delivered papers for a long time to get the money to buy 45s, and then I had an extra twenty dollars which I had scraped together—and I sat with the Fats Domino records in my little bedroom in the north end and learned some of those solos note for note. Firstly, in the Devrons I was a saxophone player and an occasional singer, 'cause they were still doing mostly guitar instrumental stuff—the Fireballs and the Ventures and stuff like that—and they'd let me play sax a few times a night and sing a few times, and I had to keep leaving the stage when it wasn't a sax or it wasn't a vocal. So one time we played at St. Martin's Anglican Church, where I was in the church choir and went to Sunday school and I had my communion there. We were doing a gig at, uh… very early in the Devrons stage. We were doing a gig there and there was an upright piano at the side of the stage. Now, it wasn't even miked or amplified in any way, but it came time for me to leave after a vocal and I said, to hell with this, I'm not leavin', I'm just gonna play along. Whether it's amplified or not, I'm playin' along and I'm gonna stay part of this band for the whole night. And that was it. Then we found a fourteen dollar Diamond violin pickup, which we learned how to hook onto the back sound board of the piano with thumb tacks and scotch tape and put it through one of the guitar amps. And at that point I really became part of the band, and it's really stayed the same way ever since.

AM So how did you hook up with those guys?

BC My best friend, Ed Smith, we went to Luxton School together in the north end through grade school and junior high, and then he was in that band already. He had bought a cheap Silvertone electric guitar, and he and a guy named Derek Blake, and they got together to learn Ventures and Fireballs guitar instrumentals, and Ed would always be telling me the next day at school—oh yeah, rehearsal went great last night… boy oh boy… and I was like, drooling, you know. I wanted so much to be in this band. So I said, Ed, you know, can I just come and hang out and hear what you're up to, you know. Of course, I had a secret agenda.

AM Of course.

BC And so I came and hung out and they did their instrumentals for about an hour, and then I said, hey you guys know all the Ritchie Valens stuff don't you? I said, let's try *Donna* and I'll sing, you know. And we did it and they were kind of impressed—I was on key, you know, and I knew all the lyrics. And then we did *Come On Let's Go*, and then I said, hey guys, *La Bamba's* only three chords—it's only A, D and E—just try it, you know. So John started layin' down this Bossanova kind of rhythm, and I did *La Bamba*, and then we did *Baby Face* by the Beaumarks, and the next thing I knew I had sung about six or seven different tunes. So I mean I was in, you know, 'cause these guys weren't lead singers, and I mean I was in.

AM Tell me about the singing. I mean that's another step away—like, you can play piano, you can play sax, but singing is a different kind of performing, right?

BC Yeah, it is. It's, well, it goes back I guess to the church choir. It was the only real training I had was the church choir at St. Martin's, and later—in high school at St. John's—I got the lead tenor role in *A Trial By Jury* one year, and then the following year *HMS Pinafore*, which… Mind you, that's skipping ahead. Those were huge, huge parts you know, with dialogue and everything, but I think the singing—I always knew I could carry a tune from a very, very early age.

AM And it was something you wanted.

BC Well yeah, I'd sing along with the guys on the Ed Sullivan show, you know, and I always loved the singers. And even when I was a kid, before rock 'n roll got really big, I remember seeing Dennis Day, this high, high Irish tenor voice, and I said to myself, you know, I could do that—uh, rather arrogantly for a seven year old, you know—I was thinking that way already. But I always had this thing like, I like singing and I always believed—and I still do—that one of the integral parts of being a singer is a lack of inhibition. I think that's a great part of it. My mother can sing and carry a tune, but God almighty if there's four people she's terrified; she can't get up in front of people and do it. And I think one thing that great singers bring to the table is a lack of inhibition. And I thought about this 'cause I'm writing a book now, finally, after all these years, and I was really trying to describe my take on singing, on being a vocalist, 'cause I've had thousands of people tell me that I'm their very favourite singer. With all the singers in the world there are to choose from, you know, if you're one person's favourite singer that's pretty good. So I thought that maybe I had that lack of inhibition, that magical place you go to when you sing. I go somewhere else, metaphysically I guess, and I think I had that pretty young. And I loved being in the church choir, because there were harmonies, and around Easter there were special hymns and around Christmas there were special hymns, and these beautiful layered voices of harmonies—I always loved that. It took me somewhere else, you know, it took me out of myself somewhere else. So very early I liked that a lot, and I could always sing fairly well on pitch, you know. That's not really… I mean anybody can really—almost anybody—can carry a tune. But to take it to the next step I believe you really need that lack of inhibition. The great singers have all had it; Elvis used to talk about going somewhere else when he sang. Bono from U2, it's the same thing. If you watch him he is somewhere else. You disconnect yourself from the physical world somehow and ethereally march off to some unknown land known only to singers. And I really believe that to a great degree, that whatever style I've managed to have has been greatly due to a lack of inhibition. So the singing really was always… I was singing along with Guy Mitchell when I was four years old, you know, and probably fairly rhythmically.

AM Holding a tune. Well, let's have your first piece of music now. What should we play first?

BC Oh well, I mean let's go right back to the biggest thing that ever hit the planet, you know. You younger folks, you think Michael Jackson was big and Nirvana was big, and I mean, there was never any, any craze that hit the planet like the Beatles. I'm around for all of it and I can tell you that. Not even Elvis was that big, and if I had to pick one Beatles song I think this was absolutely their finest moment, and it was the title of their first film, too. Plus you get to hear both John and Paul sing lead—John sings the verses and Paul sings the bridge—an incredible piece of songwriting, the Beatles doing *A Hard Day's Night*. [MUSIC]

AM Okay, so here you are. We've got you up to being about a thirteen year old kid, starting to play with the Devrons, and you guys turned into the hottest thing in town.

BC We really did gain incredible popularity very quickly. And I don't know, I think part of it would have been the novelty of our being so young. We were thirteen and fourteen and yet we were doing all the hit songs of the day. And I remember we got hired—the first year-and-a-half or so let's say—we got hired a lot by fraternities and sororities. I think that the girls that were five or six years older, going to university, they thought this was really cute—that these young guys could do Beatles songs and Paul Revere songs, and Bob Dylan and Turtles and all the stuff of the day, you know… the flavour du jour. We pretty well had it covered; we would do Lovin' Spoonful and Gary Lewis, I mean everything that was on the hit parade we could cover. And I was always imitating the singer. Whatever record it was we chose to do I would try and imitate the singer,

and, I think initially, when I was about fourteen, I think the older girls found that kind of cute—not a sexual attraction so much as a novelty of these young guys whose voices had barely changed. But they were a pretty good band, you know, and there was a novelty.

AM That's not too flattering for a young kid, you know. I mean, didn't you really want… you wanted to be the rock star.?

BC I didn't care. You know, honest to God, I didn't care. There were crowds there and they were paying us, not a fortune, but enough to buy instruments and suits—at least matching outfits, you know—and I just loved being on stage. I have always loved that idea of being on stage, being a performer. It came very easily to me, I was never inhibited or shy. I used to tell my mother, why try out for the chorus when you've got a chance to get the lead, you know. And that was always my attitude.

AM Now, kind of a funny life though. I mean, you were still a kid and you got treated like a rock star on the weekends.

BC Absolutely, yes.

AM And you were going to school and singing in the high school musicals.

BC Yeah, our parents were still paying the bills and school was taking care of our daytime, but boy oh boy, came the weekend… man, we were up there on the pedestal. And it was wonderful, and I really did like that. You know, I would be a liar to say I didn't like all the attention and the accolades, and…

AM And it soon started to focus on you, more than the band.

BC Well yes it did. It's funny, because I guess what happened was, once I got a taste of that—you know, applause is very, very addictive—and once I got a taste of that I really took over the reins. A band that had existed before I came into it—I really weaseled my way in at first—and eventually, within about six months, I was running everything. I was picking the music and there were no more instrumentals, you know. I was singing all night by that time, and I was telling the guys what the chord changes were and you better show up knowing this and that, and cracking the whip, you know, organizing. By the time I was fifteen I was really a band leader.

AM And did you fight? All the boys I know that played in bands fought.

BC Uh… a little bit. A little bit we fought, but they always acquiesced to my way of thinking because they knew that was probably the better way to go.

People were calling me one of the best singers since the Guess Who's Chad Allen, and all this stuff. And I was still a kid, you know, and I loved the attention. Boy oh boy, I don't make any bones about that. I loved the attention.

AM It was an interesting scene in Winnipeg in those days because there really was a local band scene. And there was the star, there was Chad Allen. Now, were they the Guess Who by that point?

BC Yes, they were actually, 'cause they had, um… I was still in the Devrons when they released *Shakin' All Over*, and that's when they changed their name.

AM And they were sort of the bright light of the Winnipeg scene, and then the Devrons.

BC But not only, not only in Winnipeg, but at that point the Guess Who was probably the biggest thing in Canada. You know, other than Gordon Lightfoot I can't think of anyone else that had a national presence at that time.

AM And Winnipeg had a lot happening.

BC Oh definitely… from about '64 to '67 Winnipeg was definitely the rock 'n roll capital of Canada, and anyone with a really astute sense of pop music history would never, never argue that point. See, at that time, Vancouver was still not a very big city. There was a little bit of a coffee house folk scene out there. Montreal was still very heavily ethnic French music. Toronto was steeped in rhythm and blues; it was all light shows and silk suits and dance steps, you know, and horn sections. Winnipeg was just straight ahead white bread down the middle rock 'n roll. Like, it was a carry-up from the Midwestern United States, from Chicago to Minneapolis to Cleveland, that whole general vicinity. And that just carried on up over North Dakota into Winnipeg, and Winnipeg was rockin', and the other places really weren't yet. And the thriving band scene, the community clubs and schools and churches…

AM Community halls had dances every weekend.

BC Absolutely. And plus the drinking age was still twenty-one, so the kids weren't going to the pubs yet. Drugs had not hit the street as such, so there was none of that freaked out scene yet, and it was just the music was the buzz, and it was a wonderful time and I really miss that in many ways. When they lowered the drinking age it was the end of that, because then all of a sudden a sixteen-year-old with a bit of stubble growth could lie his way in as an eighteen year old to the bars, and that left the community club and school and church scene… It finished it, you know.

So it was a sad day I think, the day they lowered the drinking age, in many ways for many reasons. But I'm just looking at it from a selfish show-biz point; but I mean obviously, for cultural reasons, it created its own problems, too. But I regret that happening because it pretty well devastated the scene that we're talking about right now. But I remember one time, in grade ten at St. John's High, making a list. I was fascinated at how many bands there were and I made a list of working bands that worked regularly every weekend. It numbered almost two hundred, if you can believe that. And that's thirty years ago in Winnipeg, which couldn't have had more than about 300,000 people at the time in its population—two hundred working bands that worked regularly every weekend. That's astounding. There was nothing anywhere near that in any other Canadian city. I mean, we were rocking boy, and I was glad to be there at that point in history. I really was.

AM So what should we play now? Let's take a pause for a piece of music.

BC Well remember earlier on we were talking about the Devrons days and when I was first a saxophone player. I think the first thing I learned how to play was a rock staple called *Wild Weekend* by the Rebels. And I mean it was just a simple record, probably cut in somebody's garage, and it really captures the essence of rock 'n roll—simple, straight ahead, no thinkin' tap-your-foot good time feelin' rock 'n roll—aptly titled *Wild Weekend*. [MUSIC]

AM So tell me about getting invited into the Guess Who. Did you sort of think it was your destiny?

BC No, I had just come home by train from Minneapolis with the Devrons. We had gone down there with Bob Burns to cut our second single on Rio Records, and I was exhausted. I had ridden all night in a train and the heaters had broken and we were freezing, and I had just crawled into bed back on Bannerman Avenue and the phone rang about an hour later. And I was exhausted. I hadn't slept for almost thirty hours and it was Bob Burns saying, I and the boys in the Guess Who, we want to talk to you and would you please come down to channel 7 TV studios right now. And I thought, oh boy, they're going to help the Devrons. This is great, they're going to give us a helping hand—wow! I couldn't believe it. I got rejuvenated, jumped out of bed, my adrenaline was flying. I got down there and they asked me to join the band. I thought it was a joke. I thought they were playing a cruel joke on a young guy, so when they first asked me—they said we want you to join our band, Burton—I got up and said, geez guys, I'd like to help you out but the Beatles just asked me. You know, I really thought that. You know—flippantly he said, sarcastically—and I walked right out of the room. I carried the joke that far 'cause I really couldn't believe it. And then about thirty seconds later I walked back in. I said, you guys, you're not kidding are you, and they couldn't believe I had been so light-hearted about it all. But it was true. And then came the horrible task of telling the Devrons this, you know. So that was ugly, and I had gigs to fulfil, too. I had about a month's worth of gigs to fulfil after I had broken this news.

AM But did you question it at all? Was there any moment of saying maybe I shouldn't?

BC I never thought twice, never thought twice.

AM Too big a chance.

BC A gift horse like that you definitely don't look in the mouth, you know. It's like maybe you're one shot at the brass ring and who knows if the Devrons would have gotten that far. I personally don't think—as much as I love the guys and everything—I don't think they were up to the quality of players that Randy Bachman and Gary Pedersen were, you know, and Jim Cayle. I mean, these guys were really good and they were pros. They had already committed; they didn't go to school anymore or hold daytime jobs. That's what they did. So, I had dropped out of high school by that time and they were kind of waiting for that to happen. They all swore they would never ask me to leave school to join the band. So when they heard I had left school, well then the road was opened for that. And I just really couldn't believe it. I wasn't even eighteen yet and I had been asked to join the biggest group in the country. It really was a Cinderella thing, you know. It would be a great script. I mean, they write things that aren't that cool, you know.

AM Okay, so we've got you into the Guess Who now. And all of a sudden…

BC Well, not quite all of a sudden. We had a couple of pretty lean years there—'66 and '67 we got into some heavy, heavy debt.

AM And there was the bad luck trip to Britain.

BC Oh, that disastrous trip to England.

AM What happened there?

BC Well, Bob Burns you know—bless his heart—he was our manager, but his vision didn't really go very far into the future, and he was hoping that once we got there we'd land a big recording contract and everything would be fine and we'd be the next big thing. But when we got over there it was mostly on speculation, and we had borrowed all this money for our plane tickets and our silk suits from the Stag Shop, and our spanking brand shiny new amps and guitars, and we went over there like kings of the hill. And there was no recording contract when we got there.

AM Did you know this? Did the band know it?

BC No, absolutely not. We thought we were going over there to a slam dunk, and you know, it just didn't happen. But, we did do a couple of recording sessions while we were there and, you know, we didn't even have enough money for return tickets at first. So we ended up staying about three weeks there on a per diem of about four dollars a day each, and so you had a choice. You could have a couple of little pork pies during the day and then maybe some bread at night, or you could save the whole four bucks for a really big meal in the evening, you know. And those were the choices. I mean, it was lean, you know. So people who tell me, oh, you've always had it so easy, you made it so young, you know, that's just not the case. You know, I was terrified. I had just left school a year before and I was in England, I was nineteen years old, and part of a hundred thousand dollar debt. So, we came home to very lean times. We were back home in Winnipeg kind of holding our heads in shame, and we had been sent off with front page accolades and a big, big crowd at the airport, and TV cameras—and then we had to sneak back into town a month later and it was really awful.

AM 'Cause everybody in Winnipeg was waiting.

BC Oh God, yeah. You know, we were sent away as the kings, the ambassadors, and it was 1967, it was centennial year. They were giving us huge bags of Canadian flags to pass out and we were the ambassadors and all this, and it was just awful to come back so prematurely.

AM Well it was really a management screw-up though wasn't it?

BC Well it was, yeah, and I mean he was rolling the dice. I mean, it could have worked, it's just that it didn't work. So we came back and at that time, you know, our price was not that much. Outside of Winnipeg we couldn't get more than about $250 a night, and that just was never going to be enough to pay off the debt. So, enter the CBC fairy godmother with her magic wand. Well boys, we're going to be doing a weekly television show right here in Winnipeg. It's going to go out nationally every week—no travelling, good salaries. Can you boys read music? Yes, we lied.

AM And you were thanking mom for those piano lessons.

BC Well, I couldn't read anymore by this time. I had let the reading go, and Jim and Randy never could read. So the only one that could really read music was Gary Pedersen. So they said, okay boys…

AM Why did they want you to read?

BC Because there were ten new songs to learn every week and they didn't think we could learn them all by ear. They didn't know us very well. But, so anyway, the funny part of this story is that Bob McMullen, who was the CBC director of music at the time, he wrote out all these charts for various songs by the Monkees and the Hollies, and we didn't know what they'd be throwing in front of us, but we said, okay, we're going to go down and fake our way through this, you know.

AM This was like an audition?

BC Yes, yes—to prove to the producer that we could read music, right. So, he puts a chart in front of us for *I'm A Believer* by the Monkees. Well, we're looking at the charts and saying, yeah, I think we can handle this. Okay Cary, count it in, right. And we're pretending to read it. Meanwhile we've learned it by ear from the radio and we're looking at the music, but we're not playing from the music at all.

AM Hoping you know when to turn the page.

BC And the guy was saying, very impressive boys— you know, yeah, I guess you'll do. And he threw another thing up there that we happened to know, so we just pretended like we were reading the music and we got the gig.

AM Let's have another piece of music now. What shall we play next?

BC Hmmm. We'll jump forward to the eighties, and here again I don't like the word genius being bantered about too frequently, but Prince is one that I really think fits the category.

Truly a gifted individual. A lot of people are soured by his image, but I'm in the business and I can separate the art from the image and, you know, he is a bit eccentric, but he's mastered many instruments—he's a great drummer, he's an incredible bass player, he's a producer, he's an engineer, he's an unbelievable vocalist, he's an incredible songwriter and a very, very good guitarist. And he just has vision that few have, that very few are blessed with. Plus he's very strange. His father was black and his mother was white and —-he's kind of androgynous and they don't know what his preferences are, and there's just such a mystique about the guy that it's, um, a lot of it is a bit too much for some people to handle. But, as far as the—just the art, just what he's left as a recording legacy—there are very few that will be remembered as geniuses, and he's definitely one of them. And then this cut is possibly his best work, I think. It's called *Sign of the Times*. [MUSIC]

AM   You were twenty-five thousand dollars in debt, but, miraculously, the CBC in Winnipeg offered you a steady job on a weekly national music program.

BC   And then all of a sudden this was regular money, very good money actually—very, very good money—and all it was, was a drive down to Portage Avenue every week. And I mean we spent most of our lives there for that two-year period, '67 and '68. In '67 it was called *Where It's At*; the second season it was called *Let's Go*, and then we went into colour.

AM   And high profile.

BC   Yes. Besides the money, the big reward was it gave us a national presence. From Victoria to Newfoundland, suddenly we were recognized.

AM   And it was really the only Canadian pop music show.

BC   It was. I mean, Monday I think was Halifax, Tuesday was Montreal, Wednesday was Toronto, Thursday was us, and Friday was Vancouver. So every week, like clockwork at 5:30 p.m. on Thursday, there we were in everybody's living rooms. Not only the salaries were great, but it gave us that national vibe. It was the first time we were known, from Newfoundland right to Victoria. When the first season ended we went out to Vancouver to play a gig one time, and I'll never forget it. Randy and I were walking downtown to get some new shirts and vests for onstage, and we started getting chased by girls and stuff, purely from the profile we had from the weekly TV show. It was absolutely fascinating—it was kind of like being the Monkees, you know. I couldn't believe it. And my grandmother on my dad's side was still alive and she was living in Vancouver, and we did this autograph session at Eatons, and God she showed up and she was saying, "and that's my grandson, Mr. Cummings," you know. And I mean, like, we had this unbelievable presence all of a sudden. Thank God for the CBC. I mean, they bailed us out of debt basically, not only—and the financial reward was the small part of this, that was the small consideration, because through that TV show in the second season Jack Richardson first saw us, and he ended up producing every Guess Who record there ever was. And he actually had the gumption to mortgage his house in 1968 and fly us to New York on the strength of what he had seen on that TV show. And on the strength of what he saw on the TV show he flew to Winnipeg to meet us and he had Randy and me play him some of our original tunes, and one of those tunes was *These Eyes*. And on the strength of *These Eyes*, basically, and the fact that we had enough other songs…

AM   But you weren't really getting a chance to play that original music though, were you?

BC   No.

AM   This was all cover tunes.

BC   Not until the second season. Then Larry Brown, the producer—bless his heart—he knew Randy and I were writing, you know, and we were trying to become writers, and he said, look, you have a national forum outlet here for your original stuff. He said, you know, I'm not gonna let you do a whole show of stuff, but you know, one or two a week maybe, or a couple every second week, and we'll see how it wears on the public. If we get any mail, well, that'll encourage you guys—well Randy and I were just like, you could have knocked us over with a feather. I mean, this was the chance to do original stuff on a national show, on TV. So, out of that writing came *Undun*—Randy wrote *Undun* for that show, and we wrote *These Eyes* together for that show. And we started writing songs like *Pink Wine Sparkles in the Glass*, and *We're Coming to Dine*—all the stuff that was on the *Wheatfield Soul* album, which was the *These Eyes* record. And then Richardson flew to Winnipeg and met us, and uh—God bless him, you know—1968, to mortgage your house, to take four buffoons from the prairies to New York city, you know. On spec! On speculation—he had no contract with anybody—produced the album with the house mortgage money…

AM   Produced it—where was it? Where did you produce it?

BC In A & R Studios in New York, right down in… oh, right in the heart of Manhattan. The studio's no longer there, but it was right next door to that club where Gene Krupa used to play, and I mean, like, this is unbelievable, you know, this was—ooh-eey—we're a block from Time Square and we're making records—well, I can die happy now, you know. And um, then he shopped the finished master around and was turned down by a few companies and finally went to RCA, and RCA loved *These Eyes*—they said, don't know about the rest of the album, but that's gonna be a smash. And, as history would have it, it was. I mean everything changed, that's when life changed. *These Eyes* changed our lives forever and it was never, ever the same.

AM So were you playing like, clubs and things like that, during the time that you were doing *Let's Go?*

BC We would play sometimes on the weekend at high schools and churches and stuff, never night clubs 'cause I still wasn't old enough.

AM Right.

BC You know, the drinking age was still twenty-one. I still wasn't twenty-one yet. I mean I wasn't twenty-one yet when we wrote *These Eyes*, so technically I was old enough to get a gold record but not old enough to drink, you know, or vote.

AM And of course you didn't.

BC No. I really didn't, actually. I was pretty…

AM You were still a good little kid.

BC Up until about twenty-two. I didn't really get wild until I was about twenty-two and started travelling—when we got on that treadmill, you know.

AM And discovered yourself a millionaire rock star.

BC That treadmill of three hundred cities a year, and then I got a bit nuts for awhile, but nowhere near to the extent of most people. But, um, *These Eyes* really was the moment, you know, that changed it for us.

AM And how did you know? Like how did it unfold? All of a sudden it started getting play everywhere?

BC No, it took a long time. Oddly enough, it broke in Canada first; in '68 it was a big hit in Canada and it hadn't been released in the States yet. And then when it broke in March of '69, then it was a hit all over again in Canada—it was like we were reaffirmed as artists, you know.

AM Now, being like the number one, having a number one song—huge record—now, how did you hear about it?

BC We first started hearing that they were makin…

AM And you're back home now at this point.

BC Yeah, still in Winnipeg. Yeah, matter of fact we were still doin' the CBC show when *These Eyes* started breaking wide open.

AM And still living with mom.

BC Absolutely. I haven't left home yet. I'll tell you an interesting story about that a little later, but we started hearing that we were getting a little air play in Detroit. We're saying, oh geez, that's exciting, maybe we can get one gig there next year in Detroit, you know. And then a phone call came—wow, they went on it in San Francisco. We're saying, geez, that's exciting. Then, a couple of days later—wow, they just added it in Boston, you know. Hey guys, three stations in Texas just went on it. And then all of a sudden it just—this was after months of promotion, it wasn't an instant hit in the States—but when it did click it really lasted, it was on the chart for six months, for twenty-two weeks or something.

AM And then you had to do something about it, right?

BC Well then, you know, you're forced to climb the mountain of comin' up with a follow-up.

AM Or do you get out? Did they call you out on the road right away?

BC Oh yeah. All of a sudden, I mean, we were playing all over the place; first small theatres, then bigger halls, and then we got invited to do the Seattle Pop Festival. We got to play with The Doors and Led Zeppelin and The Mothers and Alice Cooper and the Charles Lloyd Quartet in Chicago, and Jefferson Airplane, and—ha—we got all three days on the strength of *These Eyes*—we played for 150,000 people, which was the biggest crowd we'd ever seen, never mind played for, and got to hang out with all those people for all three days. The Byrds, the Burrito Brothers, The Vanilla Fudge—everybody that was big was on that. It was way better than Woodstock but nobody filmed it, you know.

AM So did you believe it then? Did you believe you belonged there?

BC I didn't believe it until Dick Clark gave us the gold record on American Bandstand. And I was still twenty-one, you know, and I said, my God, somethin's goin' on here. I can't believe this but I'm here on American Bandstand and, and you are Dick Clark for real, aren't you?—you know, I'm sayin' under my breath—and he's handing us this unbelievably beautiful thing. And it was twice as beautiful for Randy and me because our names were under the title, as the writers, you know. So it was twice the event for Randy and me that it was for Jim and Gary, and I, I mean, I just—I really felt like something, you know. I felt, okay, this is enough, I've done it now, maybe I'll just go and teach school or somethin'. I was just so amazingly in wonderment of all this.

AM Really? I mean, weren't you saying more, more more?

BC Sure. But the first thing, you're first fear is you're gonna' be a one hit wonder, and there have been thousands of those, you know. *Duke of Earl* by Gene Chandler, never to be heard from again. Question Mark & The Mysterians *Ninety-Six Tears*, never to be heard from again. And you can go on and on and on and on—there have been a million people like that and we didn't… and Randy and I said to each other, you know, I really don't want this to happen to us. But by the same token we wanted to be a hard rock band, so we were coming up with all these really grungy songs. And then Don Burkheimer from RCA New York said to us—he took us to the Carnegie deli one day in New York and said, look, give us one more in the vein of *These Eyes*. A ballad, you know. It'll make it easier to break it at the radio stations, there won't be any confusion about your image and you guys will never have to work again. And so we looked at him and said, Really, that's what you want? And he said, yeah.

And you won't have to be like me, busting your butt every day for somebody else. So Randy and I thought that was a pretty good prospect, you know. So we were flying out the next day; we were going from, uh… we went back to Canada and we flew to Vancouver, we played a job in Vancouver. And that very night we finished the gig and tore down the equipment and drove to the Tswassen terminal, waiting for the ferry 'cause the first ferry was about 6:30 in the morning, and we didn't go to sleep 'cause it was already 4:30. So it was a couple of hours to wait for the ferry, and we're sitting on our old highway bus—and this was just like a day after what Don Burkheimer had told us—and Randy pulled out the guitar and he said, "Butch" (he used to call me, it was my nickname). He said, "Butch, we need that follow-up." And he started strumming some chords and I started singing, and in about fifteen minutes we had written *Laughing*. And that's how that happened.

AM That quick?

BC Yeah. Sittin' on the bus waitin' for the ferry. And Jim and Gary heard it, and our road manager heard it, and he says, oh man you guys, that's it, you got it. You know, you got it, that's it. And then Randy had *Undun* already written and they put that on the B side, and then they started flippin' it over in Texas and we had a double-sided single, and then, oh man, we knew we were off to the races at that point. At that point I started realizing that we could last, you know.

AM Let's have another piece of music.

BC Well, here again, you know, it's a band that we worked with together several times in the sixties, and they took an old Bach organ prelude and played it on organ and put some lyrics to it—some very ethereal lyrics—and the band was called Procol Harum and it's the timeless classic, number one smash called *Whiter Shade of Pale*. [MUSIC]

AM You know what?—of course you know—that *American Woman* outsold The Beatles.

BC Well that year, 1970, we sold more singles than any band on the planet, so we really had quite a—phew, that was quite a year 'cause that was also the same year as *Share The Land* and *Hand-me-down*

World and *Bus Rider*, and all those songs in one year. *No Time* came out in late '69, but it was still on the charts when we hit 1970. So in one year we had *No Time, American Woman, No Sugar* was the flip of *American Woman, Hand-me-down World, Share The Land* and *Bus Rider*—all on the chart in one year. It was a pretty amazing year.

AM Huge. And did you, while you were writing— you were telling me about writing *Laughing*—and did you know that that well was not going to run dry, that it was there, that you could do this?

BC I think by that time Randy and I had— although we were still quite young—we were disciplining ourselves to make time for songwriting. You know, I was still living at home and we had a piano and he didn't. He was married by this time with his first kid, but he didn't have a piano. So, when we were in Winnipeg you know, he'd come over very often to my mother and grandmother's house and we'd… he'd bring a nylon string guitar and we'd sit at the piano. And we really tried to devote time for songwriting; we tried to put away a few hours a week. We wrote very quickly together and very prolifically, and also I was writing poems with the rhythmic structure that could later be turned into songs, so I was kind of like tryin' to stack the deck in our favour, you know. And Randy was also writing riffs that he knew I could—to which I could add lyrics, so we really fed each other very well. Randy and I had this incredible chemistry, this synchronicity that it's few and far between, you know. I miss that part of knowing Randy. We're not on the best of terms anymore, but I sure miss him musically. He really taught me a lot, too. When I first joined the band I didn't know about some of the mathematics of music, and he really taught me a lot, you know. And the writing with him was effortless; it was absolutely a labour of love, it was never, never tedious at all, or arduous. We just clicked, it was fun. It was, man, it was like our hobby almost—writing songs, writing million selling gold records. Like hey, what a hobby you guys got, you know. But that's really what it was. It was fun, it was just fun.

AM Now your life must have changed radically during those days, when everything was happening.?

BC Ooooh, the money. The money started getting way out of hand. I mean, I told ya I'd tell you an interesting story. This really happened. The cheques, usually you're about six months behind—you know, it takes awhile for the money to accumulate and then it gets to you. But the money started pouring in, especially for Randy and me 'cause we were writing the songs. Our income was in a whole other strata than Jim and Gary and I was living at home. Still. Still living with my mother and grandma; my mother was still working at Eatons, you know, and I used to go get the mail and bring the mail in for everybody. And I got a couple pieces of mail one day and I didn't think much of it and I shoved it under my bed and I forgot all about them, a couple of envelopes for me. And they sat under my bed like, in piles of garbage and comic books and magazines and hockey cards and stuff—they were just lyin' there for maybe four or five months. And one day my mother was forcing me to clean up my room and I opened these envelopes and it was fifty-seven thousand dollars in cheques, and they'd been lying under the bed for about four or five months. Now, you know, nobody in my family ever had fifty-seven thousand dollars at one time. And I hadn't even left home yet, you know. And my mother's forcing me to clean out my room like a nine-year-old and, what a… Okay, I'll clean out my room. And what do I find, fifty-seven thousand dollars. It was ridiculous, you know. That's the— that's the fantasy part of it all; it was just nuts. The money meant nothing anymore.

AM Then what do you do? I gotta start spending it?

BC No, I never did because I really knew the value of money. I saw how hard my mother had had to work and we never had affluence, so I knew that… My mother gave me a great ethic when I was young: she said, money is for spending, but not for wasting.

AM And you kept that.?

BC That was one reason I never got into dope big time. It was one reason I never got into gambling. I never got into silly clothes and silly, flashy lifestyle. You know, I bought a beautiful Jaguar and paid cash for it and bought a big house in Tuxedo. But these were not frivolous things; this was just something that was afforded me by my success. But I was never stupid with money. The way I saw other people go through fortunes, you know, and dope and gambling and crazy yachts. Nonsense, you know. I never fell into any of that 'cause I think, really, seeing how hard my mother had to work and how great she was with managing money—it was great to watch her get through life making the most of a kind of a down situation, you know. So she gave me a great ethic as far as money.

AM Let's have another piece of music now, Burton. What shall we play?

BC Just about, hmmm, a few months before I got into my first band, the twist was the craze in North America, and of course Chubby Checker had the original record and then there were all kinds of twist records. I don't think anyone hit with such a bang as Joey Dee and the Starlighters, with that live album from the Peppermint Lounge in New York. I remember running to buy that—I had to save my paper route money—running to buy that record, and the big hit off there was called *The Peppermint Twist*. And musically, and production wise, this still stands up very, very well thirty-six years later. Joey Dee and the Starlighters with *The Peppermint Twist*. [MUSIC]

AM Was it a shock when Randy left?

BC Um, no, because we kicked him out of the band.

AM Oh, you did?

BC It was quite simple. I mean, he'll tell ya that he left; that's just not true.

AM What happened?

BC It just was a lifestyle clash. He was doing other things, extraneous things to the band. He was doing some crazy publishing thing with Steve Cropper from Booker T and the MGs down in Memphis. He was wanting to produce other acts. He put out a solo album while *American Woman* was still out. I mean, he did all this stuff—he wanted to be more than just part of The Guess Who, and we were content to be band members, team players. And it all finally hit the fan when he said he had to go home to Winnipeg to have an operation, and we had three weeks of bookings left in the States. And we couldn't cancel them 'cause it would've been lawsuit time, you know. So we got this kid from Philadelphia to fill in on guitar and we were in San Francisco somewhere, flying to New York the next day, and we found out that while we were on the road with Bobby Sebelecko filling in for Randy, Randy was in New York doing business. At that point I just said to Jim and Gary, I said, guys, it's either him or me—that's it, you know. I would have been a solo artist in 1970 if they had decided to go with Randy, but the three of us got together in a room and clasped hands—like 1,2,3,4,5,6 in a pile—Jim and Gary and I, and we said alright, when we get to New York we tell him, that's it. And no matter what Randy tells you, that's what happened, you know. We kicked him out of the band. It's quite simple. We weren't gonna have that kind of stuff, you know; it was far too—it was far too religious to us—it was a spiritual thing we had going. I mean, we knew how we had beaten the odds and we didn't want to jeopardize it and we didn't want someone who wasn't a team player. So quite simply we kicked him out, you know.

AM And then it was your band.

BC Then I inherited the reins and we got two other guys from Winnipeg, Kurt Winter and Greg Liskew, and then, oddly enough, that's when we cut the biggest album in Guess Who history. *Share The Land* was the biggest album we ever had. And everybody was waitin' for the band to fail, you know.

AM More Winnipeg boys. You went back home to get 'em.

BC Absolutely. Well, it made it easier, you know, geographically. We didn't want to get a guy from Vancouver or Toronto. We had different ideas; we even knew a guy in Minneapolis that would have fit fine, but it's just, you know, for local rehearsals and stuff it was much easier. And I knew Kurt's playing, I admired Kurt's songwriting very much, and I knew he and I would hit it off. We had partied together a little bit and we were kind of friendly, and neither of those guys could believe it, you know, when they got the phone calls—it was really funny. But it clicked, it really clicked. *Share The Land* is one of the best albums the Guess Who ever did.

AM And then you did start your solo career, after mid-seventies when the band finally dissolved.

BC Yeah, well, we went through a few more personal changes and then it started getting away from what it had originally been, and then we finally recruited the first non-Winnipeger, Dominic Troiano from Toronto. And that was the beginning of the end 'cause he was really a jazz fusion guy and we were a very, very straight ahead commercial band, for which I made no apologies and still don't, you know. That's the kind of stuff I loved—three-and-a-half minute songs with good hooks, man. That's how I was raised and that's what I knew. And when it started drifting into this fake jazz syndrome, I said, this is enough for me, you know, I—plus, I will tell you, very quickly—I had written a song called *I'm Scared* when I was still in The Guess Who in 1975, and I showed it to the guys at practice and they didn't wanna do it and that really broke my heart. I said, there's something wrong here, Burton; this is a really good song and they don't wanna do it, and you're the lead singer and it's your band—I said, what's goin' on? So that kinda—at that moment I kinda quit in my head, you know, and then a few months later I did physically.

AM Okay, the two different styles that you're really noted for—the real rockers and these great ballads—what do you like singing best?

BC Hmmmm. It's physically easier to sing the ballads. If I had the kind of throat that Robert Plant has I would like to sing like that all night. But physically I can't, you know. But I always wanted to be Robert Plant. I mean, he... When I first heard Led Zeppelin I was just nailed to the wall. But I do like the love songs. You know it's funny, they call Elvis the King of rock 'n roll, and yet, historically, his biggest records were the ballads—things like *Are You Lonesome Tonight* and *Love Me Tender*—and I mean, *Can't Help Falling In Love*... those were the biggest selling records he ever had. The King of rock 'n roll, his biggest records were ballads, you know. So, I really like both, but it's physically easier for me, I would probably say—believe it or not—the ballads, you know. And I've had my biggest solo successes with ballads, and I mean *These Eyes* was a huge record, too, you know. It's just that *American Woman* was such a fluke—I think they expected us to be, like, more Zeppelinesque because of that record, but I mean *Stand Tall* was huge for me, *Break It To Them Gently* was huge for me. *I Will Play A Rhapsody* was a big record. *I'm Scared* was a big record for me. They are all kind of softer songs, you know, so probably I lean more towards the ballads. They seem to have a more lasting effect with people; they seem to get under their skin deeper than the rock stuff, which I still like. But, especially with my female fans, they really like the love songs, you know. So you don't fight your strengths, you know.

AM Well, I'm afraid we're going to have to send you off to the mountain top now, so if I was sending you off anywhere, where would you go to live out the rest of your days.?

BC Well, if it weren't for the ozone hole I'd probably say New Zealand, 'cause I was there once before there was an ozone hole over it and it was one of the most spectacular places I've ever seen, although now there is a problem with the sunlight, you know... So, maybe, hmmm... gotta go pretty far to beat Maui, although I was in Cancun earlier this year. I might say Cancun.

AM You're sounding like a beach kind of a guy here.

BC Well, I mean, I grew up in Winnipeg. This is just a natural progression, you know. I really like the Carib-be-an, or Ca-ribbean—whichever way you say it. I would, you know, right now as I speak to you I'd have to lean toward Cancun—I was fascinated by the Mayan ruins and the water was really the colour it is in those postcards, you know. And I went parasailing and I had a wonderful time, and the people were friendly and the music was good, and the food, and... Yeah, I could get by in Cancun very, very comfortably.

AM And what will you be reading?

BC One book only?

AM One only.

BC Oh, there's no question. *The Naked Ape* by Desmond Morris. If I ever read one book that changed my life and everything I thought, and every subsequent action was tempered by that book, it was *The Naked Ape*. I really woke up when I read that book, and anyone within earshot of this broadcast, I would highly recommend that you read *The Naked Ape*, because it pertains to every one of you.

AM So what's your final choice of music.

BC Final choice? Well, when someone asked me the other day about this I didn't really have to think too hard because it's a song by Ray Charles that really changed my life when I first heard it, and uh, I don't like the word genius being bantered about too flippantly, but in his case it really applies. I think he's influenced probably more people than any other single pop music icon, and my choice would be *What I Say* by Ray Charles, which is an absolute classic.

AM Do you remember the first time you heard it?

BC I was very young, because it came out I think in '58 or '59, and I heard it about a year later I think, on CKY radio in Winnipeg, and especially that part where it broke down and he would go, ahhhh, ahhhh… and the Rayettes would answer him, ahhhh—and there was this interplay… and I mean, it just took me to space, you know, it was wonderful. I finally got to meet him one time when we did a Dinah Shore show together—and bless her heart she's gone now, too—but she had the foresight to sit me next to him through the whole hour taping. So every time they broke for commercials I got to talk one-on-one with Ray Charles, and I just turned into mush, you know. It was wonderful.

AM Burton, it's been a real pleasure meeting you.

BC Thank you, it's been really wonderful talking to you and I had a lot of fun covering all this ground. Thank you so much.

CINDY CHURCH
WITH ANDREA MARANTZ, 1996

AM So you just got home from Germany?

CC Just a few days ago. I was doing a promotional tour, just Nathan and I. It's been a long time since he and I worked as a duo but because it was a promotional tour we'd decided to do that. We were gone for about two weeks and did seven dates over there. It was very interesting. Country music over there, it has a cult following because it's not part of the indigenous, German make-up. A lot of people don't like it and I think a lot of people over there listen to traditional German folk music and techno-pop and pop. And they still have huge discotheques over there, in fact, the town where I was staying had the biggest discotheque in Germany in this town. So I think for a lot of people they just go country, oh yeck, so the following there is very small.

AM But they're fascinated by the west.

CC Well they're fascinated with the music and the performers as well and they know everything about it and everything about the history of it, a lot of them do anyway, and a lot of them dress up. I heard about this where they dress up, kind of in costume, and its their statement. I'm a country fan and this is how I look – bad hats, chaps and six guns and knives, and that's their country music statement. And then there's other country music fans which are normally dressed and don't want that to be their statement. We play places from little, hard-core country bars to bistros to concert halls. Just a whole gamut. The people who booked us kind of wanted to see where we would fit it so the next time we go over they would have a better idea, and they all seemed to work, all the places.

AM Completely different kind of experience than what you have here.

CC Totally. Then the language, not a lot of the people, because we were in a lot of small towns, spoke English. So I was glad I bought my phrase book before I left. It was interesting too. I was never in a situation where I finally got a clue how immersion works because by the end of the two weeks, I'd find myself sitting being in a conversation with two people speaking German and actually understanding what was going on, where it was all starting to sound normal to me and it would have been interesting, had I stayed longer, to see what the next step would have been. The light bulb went on. So it was very interesting on many, many levels being over there.

AM So let's go back to your childhood now. From Germany to Nova Scotia. Tell me about your hometown.

CC I grew up in Biblehill, which is a village connected to Truro. Truro is very much a business town, was then and still is. It's very pretty. My life growing up there was very much the lower part of my street. The neighbourhood at the bottom of College Road and I lived there and my cousins lived beside us and other cousins down the street and my school was right across the street, and my grandparents had a little lunch counter restaurant at the end of that street. So my life was very much right around this area and I look aback on it now and think, it was pretty neat growing up there. And a very, very close relationship with my grandparents. We were their only grandchildren, my brother and I, and we were very connected.

AM Musical family?

CC Well somewhat. My mom had always aspired to be a singer. She sang in high school with two sisters and they had a little trio, hot professionally, and would just get together and sing and sing. They did do a few radio shows in Truro, which I would love to get my hands on; I would love to find those tapes. I don't know if they exist anymore.

AM What kind of stuff did they sing?

CC Country. And probably the popular country music of the day, in the fifties and we would have people come over to the house on weekends, the odd party, where people would bring their fiddles and play piano, and play the traditional Maritime music and I can still see my grandmother and her sister hop polkaing around the basement. So it was musical. My brother and I had to take piano lessons when we were kids and I was in the school band – played bassoon in the school band.

AM And would you get up and sing at these little gatherings?

CC I would. We would, my brother and I both, would sing together.

AM Did you think you would become a professional singer when you were a kid?

CC No. It never occurred to me.

AM What was the dream?

CC At that time I wanted to be an artist because I drew a lot and that was what I thought I would do. I used to get up at six in the morning and just be drawing, drawing, drawing. It was probably more conducive to my nature to do that too.

AM What do you mean by that?

CC Well, just that it appeals to the loner in me as opposed to such a public figure.

AM Do you still paint?

CC Every now and then. About six or seven years ago I got into doing watercolour and ink, and then I just got too busy. I haven't done anything like that for awhile but I hope to someday go back to it.

AM So how did you move west?

CC I left right after high school. I was eighteen and I really wanted to leave badly. I had romantic notions about moving west, and a lot of people were moving west at that time. It was 1977 and the big boom was happening out here in Alberta and a lot of my friends had moved out. My best friend and I just decided that was it, we were heading out, and we did. We went to Edmonton and I was there for a year. Saved up our little pennies and came out. Then a friend of mine was going to Vancouver Island and that sounded even more intriguing. Having grown up on the east coast, I missed being on the ocean, and I went to Vancouver Island and was there for six years. I spent most of my twenties there. Drifting around. Waitressing, we were either working in a restaurant or a bar and singing a little bit on my breaks or on weekends.

AM Did you start getting up in places you were working?

CC Started doing that and eventually… I was always encouraged to go sing for a living but it was scary and I was very shy in my twenties.

AM Who was it that gave you that encouragement?

CC Just different people who I would come into contact with, and Nathan, who also lived in the same town on Vancouver Island and who was off doing musical things. His band would play at the bar where I was working and he had heard me sing and would always coax me to come up and sing a couple of songs. In the meantime, he had been out in Alberta working with Ian Tyson and doing various things and at one point he had come back and was looking to do something, and at that point I had learned how to play bass and was getting a few gigs as a bass player, and was looking for something to do too. Then we decided to do something together.

AM So this wasn't like a conscious decision "I want to be a musician"?

CC NO, no- it wasn't something where I knew from the time I was a kid this was what I was going to do. I wish it was that. No, I kind of half drifted into it.

AM So you started singing professionally kind of late in life, a whole old twenty-five. Were you and Nathan romantically involved at that point when he came back and said, "Cindy, I think you should sing."?

CC Well that became part of it, yes. Originally it was to work together and do something but the romantic part came about.

AM And then together you came to Alberta?

CC Yeah, we went to Yellowknife first to put our repertoire together and he had a piece of land up there that he had won through a lottery system where your name goes into the system and you could get it and you have a piece of land offered to you. You have to build something on it within two years and he had this little piece of land on a lake, thirty miles outside of Yellowknife and the time was almost up that he had to build something on it so these people, partners of his, put up the money to build the cabin. He's a carpenter so he built it, and we were both out there on this lake, thirty miles in the middle of nowhere, in the bush.

AM And where were your audiences for you musicians up there?

CC Well, we would hop in the canoe. We had a six week gig at the Explorer Hotel in Yellowknife and we honed, and put our repertoire together, and we played every night and stayed there some, and stayed out on the lake. It was quite the experience. Being on the lake was a real experience. Just us and the loons and the mosquitos.

AM Is it beautiful up there?

CC It is beautiful. Lots of rock and small, stubby trees, but the skies and the northern lights that we saw being up there and we were the only humans out on the lake at the best of times and it is just its own special beauty. I think I appreciate it more now. At the time, I appreciated it but not really. It was really isolating to me at the time. I was just back a year or so ago and I thought, I'd love to spend more time here now. It's a different place in my life and I could really enjoy it. I just remember seeing the best thunderstorm I've ever seen, and the biggest mosquitos. The relentless mosquitos. We arrived in March and left in August and came to Alberta. We played for a little bit as a duo in Edmonton. Then we heard that Ian was looking for a new band and began working with him.

AM Now your partner, Nathan Tinkham had worked with Ian Tyson before, knew Ian already?

CC Worked with him and recorded and was part of Ian's first contemporary cowboy album, which was *Old Corrals and Sagebrush*. So he knew Nathan could play, he just wasn't sure about this gal he was bringing with him. So I went and auditioned and passed.

AM It must have been something. Ian Tyson was legendary at that point and this is a starting out singer in many ways.

CC It was a big deal. That's when my parents first went, OK, we like what you do now, we get it. It was my first big stepping stone to be where I was and then to be elevated to this situation, working with someone like Ian for his audiences. I've always said that he was very gracious in that he would always allow me to sing a couple of songs during his sets and really encouraged what I did and respected what I did and really exposed me to his audience. I made a lot of really good connections during that time and a lot of really great friends that I'm still in contact with, so that was a very important part of my career.

AM Let's have your fist piece of music now. What would you like to hear?

CC This is a tune from Jamie O'Hara and he was half of The O'Kanes in the eighties. I don't know if you're familiar with them, Kieran Kane and Jamie O'Hara. They had a great little album out and now they do things separately. He's just one of my all time favourite writers and I think he's a great singer and this is a song from him called *The Cold Hard Truth*. [MUSIC]

AM Now, Peter Gzowski has made a bit of a difference in your career. How did you run into him?

CC Well, I guess the first time was when he phoned me up to do a national hymn-sing. They get people from different parts of the country in the studio, and you're all hooked up through headphones and you sing together and it sounds bizarre but it actually seems very normal when you're doing it. You're just so in tune with everybody else and…

AM I've heard those and I think it sounds great on the radio because it sounds like you're all in the same room but I kept thinking, she's siting there all by herself in Calgary or Vancouver or… you know…

CC Yeah, at five in the morning usually I might add but it seems very normal when its happening and that first one we did, this combination of people, really took off and we did three, three or four more and so that's how I became… oh no actually, the fist time we met him was with the Great Western Orchestra. We did an interview with him but that was a long time ago so he was familiar with…

AM He became an instant fan?

CC He was a fan and he has remained so and a very big supporter and…

AM Speaking of the Great Western Orchestra, that was the first step away from Ian and into doing something different.

CC Yeah, both Nathan and I felt after three years working with Ian, we really wanted to do something on our own and at the time David was looking to do something and…

AM David Wilkie?

CC Yeah, and we decided to do something together.

AM And that was a very successful album.

CC It's funny, when I was in Germany people were coming up to me with vinyl copies of that album wanting it signed. Now where did you find that? I can't find those. Where are you finding them? But I still think it was a classic, and is a classic little album. It was made for so little money and I think in such an innocent, naïve way. It was just doing an album that, you know, was representative of what our sound was at the time and it was one of those little things that took on a life of its own and did well.

AM You were with that project for a couple of years?

CC Three years, the magic number. And then that ended.

AM And its just been really soaring since then. I mean you've just gotten busier and busier and busier.

CC Soaring? OK. Well, it seems with me its always kind of like a steadily moving thing and it seems like in the last couple of years things have really started to feel like they're beginning to work. It's a very interesting and exciting time right now… in many ways.

AM You've been a solo artist, part of a trio, a member of a large group, and most recently, a part of Quartette. Now, the success of that particular combination must have been exciting.

CC Quartette is one of those situations where it seems that certain projects have a certain chemistry and a certain thing about them that makes them work and makes them take on a life of their own and, I've said before, if you would have told me, you four singers are going to get together and this is going to happen, I would have thought—huh, right—those voices won't work together I don't think, but…

AM How did that happen, how did the four of you get together?

CC Well, we all knew each other. Certainly Colleen, Sylvia, and Caitlin knew each other well because the all live in the east and they have history together. I knew Sylvia through Ian. I had met her a couple of times and when we would run into each other, we'd chat. Caitlin had met me when I worked with Ian and we did Maraposa one year and she became a fan and we became pen pals. And I had always been a fan of Colleen's since, I remember when I left Nova Scotia, I had a Colleen Peterson tape which I used to play all the time and she was just an idol. I was such a big fan of hers at a young age and I had met her a couple of years before Quartette got together at the Edmonton Folk Festival and she stayed with me a couple of times when she had gigs in the west. So, you know, I had, you know…

AM You were friendly.

CC They were acquaintances more than anything and we had all submitted material to Harbourfront in Toronto, looking to work there individually, and Derek Andrews who books Harbourfront was having a Music Women Weekend, where he was bringing women from all over the world and he was looking for a country representation and was talking to Colleen, and Colleen suggested doing something with Sylvia and Caitlin, and Caitlin suggested me, and so here we were getting together for just one gig. And we were originally just going to do it as a songwriter in the round, all individuals singing their songs. We started thinking, we all sang harmony, why don't we sing on each other's stuff. So, we sent tapes back and forth and like there were twenty-eight songs or something and I went out a week earlier and rehearsed them, and immediately had that chemistry. It was immediate. Just sitting around the house singing. All the voices would fall into place and it's just one of those strange and wonderful things. And we did the gig and it just went over like gangbusters. We thought, hmmm, this is interesting. Then we did a Gzowski show, and people were phoning in across the country wondering where they could buy this album and there was none, of course. And we just decided to do one. It really has taken ,and there's two albums, both of which are very successful , you know, being put out independently and not having a big machine behind you. But CBC Radio has been a big part of that because Quartette has not been embraced in a big way by country radio in Canada because, it's no, it doesn't fit into that narrow little vision that's happening right now.

AM Does everyone bring material to the group?

CC Everyone does and everyone brings their own influences. Like, Colleen certainly her roots are in rhythm and blues and she brings that to the party. Caitlin brings a more blue-grass edge to the thing. Sylvia just brings herself. Sylvia is Sylvia. She brings those little novellas that she writes, her story songs and her bass boys. She loves being able to sing all the bass parts in the group.

AM It's amazing. She can really get down there.

CC I know. How do you do that? And, it's just been a lot of fun. It's really been a lot of fun and continues to be and we just take it as it comes and see what happens with it and try to make it all work with our individual stuff, too, because it's, it can be… There haven't been any major conflicts yet, but its certainly a matter of communication and knowing what everyone is up to a long time in advance so that the calendars don't get all amuck.

AM Right, because there's no commitment to do this as the whole focus.

CC No, No one… I don't think anyone really wants to get lost in the group situation like that because – you can't – you still need the momentum to keep going with your own stuff.

AM And that's part of what really feeds Quartette is that you are each maintaining these individual personalities.

CC Yeah, and I think too, I think it's part of what makes a lot of stuff that would normally crop up, petty things in groups that pop up that you have to deal with, a lot of those are alleviated because you do have your own thing. You don't get, as I say, we've all done this for years and we're not twenty. And you just see this stuff coming. You see it coming, and you go, it's not worth getting upset about. It's a very mature – it's four adult women working together and I got to say, I'm proud of how it comes off. I was really proud of how those tours worked – you know, the cross-Canada tour. And I said at the end of the tour, I'm just so proud of us, how we made this work and how there was no silliness, and no pettiness, and no… it was a lot of fun and everyone put their best foot forward and everyone was a trooper. I was just really proud of that.

AM Turner Valley Albertwhere you live, that's become a real little music community. So, what's the appeal for you? Why are you in Turner Valley?

CC Well, again I kind of drifted into it and I first ended up in southern Alberta because of my affiliation with Ian. We originally lived in Longview. It 's beautiful in Longview and I love it there and we were right on the edge of town overlooking that southern expanse of foothill and mountains and I love living there but it was just that much further to go out of the city and we decided to move to Turner Valley about seven years ago and have been there ever since. What appeals to me about it, like I think this part of Alberta is so special anyway. It just has everything. It has mountains, it has foothills, it has prairie, it's temperate – normally it has temperate winters, this one is an exception – it's just so beautiful there. I love the balance in my life. Like I love zipping off to Toronto all the time and I love zipping off to Germany and I love travelling. It's a big part of this life that I' like and I've always liked travelling since I was a kid. And I need that excitement and that buzz to feed me, but I also really need solitude and to be away from all of that and to kind of store up energy again, and this is what living Turner Valley does for me and I love all the small town things, not the small time things you can find with living in a small town, which I just ignore. If people are talking about me, I don't know about it and I don't care but I love all the small town things like the gals at the post office knowing that I'm going away and keeping my mail for me and wondering where I've been and being on a first name basis and the gals at the bank and just kind of having this neat, friendly…

AM   Let's have a piece of music.

CC   How about Jennifer Warrens.

AM   Beautiful voice.

CC   Her stuff – this is from the album called *The Hunter* and again, it's the one tune that I played over and over and over. She co-wrote this with Leonard Cohen. She is one of the few people in the world that I would love to meet and to pick her brain about how she creates music. She's so much involved in the production of her albums. She's so quirky and so artistic and so musical, I hope to someday, someday I would love to meet her. But this is one of my favourite songs from that album called *Way Down Deep*. [MUSIC]

AM   Jennifer Warrens' *Way Down Deep*. The choice of my guest on Mountaintop Music, Cindy Church.

CC   It's so nice to hear these. I haven't heard some of these songs for a long time. This is nice.

AM   And you'll go home and put them and play them over and over.

CC   I just may.

AM   Now before we send you to your mountaintop, we let our guests take one book with them.

CC   I'm been thinking about that. That's a toughie. I was thinking about what authors have I run across who have just really hit me over the head with not only the story they were telling but they way they write. How you form a connection with the way somebody is writing. How their style really stands out and affects you and I've had various authors where I've had this happen where you want to read everything they've written. Larry McMurty was one for me and another one was Pat Conroy who wrote *The Prince of Tides*, so I picked that. I picked *The Prince of Tides*. I remember when I was reading that book I was on tour in B.C. and I would not come out of my room in the daytime. I couldn't wait to get back to this book but I didn't want it to end either because the whole experience of reading it was so great. I wanted to find out what was happening but I didn't want it to end. But his writing really knocked me out. His power of description – I just appreciated his whole working of the language and the sense of vulnerability with his writing that I picked up on. But I also loved the story and the whole dysfunctional, psychological, Southern aspect to that book.

AM   You also get to choose where you'd go if we cast you away.

CC   Well, again I was thinking about this on my drive in, and I was thinking I have done enough travelling in my life to actually know of a really spot where I've gone, I could live here forever. So I was thinking back to a fantasy that I have lots of times about where I'd like to be at certain times and it again appeals to that part of me that craves solitude, and again this may come from growing up on the east coast but I always picture being in a place, it's a cabin, kind of like the one in *On Golden Pond*, for instance. Like that, kind of old-fashioned, big veranda and I'm up really high, almost on a cliff, over looking ocean. I always envision myself getting up in the morning, being in my robe, and having a big mug of coffee overlooking the ocean. That for me – and I'm alone, there's no one around me, no people – and that's a really peaceful thought for me. I would still someday in my life love to have a place where I would have that. Where I could wake up in the morning and have coffee overlooking the ocean. And I don't even know what ocean at this point, but that's where I'd like to be.

AM   What's your final piece of music Cindy?

CC   My final piece is a Steve Earl piece. I'm a big, big fan of Steve Earl. Interesting, when I was in Nashville, I ran into a publishing company that handled his sister's material, Stacey Earl, and she's a very interesting writer. I'm looking at a couple of her tunes for my next album, actually, but this is from his album *Guitartown* and I love this song. When I was in Germany, I was playing this seedy, little bar called Alabama in Berlin and we were having a couple of German beers after the gig and this came on the jukebox, and it's called *My Old Friend The Blues*.

AM   Cindy, thanks a lot for coming in.

CC   Thank you, Andrea.

JH   Does this feel as strange for you as it does for me? I'm usually sitting in my easy chair listening to you, you're usually on the other side of the microphone.

PG   Well, we could change roles if you want.

JH   I have a feeling that…

PG   What music did you bring?

JH   Your life might be more interesting than mine to this point.

PG   Longer, so far.

JH   So, as Shelagh Rogers says in her introduction to your fifth *Morningside* book, people are always asking her, *what is Peter Gzowski really like?* And I guess we could start on that note—what is Peter Gzowski really like?

PG   Much like the guy you hear on the radio, with certain modifications. There's a certain degree of smoke and mirrors—a lot of smoke, maybe not many mirrors and fraudulence. I mean, there is… you can make a definitive difference right from the very beginning that away from a microphone I swear a lot, and swear a lot, and easily, and do not on the radio. So we can begin with the bald statement that there is a difference between the private and public person. I also have a… I would like to think that in real life I have good manners that my grandmother would be proud of, and I like to think that on the radio I have good manners. But I know away from the microphone I can be grumpier than I sometimes sound, and snappier. I hurt people I am told. I know it's unintentionally because I can't think of many occasions when I have deliberately wanted to savage somebody, but I have a bit of a smart and quick tongue which does, and often, show away from the air. But I also have… I'm much shyer than anyone would believe and do not like, sort of, public encounters and things, you know, so I tend to shrink from them. And I also have an awful memory for names, so I appear to cut people whom I don't intend to cut and I know that there are several wounded souls around the world who think I'm a real (I won't say the word on the radio), and much different from the front I present. But I don't think there's too big a difference. Well, sometimes I'm faking my enthusiasms, too.

PETER GZOWSKI
WITH JUDY HAMILL, 1994

JH   Well, after a long haul like that I guess that's true. I think it's true also, you're with people intensively for three hours every day, you can be a bit antisocial when you leave the studio. You don't want to go out and have a crowd of people around and talk with them.

PG   That's exactly right. People call me antisocial, but the truth is I'm social, as you say, for three hours a day, and at a lot of other meetings and public encounters, so solitude becomes pretty important to me. I should say probably a bit more about faking my enthusiasms to people because I am, I guess, reasonably well-known for maintaining a certain level of enthusiasm and curiosity. Most of it is real, 'cause I've learned over the years that even stuff that I don't think I'm interested in, when my tyrannical producers forced me look into something that I wouldn't maybe have done out of my own natural curiosity, I discover there's really interesting stuff in there—*oh, no kidding, that's how that works.* But occasionally I do have to say, hmmm, really, another sparrow, eh. That's three sparrows I think now.

JH I want to talk a little bit now about the young Peter Gzowski, and the young Peter who actually spent some years as Peter Brown. Tell me that story.

PG My mother and father were divorced very early, very shortly after I was born. I scarcely knew my biological father as a child; I came to know him in later life. It was mid depression, the height of the depression (I was born in 1934) and they were both from middle class families, but there was simply no work. They traveled around a bit together and then my father kind of took off to Red Lake, Ontario, as a miner, and across the prairies, and he really didn't get anything solid until the war broke out. So they were divorced. And my mother, who had a masters degree in library science, was a graduate of St. Andrews University—'cause she had gone there because she was too young to be admitted to the University of Toronto, and was, in fact, brilliant—she was working in a book counter at Eatons and trying to support a young son. We didn't use things like single mothers in those days, or working mothers, or divorce was really, really uncommon. But she remarried, and I often think largely so that I would have a home to grow up in. She married a nice guy named Reg Brown from Galt, Ontario, and when I was four or five we moved to Galt. And she was smart enough to realize that someone in a small town like that, would have a very difficult time with a different name than his mother and stepfather. So, though Reg never adopted me, my mother had me take his name. So I was Peter Brown in all the years I was in Galt, which was about 10 years. That's where I had a childhood and it was this wonderful, solid place to have a childhood. It was a great place to be a kid.

JH You mentioned in your journal that you'd like to write a book about each of your parents one day. Are you still thinking about doing that?

PG I struggle with it from time to time. I've never understood the process of writing fiction or how it would appeal… how to handle it. I mean, I think there's things I would have to deal with that probably only fiction, only a novel could deal with. They were both very interesting characters, people out of their times very much. My mother died when I was 14. She was the children's librarian in Galt and I don't think she was happy in that town, and there are some very personal and difficult things to write about both of them and in a way, their characters are right out of the literature of the time. I mean, my mother could have been written by Dorothy Parker or Scott Fitzgerald, and my father was like many men of that time, who really… the war in fact was the highlight of their lives. Then, when they came back from the war, they were never able to recapture that romance and that excitement, so my father didn't do well after the war. He was a very nice and very charming guy as I got to know him, but he was also I think in a sense a victim of the times, so that… not a victim—we do too much victimizing in the world—but a product of that time. There were many people like him. And they're very interesting people.

JH Your mother being a reader and so involved in literature, books and so on, she influenced you strongly toward becoming a man of letters, wouldn't you say?

PG Not consciously. I mean, she just… words and writing and books were so much a part of her life, she couldn't imagine that there would be such a thing as a world without them. So our house was full of not only the somber and classical books, but of books of joy and humor and pieces of poetry and cartoons and the *New Yorker*. And I was taught early on not to have very much respect for books in the physical sense—you can take them into the bathtub with you and chew them if you want, and take them to bed and bend down and write all over them if you feel like it, they're part of your life. I wrote stuff as a kid, little bits of verse and things, but I was going to be an engineer at one point, too. I had all kinds of other career plans, I never… I used to dream about being a writer as a young person, but I didn't… I mean, I took several other turns before I set on that path.

JH Your first step into the world of journalism—well, you can't call it journalism, can you—was as an ad sales journalist with *Timmins Daily Press*. You weren't very good apparently.

PG I think I may have been the worst ad

salesperson in the history of not only the *Timmins Daily Press,* but possibly the entire Thompson daily newspaper chain. I was 19, I had no interest in advertising (I didn't think it worked, I didn't think it was a very good idea); but it was the only way I could get into the newspaper business. It was actually a friend of my mother's from Galt who was at Thompson, who when I went looking around for a doorway said, well, go to Timmins and you can sell ads for awhile, and when there's an opening you'll be there and you can get onto the editorial side. But they assigned me, oh… you know, the ad department… all the other salesmen would give you when they distributed all the clients, they'd rip off the bottoms of their lists. So you got all the worst candidates, all the deadbeats, all the ones who couldn't… And I would go into these merchants at age 19 and try to tell them that advertising would save their business. And they would spend most of their time telling me how bad things were. I was making $40 a week, and from a haberdasher (a men's wear place that was on my list, a guy I quite liked) I bough a $19 black homberg hat because I felt sorry for him, and because one of the older ad men told me that if I wore a hat I might look older. So for a couple of weeks, walking around Timmins, Ontario was a guy whose teenage acne had not yet disappeared from his face, wearing a pompous homberg hat that he couldn't afford. And the guy never did buy an ad. The only ad… I sold a half-page of advertising once, I was so excited I ran back to the office and they said, oh, he hasn't paid his bill for 12 years, he's looking for a place to get in. No, I didn't do well at that Judy.

JH How did you get your first break to write some copy?

PG Well, I pestered the guys in the editorial department in the newsroom into letting me, you know… can I do anything, can I cover a meeting of the Beaver Club (which I think in fact was my first—covered a speech for that) and I would… anything. And I mean, I could type a little bit, but I hung out with them and would go and sit and their table in the pub, where I was drinking illegally, and pestered them and pestered them. So I got a chance and then I got to actually write some stuff, and they published.

JH Did you fasten on a moment when you decided, yeah, this is what I want to do, whether or not it was the minutes of the meeting of the Beaver Club or whatever—but journalism, this is it for me?

PG I still don't use the word journalism. I mean, I never did set out to do that. I wanted to be a reporter and a writer, and I never thought of anything as pretentious as journalism. I don't think there was a moment of epiphany. There was… I remember when I got my first byline, when all of us went out for coffee after we had 'put the paper to bed' (as we never said, only the outsiders said that)—and they went around and I was thinking that I had seen the city editor write, "by Peter Gzowski, Daily Press staff writer." I had seen him write that at the top of my copy, so I new when the paper came out I'd have a byline. So they went around the table and Chris Saltzan, who later came to Winnipeg, had, you know, a milkshake, and Bob Regulee (who later won three national newspaper awards and whose son is now a good journalist)—Bob Regulee had fried potatoes and a cup of coffee. And Bill Bothwright, who later went on to the San Francisco Chronicle, would have a cup of tea and pancakes. I said, by Peter Gzowski—that was the only thing that was on my mind. In other words, no moment of epiphany, I just knew I liked it, and I learned also that I didn't know enough to do this, so that's when I decided to go back to university, out of which I had dropped.

JH Did you listen to CBC radio when you were a kid?

PG Yeah.

JH Did your mum have it on?

PG Yup. Although it was very different in my childhood years because it was still predominantly American, so that most of the programs that I would remember are Jack Benny and Fred Allan. But I do… I remember the wartime drama about an RCAF Lancaster bomber, and I remember Lux Radio Theatre with Cecil B. deMille, and I think it was Monday nights 'cause my mother always ironed to Cecil B. deMille. But it was at that time, and then later when I went to Moose Jaw, would I realize that there would never be a better expression of the prairie I was discovering than *Jake and the Kid* that had been on CBC radio, 'cause I could see the land that W.O. Mitchell was writing about under my city bred shoes. So CBC radio… I never dreamed of working there, but I had some unconscious understanding of what's important to its relationship to who we were and how we were growing, and a place to tell our stories, our own stories to ourselves.

JH   Let's take a break for a piece of music. What's the first thing you'd like to hear this morning?

PG   I'd like to hear that I can sleep for another two hours.

JH   I don't know that one.

PG   This is a piece by Beverly Glenn-Copeland, who's not really well-known, but there's so much joy and good feelings in this. Beverly Glenn has been around for a number of years and has a number of songs out. She's a black singer and writer from around Toronto, and I don't know where else she's played except on Morningside. And from time to time—we have done for years—we play her wonderful *Onward and Upward*. [MUSIC]

JH   I guess you've probably traveled and seen more of Canada than even Joe Clark, but you've sure traveled a lot less internationally than he and many others?

PG   I've traveled a lot less internationally than practically anyone I know.

JH   Where have you been outside of Canada? Anywhere?

PG   I've been to the Caribbean. I've seen France.

JH   Sounds like from the plane…

PG   No, from the ship. I took my five kids to England one time when I was between engagements, as they say. Somebody folded a magazine on me, of which I'd been the editor, and gave me a lot of money after. I'll come and fold your magazine anytime if you'll give me a year's salary, which was $35,000 at the time (in case anyone's thinking of untold wealth). So we went to England on a ship, so I saw France. I've been to Moscow to see hockey, I've been to Warsaw to try to learn to pronounce my name—I am 'Jevoski'. I have not been to California—isn't that amazing, you know. For me, L.A. remains Lethbridge, Alberta. I just haven't been to the other one. I'm the only person I know… Have you been to California?

JH   Well, Disney World.

PG   Well, that's California. But, you know, the funny thing is many of the places I have gone, England being a notable place in point, I've already been. I've been there in films and books and poetry. And I mean, I knew all of London when I was walking the streets. Why, Sherlock Holmes lived right up that street right there. So that's true, so I think, well why go there? Besides, I haven't yet finished discovering this country. It is very provincial. On this book tour I was in Winnipeg, and some friends of mine who are going to Germany to run an international school there, and they had some other friends and an Air Canada pilot who lives in Winnipeg and commutes to where he takes the next flight to New Delhi ('cause he thinks Winnipeg is the best place)… and they were sitting around, and a couple of other people, and they were saying the traffic's worse in Bangkok than it is in Manila, you know, and the other one would say, well, in Saudi Arabia where I was playing golf… oh, golf, is that as good as it is in Argentina. And I'm thinking, you have to go to Winnipeg to feel really provincial. And I am really provincial and I'm not proud of it, but I wouldn't exchange the experiences that I've had of this country for luggage covered with stickers from exotic place names. I've been to Iqaluit seven times.

JH   I haven't been to Iqaluit once.

PG   Well, you should. No, it's too bad Canadians don't… that we don't know our north better. It's not all our fault, partly because, if any rational person is given a choice in February—would you rather go to Arizona or perhaps Iqaluit—I think the rational person would say, oh, I'll go to Arizona. Also, it's cheaper to fly from Calgary—I haven't looked it—but I'll bet it's cheaper to fly from Calgary to Amsterdam than it is to Cambridge Bay. But it's spectacularly beautiful, it's full of warm, interesting, fascinating people. It's politically one of the most interesting and volatile areas in the world, and I just wish more of us knew it, the north alone. But I'm never in a part of the country I think I know without discovering a corner of it that I didn't know about. I mean, as anyone who's ever been to Cape Breton has, I have a crush on Cape Breton. But the last time I was there, which was in June, I went to a little place called Dundee, a resort, and I hadn't heard of it before.

JH You should have some book tours in places like Dundee.

PG Absolutely. Because one of the drawbacks of the book tour is you're never anywhere—you're just in hotel rooms and radio studios and book stores, which are, except for the people, fairly uniform.

JH You collectively talked a little bit about Maclean's, the youngest managing editor, the astronomical salary that you had there at 28 years of age. Were you really in the deep end?—do I know what I'm supposed to be doing. I mean, was it a case of having any idea…

PG No, I had no doubts. No, I was… God, I wish I knew now what I knew then. I mean, I wish I had the untrammeled confidence of youth. I was quite sure I was up to that job. I thought Maclean's was the most important institution in the country, 'cause I'd hardly worked anywhere else. But it's a funny thing about that confidence, 'cause I think in a way my greatest lifelong gift at journalism has been my lack of confidence. So I don't know when I developed my lack of confidence, 'cause I don't think I had much then. I had far too many jobs too young. I mean, I was the youngest this and the youngest this—the boy wonder of Canadian journalism.

JH When you say your lack of confidence, you mean, so, you go into an assignment with this lively curiosity and you're open to it, and then you sit and think it over and make up your mind how you stand on it, how you want to approach it.

PG That's part of it. It's more… I turned 60 last summer and my incomparable assistant, Shelley Ambrose (who comes from Alberta) organized the best imaginable birthday party for me (60th birthday party for me) because nobody came to it. What she got was… knowing that I do not like either to be the centre of a lot of public attention or that I don't like large parties. I like my gatherings to be six or eight friends for dinner. And knowing that I didn't like that, she nevertheless organized a huge party for me to which nobody came because it was a party by fax. She got friends from much of my lifetime and many parts of this country, to write or fax me poems or thoughts or stupid things or parodies or cartoons and things, and then they were all assembled in this beautiful box made by my wonderful friend, Peter Brown, the book designer, and he'd made it all elegant. And that was waiting for me when I got to the cottage on my birthday morning, and I spent many hours of laughter and tears and things, and it was just the best birthday party I've ever had, by myself with all my friends and my kids and everything there on paper. But in that, Bob Fulford, who has been my friend for 40 years, did a little piece about me. Fulford's very smart. But he said that the reason I'm good at what I do on the radio is that I still have that fear. 'Cause he said… he remembered a conversation he and I had had when we were young magazine people together at MacLean's and talking about another young magazine writer whom he was very high on, and my saying, he'll never get anywhere, and Fulford saying, how come?, and me saying, 'cause he doesn't know how hard it is. And Fulford said, I've always thought of it as hard, and I still think of it as hard. And even after 30,000 interviews or more on the radio, I work very hard preparing myself 'cause I'm scared that I'll mess up, you know. I read the book in case the author will challenge me about some perception; I think my way through. So I think that it's lack of confidence that I've somewhere learned after being this uppity young guy. I had a couple of spectacular failures, which help a lot.

JH I'd love to hear about them. We'd all love to share in the agony.

PG Well, many people have seen one of the most notable, which was my incredible late night television career.

JH Oh, the TV thing; oh, I thought you were talking about live on air. Well, the TV thing of course was just an unfortunate set of circumstances in a way.

PG Yeah, me and television.

JH It wasn't your fault.

PG Sure it was. I said, yes. I mean, I wasn't raped, I was seduced. I said, this sounds like a good idea. It did sound like a good idea, it still sounds like a good idea. I think I could do late night television.

JH I think there is still the perception of what's so good about, let's try and translate it to television 'cause that can be so much better than the little bursts and clips and cutaways.

PG Yeah. Where is it written that you couldn't have a nice conversation. Why couldn't we be doing this on television?

JH People's brains and ears aren't different because they're watching…

PG Yes.

JH Are they?

PG No, no.

JH But they seem to be the way it's packaged for them.

PG And they could see how cute I am.

JH Well, that's only my privilege this morning. Let's have another choice of music. What would you like to hear next?

PG Well, I want people to know that I'm not just interested in sloppily sentimental and 'feel good' music, and I want to play… I love Buddy Wasisname and the Other Fellas. We had a… the sort of epitome of my 'raise funds for literacy' career, which is mostly golf tournaments but now has a number of concerts in various places. And we had a kind of all-star concert and we took over the Winter Garden Theatre in Toronto and sold it out for $200 and more per seat, and I was able to bring people from all over the country, I mean, including the very distinguished Oscar Peterson and Karen Kain—look at that, two people I brought all the way from Toronto. But others, I mean, Valdy and Tom Jackson; but there was no one I was happier to bring to the hallowed halls of distinguished, 'let's wear a black tie to the concert tonight, Mollie,' than I was Buddy Wasisname and the Other Fellas from Newfoundland. I think these guys are geniuses, and this is a very seasonable song, too, so I think we should play Buddy Wasisname and the Other Fellas.

JH And the name of the song?

PG I'll tell you, the song self-identifies, you don't have to do it… I hate that. Don't you hate that when the guy says, and now, here's Cole Porter with *It's Only Make Believe* [PG singing]—oh God, I almost sang. Here's Buddy Wasisname and the Other Fellas. [MUSIC]

JH So, will you always be the writer first or the radio host first now? When you say you're afraid of messing up on the radio; because your input is always considered to be crucial to the success of the outcome, like a writer—for the research you've done, for the preparation you've done, for your conversation and your input back and forth and the dialogue. Like a writer, if you don't know your subject thoroughly, you'll mess up. What did all that mean anyway?

PG I was trying to sort my way backwards through the question to find where it's core was. You started to talk like me, just flap your gums until a sentence comes out. Then put a question mark at the end of it and look at the guy. I am still a writer in my own mind—maybe no one else's—I'm still a writer who's working on the radio for awhile. But I'm not a satisfied writer in that, you know—and this is probably a really stupid thing to say on an interview on part of a tour that is flogging books—but there are many that I'm very happy with. When people bring the *Private Voice* that you're quoting from so thoughtfully today, up to have it signed in a book store, I sometimes want to say, it isn't as good as I wanted it to be, you know. It's got a lot of stupid stuff, I should have taken another year with that. Well, we've unsold that one, now let's try… There are others that… I mean, I love the little *Canadian Living* book, although it's only a collection of columns, but I found a voice in there that I'm quite happy with. But other books, no. I had a very successful hockey book, it was based on the Edmonton Oilers—it should have been much better. So I am an unsatisfied writer and I still need to fulfil that somehow, I need to get at a project that I do properly take the time and the care and the thought, and the rewriting that is necessary.

PG   Did that not answer your non-question?

JH   Oh, it did perfectly not answer the non-question. When you first got onto radio, filling in for Bruno Gerussi, *This Country in the Morning*, there you worked with Allan McFee at your side. Talk about the good old days—he, the famous trickster?

PG   I wasn't present for it, but I know this happened. There was something called *The Honer Harmonica Hou*r, which Tommy Tweed was the host of, and Allan was what he always is, the Allan McFee of (God bless him), and only Tweed… it had a live orchestra and actors and everything, it was a real production number from studio, probably G, in Toronto, which was huge. Big. And we had, like, two script assistants and two directors—I mean, big ambitious stuff a couple of hours long. Tweed and McFee and the engineer were the only three people who knew that they had set all the clocks in the studio and the control room two minutes ahead of real time. So as the clock came up to what everyone thought was the opening moments of *The Honer Harmonica Hour*, Alln McFee came on, and in that wonderful mellifluous voice said, *good afternoon and welcome to the Horman's Horrific Hour*. And then Tweed said—I can't repeat what Tweed said because it included a number of curse words… *you stupid, son of a _____, I knew you were* going *to _____ this up*. And McFee said, *I'm not takin' that from you, Tweed* and they're yelling this. Everyone in the control room thought it was all live to the network—obscenities, everything. And then, of course, as the clock came around to what was the real time, McFee said, *good afternoon and welcome to the Honer Harmonica Hour, with your host…* and they did it, they just… the trouble they took to do that. He did all kinds of things like that.

JH   Stuff like that doesn't happen anymore. We're all so deadly serious, aren't we. Correct.

PG   You think this is on the air, don't you. You don't know why I just set fire to your script. See, they used to do that to each other, too, in the newsroom, set fire to the guy's script as the guy was reading it.

JH   Can't even smoke in the studio, never mind set fire to.

PG   Tell me about it.

JH   Is there another piece of music that you'd like to hear now, Peter?—something again special for you?

PG   I think Murray McLauchlan is a genius. Murray McLauchlan has become a very treasured friend, and people got to know him as a radio host when he was doing *Swinging On A Star*; but I've seen Murray in concert situations as an emcee. They would take him to the north on the Arctic things, and the guy gives so much of himself, and he's a poet as well. Let's play this song, which I saw Murray McLauchlan sing in (among other places) Inuvik, Northwest Territories. And all the kids from the north—the young Inuit and the Dene and the southern kids—knew the words to Murray McLauchlan's *Farmer's Song*. [MUSIC]

JH   You admitted very readily that your verbal style, your oral style is somewhat halting and run-on and so on, and I suppose if you were to hire a radio host, you wouldn't pick yourself in your present style of speech.?

PG   No.

JH   But it works for you, you're comfortable with it. It doesn't matter anymore?

PG   I still don't like it, it frustrates me when I listen to it and I'm very conscious of it when I hear myself on the summer reruns, or sometimes on the *Best of Morningside*—*get to the point!, think what you're going to say before you say it, you idiot!* But, I think what I have been able to do is make thinking aloud be an acceptable part of the radio style, and so I think it draws the listener in, in some way. At least that's what producers tell me. People tease me about it all the time. People think they can do satires of it. I mean, the *Air Farce*—very good—Don Ferguson can do a pretty good me, and other people can write a pretty good me, buy nobody can do me better than I can do me. My style is so close to being a self satire as it begins, that just pushing it over the edge scarcely changes it. You should see… read the first sentence of the fifth and probably last *Morningside Papers,* which takes practically a page-and-a-half, just that one sentence. Well, I did that mostly with my tongue in my cheek 'cause it's me.

JH It's expected. But, if you could hire a speech pathologist to change it, would you?

PG I don't know if it's speech pathology; I think I'd need thought surgery.

JH I want to go on the record, Peter. You brought up *Ninety Minutes Live*, I didn't; but I do want to talk a bit…

PG Did I?

JH Yes, you did. I want to talk a bit about…

PG Then can I un-bring it up?

JH No, because I'm not going to ask you about the bad times on the show; I'm going to ask you to acknowledge it was a very ambitious project and there were some good moments. There were moments with Robin Williams, for example, that were hysterical.

PG Do you remember that, or have people just told you that.

JH Sure I do. No, no.

PG 'Cause it was fabulous.

JH I saw this.

PG Robin Williams was nobody at the time. I mean, it certainly was before *Mork and Mindy* or any of the things he did. And one of the producers had heard of him and brought him up, and I can still remember that night. Who's that little?… he was then a teenage phenom…

JH Rene Simard.

PG Rene Simard, good for you. And he had come on with his record, and Williams came out and picked up the record—it was a gold record or something—and set off on the most maniacal monologue in which the record became a discus and a bishop's hat and a bowling ball and a halo; and it just was that the incredible imagination in that guy was evident there. Yeah, there was that good moment.

JH Margaret Atwood.

PG Standing ovation.

JH There was this aspect of Margaret that we didn't know, a bit of a cartoonist.

PG Margaret… The two longest standing ovations from the studio audiences over those largely uncomfortable two years for me—and they've been worse now in retrospect than they were—were for Margaret Atwood and Maurice Richard. I don't know what that tells us about who our heroes are, but I've often thought, what American novelist would get a standing ovation on Carson or Letterman or whatever, you know.

JH And the moments that are over the top and yet just could be incredibly tragic—when Pierre Berton chopped his finger off in the…

PG No, no, he didn't chop it off.

JH Well, he nearly chopped it off.

PG He tried to chop it off. We were having a cuisinart demonstration, live. And it was spinning around and Pierre, who knows of course… One of the things about Berton is he never lets lack of knowledge or understanding stop him from having a certitude and explanatory attitude. Berton knows more about anything than anybody. He's convinced, and often he's right, but not about how to stop a cuisinart that's spinning. You do not put your finger in, Pierre, to stop the blade. Oh God, that was awful.

JH And the producer had said, everybody, don't pull the top off, leave the thing alone.

PG I think they had, yeah. But I was standing behind Pierre, and as soon as he did it—'cause he's such a trooper, you know, he brought his hand around behind his back with these great, throbbing rivulets of blood dropping, things the size of loonies although there were no loonies at the time, blobbing on the floor behind him. I could see this, so I quickly went to commercial—except we didn't sell very many commercials, but we did have two minutes of black tape to go to, so I did that. And fortunately, the next guest was a doctor, John Tyson from Winnipeg, so he took Pierre and he gave him the equivalent of… he used his thumb as the equivalent of a tourniquet and stopped the bleeding. We rushed him to hospital and he went downtown and got it stitched. But I'll tell you something. I was once at the MacLuhan Institute in Toronto. I was asked to give a little talk about the differences between radio and television and some other portentous things, so I got some examples and I thought I would use that moment. Well, I'll tell you, I don't know what it was like to see it live, but when you know it's coming and you're sitting there and waiting to see it—watch the man amputate his finger (of course, this is now very popular on television). We now have… Have you seen Operation or whatever it's called?

JH   Yes, once.

PG   God, not me. I've seen about 30 seconds of it. But when you know your finger is about to… whoa, don't watch.

JH   Two seasons…

PG   I wanna say John Candy. Because a bright and nice young man who is making a film about John's career, came to talk to me about *Ninety Minutes Live* and had some of the tape clips of John's appearances there—'cause he, too, was brand new. You know, that wonderful, funny expressive face that could make you laugh just by his reaction to the University of Calgary law school gastrointestinal marching band, which was very funny on its own, but funnier because Candy would bring them out, and he was… Or, the day we did The Twelve Days of Christmas, live from Halifax. Chaos in the studio. We actually had five lords 'a leaping and that stuff, prancing in this tiny little studio—but John was there. And so, no, it wasn't all bad. You know, I do tend to dump on it too much. One of the things it did was, it tried. And I think in many ways we cleared some paths that *The Journal* was later to follow. I'm sure we decreased the chance of having a successor; I felt nothing buy sympathy for Ralph Benmergui who while a very different guy with very different ambitions and a very different sense of himself, nevertheless suffered much of what I suffered, including that awful feeling of getting yourself beat up. Because one of the things… if your books are criticized, that's okay; you know, it's, *what do you mean, it's better than that?* Some of my books have been over praised and some have been under praised in my view, and so on. But when somebody really kicks you around on television, it's not your work they're criticizing, it's you, and it's very difficult, very painful to read. And Ralph had to go through some of that.

JH   Your intro to the *Morningside* following the announcement of the Benmergui demise was very touching, and I hope very truly felt. You sympathized with him as only you could, having been through it.

PG   Well, the *Globe and Mail* phoned me. Liam Lacey, who's a good reporter from the Globe, phoned me after Ralph had been cancelled and said, what would you like to say. And I said, oh nothing that isn't predictable. 'Cause the truth is, I thought the show was appalling, I though it was awful; but I certainly wasn't gonna say that on the morning after its cancellation. You know, it was not the time to say that. So I said, you know, we try to do things we're not very good at (it was another interpretation of an American medium). I said a couple of things about stand-up comedy and stuff, and Liam wrote it with his usual affable accuracy, and the next day the lead editorial in the *Globe and Mail* jumped up and down on my head for saying what they thought was my comments about Canadian humour. I'm taking lessons in Canadian humour from a newspaper that puts your morning smile on the front page? It was the most outrageous thing. This is a country that gave us Stephen Leacock.

JH   I want to hear another piece of music, Peter. What shall we hear next?

PG   Well, we've got my song cued up. Shall we do that?

JH   Ian and Sylvia and Peter Gzowski.

PG   Pete.

JH   Oh.

PG   That's what it says on the recording: Pete.

JH   Now, the opening lyric isn't a *Song for Canada*, so you have to announce the title, which I just did.

PG   Can I introduce my song here?

JH   You better, this is your job.

PG   No it's not, I'm the guest.

JH   No, the guest introduces the song.

PG   Does he?

JH   Yeah.

PG   Alright. This was in 1964. Ian Tyson, whom I had become friends with because I'd known Sylvia when she was in Chatham, Ontario, the daughter of the choir mistress, Sylvia Fricker; and Ian said, *should we write a song together?* And I said, sure, 'cause at that time he had more melodies he said than he had lyrics. Ah, he's a wonderful writer now. And I said, sure, so he played me this melody. And of course I can't carry a tune in a bucket, so I wrote nonsense words to it and memorized the nonsense words and went home and wrote the parallel to that. There was a song that was deeply felt about the way the country was going at the time, 1964, and as corny as it is, I think the lyrics to this song still apply, although it's almost never heard. When that song was made it was revealed to the world, it was Ian and Sylvia's first concert at Massey Hall in Toronto, a major moment in their lives. They were still not at the peak of the way they were to become. Ian and Sylvia, God they were wonderful, and still are. And toward the end, right near the honoured spot of all at the end of the concert, Ian came up and in that, you know—this is a guy who grew up in Vancouver and has the best Oklahoma accent— and he said, *and now here's a song that my friend, Pete Gzowski and I wrote together*. And I was sitting in the audience. And then… so they played what we just heard, and then we heard, *how come we can't talk to each other anymore*, and because my name had been there, or something, people thought it was funny. Now, there is no fate worse than exposing yourself in a serious, if somewhat sentimental vein, and then have people snicker. Oh, it was awful, I wanted to crawl under my seat. Didn't go to the post concert party. And the song didn't last very long, although still, when I go around the country I will find occasional people who are touched by it. It's not a bad song, eh?

JH I think it's just a fine song and I'm glad we unearthed it.

PG I feel it will get earthed again fairly soon, but it was nice to have it stick its little head up above, under the mountain top—for a moment on Mountaintop music—my song. Ian and Sylvia, with a song co-written by Ian Tyson and his friend, Pete Gzowski, *Song for Canada*. [MUSIC]

JH I don't know where to begin with all the people that you've interviewed in your 13 years with Morningside, but can I throw some names out and you tell me what comes to mind: Eric Kierans, Kierans, Camp and Lewis.

PG Oh, unbelievable. I mean, it was the highlight of my week, every Tuesday morning. I remember somebody asking a friend of mine why Gzowski worked so hard, and he saying, well, wouldn't you?—it's not work to go in and say good morning Dalton, Eric and Stephen, and then just enjoy their company. There were so many qualities about the three of them that we've never been able to match. One is genuine affection for each other and respect, and a sense of conversation as opposed to debate or interview—they would actually listen to what one another said. And Eric Kierans is a font of wisdom. Eric would go into the most convoluted answers— and usually Stephen would be with me, Dalt would be in Fredericton, Eric in Halifax—and he could practically, you know, see our eyes rolling. And I would ask him something, he'd say, well, and he'd go off. But it always came back to the point and he always had something fresh and interesting and wise to say. It's still missed by me and many other listeners. It's largely gone through matters of health and age and difficulty in doing it regularly. But I miss them and it was an honour to be among them.

JH Pierre Trudeau, the last interview with whom won you an ACTRA award.

PG Did it?

JH Yeah.

PG Remember ACTRA awards?—we don't have those anymore.

JH Not personally, no.

PG Well, they should have given it to Mr. Trudeau 'cause there was… I loved interviewing Pierre Trudeau. He's so smart, he's so smart. I don't know if that was the last one or not. There was one I went down to Montreal and into the room at the Ritz-Carlton and I just sat down and the tape was rolling. And he just started quoting T. S. Eliot, off the top—I hadn't asked him a question or anything—he started with the T. S. Eliot, and I can't remember the exact quotation, not being as scholarly as… Imagine having a prime minister who could quote T. S. Eliot.

I mean, the people who followed him, don't, or haven't been able to. Look, I mean, I disagree profoundly with many of the things that he wanted to do to this country, and some that he did—and not just to curry favour when I'm in Alberta about the NEP or other things—I think he had a wrong vision, and I think a misunderstood vision about a bilingual nation and so on. But what a towering intellect. And his interview alone, oh, it was just so much fun. It was like playing chess, you know. You had to be one step ahead of him. Surely the most intimidating ski hills at Banff are the most exhilarating. And when you skied Mount Trudeau you were at the edge of control. He got mad at me once. I'm not letting you get through your whole list; I'm a terrible interview, aren't I?

JH   I never know when you're finished.

PG   "I" never know when I'm finished. You can say shut-up if you want. Do you want to hear when Trudeau got mad at me, or not?

JH   No, I want to ask you about Joni Mitchell.

PG   She smoked in the studio.

JH   Along with you.

PG   No. I haven't smoked… I did… I haven't smoked in the studio since they made it against the law, except during the Gulf War, when in order to do three hours we had to be for the seven hours. So I lit up when I was doing live Gulf War stuff, and who should walk into the control room but the vice-president of radio. It was the first time she'd ever been there, it was the first and only time I ever smoked, and she walks in and, *does he smoke in there?* I said, yeah, if I'm here for seven hours, I smoke. Well, so what.

JH   Well, speaking of getting in heck and people getting mad, everybody in the control room is mad at me because I haven't, in fact, let you tell me why Pierre Trudeau got mad at you. So would you please?

PG   Look, you and I are in control. The producers give the orders and tell you what to do, and you say, yes sir, yes ma'am; but when you're out here, you do what you want to do. Because I said to him, did it ever occur to you that if the War Measures Act had been imposed when you were the young lawyer that I wrote about in Montreal in the early 1960s, that you would have gone to jail. And you know what he said: *Yes, I would, but I wouldn't have bitched about it.* What a guy.

JH   Lastly, Northrop Frye. And you mentioned in your *Peter Gzowski The Private Voice* that he was tough. You were intimidated a bit there, too. I mean, who wouldn't be.

PG   What do you say to Northrop Frye? Northrop Frye had no small talk. I mean, what do you say to him?—read any good books lately?—the world's foremost biblical Blake and Shakespeare scholar, you know. I, with an old B.A., a guy… My last university English teacher said, I don't know what you're going to do with your life, but it should have nothing to do with the written word. I'm interviewing Northrop Frye.

JH   And all this flashes in front of you as you sit down.

PG   Well, we pre-taped him, 'cause he was painfully shy. Shy and unassuming. And honest. And I worked so hard getting ready for that interview… oh! And I would get these really scholarly, incisive questions about the underlying meaning of MacBeth in his biblical overtones, and he would finish, then he'd say, *yes*—that would be his answer.

JH   And then, after all that work, really, what does a listener want to know? I mean, what do you read in your spare time, Northrop.

PG   Norrie. I think his friends actually call him… He was a lovely, lovely man. Then, I went to stop the interview because I'd broken into a fit of uncontrollable coughing, and when I was finished and I waved everything to a stop, and then this sweet man looked up at me and he said, *sorry*. He was sorry that I'd screwed up.

JH   The ultimate Canadian intellect.

PG   Yeah.

JH   Something very dear to your heart I want to touch on now, Peter. The golf tournaments, the Peter Gzowski golf tournaments, that you vowed in the beginning in '86 to raise a million dollars for, and which have exceeded three million dollars. But I wanted to ask you why that's become so important to you?

PG   I don't know. Literacy has become important to me, that's what I didn't understand at the beginning. It's almost serendipitous that I fell into the cause of literacy. I had the original tournaments just to get some friends together, and realized if I soaked them a few bucks we could make a few dollars, and looked around for a place to put it. We made $18,000. And the people from the literacy movement, which was not on the public agenda at the time at all, had been coming to me. And I felt sympathetic to it for a number of reasons: my own mother's early days as a librarian, my own joy in books, my sense of what would a world be like if, God forbid, I couldn't read. I had an emotional sympathy for it, but no understanding of it at all. And as I began... But I thought, well, we'll give the $18,000 bucks to Frontier College in Toronto. I don't do them all anymore 'cause it's too much for me. I've been playing more golf tournaments than Fred Couples, and Fred and I don't play in the same league. So I stepped back about it... and I wish it had made more of a difference, you know. We have raised three-and-a-half million bucks or something, but there's still five million Canadians who have problems reading. And it's going to get worse, 'cause the more the age of technology comes upon us, the greater the need for literacy and retraining, and we're gradually waking up to that. We need much more than some golf tournaments, but I think they may have raised some awareness.

JH Well, you've seen the money put to work, haven't you?

PG Oh, I've seen people learn to... I've been really moved by individual stories—and there are hundreds of them, thousands of them—of people whose lives have been turned around. And I've seen equipment put into places and I've seen courses and I've seen people line up to become tutors. But the problem isn't going away.

JH Has your literacy in golf improved any?

PG I'm a terrible golfer and I'm getting worse with each passing year. It's awful. We play this marvelous game in the tournaments called a scramble, where everybody's even, but I'm no... I won a tournament, in Calgary.

JH You did? Which one?

PG The PGI, the Peter Gzowski Invitational 1993, you're looking at one of the first place team people.

JH You're talking aggregate score here?

PG No, we're talking the best score, best thing—and what they did was, they put together this conspiracy. You could buy me to play in your foursome, and some people bought me. But it wasn't so much that they bought the best golfer, they bought an extra shot on every hole. So we had five shots at everything, everybody else only had four shots. And you know who can hit the ball forever?—Harve Andre. He hits the golf ball about 325 yards, he's amazing.

JH He probably has that technique where you picture a face on the ball, you know.

PG He thinks it's a liberal.

JH Exactly.

PG Yes. So he was on with me and we won.

JH Do you see *Morningside* carrying on? I mean, every season you have to sort of punch and pull yourself back to it after your summer break, or so you have written. Do you still feel you've got that reserve to get yourself back on air every fall and go some more seasons?

PG I sound to me good on the air this fall, which surprises me, because I wanted more summer when I came back. The unit itself has gone through some changes, which often means a slightly added burden for me as I work with new producers again. There's almost no one on the program who was there when I started, just as there's no Premier who was there when I started or no, you know—I've outlasted a lot of people. There are two conflicting forces in my life: one is the gravitational pull of age (I am 60, as we have discussed at length) and 3:15 in the morning (when I get up) gets earlier every year. And I won't do it if I'm coasting, I won't fake it. That's the one thing, when I know that I'm faking it I'll be gone, and I hope no one will have to tell me. But I don't know how to face the day when I can't go out, go down there and look at that mail and press the little red button and meet the next L.A. Daneka or Carl Johanssen or Donna Williams or John Polanyi or Pierre Trudeau—you know, every time I think I've interviewed everybody, somebody else comes along.

JH Not necessarily a big name either.

PG No, no.

JH The most surprising Canadians.

PG Oh no. I mean, occasionally you'll get surprises like Donald Sutherland, who I thought was aloof. I had some problems with Donald Sutherland in my television days; I think I stupidly asked him about the women in his life or something, that's what you do on television. But when he came on, he came for 20 minutes and we spent an hour; he was anecdotal and warm and funny and I could have gone forever, that was a delight. But more often the surprise comes from Linda Crabtree, who was a woman who got an honorary degree from Brock University because of her work in doing a newsletter for—I hope I get it right—the Charlotte Marie Tooth Disease (CMT). It's not the tooth disease, it was Dr. Tooth, and she's very debilitated. A story of triumph over physical handicap. She's funny and rich and sexy and good. So there's always another Linda Crabtree.

JH Let's take a break for a piece of music, Peter. What shall we hear next?

PG Let's play... well, let's play Tracy Dahl, 'cause this is another undiscovered gem. There's so many musicians in this country who I've had the pleasure of discovering, not only for their musical ability, but for their joyousness and persons, and Tracy is one of them. [MUSIC]

JH Before we send you off to your mountain top, we let you take one book with you, just one. And if you could only take one, what would it be?

PG Couldn't do it. I have all the same cliché answers as everybody—the works of Shakespeare, the Bible, the books that have been most meaningful in my life—anywhere from *Who Has Seen the Wind* to Catcher in the Rye to Alice Munro's *Open Secrets* to the writings of A. J. Liebling, to almost anything. But the thought of life with one book is beyond my imagination. I mean, I couldn't... I have the attention span of a gnat; I need to have Jane Austen on one side of my bed—the book that is—and Alice Munro on the other, and a paperback about Kinsey Mahone's latest crime adventures, and the memoirs of Scott Young and Joan Baxter's life. They have to be all over the house and I have to be able to pick them up one at a time and dip into them. I only have one characteristic for my book, if you're really gonna make me take only one book. It might be, *Who Has Seen the Wind* just because there's so much of us and my own... I have so many memories of Mitchell and of that landscape. But no, 'cause see, I don't want to read a book whose author I have to interview the next day, 'cause I'm sure that if you put me on a mountain top with one book and I spent three hours reading it, that on the very next occasion Catherine Mansfield would come up on a ladder and say, well I'm here for my interview, Mr. Gzowski.

JH You also have a choice in where you spend the last of your days. It could be on Lake Simcoe, it could be on the prairies—anywhere you like. Where do you want to go?

PG On Lake Simcoe, on the prairies, Cape Breton. Lake Simcoe then. If I really only have one, but...

JH Here we go again.

PG What?

JH Well, you can't narrow it down. But try. This is an imaginary exercise.

PG I just narrowed it down for God's sake. Lake Simcoe I said.

JH On the prairies, you said.

PG No, I said, I said...

JH You said Lake Simcoe on the prairies...

PG Well yeah, I know I said Cape Breton and everything, but I agreed to do one place and I said Lake Simcoe. I'll tell you why, although I have a much better story about once running a contest for a newspaper column that I wrote about how would you spend tomorrow if it were the last day of your life. Can I tell you that story?

JH Sure.

PG I was writing a column for the Daily Star and I thought, Toronto. And I thought, as with *This Country in the Morning*, which I was undergraduate of, I can get the readers to write my columns for me. So write me letters about how you would spend... And I got a lot of really good letters, but the one that struck my heart strings was from a young woman who had put together a very appealing and joyous and imaginative list of things: riding the roller coaster at the exhibition gounds, going to the Mars café in Toronto for a bran muffin, dancing and jitterbugging with her brother in the living room—it was very sweet. And I called her to say, you've won the prize (which the prize was to actually do all the things you wanted to do)—I'd arranged that, got Jimmy Conklin to open his roller coaster and stuff. And she couldn't hear me 'cause—her name is Rhonda Tupper and she's become a friend I treasure, and she's got about two percent hearing. But she's learned to play the piano, she's married a neurosurgeon, they're living in Montreal. She went to Paris to live so that she could lip read in her second language. She's got two university degrees, she's teaching people. I spoke at her wedding—I was honoured to speak at her wedding—but she made me get my moustache trimmed because she said when your moustache is too long I can't hear you. And Rhonda became a very important part of my life just because of… And the other thing is, it's a friendship that survived with someone who can't hear me on the radio. So, Lake Simcoe, that's where I'd go for my home.

JH And the music to play as you head off to your cottage?

PG Well, this is a song that speaks for me. This is Leonard Cohen, who's exactly my age. I have a tape of Leonard Cohen and me at one point saying together: *I was born like this, I had no choice, born with the gift of a golden voice*. This is the greatest song every written: Leonard Cohen, *Tower of Song*.

JH Before we go to that song in…

PG I just gave it a perfect intro and now you're doing this thing.

JH Well, I have to say goodbye, but before I do I have to anticipate that line, you two of the same age: *I ache in all the places where I used to play*.

PG That's right. So you realize the wisdom of this song.

JH Exactly. Thank you for being my guest on Mountaintop Music, Peter. It's been a pleasure.

PG I've had a really good time, Judy, thank you. Very self-indulgent.

AM Have you picked up your guitar yet this morning.

OL Ah, to be very honest with you, not yet.

AM Too early.

OL Yeah. And sometimes I do pick up early, but I haven't done it yet. But I will when I get back home. You know, it's my baby, and it fill my soul and give me all this wonderful feelings to be able to express myself. So, it's part of me and, I don't know, I'm part of her.

AM So it would be like asking you not to speak if you didn't play your guitar every day?

OL In a way I would say, without being too cliché here. But, I mean, I've been doing it since I was 10 years old. Not obviously with the same guitar because they break very easily, but with that instrument, so it's part of my life—completely part of my life.

AM Well, let's go back to your childhood. You grew up in Santiago, Chile. Was your family musical?

OL Yes. Not professionally, but very inclined to all these instruments—guitars, harps, accordions. I remember when I was about 10 we used to go to a church, a Pentecostal church, and my father was kind of the musical director of a little group in Santiago. And we did have our own personal group, like all my family—my sisters, my father, my mother, myself—and we used to play in churches. And we was kind of the attraction there.

AM And what did you play?

OL You won't believe this, but I played violin. That was my first instrument and I was playing that instrument actually in this little group and my father used to be the big boss.

AM Now, was that your choice or did mom and dad say we need a violinist?

OL No, no, no, it was my choice. The reason it was my choice was because I really loved the sound. And one of these Sunday morning church, we went, but it's a little man playing this instrument and I really like it a lot. And I ask my father at the time, I said, I wish some day I could have one. Well, he surprise me. He did bought one for me and he actually bought this man's instrument, I mean violin. He

OSCAR LOPEZ
WITH ANDREA MARANTZ, 1997

bought it from him. I don't know how he did it.

AM The very one.

OL The very one that I like. And he bought it from him and I play it.

AM Right. Do you still play at all?

OL Once in awhile I do, yes, when I get, you know, to do concerts sometimes… other musicians and they have a violin, I say, can I play a little bit. *Sure.* But, for that instrument you need a lot of practice because it's such a sweet and a precise instrument, you know. You have to watch out where you put your fingers or you will sound totally out of it.

AM Now, we think of Chile as being a Catholic country, primarily a Catholic country. How did your family end up in the Pentecostal church?

OL The way I ended up in there, my father ended up in there—from what they told me, the stories they tell me, and I believe it. My father got sick. All the doctors told him that he didn't have long to live.

Well, they told me that one time he just wake up in the morning and heard the evangelists outside—because that's the way they do it there, they go in the street and play instruments and preach and all this stuff. He say if the God of the evangelists cure him, he will go the rest of his life with that particular religion. Anyway, that night he think he fall asleep and he saw Jesus come and operate on him, and told him he would give him 10 years to live, to raise his children and everything else. The next day he wake up, he start feeling better, much better. And that's the story. And then after, I think it was about 10 years—a little longer than 10 years—he died.

AM And you were just a little boy?

OL Just a little boy, yes. And now I tell you it will sound a little bit of fantasy story, but I'm not sure, but I do believe in that. Call my crazy, but I do believe in that. I believe in what my father and my mother used to tell me, because a lot of miracles happen if you believe. And I'm not trying to be an angel here, but I kind of believe in that and that's the way he came to the Pentecostal church.

AM So, is that sort of spirituality important to you?

OL It is very important, and I left it for many, many, many, many years. I went off that because I became more rebellious. At the time, you have to remember, I was a little boy and I used to go to church just because my father used to take me. I mean, I had no choices. If I didn't went I get a spank in my behind. So I went to church because he took me, like it or not. But I did have a great time. Somehow they put that feeling in my heart, in my soul. Still now I remember all that and it's really very important in my life because, I mean, somehow I believe that God is helping me through my career, through my life. Even if sometime I don't deserve it, but he is with me, I know he is with me, and once in awhile every Sunday—and to tell you this, it is new—but I go to service still in the morning, you know. And something make me feel good. And I don't know if it's coming back to when my father used to take me to church and I go back in history, and I feel like I need that. It's a necessity sometimes the human need; we don't know what it is and we're trying to discover that, you know. But I born, spiritually, I born in that Pentecostal church, and maybe I need that sometimes.

AM When did you turn to the guitar?

OL I was 10 when I got the violin, and I kind of really feel uncomfortable with that instrument. And then I pick up the little mandolin, and that really help me to develop, to be fast with my fingers. But the real instrument, when I discover my real instrument, was when I pick up the guitar at that early age. I do have a very good friend of mine, he is still back in Chile—his name is Miguel—we grew up together. Well, I can tell you we play every single day. We play for five, six hours of playing, playing, playing, playing.

AM So, it was Miguel's guitar?

OL No, it was my guitar. My father—I used to borrow his guitar—took it and go to his apartment, and we close the door in his room and we just play for hours. And he became my musical partner for a very long time, and we even made an album together in 1973. He was the guitar player and I was the bass player believe it or not. That was how the guitar became my friend. So I've been doing it—and now I'm 43 years old and I've been doing it since then.

AM Do you remember your very first guitar that was yours.?

OL Oh boy, that's a really good question. I don't remember my first guitar. I don't know how I got it… boy, that's a very good question. If I remember I promise that I will call you and let you know.

AM But I'm sure you remember your first recording?

OL Yes, yes, obviously I do remember that because Miguel, he had this connection with these couple of guys, one was from England and the other guy was from England, too. Fernan and Bert both was from England, except Fernando was more Chilean than anything else. So Miguel, I don't know how he did it, but we ended up in this basement with the drummer—very rich people, have everything in the basement, all you can imagine instrument wise. So we start practicing and these two real songs, so all of a sudden we got this record man. He came to our place, I don't know how he got there; but he got to our place and he listened to our practice and say, I want you guys tomorrow morning at ten o'clock in the studio. That's my first, actually one of my first professional experience, in the studio. I didn't know nothing about it, I have no idea what this thing you put on your heads are for. So we did it, we record two songs actually, and believe it or not it was three time actually we were first in the ranking in Chile, playing on the radio. And nobody knew who this group was, nobody knew nothing about us.

AM And it was just the two of you?

OL No, five of us—the drums, rhythm, guitar player (myself), the bass player (Miguel) and the singer. So, the thing is… the funny thing when we went to the beach and walking around—there's a lot of people and it's a great place to be—and I was walking and I listen to our song on the radio. So I stop and I kind of went to ask these ladies and teenagers in the car; I say, what is the name of that group? *I think it called Grace of the King*—because we used to call ourselves in English and the song was in English actually, I didn't have no idea what he was saying because this song was all in English. So I say, who are this group? They say to me, well this is *Grace of the King*. And I ask her, do you know where they're from—and we all kind of want to know if they knew who we was, you know, because we know absolutely nothing. So I said, no, I think they're from England. And I said to her, do you believe I tell you this is ours. *Sure, get out of here*—you know? Nobody believe, really honest to God, and the thing is, the neighbours, even the neighbours, was going and knock on my mama's door and say, is Oscarlito (they used to call me Oscarlito) home? Because they are mention on the radio, if anybody get in contact from this group—they know they are from Chile—please to contact them and tell them to come to the radio station; we need to interview them because this is something big that's going on with this group. And nobody know nothing. We did absolutely nothing. And sometimes, you know, sometimes I ask myself if I knew what I know now at the time, we could have lots of money right now to tell you the truth. Because we didn't get money at all whatsoever.

AM Why didn't you? Why didn't you want to sort of persue it?

OL I was not interested in that. We used to do it together within the community, you know. I mean, these people they have lots of money. I mean, the lead singer, his father he was in the government, and so the place where we practice they have swimming pool, they have everything, you know, about ten rooms. And we stayed there, we swim, we just… I mean, it was unbelievable. It was no really interesting for me to go after the money, but I should. Nobody really did; we all kind of went like birds fly, you know. We just enjoyed…

AM How old were you?

OL I think I was about 17, yeah. So, you know, at that age it just was, yeah, let's do it, have fun, you know.

AM There's no 16-year-old business men, thank goodness.

OL I should have been, I should have been, because that's my nature. I mean, I like to put my hands in those things, you know. But at the time I just was blown away just to do the recording. And I don't know if I would ever make money with that guy who make us record, but I still have the contract and I still have the 45. Actually, my sister has my 45 because she doesn't want me to touch it because she say I gonna break it. So she actually is protecting it for me.

AM Let's have your first piece of music.

OL Sure, it's a song that I love from the Gypsy Kings, and I know sometimes get sick and crazy, I mean, to listen to Gypsy Kings, but this song has a particular beautiful melody called *Guitarra Negra*. It's an instrumental and I really hope the people out there enjoy it. [MUSIC]

AM You have had many different jobs including selling carpets?

OL How you know that?—it's supposed to be a secret.

AM But you also played your guitar while you were selling carpets.

OL Well, yes I did. You know what, I was actually working for this gentleman. We used to live on the fourth floor in the building where I used to live back in Chile, Santiago. And I was needing a job because I used to do music part-time, I never did it full-time. So he offer me to be his helper selling carpet, you know, so I was working for him and eventually ended up working for the company; but I still was working for him, he was my boss. So, because him and I was one of the best sellers, and I mean we got the top of the sellers of all the people, you know, we are number one. They send us to this trip to go to the entire north of Chile to sell carpet, I mean door to door. So we went on this big, big bus. We both was driving, and we got there and I started selling, and you know sometimes you got one of those days, they are very good, and one of those days that you don't feel like doing it. So I don't want to get that door stuck in my face again, you know, or slapped in my face again; and I always remember, every time I got the chance, the opportunity to see a guitar—because I went to many, many, many houses—and sometimes these houses, they treat me really good. I say, I'm representing "Carpet Winners"—a big name in Chile, it's no longer there—but this was a humungus, very good reputation. And people know that and sometimes say, oh, come in. So I got in and talk about, you know, show them the carpet if they need a carpet, and well, I have to ask my husband. I say, well I can leave it here if you don't mind and you can ask your husband and show it to him, and if he likes it, you know, call me. So I give him my name and next day they call me and say, yeah, he likes it. So I go back, get the money, or whatever he's going to buy; and sometimes they have this guitar and there was a husband and wife in there, and usually the husband is the one—we are the ones usually to say, what are you doing, what do you want to buy that for, we don't need it, you know. And women, typical, you like things, and for a good reason because they want the house to look good. But I had a really good talk, I was very good in that, and I still am, but I don't sell carpets anymore. But sometimes they had this guitar in there and I say to them, can I try it? *Do you play guitar?* I say, a little bit—can I try? So I pick up the guitar, sit down, try to break the ice, you know, and people get more comfortable—we all get more comfortable, ended up with a cup of tea, cup of coffee, whatever, and just playing the guitar. And believe it or not, just because of that I sold a lot of carpets—just playing the guitar.

AM And then you came to Canada, to Winnipeg in 1979.

OL My goodness, yes, in 1979 I arrived to Toronto for a little while and I came to Winnipeg—'Winterpeg' what they call it.

AM Yes, quite a change from Chile.

OL Quite a change, but in the beginning, you know, it was such an excitement. And I came in October.

AM Why did you come to Canada?

OL Why? Ah… my sister was living here and I follow her. And I think I wanted to move up in my musical career, I wanted to be able to experiment with different styles. Learn. I hear so much about North America back in Chile—you know, groups like Led Zeppelin, Grand Funk, Ten Years After, and all these—very popular there, and Canadian musicians. And I wanted to be able to be here and learn things. So, that's the reason, major reason why I came here. And believe me, when I made that decision, I got here, I was not sorry at all. Except, the first couple of years it was very hard on me getting used to the new society, the new language—it was very hard.

AM And you were still playing music, though?

OL Well, when I got here in the beginning I had to do other things. I was working in a body shop, I mean working on cars and things like that. And thank God for that. That's why… it's weird how God prepares things for you, God prepares things for you, you know. It's weird, because I was working in that—and I always remember this—the owner was a little man, his name is Henry. And I was working there and doing my job, but I was not really into it. So somehow he find out that I was a guitar player. To make a long story very short, he actually one time call me to his office. He say, you know, I been seeing you working here and you're not totally into this, and I just want to let you know that you're fired. And I say, Henry, you know that I need a job, I need to work, I need to make some money, I need to survive. (Henry: *Tonight we're going for dinner to my place.*) And he kind of confused me because, *we're going to dinner to my place.* Okay, I say. He was a wonderful man. He took me to his place, he have about five guitars in his room. We had dinner, we got to play the guitar. He asked me if I play, I say, I play a little bit. So he start playing this Portuguese music. And I'm good in improvisation and stuff like that, so I start really… I just let it go, I start improvising. He just with his mouth open, he say, *Jesus Christ, man you are fantastic.* Anyway, a couple of days later I was still working for him. I say, just give me a week. *Oh, no no, don't worry,* he say. *But you, I don't want you to work here anymore.* This guy came, I saw him go into the office. That was a guy with a band, a rock 'n roll band; he was needing a lead guitar player so he actually came and talked to me. But I didn't speak English very well, so anyway I ended up playing with these guys. And I ended up, you know, making really good money, and…

AM So this guy just knew that this wasn't the place for you, that you were not going to be happy?

OL No, he knew. He knew. That's why I love him so much. We never really… You know, when I got back to Winnipeg, I went to do a concert there about a year, maybe two years ago in a folk club. It was a beautiful place, it was packed. And I was doing my performances and half… the second show, actually second show they call me—I was in my dressing room—they say, there's a little gentleman who wants to see you outside. So I went outside and there was my ex-boss. I give him a humungus hug—we talk, we cry. So he came and was sitting in first row. And I had to tell the story to the people how my career start, and I couldn't help him, but I make him stand up and he start crying. And I'm very emotional and I start crying too. And I say, I'm sorry that I'm doing this, but this is the man who put me in my music. And it was the most beautiful moment.

AM And sometimes we need that, just that little shove.

OL Yes. And he was… I mean, he is very important in what I'm doing right now. I mean, just a little man say to me, *you fired, I want you to play guitar, I want you to play music, I want you to be up there.*

AM Let's have another piece of music. What would you like to listen to now?

OL Well, it's a song you know, I guess it's a classic, and it's a traditional thing—you guys probably already know for a long time it's been around. And I used to play this song, believe it or not, in my own style, and I really, really like this song even though it's been done many times. But who cares. It's called *Classical Gas.*

AM What is it about this one?

OL Just instrumentation. Just the melody, the melody line and it just get to you, it get to me. I mean, like I say, it's been done many times, but when a song has a power to stay with you in your mind, you know, it's something else. So this song has been around and I love it, it just feels good.
[MUSIC]

AM So, the band that you started playing in, you were playing rock 'n roll'.

OL What we just play was, you know, middle of the road country music, calypso, reggae, rock 'n roll—no heavy metal. I mean, you know, I remember when we play, they always screamed, they say ACDC! And I didn't know what the hell was that. You know, I say, what? We just let it go, but this one time I ask the drummer, I say, what is ACDC? Why they want to hear..? What the heck is it? *It's a heavy metal rock band, they want us to play a song, but we don't play that music.* This is a funny thing. Now I watch them on TV and you know what, I don't mind those guys…

It's different… You know, I'm not great musician, and we're talkin' about probably what?—50 years old now. I mean, 45, 50, how old do you think they are? And I always take my hat off to people like that—like *Rolling Stones*—I mean, people who have been around for generations, you know. They transport their music to different generation, and I always respect that. If you can keep that, that means you have been doing all your life something unbelievably good and you are a great musician, to be able to do that. Not many people can do that, you know.

AM So, you were learning English through all this?

OL Through all this process, definitely. It's entirely a process. And one of the good thing I did have on my side actually, I was never afraid to speak my mind or to try to tell people or to ask, what did that mean, what did this mean? We tend to be embarrassed sometime—especially myself when I ask for a package of cigarette and they understand, but they didn't understand the kind that I want to smoke. So, when they say, *pardon me?*—that really screwed me up. They say, *pardon me?*—and what am I supposed to say after that? You know, I didn't know what that mean, so I kind of have a hard time. And I know sometime they was pulling my leg, so I learned the bad words in English. That's the first thing you learn sometimes, to protect yourself. And actually I learn it and when I knew they was giving me a hard time I just went and say, you, you know, you go to—whatever.

AM Did you want to go home?

OL I wanted so bad to go home. I really want to get out of here. I just say, what am I doing? Okay, I'm here for a reason and I'm here because I want to learn, I want to play music and I want to have these new experiences; but in the meantime I was suffering with the nostalgia and the sadness, and all these things they attack you when you are in a depressed moment. Get up six o'clock in the morning, go to work, come home, watch TV, go to work, come home, watch TV, go to work—totally depressing. And I wanted to go home. My sister, my oldest sister, stepped forward and she just grabbed me and she say, you gonna stay here, you gonna go through this, you gonna be okay—listen to me. And then she just slapped me, like—no physically—but she slapped me, she just moved me. And she was very, very, very important—a very important part of my life in Canada. Without her I think I probably could… maybe without her I would go back already. But she made me stay here and it was a wonderful thing, you know.

AM Somebody that could just sort of have that faith in you when you didn't have it in yourself.

OL Yeah, exactly. Because I was lost; I mean, I was totally and completely lost. I mean, I say what am I doing here. You know, I used to cry a lot because I say, you know, okay I came here, but what for? What am I doing?—I don't speak the language, how am I gonna… Things start changing completely. That's why I say to you, I mean, how I can… I can't leave my guitar away because things change completely when I start playing music. My life completely change, just went 90 degrees, you know. I start meeting friends, I start speaking the language a little bit better, I start understand what they was trying to say to me, I express with my music, I have fans. The first time I ever sang , I have fans come just to listen to this group because it was a Latino playing rock 'n roll with Latin roots, you know. So it was… my life change completely right there, in Canada.

AM Oscar, let's have another piece of music. What shall we play?

OL Hey, *Concierto de Aranjuez*.

AM Oh, that's a beauty.

OL It's beautiful music, it's so powerful and so strong, I like the orchestration. It's another song… I mean melody, it's been around the world, and, like I say, it's a wonderful piece. And I even play this song, too.

AM Do you?

OL They have it in my repertoire when I was playing in a restaurant and things like that. I'm not sure if I should say that, but I was playing in a restaurant and this song was in my repertoire.

AM Wouldn't it be fun to play it with an orchestra?

OL Oh God. I tell you something, it will happen. It will happen because that's one of my dreams. I have many dreams, but that's one of my dreams. It will be great to be able to play with symphony, with orchestra, you know. You have all these great musicians backing you up. [MUSIC]

AM So, from Winnipeg to Calgary, what brought you here?

OL Well, there we go again. Follow my sister. I was in Winnipeg and doing very well actually, but she move away and we're a very close family. And I wanted to… I hear a lot about Calgary and I think, well, this is time that I need a change. I was playing so much in bands and electric guitar and things like that, that I say to myself, maybe there it will be different. And always seem like when you go to a new place it's always hard in the beginning. But I made my choice to come here and this be my home for about 15 years.

AM   And this is where you really started playing the music that's the closest to your heart?

OL   Calgary is the place that I really got my nylon string guitar. It's the closest to my heart. Exactly what you say, the instrument that I feel like, to me, without offending anybody, is the real sound of the guitar, the sound that you play and the sound that comes out. And here, when I start doing that, and I used to play in a lot of bars and restaurants around Calgary. I'd play in there and I'd have a friend of mine backing me up, Manuel used to play with me—a wonderful guy, a wonderful guitarist—and I made a decision to go and try and play in restaurants and things like that. So that was my first step, and it was the right one. And slowly we started getting a lot of followers and the restaurant was packed. Every time more people and more people, they are going to see this guy who plays Latin music (they're good). And one of those moments Les Siemieniuk show up in one of the restaurants, from CBC.

AM   Our music producer.

OL   Your music producer show up in one of those places, and from there things change too, you see. It's always been a process of life, a musical process. If you continue and you're strong at it and you're very good at it and you keep going and never give up, things are getting better.

And I remember that time… I think I do pay my dues a lot because I play a lot in restaurants. And it was a beautiful thing because I got to build a wonderful audience. And from that moment—and I'm going to mention this because it's such an important step—from that moment that I start playing to the moment with the concert with my brother, my brother James Keelaghan in Jack Singer Hall, I say to myself, boy, it's a long way from there, you know.

AM   Tell me, tell me about meeting James. When did you meet him?

OL   We met actually about five years ago. We keep saying that every time, five years, yes. We met actually about 35,000 feet in the air. We was going to this festival in Sudbury, Ontario—Northern Light Festival—and we met in the air. And he kind of look at me and I look at him and we just, we connect.

AM   Did you know who he was?

OL   Oh yes, you know why?

AM   Because he'd been playing around, too.

OL   Well, the thing is, one time I went to a place—and I don't know if you remember this place, used to call Monty's Restaurant, it was on 17th Avenue—and I went one time there because that's one of the first place I ever played, actually. On Sunday morning they have this performance and that's one of the place that I would play. My first place. And I went, but I went at night this time, and they have this music going on—great place to be, you know, coffee and all the stuff and having a good time. And there was this guy, you know, to my left, about 10 people from me, with glasses on, and all these people surrounding him and talking to him and quack quack quack quack. So I said to one of the persons, who the heck is that? *Ah, that's James Keelaghan.* Who is James Keelaghan? *Oh, he's a very popular folk singer, he's very famous in Calgary, he's very… you know.* Oh, really. Hmmm. But he's ugly, I say.

AM   Nice guy.

OL   Who will know now we're the best friends in the world, we are brothers, you know. But I was just joking, I mean.

AM   Sure. So here you are at 35,000 feet.

OL   Here we are going to that festival, and then we start playing music together. We met in there and we start playing, and from that moment on we say, well, we have something going here, let's keep going. And now here we are, came back from the studio and we've recorded our first album together, and we are very good pals. We've been travelling together everywhere, most of the places.

AM   Now you've been playing, before you got together with James—well, you still do—you play on your own a lot. You have your solo career.

OL   Oh yes, yes.

AM   What's the differences between playing on your own and playing with somebody like James where it really works?

OL   Playing on your own, it's not like you have to work double. But playing on your own you are by yourself up there, okay. Nobody's helping you out, so it's a good thing to make you stronger and to be able to work your show much better. And it was very scary for me to be very honest to you, and it still is scary.

AM   To get out on stage as such.

OL   Yeah. No scary in a bad way, it's scary in a good way because it made the tiger come out, you know. Come on, do it. And I always claim to have my invisible friend, actually my invisible brother, my twin brother—his name is Carlos, he's the bad guy of the family. So I always got him in there playing the percussion or playing guitar or whatever. And I talk to him and people say sometimes, hey, these guys going crazy on the stage. But I explain to them and they just laugh their face off. It's quite neat to be able to play by yourself because, ah, I mean, it's a process you have to learn and to be able to control all the things on the stage. And sometimes it's harder than other concerts, but I'm getting much better all the time. I think I'm good at it. I try to accompany a lot my guitar performance with my vocal performance. I use a lot of vocal performance when I play by myself. And I use a lot of humor, spontaneous humor—sometimes it work, sometimes don't. But a lot of the time it works a lot because I like to be spontaneous, and that's the way I am. I mean, take me or leave me, but that's the way I am.

AM   So, when you work with James, then, it changes that dynamic. Why does it work well with the two of you? What is it about that?

OL   Well, I think we have the same goals, musical goals. I think that we have the same emotions and we have the same passion, and we are very aggressive. Even if he sing ballads and all this stuff, but he's a very aggressive son of a gun—I mean on the stage—and I am, too. So we can fit with each other. And technically speaking, when he play we have a rhythm guitar, and when he play the rhythm I have much more freedom to move my fingers all over the place and just, to tune my guitar in the air if I wanted to because I know somebody is there—ba ba ba ba ba ba ba ba—backing me up. And in the meantime he's put strong rhythm on me, and when I'm trying to mellow down, I hear him going, raaaaa screaming. And I just wake up, so it's just a feeding frenzy. You know, he feed from my music, I feed from his music, and it works. I mean, a lot of people have been asking us why. We don't know how this things work, man, but it works unbelievable. I mean, it's a nice connection right there.

AM   You've played in some really interesting places. Tell me about Hong Kong?

OL   Oh boy, that was a good one. Well, you know, the things is that I was not supposed to be there, but ah, they hear James' music somewhere in London, I believe, if I am correct in this, and they like his music. So they want to have him in Hong Kong for festival, so James says, well, you gotta hear Lopez. So they got my album and we was playing alone in England, doing a concert there, and one of the important people of this festival were with his wife vacationing there, and they came to see us in the concert. And the guy just went bananas. He said, you both have to be there, you both of you—please, please, gotta be there. So we went over there and we was the first Canadians to be in the Hong Kong folk festival. And we'll probably be the last ones because I don't think they're gonna do it any more.

AM   Isn't it great that you got there.

OL   We were very lucky, very lucky.

AM   What were your audiences like? You don't think of this style of music in China.

OL   Well, most of the audience—to be very honest with you—most of the audience was British people, ah, a big colony obviously. There was a lot of Chinese people and stuff like that, too, but most of the audience was British people. It was just a great experience all around, just to go, you know, to the market, just to go to see the Chinese opera. In every corner of the street was this Chinese people singing and with this weird instrument, this guy with a cigarette in his mouth with, you know, he's playing this weird instrument. He's just so relaxed and making this unbelievable sound. I stop in there for hours and listen, then I just move to the next corner and there was another one. Just great. All the experiences, you know, to be able to be there and to see those things. Now, that's a different culture right there.

AM   Now, we were talking a little while ago about how the world is such a small place. You ran into somebody in Hong Kong that had heard your music in the Middle East?

OL   You know, we actually went to an interview on the radio—a British radio station, you know, a really big station and they play a lot of commercial stuff and things. So somehow we got this interview and then this lady have our album—James' album, my album—and the first thing we say, well how you doin', how are you, and she say, I have to ask this question, but are you Oscar Lopez? Well I believe so. By this time I say, well, what, did I do something wrong? I don't even know you, I said, did I do something wrong?—and just laugh your face off. Anyway, she say that it was such an honor to meet me. And that was James' and I interview, but that was a surprise to me now when she say, such an honor to meet you. And I say, will you explain why? And she say to me, well, you know, I was in the Middle East—she did not mention which part in the Middle East—I was in there for holidays, and I was lying on the beach minding my own business on the sand. Beautiful. And I heard this music (and I had enticed her to my music) and I didn't know where it was coming from. So finally I get up, she said, because I love this music very much. Finally get up, went to this restaurant where this music was coming from and asked this person in there—I don't know who he was, the manager or whatever—who is this? And the guy said, *this is Oscar Lopez*. Oscar Lopez from where? *From Canada*. How I can get this album? *Well, you can't. I don't know if you can or not*. But she was telling me this and I say, you know, one of the thing that really surprise me, is that I have no clue and I have no idea how my album got there.

AM   Let's have another piece of music.

OL   Sure. Well, this one is a song that I used to play when I was back in Santiago and I was playing in this group. We used to love, and I still love this Beatles—one of my favorite groups—and we used to play this song. It's just a gentle song and I want to… if you can play it for me because it's a great melody, good lyrics and talk about the guitar. The only problem is that I have problem to pronounce the title of this song, so may be you're going to have to help me with this one, okay.

AM   I'll help you Oscar.

OL   Okay. I think it's called, *While My Guitar Gently Weeps*. [MUSIC]

AM   You've never been back to Santiago since you left. How come?

OL   How come? Hmmm, how come. Timing. This is a very important thing. I don't have a lot of time to go, and the thing is to go to Chile at least you gotta go for a month, or a couple of months to be able to really enjoy. Secondly, the money situation. I mean, it's not cheap to go over there.

It's a long way. And thirdly, you know, it's not really been the right time for me to. I want to go back and I want to be able to do some shows and concerts there.

AM   Is your music played in Chile?

OL   I don't think so, no. They have my albums actually. They have *Dancing on the Moon*, but I think they are playing on FM, and the big things there are AM radio—they are very big there. So I want to go back when I really feel one hundred percent; it's gotta be the right moment, the right time.

AM   You want to go back as the big success?

OL   Well, not so much big success because, you know, I don't want to do that. I mean, if you wanted to do it, I mean it's very hard to do that. What I want to do is just to be able to go over there, you know, and play in a few places, do a couple of shows on TV and, you know, I'm not sure how they will receive me; but just to, you know, just to go back and see how many things have been changed.

AM   Hard to go home, though, isn't it?

OL It is. You know, what the thing is, this is home. I was 26 when I got here and now I'm 43. Half of my life has been in Canada, and to tell you the truth it's sometimes very scary and sometimes I dream and think, if I go back, I mean, will I feel comfortable now. It's almost like, ah, I learn everything, my other half is here you know. Ah, always… Chile's always gonna' be in my heart because it's the land that I born, but this is home, the country who open the door for me. And without trying to be a nice guy—I always say this—this is home, and that's why I became a Canadian citizen six or seven years ago. Because when I did that I was sure I made my decision, this will be home, you know. And it is home.

AM Do you look on your talent as a gift?

OL Definitely. Oh, definitely. I cannot tell you nothing more than that. Yes, it is a gift, it is a gift from God.

AM How much do you practise a day?

OL Well, like I say once again, I don't practise. If you want to call it practise, I take my guitar and play, trying to work on songs and things like that. I think in the process of an entire day I get my guitar about maybe 15 times—pick up my guitar for half an hour, an hour, sometimes for 10 minutes, sometimes for 15 minutes. But it's a process I do every day, all day, without doing it for hours. You just pick up the guitar, play, record a little bit and play and play, and that's the process that I'm doing most of the day.

AM Do you have to kind of keep in shape for it, though? If you didn't play for awhile would you be clumsy?

OL Oh, definitely, definitely. I remember that I went to Mexico one time and I made a big mistake not to take my guitar with me. I went for holidays and I didn't play for three weeks. I got back home, got the guitar, and believe me, I felt it. My finger was really, ah… I had lost the calluses and I still feel the… It's a hard thing, you know, when you don't do that, when you don't play, don't practise. So, it definitely affects you, and it's something I'm not going to do again. It's important to play all the time.

AM Let's have another piece of music.

OL This guy's a very good friend of mine. He's an amazing guitarist, his name is Don Ross, and I select this music because I think it's a wonderful piece. It's called *That'll be the Phone.* [MUSIC]

AM You met Don Ross at the same time as you met James and that's something that you're really noted for, especially at folk festivals. You really enjoy playing with all kinds of other people.

OL That's my favourite thing of the entire festival to be very honest with you. I like to play main stage—everybody like that—but my favourite part of the entire festival is doing this workshop, because you get to meet such incredible people like, here we go again, Don Ross, James Keelaghan, Amos Garrett, Dave Lindley. In Canmore, for example, I got to do a workshop with a Chinese girl, she play the pipe. I was playing one of my tunes and it's not difficult to follow that kind of thing—very fast and different things. I think her name was Chucha (she's from Vancouver), and actually I was playing this piece, and all of a sudden I hear this weird instrument, and I look on the side and I say, take over baby, go for it, you know. And that's when you create an atmosphere, you know. And I'm good in that. I think I am very good in this kind of… If everybody else, like I say, have an open mind, I'm willing to… I've always been willing to participate and just make people go home happy or come back at night, you know. It's part of the… I mean, because a workshop is great, you have to explain… It's good to explain what the instrument come from, what type of instrument—it's a great thing if people ask questions. But to tell you the truth, most of the workshops turn into like a mini concert, most of the time. 'Cause that's what people want to hear, you know. They want to know a little bit about the instrument, but they want to enjoy the connection of different styles of musicians, you know. That's my opinion anyway, my personal opinion.

AM Now, before we send you off to your mountain top we let you choose one book to take with you.

OL Well, you know, I'm not a big reader. Music, whatever you want. Books, I'm not sure. But I will take this one with me and I'm gonna tell you why.

It's called, *La Casa De Los Espiritus*, mean the house of the spirits, by Isabell Allende. This book's about… there's a lot of love and passion and it's a family and it have to do with different step of life and people's lives. And it's a great thing, you know. The reason that I got this book and I will take this book with me, because it's given by a very strong and very good friend of mine. And should I have to tell you his name, or not necessarily.

AM Oh, you can tell me.

OL Oh, what the heck. James.

AM James Keelaghan.

OL Okay. Well, he's an historian, you know, he's interested in books. So, I think it was somewhere in the United States. And he say, well let's go into a book store. And he look my face. Oh, he says, I see the excitement in your face, Mr. Lopez. And I say, sure, okay, let's go, let's do it. So anyway, I went over there and he went to do his own thing and I was looking in the Spanish section, looking for some Pablo Neruda poems, because that's another thing that I really love, and I look at this book. And I took it out and I started reading it and I said, wow, it's in Spanish. Because it's an unbelievable thing, but I never read this in English, but I read other things in English and the translation from Spanish makes a big difference. You can read in this book things the typical thing the way we speak, the way we say things, you know, and it's just great. So anyway, I look at it, I read a little bit and I put it back. So James went to pay his stuff and we're ready to go. I went to the car, we got into the car, and he say to me, this is for you. And he hand me this book in my hand. And I say, why did you buy it. Happy birthday, he say, it's for you. *Now you're gonna have to read it.* Okay, well, I'm gonna read it, so I will take this book with me because, like I say, I started reading it—it's really nice, it's beautiful, it's a great book and I gonna' finish it. I promise that I gonna' finish it. So I will take this one with me.

AM So if you were going to be cast away somewhere off by yourself for a long period of time, but you could choose any place in the world, where would you go?

OL Well, you know, well I would like to go to be in a place… Le Mer is a beach actually in Chile, on the coast in this magnificent place. They call it the city of gardens because it's just a killer, it's just beautiful—a beautiful place to be, relax, great people, great food. Everything.

AM Oscar, thanks a lot.

OL Andrea, I would like to thank you so much for this opportunity. You know, I almost been feeling like I'm talking to my therapist. Now you know everything. I like to thank you for the opportunity. This has been great for me, a great pleasure to be on your show.

AM What's the final piece of music that we should play?

OL You know, I really like this song, and what else I can say about this gentleman. I call him Garnet Royer. He doesn't like when I call him Garnet Royer, but this is song by Garnet and it called *Night Drive*, and I love the instrumentation that he does and the sound he make come out from the guitar. The lyrics are beautiful, but my main thing is just I love the arrangement he make in this instrumentation. So I think I will have to leave you with this beautiful, beautiful piece of music by Garnet Rogers.

GORDON PINSENT
WITH DAVID GELL, 1991

DG Now you were born and raised in Grand Falls, Newfoundland, 1930—that was the height of the depression. Reflecting back now, what are your memories of that time? Were they happy memories?

GP Yes they were, and I'm almost ashamed to say that they were because, in fact, we were going through some very troubled times. My father had been off work at the paper mill. Even if it were not for the depression, he was not well at that time he had spent 11 years of my early childhood fixing shoes and things, and it was not a very proud time for him because he was trying to raise a family and so on. But I do remember being happy—and this is the most curious thing—at about that time.

DG Was it a large family?

GP We had six; we had three sisters, three brothers. I had rickets of all things—couldn't walk 'til I was about five. That lack of calcium business, you know, and you find out more about it as you grow older I suppose. But at that time it just seemed to be a curiosity for me, how I was… the fact that I was able to throw snowballs from sitting down or something, you know. It was just a very invigorating time. I had no answers to anything, but I had lots of questions and they were all being answered by the people around me. I adored adults. I loved the family. We weren't demonstrative in that sense, but ah, I spent a good amount of time just simply in the company of adults and, like many other kids I suppose, wanting to grow up a little faster than I should have. But at the same time I had a great time just being my own age. And Grand Falls, this town that I remember so well, was ideal for those purposes you know.

DG One of the things youngsters love to do of course is play act. You had a vivid imagination; did your future life sort of suggest itself, although at the time you may not have recognized it?

GP Oh yes, very much so. And in fact I did recognize it even though, again, the drawing, the arts, seemed to be there at my fingertips, and I sort of fell in with it naturally. I was pretty sure in my head that there was something else going on, that I wanted to be elsewhere. I would put on little plays in the back shed, I would spend my time at the movies, and suspect probably that's where my reality was, far more than out in the streets. I did imagine this cardboard cutout kind of existence beyond Grand Falls, called Hollywood, and it was a very big thing for me. My imagination took over by the time I was, well, into my early teens. By then I had lived a full lifetime of experiences.

DG Was there a moment in your life, at that stage perhaps, when you said, yes, this is what my life will be?

GP I think so. I'm not sure I ever voiced it; I was quite sure that there had to be a reason for this attraction to be held this tightly by an idea. It just seemed to… And I suppose at that time I was simply like anyone else going to the movies, captivated by this particular… kind of the magical wall kind of thing, you know—I knew that somewhere, somehow, these people were living this existence, with two-tone shoes and lots of money to spend, and cars to drive and beautiful women around them, and all sorts of things.

DG Was there any history of the theatre in the family?

GP No sense of theatre at all. We had singers in the family—choral, you know, choir-type sisters and so on, but really, no. And very little theatre in town. Every so often something would come through town, but really not at a great rate at all. It was very, very spare in those days. So again, it was up to the individual, and as they say, you know, we entertained ourselves. Television, film, things of that nature just went by your window every day in the characters of the town and the marvelous atmosphere.

DG What did your parents think then when you said, I'm going to be an actor.

GP My mother was the sweetest, quietest little woman ever, and ah, I think it was her being so silent that sort of made me speak up a bit in life. And I was always able to surprise her. I came to her at age 13 and said, I'm engaged you know. You know—*oh yes, are you?,* she said. It wasn't as though she was in shock, it was that she didn't know quite how to behave or if she should, you know. Um… I just robbed a bank. *Oh, did you? I see.* You know. So when I said, I'm going to be an actor—*Oh yes, well.* That seemed to make sense because she gave me 10 cents a week for something… go to the movies, obviously to find some kind of a career.

DG Your father died when your were nine, but what about your brothers and sisters reaction?

GP Well, I hadn't said enough at that point for them to take me too seriously. They didn't take me seriously anyway, you know, so there was never a problem there. But I was really getting in everyone's way at that time. All they knew was that I was the member of the family who laughed all the time. I laughed at everything. When my father was lying in state in the front room in his coffin, and everyone was sitting around quite sort of dour faced, I was the one trying to get people to smile or laugh or whatever. Not that I didn't understand what was happening, but ah, I don't know, for some reason I felt that this was all kind of necessary at that time.

Later on it was very curious because, in fact, when I got into the business and returned home from time to time, their reaction was quite peculiar. They would say… I'd say, well, I'm back in town—oh yes, pick us up a pack of cigarettes—you know.

DG You're back to being the junior member of the family.

GP I was back to the kid. I was back to this person.

DG What was your very first stage appearance? Can you remember?

GP Yes, I do as a matter of fact. I was then… ha, ha… not to give you a long list of jobs that I had done leading up to that point; but in fact I had been three years in the Paratroopers in the Army at that time. I had also taught dancing at Arthur Murray's. I had been a commercial artist part-time, and other kinds of jobs, leading up to this peculiar profession. But then again, I knew that at the tail end of it all was this profession. I was walking down a side street in Winnipeg, and a small group called the Winnipeg Repertory Theatre, run by a woman called Lena Lovegrove, whom we loved to call leaping Lena Lovegrove, and she had that sort of dowager appearance to her, and she put on these plays, three nights per play. And I was there at the tail end of one of those plays, and the audience had left and they had come out to read the following play (the play to come on next). And I was sitting there and I had never appeared on stage, ever, but I knew I had this deep abiding love for it. And she said, oh, I thought the place was empty. I said, no, I'm leaving now. She said, well, we're about to read our new play, our next play; you seem to be fairly presentable, would you be interested in taking part in it? I said, oh gee, I don't know, and I looked at my watch, and she said, well, you know, a small part (the part of a doctor or something). And I said, well, I really should get home. And she said, have you ever acted before? I said, oh yes, many times. Oh, you have? I said, oh yes, down East. Well, you know… I've done a lot of varying things. So, I got up on stage, kept checking my watch as though I was the busiest person in the entire world, read the part of the doctor. She said, that was very good, would you like that? I said, no, I live too far out of town for that. I'd come in for a larger part, I said. She gave me the lead. I had never been on the boards before, I now am playing the part of the father in a Ruth Gordon play called *Years Ago*, which they turned into a movie called *Angel Street*. *Years Ago*, with Spencer Tracy, and I played the Tracy part at the old age of 22 I guess.

DG Did you have any difficulty, since it was your first time, with the mechanics of learning lines and delivering?

GP No, I didn't have any trouble there whatever. The reviews, I remember, said, despite his obvious youth and not very good make-up, he did quite a credible job.

DG Well done. Well done young Gordon. As a young person growing up, of course, the Newfoundland you were in was not yet part of Canada. Were you a Joey Smallwood supporter?

GP At 17, no. I'm not quite sure what I was. I remember tales of Smallwood at that time, going from place to place and being kicked out of a lot of them, and eventually coming to roost as premier. I remember the banners, I remember the referendums. I most distinctly remember the second referendum that brought about confederation, by a slim margin, because in fact there was a commissioned government—England, economic union with the United States, and confederation. Those were the three. And I left Newfoundland six months before confederation rolled in. You needed $250.00 and x-rays. I had my x-rays, I had no money, and I remember sitting in North Sydney, and this man asking me if I had any… you know, to put my money on the table. And I think I pulled out 13 cents or something. He said, if you're not working in three days you're going back. So that's how it was in those days. Canada might well have been across the earth.

DG Did you get a job within three days?

GP Yes, in three days time I was working, pouring cement and mixing and working on the basement… enlarging or something, helping to work on the basement of a man's store. And I remember seeing these three people come by—these suits—and they sort of… One crouched down and said, um… (and I'd put a little extra dirt on my face to make it very impressive) they said, *oh, you're working?* I said, yeah, and I love it, love it. And they walked away and I quit. I quit and joined the circus for about three or four weeks. Then I went to Prince Edward Island picking spuds, and then across the country, ending up in Toronto with three cents. Stepping out of Union Station and saying, where am I?—you know. But having a fairly good idea.

DG Where were you the day that Newfoundland became part of Canada?

GP I was in the unemployment office in Toronto. This man said to me, *what can you do?*—you know, what do I look for in the way of work? I said, I'm an actor. He said, *no, seriously, what do you do? I can't get you work as an actor*. And of course, then I hadn't been, you know, but I knew I was going to be. So he said, *what were you before that?* I said, a shepherd.

DG There's not much call for that in Toronto.

GP He said, *there are no sheep in Toronto*. Oh!—then I must have been misled, I'll have to look into that. I just came from shepherd's training school in Grand Falls, Newfoundland—what is this? So… [laughing] he couldn't find me work as a shepherd and he couldn't find me work as an actor. I lowered myself to a few other jobs before I joined the Army, for three years.

DG What were you in the Army?

GP A private.

DG For three years?

GP Oh, very much so, very much so a private.

DG Did you enjoy the life at all?

GP No, not a bit.

DG No, I would have thought discipline, from what you've told me, would be your long suit.

GP No, totally unlike me, and my brain began to turn the colour of my uniform, so I got out after three years, ended up in Fort Churchill. Was foolish enough to think that I wanted to go to Korea (don't ask me why)—and anyway, we were not sent because I was in the First Airborne, and at that time they were sending the Second Battalion. I ended up in Fort Churchill and discharged in Winnipeg, closest possible spot to Fort Churchill. I had an early marriage there, in fact, with a couple of children, and went about going about the business then of going on stage. I was lucky to do the first live television out of Winnipeg, and a lot of radio work.

DG Sounds like a new career beginning. Let's break off at that point and have your first choice of music. What have you chosen and why?

GP Roberta Flack, *The First Time Ever I Saw Your Face*, and I believe it has mostly to do (in fact, I know it has) with meeting my wife, Charmaine King, the actress, for the first time.

DG When was that?

GP This would have been in '60 in fact. She was doing *The Mad Woman of Chaillot* with the Crest Theatre in Toronto, and I played the love interest. She needed someone to whistle, she couldn't whistle; she raised her fingers and I whistled from the wings, and I've been whistling ever since. [MUSIC]

DG Gordon, we've got you to Winnipeg, you're out of the Army, your theatre life is beginning for real. What, ah… your first experience in acting, perhaps at Winnipeg's Theatre '77… Did a kid from 'the rock' feel comfortable in the mid-prairies?

GP Yes, there was something in whatever this attitude I had, that made me think it's perfectly normal. Perfectly normal. I knew that to be a performer, performing artist, you had to have a sort of a world feel to it, a universal feel. You couldn't afford to go around doing Shakespeare, saying, *hark, I hear the cannon roar*.. You know, you had to be very careful about where you were going. And I felt that we all had to sound a bit alike at least, and so we did. I did a fair amount of early radio work as I said, in Winnipeg, and ah, I've used that and a workshop—workshopping situations—in order to level out whatever vocal problems I would have along those lines.

DG Did you have (when you were a youngster)—did you have a Newfoundland accent?

GP I suppose I did. I must have, because a brother of mine looked me up not that long after I'd gone into theatre, and he sounded completely different to the way I sounded, and I… and of course I did, you know; and I was able to dredge it up at a moment's notice. But it was important for me at that time, if I were to continue on I had to make sure that the accent wasn't too strong.

DG It's interesting. When I mentioned to people that I'd be talking to you, the first thing they mention is that you are from Newfoundland. Have you found in your career that people plan roles for you because of where you're from?

GP There has been a bit of that, but I've been lucky in the last… I wanted to make sure at the very beginning when I worked on Newfoundland pieces, that I didn't want to make a career of it. It was important for me to get certain things off my chest and write them myself or take part in them. But also, I knew that I shouldn't kind of stay there. I mean, the reminder came back from my early days as an actor, don't get stuck in one place, don't hang your hat on one nail in this country or they'll keep you there. You know, it's a very tricky situation for a performer, so ah, it's very important that I centre myself, with the sensibilities of a Newfoundlander in mind, whether it has to do with writing or performing or whatever. But then I have to branch out and be other things.

DG And yet some of your greatest success derives from that; I'm thinking of the work you did as *The Rowdy Man*, which you wrote as well as starring in that. Was that, for you, a way of getting back to your roots?

GP Well, it was in a sense. I wrote that on a hilltop in Sherman Oaks, California. I knew that I wanted to take my career in a different direction to where it was going. I thought I could stand in line forever in L.A., even though I was sort of working at the time and doing my… making the rounds on episodics and so on, episodic television. I thought, well, I better start taking writing seriously and perhaps try to conjure up the kind of thing that I'd like to do. Following the first rule of writers, write a thing that is close to you. I thought, what do I need for a premise here? And the one I arrived at was *The Rowdy Man*. I asked myself, how I would have continued had I stayed in Grand Falls, Newfoundland—not that I would have become this particular person, but the premise itself was an interesting one. Had you stayed, how would you be today? What would have happened to you? Where would you have gone? And I find that an interesting kind of way in. So I wrote the piece on that basis, and then it was simply a matter of getting the money, finding a way to put the thing on, and perhaps then that would help change gears for me. I've always been interested in sort of turning left when they think you're going to turn right. I didn't again want to be labeled or stuck in a corner at the mercy of the business. I wanted to help, well, move myself around a bit. It's really got to come back down to yourself. It's got to come back down to you the writer, you the performer. I've always believed that there has to be two of you: one, certainly from the standpoint of performing. It isn't enough to be the ambitious whatever, it isn't enough to be the performer who wants to go and conquer. You've got to have yourself standing nearby—another you, a reality, a big brother almost, holding your hand saying, no, don't do that, this is real life after all, you can't get lost. You can't run your life according to others' perception of you. You mustn't go out there and just sort of wander, or be thrilled that somebody would think something of you or supply advantages and opportunities. They can take them back again. You've got to be careful. You must be very real about it as well. So big sisters and big brothers to help you through, I think, are important for young performers, otherwise they tend to go and get lost in that other strange business. But this is pretty well the way I've done it, so when I backed up into the writing again and learned properly, I knew I was doing it the right way. I didn't have much patience for it because I never did—scholastically I never did and so on—so this to me was the great test of all time, and it would eventually pay off. Learn properly. Always learn properly, you know.

DG Is there still anxiety or anguish waiting for offers to come in, or deciding which role to accept?

GP Yes, because I think in the last 10 years I've been fond of saying that I've been selective. In the meantime, my rejections are like anyone's rejections: if the country's not ready, or the economy's not ready... If the industry is going in a certain direction and ah, you know, you're not with it, you can simply be remembered for things you did, and they let it go at that. My trick is to try to get up and climb those stairs and write something out that I feel still I would like to do. It's a very peculiar time, it's an odd time. People in our business who have done well, have done well because they have managed to enter the mainstream, either copy-catting American or doing things that have been done. I'm far more involved and far more concerned with the idea of trying to at least, help create breakthrough Canadian films or ideas that will stand on their own, without having to copy anyone, and to attempt to just get our stories told before we lose our storytellers, before it's all part of the one great pattern that we're so familiar with—you know, from the States. And this is not easy to do, as you know, and it's tough enough to get anything off the ground in this country. But we have a business of stops and starts that is unlike anything. It's quite peculiar, and to stay part of it, and to get up every morning and explain who you are and what you do, is something that, well, it has to be done. And you have to see the good in that because, in fact, you may even need that to survive properly and not be complacent, you know. I feel good about that. I go back home, my brother, Harry, says to me, *ah, now obviously I'm not gonna ask you to retire and come home and live next door, but ah, do you think you ever will?* You know. And they're all kind of talking this way, they think it's time now. They're all getting on a bit and what am I doing? What is this foolish man doing?

DG So, we'll break off at this point for another of your choices of music. What would you recommend next?

GP Well, we've been talking about *The Rowdy Man*, And I've been hearing this on radio stations across the country. That film was made in 1971, and I'm constantly surprised to hear this thing. It doesn't happen often, but when it does it brings back a lovely thought. Theme from *The Rowdy Man*, written by Robbie McDougall, produced by Ben McPeak, who's no longer with us. And it's in his memory that I would love to hear it again. [MUSIC]

DG Gordon, you've already mentioned Charmaine King—you're been married for nearly 30 years now. You also have a daughter who's chosen to become an actress, so you've got a whole family of thespians now. How does that work out? I mean, are your interests divergent?

GP They are not, oddly enough. I was not surprised that Leah, our daughter, moved into these circles, took on this peculiar persuasion of performing. But, ah, I turned immediately into another kind of dad, and wasn't thrilled by the idea. I've seen the way it has gone for an awful lot of young performers, and I didn't want her to waste the time. And then I realized, of course, it's not a waste. Everything is a search, everything is an experience. I just didn't want her to make the same mistakes that I did and so on, and I wanted to give her a whole list—don't follow those, don't follow those, do try not to do all these things. And, ah, anyway, there she was and there she is, married recently and I have just become this other kind of person all over again. I think I was kind of tough and a bit scared to begin with.

DG Did she notice the difference in you?

GP Oh, the minute she moved away and she realized, of course, I was no longer on the phone all the time, she knew that I had eased up and probably was not as scared. And she also realized that, as a parent, parents are scared; this is why they want to do the right things, even though they're not sure what those things are. And so, ah, we had a very interesting period of time while she was growing up. But in fact I had gone to lunch one day with the director of *The Bay Boy*, a film called *The Bay Boy*. Dan Petrie called and he said, let's have lunch. And he said, I'm looking for these... He said, I've only got two or three girls to cast now—young girls—and he said, you have a daughter. I said, stay away, don't even mention it. And he said, no, seriously Gordon, I've seen her picture and, you know, is she going into the business? And I said, well, as a matter of fact she wants to, and so on. And I made the decision there and then that he should probably... that it would be unfair of me, since he asked to see her, to not suggest it to her. And I did, and she went down, got the role, and has sort of kept moving ever since. But I had gone through this very special horror film of my own trying to watch her take the stage.

DG Did she pay attention to what you say in your list of do's and don'ts?

GP A lot of it has come later: the business of, *gee, I guess you were right; or no, you were wrong*—you know. We speak quite openly during these various phases of hers, and now she's a young woman of 27 and knows her own mind, has grown into a wonderful personality, has a great sense of humour, and she and Charmaine look at each other and continue talking, even though I'm talking about something quite different.

DG What about working together? That must be a temptation, to do it, and a temptation never to do it.

GP Yes. Very strange about that. Charmaine and myself have only worked together a few times. I'm not sure that we do our best work with each in that sense. I'm not sure we get deep enough within characters to make it all work. I think we can be effective, but that's the end of it. I've never worked with Leah yet. I would like to have been the first to direct Leah. I'd like to have, sort of set a few ground rules for her, and not have this girl arrive on the doorstep later on having known everything, you know, and have gone about it her own way. I'd like to have taken a part in that, and I will yet, I think. Maybe the answer is to, again, go up those funny stairs and write something that she and I can do together. It would be interesting.

DG Were there any moments when you were... Obviously, because you love your craft so much, acting is so important to you, was there ever a tendency or temptation to devote too much time to that, so that your family life suffered?

GP Yes there was. I tried to balance this; anytime I got awards or something, and Leah would probably put them up on mantle pieces. And I'd say, oh no, don't do that, you know not that I wanted to hide these things, but in fact I wanted Leah to get the balance, I wanted her to know that it was not all about those things. It was about how you felt about doing them. It is not in the results; it is in the travel, the journey, the pleasure in knowing that you are doing what you want to do. That part was extremely important. But these days, there is the tendency for young people, because of the television possibilities— endless… the Hollywood picture and so on—there's still a bit of that over night thing that they would like to happen. And it's too bad in a way. A good amount of our young people are learning (what I would like to call) Malibu acting in fact, and performing. They're not interested really in the tradition or history of Canadian theatre and Canadian expertise in that sense. They are mainly interested in getting on with it. It's kind of heat and serve, you know. Heat and serve art. And they get on with it, they go about their merry way and they either make their mistakes or they don't. Hopefully they turn into human beings before they get lost, lovely men and women before they lose themselves, you know.

DG As Leah was growing up, did you ever have moments when you were resting, so you could drive her to school, take her to ballet?

GP I did. But it seemed to me there was always advice involved. I mean, yes I would, but always she had a question. She would say, *daddy, I'm going to ask you something,* and I'd think, oh heavens, is this the next phase? Is this what happens to young girls, you know? What is she about to ask? I was terrified—terrified of being the father in that sense, because I had been so wrapped up in my own work, and so it really bothered me greatly. I remember a young boy once, and, you know, she had talked about him so much—she was only 12 for heaven's sake. She talked about this boy so much, I thought, in my mind, that Anthony Quinn is going to come through the door, you know. I didn't know who this person was. And in came this little drowned rat out of the rain, whom she immediately ordered around. Charm, who went by in the background, said, *oh, is that the rapist?…* [GP laughing] In the meantime I had conjured up this terrible picture, this Jekyll & Hyde—this Hyde man—and I'd had nightmares that she would parade people through the room, saying, how about him? You know. Does it matter that he's 75 years of age?

DG Are you going to be a much more relaxed grandfather, then, when the grandchildren come along?

GP I think, perhaps. Maybe I can start again or go backwards; I'll try to do it right this time. Maybe I did some things right then—I'm sure I did—but again, it was, you know… by trying, not by knowing. And I never did know. I barely was able to raise myself, let alone anyone else, you know. And certainly as a performer.

DG Let's get back to music. First of all, we haven't asked this of you: do you play the piano yourself?

GP No I don't. We have a wonderful piano— nobody plays. I remember inviting a pianist once to a dinner. He said, my piano does not eat. So that was the end of… I can't even get anyone in to play.

DG So what is your next choice for us?

GP Delibes *Lakmé*. It is a piece that was played at Leah's wedding. [MUSIC]

DG Gordon, in 1968, you and your family moved to the States, and for six years you continued your career in Los Angeles. Why did you go? Was it the old thing of simply not enough recognition of your work in your own country?

GP No. In fact, it was very curious. I was in my late 30's. Had I been 20 or 21 it might have been a different story, but I had finished doing the three-year stint on the *Member of Parliament* series in Canada, and in those days, definitely, if you had one series you wouldn't get another. So I thought, well, let's take a shot now, just for the fun of it, just to see what will happen, or until the sense of humour runs out or whatever. And I think that's probably what happened. I became very scared of the idea of living their career, not mine, and it really would have been. It would have been again at the mercy of the telephone, and you were only as good as, and all that stuff. How long would it be before you were able to get a choice of script or whatever. I didn't do too badly at the beginning as a matter of fact, and I suppose if I'd pushed it properly I could have continued. I was cast as the president of the United States in a movie called *Colossus, the Foreman Project*. And we shot it in '69 I guess. It was shortly after Robert Kennedy was shot. And I was to play the lead in the film. But they felt that I had a Kennedy look at that point, when I was doing that *Member of Parliament* series, and I think that association helped.

And when Kennedy was shot (Robert Kennedy was shot) at the Ambassador Hotel in Los Angeles, they, this movie came about, they shifted everything around—as Hollywood is known to do—now I become the president, and in fact we shot scenes at the Ambassador Hotel, passing that kitchen table, in the kitchen area where all this happened. You know, those wonderful people, they take advantage of everything. So, that was the beginning of that. And then, a few other things; got my Green Card, waited around, did a couple of other… a few other bad movies, and lots of episodics—the Marcus Welby's and the Hogan's Heroes, and the usual—you do the rounds. And then it became too much, and I saw it going by too quickly.

DG How did you wife take to the years in America?

GP We were together, Leah had just come along—she was four at that time—and she was quite fine. She is so stable within herself, and within herself in the business. There was a time, many years before when she was quite young, she'd been offered some sort of contract, in fact, in L.A. No, didn't go, finished school instead. Did a lot of stage work, did some wonderful, wonderful roles—still does—and that was fine for Charm. I'm the one who gets up in the morning and screams and shouts about the business and what's wrong with it and everything. Charm will take things… She is truly the actor in the family, and a very generous actor. They'll call Charm for something and, ah, she'll say, no, that's not right for me, give it to someone else. You know, she's an extremely generous person in that regard—and performer. Great to work with. Those qualities are qualities I would like to have a bit more of. I guess I'm sounding a bit like the breadwinner at times, and I'm not, but I really see the need to keep proving to myself this is a good way of life. It is a fact, it is here. In the States it's different, it's been around as long as General Motors, this particular industry of ours. Here we have to keep getting up and explaining why we do what we do, and so we're on it at all times. But Charm was fine. She did a bit of work in the States as well, but in the meantime raised Leah, and wanted it that way.

DG Your time in the States, by any judgment, was successful. I mean, if you end up being the president of the United States after living there for a few years, it's not bad at all. Why then, having been successful in one of the most challenging places in the world, did you decide to return?

GP I thought I was beginning to believe them and not believe me. When they said, excellent, they really meant fair. They might have even meant excellent, but I was only living up to whatever those limits were—the limits of television, the limits of weekly episodics. I did four pilots, which could, God forbid, have become series. I did one, it was like a medical bonanza—a father and four sons, you know—which went on forever in the way of a movie, while they tried to find solutions to turn this thing into a series. And I had five agents, changed them like shirts, you know, just to try to find the right way through. But I don't know. Well, the reason I wrote, obviously, was to break that pattern. I did that and out came *The Rowdy Man.*

DG The lure of U.S. television and movies is in many instances irresistible to young actors. Is it inevitable that we'll continue to see a talent drain from this country, specifically to the States?

GP I think probably we will. I don't know, somebody was saying the other day, when world satellite takes hold—whatever that means in its full form—that in fact we will rid ourselves of an awful lot of the usual stuff, the trash. There's an awful lot of stuff that's happening in staccato television land. There will come a time, however, when you'll say, well, I wonder what they're doing in Germany, and press a button, and there will be the best program from Germany and Japan and wherever. And maybe, then, people will have to fight harder—the schlock people—to keep the schlock coming. There'll always be that sense of, oh, give them what they want. But what they want is really what we gave them in the first place.

DG Do you think we're going to end up with a kind of world theatre musak?

GP Yes, I think that's probably what's going to happen. If we return to being more selective, and choosing to use that medium for what it's best meant. And we're just choosing it now; it's a trick, it's a game, it's just the thing to have around the house, like, well, you know, a board game or something. Whereas I think it's far more useful than that. But good is good anywhere, and I think we have to return to that idea; not only that we can do it in this country, but that we will.

DG Why is it the Australians have done it? There is an Australian theatre, an Australian movie industry which is distinctly Australian. Why—apart from the fact we're in bed with an elephant—why doesn't Canada succeed? Because, goodness knows, we've got the talent and we've got the stories.

GP Well, there's a silly little song in Newfoundland called, *Thank God We're Surrounded by Water*, and I swear to you, it's that peculiar kind of isolation that does it. I've talked to the producers in Australia, many of them responsible for some of those earlier great films of a few years back, and they said, you'd been amazed at how this thing happened. Even in television terms it only took them one year to turn everyone around from watching American to watching Australian. Now, they say it's sliding again, it's going back the other way. If it is, then that's a shame, and it just means that schlock merchants or somebody got in there. Or, it meant that maybe Australia did not, in economic terms, support what was going on. But they did their best work then. They may again, and they certainly proved it can be done. We have not been able to do that with that elephant as you say, and I think that is unfortunate. We've given them the space and the fallen dollar to shoot film, to distribute their film, to do whatever they want. And I'd said before somewhere that, in fact, if they come in to a country like ours and say, oh, gee, you don't have a culture?—oh, well, then we'll interpret your culture for you. And away they'll go. They have the power, the movement, the expertise and so on, to continue on. This can simply be an appendage of what they've been doing down there for so long. And it's awful to talk of borders and barricading and things like that, but, to barricade our culture, to sort of know it first, to get to know it, to bring it about. Otherwise it's cultural genocide in a sense. I had to have a reason personally why I came back here. I know what those reasons are, I'd like to feel that there are those that still think in those terms, but in the meantime I don't want us

to be trapped into that sense of, oh dear, if you're not mainstream, you're nowhere. Because it's so easy to follow that other game. I think anything breakthrough that's going to be Canadian will have to be different, and we have the courage to know... should have the courage to know, that to be different is also good business.

DG Are there any young people out there you've seen—young writers and actors—who are confident in telling their own stories about our culture?

GP No.

DG They're just not there.

GP They may be there somewhere, but I certainly don't run into them on a daily basis. I know of a lot of singers and dancers and wonderful talent that come out for shows and do things, and they're as good as... I mean as anywhere, and really we're quite bountiful. But they don't... And they would like to say, some of them, I'd like to do it here. And I remember hearing myself say it, I heard many people say it over the years. I would like to do it here as opposed to go abroad. What they're really saying is that they're either scared, or they don't want to leave home, or whatever. If the opportunity was there, probably they would go and have a stab at it, as we all did to some degree. I think what it comes back down to, though, is you simply have to stay, if you feel like staying, and become part of something far more satisfying than simply, okay, let's all play that same game until it runs out.

DH And at that point, let's break off with some more music. What's your next choice?

GP Don McLean: *Vincent, Starry Starry Night*.

DG And what's the story behind this?

GP Well, basically, I think we were wading through a period of music that I had not felt as close to, or near and dear to, as I had music in the past, or whatever, and suddenly out of nowhere came this tune. Well, this man seemed to be in touch, not only, with the need to bring about good melody again, but, there's something quite sort of, very familiar, in the sense that he was familiar with his subject, Vincent Van Gogh. And it just did something for me, because I'm a painter as well and, it just hit me at the right time, at the right place, while I was doing a bit of painting, and, I began to remind myself, gee, I wonder if this is what I should have done for a life's work? Should I be painting instead of performing. But, I was just thrilled that he chose to do… to deal with Vincent as a subject. [MUSIC]

DG At your stage, having given a performance, are you able to simply think, I feel good about that, that was successful and I feel right? Or, are you still evaluating yourself every single time you set foot on the stage?

GP I don't evaluate as much as maybe I should. I am happy with a good evening's work for the most part, a 90% good evening's work or a day's work or whatever—I feel good about that. I don't want to get to the end of the year and say, it's been a good year because of how much money I made or something. I want to get to the end of the year saying, this year I did that—I did that and that and that. Or, maybe even one special job or something. That's important. And I think probably, to try to keep whatever reputation there is going, and to keep those doors open, it's important to do things that mean a great deal to you. Now I'm doing it for the sheer love of it—who's in it, what's the name of the play, and let's go and make something happen. I'm desperate in the idea that the best times are ahead and that I, in fact, have a lot more to do and probably my best jobs are tomorrow's, not the last.

DG Gordon, back to music, what's your next choice of music?

GP Ha, ha… Well, I've always liked to think that I've liked all kinds of music. This is Hank Snow, of all people—*I'm Moving On*. Don't ask me why this came about or immediately of a quick memory of the army came about, where in fact the way to stay out of fights in the army was for me to impersonate various people. Hank Snow was one of those, he was a favourite. I learned very quickly a few chords on the guitar and I began to imitate Hank Snow. It's a wonderful way to not get your teeth knocked out in a fight. They had to save me because I was the one that sang these songs. On the other hand, it backfired a bit because they had some sort of celebrity touring show on at one point, and guess who the star attraction was?—Hank Snow. So suddenly I was not such a special case anymore and I had to learn something very, very quickly to take its place. And I did. I began to sketch their pictures and I got away with another year in the army without getting beaten up. [MUSIC]

DH Gordon, before we get to hear your final choice of music, we always let our guests take one book with them. What's your book and why did you choose this?

GP Well, very interesting. I suppose the first thing I thought about when I think of books, is to try to finish the one that I'm writing myself. If I don't get it finished I'm going to be in trouble. I've written a couple of books, and this thing that I'm trying to do now is an autobiography, without really turning it into an autobiography, and it's driving me crazy. I thought if I ever went anywhere, to be alone to finish something or to read something, it would be this. My title for it is, *Now Why Did I Come in Here*. I don't know if I'll ever get the thing finished. Reading as such, *The Deptford Trilogy*, the Robertson Davies—almost anything Robertson Davies for some reason—that appeals to me greatly. And it's the kind of writing, the kind of man, I find myself… if I think of the sort of thing I'd like to do, and I think it reaches or touches home, closer than ever, of things that spring from the roots. And there's something familiar in his writing treatment and his writing technique that tells me here's a man who's writing precisely how he wants to. And I don't know, there's something about it, it reminds me of the kind of thing that I would like to do if I were as expert in writing as Rob Davies. And *The Deptford Trilogy* has helped me through a number of things. I take it with me and reread *The Fifth Season*.

DG When you read like that, is it just for pleasure? Or are you busy casting yourself in one of the roles and seeing the staging problems associated with telling the story?

GP There's that as well. I think I'm doing that as well, which is a very good point. I'm not sure I've ever done any one thing, outside of performing, where I have totally devoted time to that one thing. I think there's always something else going on in my head. Concentration is a huge part of performing.

The fact that I've chosen to do other things besides perform, has made performing even more difficult for me. So in reading, yes, I can dream up scenarios like mad.

DG   Well, we'll give you some extra paper to take along, and lots of pencils so you can add to it. You also get to choose where you're going to spend the rest of your days, or at least the time of your isolation. It doesn't have to be (although we call it Mountaintop Music) the top of a mountain. It could be a desert island, or off a blustery coast of Newfoundland if you wish. Where would you choose this isolation to be?

GP   I think probably in Newfoundland. When I think of islands, however, and certainly for periods of time, Delos comes to mind—a Greek Island, Delos, where in fact one is not allowed to be born nor die. This is where the festivals used to occur well back in time. Every four years there was this incredible festival where the Greeks would go to Delos. Sophocles, as a matter of fact, went into prison and had to wait for his sentence because the festival was taking place, all because the arts were that important. One particular house—various houses in Delos devoted to areas of life—one is called the House of Masks, with an incredible floor of tile made up of masks of actors and the jobs they do, and the importance of art to that culture just meant a great deal to me at that time. There's something in its stillness, of course, which is just astounding, and I found myself sitting and staring, or stepping softly, and everything everywhere is standing still, and it's the only thing I think that's ever been able to, or the only place that's ever made me stop and get a hold of myself and really think, now wait a minute, you don't have to hurry through life, you can sit and stare, study and enjoy and learn from what you are seeing. And I practised there—and quite successfully—to see things again for the first time.

DG   Your final choice of music.

GP   Beethoven, *Ninth Symphony, Ode To Joy*, which Charm and I played at our wedding. And Charm is one of the most beautiful people I've ever met—probably the most, yes, the most beautiful. Charm does not have a singing voice. Now, she doesn't know this. Well, she does, but still, it's very curious. We were planning our wedding: she said, *now, we're going to have two tunes Gordon, and you and I are going to sing one—we'll join them on one—and they will sing the other*. And terrific, I said—which one? She said, *so we'll join in with Ode to Joy*. I'd never heard Charm sing. So we're standing there, being married, in front of the minister, and this voice entered my left ear—I did the slowest take, and then turned to Charm. Her bridesmaid had known her all her life, and she sort of gave me a little look beyond Charm. And Charm, with all the regality she could muster, you know, just pounding this song out, in a voice that was so unlike her that one would never have known that she could not sing. And she certainly didn't know. But it was quite wonderful, that we were being married at this precise moment and for some reason I had not heard her sing. I tried to alter it and go into alto, and tried to do harmony, and that didn't work. She went with me every step of the way, it was quite interesting.

DG   I don't think I shall ever listen to *Ode To Joy* without remembering your story. Gordon Pinsent, thank you very much for sharing some of our anecdotes and your music with us today.

GP   You're more than welcome. A pleasure.

AM We've got a lot of ground to cover in your life, you've done so many things; so maybe we should start at the very beginning. You were born on the Piapot Reserve in Saskatchewan. Then you were adopted?

BSM I was adopted as a baby, yeah.

AM Adopted as a baby and taken to the States. What was it like to grow up in a non-native family?

BSM Well, the race of my family didn't really matter so much as the fact that my mother was very very good to me—she was part Micmac—and the men in the family were very very bad to me. So it wasn't really a racial issue so much as that's the way they were. And I managed to survive that, thanks I think to my mother's, she's real smart—she's an intellectual, she loved to read. And she told me so far as racial things go that, you know, there's an awful lot in the world that the schools didn't teach correctly, and that the things that I saw at the movies and TV were not necessarily so, and she inspired me to go out and find out for myself. She really inspired me to get out of this place where I was growing up and find out…

AM What was the place that you were growing up, and what was it like?

BSM Oh, it was just an ordinary east coast town where people had never met a native person and didn't believe in them, and all I learned about Indian people when I was growing up, you know, it started with paper feather hats and lies about Thanksgiving. You know, native people were not invited to the pilgrims table at Thanksgiving—that's just a lie, it's just a myth—and it continued and, you know, the only time that we ever got to see Indian things was not in a cultural museum, it was in the museum of natural history. And we got to see dead Indians stuffed next to the dinosaurs, you know. So it was horrifying, it was horrible. And there was one Indian man in the town where I grew up in—he was a Chippewa—and his kindness and his intelligence and just his reality kind of counterbalanced for me the myths that we were hearing, because you know, as you probably know, around the world where it comes to indigenous people there's such a lack of self-identity, you know,

BUFFY SAINTE-MARIE
WITH ANDREA MARANTZ, 1996

that it leaves a big hole in most people's hearts. I mean, who are we? Are we *Dances With Wolves*?—I mean, no. Are we Disney's *Pocahontas*?—certainly not, you know. So I did find out for myself, I was reunited with my Cree relatives when I was in my late teens.

AM How did that come about?

BSM Well kind of by accident, and somebody just happened to know some people who had spent their time in the east, and they came east every year for a cultural event, and put me together with them. And they did believe that I probably had come from their area, and so…

AM And by this point you had started exploring that, trying to find out more?

BSM Not much, not much—'cause you know, I was only a teenager.

AM They reached out to you?

BSM Yeah. But you know, over the years I continued to check, and… It wasn't a big deal for me to, you know, it wasn't as though I had to find my birth parents, you know, like… Did you see Gil Cardinal's movie? He did a wonderful documentary on trying to be reunited, you know, trying to find about his birth parents. That wasn't like that for me, it was quite different. And I always had accepted my situation for what it was. But then when I was reunited with my relatives—not my birth parents but my relatives, or at least those I believed to be my relatives—we just all accepted one another and it was just wonderful. I've had two families and it's good.

AM So did you just hop on a train and go out to Saskatchewan?

BSM Essentially, yeah. But, no, I had met them in the east, I had met them… I had spent lots of time with them before I ever went to Saskatchewan again.

AM So it was something that you were ready to do when it happened?

BSM Oh yeah, yeah, I was… By the time I was in college I was… although I was a philosophy major, I also got my teaching degree, and I thought I might some day teach on a reservation, but I was pretty hip to the fact that a teacher's hands on a reservation are very much tied, and I'd be teaching kids the same lies that I had learned because that's what was in the curriculum. Dead Indians. And I was interested in live Indians. I'm interested in Indian history, of course, but insofar as first nations people go I'm very much interested in the present and the future as well. I'm involved in various telecommunications projects with other native people, and really with people of all backgrounds. I'm thrilled with telecommunications as an artist and as an alternative person. I don't think of myself as a minority person because I think really there are more noncorporate people than there are corporate people in the world, and when I say an alternative person I mean, you know, I don't work for NASA. I don't work for a phone company. I have no vested interest, I don't make any money off turning people on to computers, but I really do feel as though the new technology ought to be in the hands of artists and mommies, native people, teachers, kids, students, intellectuals—who are not necessarily in the mainstream—and it's a lot of fun for me to be using telecommunications and to be using computers as a digital artist. I teach digital art in several different colleges, and I teach electronic music, digital technology in music.

AM Let's have your first piece of music now. What shall we play?

BSM Oh gee. Let's see, let's play something from *The Visit* by Loreena McKennitt.

AM Now why do you pick this one?

BSM You know, because… I think of it right now because when I'm doing digital art, when I'm sitting at my computer for hour after hour, playing with light and colour, I can really get into the stories as well as the sound of her music, and I have a lot of respect for her as an individual who does her own thing. I think she's an example of someone who's done very well in her own business. You know, she has an independent record label and she's an individual and she reflects not only her own culture, but also the culture of, you know, the whole Celtic peoples. And she not only has a big respect for folk music and traditions and is a wonderful instrumentalist, but also she's not afraid to add to that tradition by putting new words and new stories into that kind of format. So I like her a lot. [MUSIC]

AM That was *Old Ways* from Loreena McKennitt's CD, *The Visit*, the choice of my guest, Buffy St. Marie.

Was there music around your house when you were growing up?

BSM A little bit.

AM And you got interested in music right away?

BSM Oh yeah, from the first time I saw a piano. I wasn't interested in dolls and I wasn't interested in sports, but what I wanted to play, all the time, was music. And what I wanted to play all the rest of the time was any kind of art. I was just a typical little kid, you know, like all five-year-olds. If you take 'em to the beach they'll make sculpture—they don't have to go to school. They'll write their names, they'll make up stories, they'll dance, they'll pretend, they'll be creative.

AM And your mother gave you, sort of, space to do that in I guess?

BSM She did. Yes, she did.

AM Did you have a piano in the house?

BSM Yes. By the time I was about, oh I must have been about three-and-a-half, and I sat down and taught myself how to play, just as children do teach themselves how to play. You know, for me it was the same as Lego's or any other building block tool. Music and other creative arts I think are natural; I think that it takes a lot of work on the part of the system to divest us of our creativity, and I think it's set up to do so. By the time you go to school you find out that the music teacher is usually in some kind of competition with the art teacher; you know, certainly for time. And all creative endeavors are in competition with the mainstream curriculum that teaches us how to work in the system for coins and to learn how to shovel coins into the corporate pocket. And I feel as though, in the future, when more people are contributing to the overall creative options of the human race, I think that things will be a little bit different than they are now. I think we're still quite primitive in most of our schools in encouraging the best in our kids, 'cause I really think they're born with a lot more. I think we stomp a lot of things out of them when it comes to natural skills.

AM You had this enormous thirst and hunger for knowledge when you went to college, and you took three different degrees. Where did that come from, that energy to learn?

BSM Well, I think that's a little bit different than the way it really happened. I went to college because I wanted to get out of town and because I just had to get away from the men in the family who were so cruel, abusive, humiliating and totally out of line. And I'd just like to say right now that anyone who abuses a child, emotionally or physically, is to be scorned and hopefully re-educated. Because it's never right. So for me, I just wanted to get out of town. No one in my family had ever been to college, I was the first one. It was definitely a blue-collar situation. Only the father drove a car, you know. It was sort of a typical situation, kind of low class situation of the times, and when I first went to college I thought I might want to be a veterinarian 'cause I loved animals. And I thought it through, like in the first couple of months, and I said, no, if I'm gonna be a veterinarian I'm gonna be with sick and wounded animals all the time, and I'm sure not a scientist. And I discovered philosophy. I took a course in philosophy and I said, oh: thought. That's what it's about—thought. 'Cause I've always been interested in people's personal relationship with the creator. Whether or not they're affiliated with the church, you know, is not the point. But people's innermost thoughts, and really, what they really aspire to and what's most inspirational and how to solve the basic life problems has always been fascinating to me. So I became a philosophy major and got my teacher's degree. And it was only after I got to college that I became hungry for knowledge, because when I would read through the catalogue of what you could take in college—ooooh, this was not your father's Oldsmobile, you know. This was not high school.

AM Kid in a candy store.

BSM Wow, yeah. There were all these things that I couldn't wait to find out about, so I loved college. I still do. And I went on to get my teacher's degree, and later on, after I'd been, you know, after I had had a career, I got my PhD in Fine Arts. But by that time I was into digital technology and that came quite a bit later.

AM When did you start singing?

BSM In college. But not as a singer, as a songwriter. I wasn't trying to write songs about whatever was the flavour of the month and already on the radio, 'cause somebody already did that. And I was so naïve. I only wanted to present things that were a little bit different. And when people would hear them they'd say, oh, I never thought of it, but that is the way that goes. So I was writing about leaving space in your life for life to happen and for love to happen, like *Until It's Time for You to Go*, which was on my very first album. I wrote it while I was in college. And *Universal Soldier* I wrote, you know, during the first year after college. And *Now that the Buffalo's Gone*, you know, which was about the way things really are for native people, and the broken treaties and the mixed up legalities of being a native person having to deal with the system.

And I started off as a young folksinger in Greenwich Village; I wasn't singing folk songs, but they were calling it folk music. And I think the reason why they called the new songwriters folksingers is because some of us were writing in a way that seemed to be very long lasting. And it was my intent as a college girl to write songs that would make sense in another hundred years, and that would make sense in any country of the world, and that was kind of a college kind of project. And my goal in a song was to say something in three-and-a-half minutes that it would take somebody else a four hundred page book to write about. I was trying to stimulate the imagination.

AM And it really illustrated the time that you were living in as well as having that sort of... I think any time that you write something really well it's very pointed to a particular moment as well as having that, as you said, can last for a hundred years.

BSM Yes. 'Cause there are some universal things that happen. I mean something today is gonna happen to everybody who's listening to us. Some one thing is gonna happen, that could happen to anybody anywhere, that has an importance for right now, but it's a timeless kind of thing. The same things keep happening over and over again. You know, they'll always have their own originality. I mean, not everything is like that. But there are these, like, paradigm moments that happen all the time. And I think what a songwriter does, or you know, a writer or a painter—what we do as artists is we have these little cameras that are on most of the times in our heads, taking pictures of our experiences, and what the creative person does, and the things that make us successful whether we're painters a hundred years ago or songwriters of the future, I think we learn how to recognize those moments that would make sense to other people as well. So when I do my big paintings in my computer—you know, they're giant, huge nine-foot tall paintings—I do them very much the same way as I'm doing my songs. They might be about native issues or they might be about something very universal, you know, like the songs are love songs, or the paintings might be something that anyone could see from their own point of view. What I'm capturing is something that anyone could see. You know, I'm capturing the obvious that nobody is noticing because it's, you know, it's my own point of view, it's my own little camera. And I think most people are artists. It's just that almost everybody's been turned off to it by the particular way that our school systems are still kind of learning how to best serve our children.

AM What took you to Greenwich Village? Was Greenwich Village just the place to go to hear folk music, to sing folk music?

BSM Well actually, I had been singing in college in a coffee house called *A Salad & Coffee House* just off campus. And I'd been doing that for several years and enjoying it very much and, you know, they passed the hat for the various singers and most people were singing folk songs. But I was singing songs that I would write, and I found out that people liked the songs that I was writing—they encouraged me to keep on writing. So I was on the way to India. I was supposed to go to India, I had a scholarship to go to a school that was founded by Ghandi for people like me who had a strong attraction to the things of the creator. And for me creativity is in a way a metaphor for my religion, you know. It says in the bible that we're made in the image of the creator. What does that most obviously mean to me? We're creative. Our creativity is what makes us better people, and our recognition of creativity in other people is what really connects us to them, see. But this is not advertised because it doesn't make anybody any money you see. It doesn't really, so you don't hear about it in this way. So instead of going to India immediately, I decided to go to Greenwich Village and sing my songs there, and have some fun and see what that was about, and hear some other music, and then I'd be done with it. Sure as shootin' everybody in the world wanted to hear these songs. I wasn't much of a singer, and I don't... I mean, my records received a lot of attention and a lot of acclaim and awards and things right off the bat. But I've always thought that it was because of the quality of the songwriting, 'cause I wasn't much of a singer and it was only out of embarrassment at listening to my records that I became a better singer.

AM Your voice always had an absolutely unique and distinctive quality to it. I think that that's one of the things that people plugged into, that you sang unique things and in a unique way. I'm sure people have said that to you before.

BSM Yeah. Also, I had a curiosity about sound that made my guitar sound very different, 'cause I tuned my guitar all inside out and upside down, which I wasn't the only person who did that, but I was probably the first to become famous who was doing that. Joni Mitchell also was doing it, but it wasn't for a few years later. The Mississippi blues delta singers were also doing that, but nobody was really… they weren't playing them on the radio, you know, so… The Hawaiian slat-key players were doing it, Ry Cooder was doing it, much better than I was, but you know, he hadn't really hit yet. So there was an unusual sound. Also I played a mouth bow, which was a very curious thing to play, relying on harmonics and using your mouth as a resonating cavity like the sound hole in the guitar, and coming up with, you know, really strange sounds.

AM A funny instrument for you to get interested in. How did that come into play?

BSM Well, the mouth bow's found all over the world, and anywhere where they use a hunting bow. And I've always said that sooner or later the musician in the group figures out that you can make music on a weapon, you know. It's just a bow. And if somebody gives me a hunting bow I can play music very well on it.

AM You plant it in your cheek, right?

BSM Well, you just rest it against the corner of your mouth; it doesn't go inside your mouth, it just sort of rests against the side of your mouth.

AM And then as you change the shape of your mouth it changes the tone?

BSM Yeah, it does. Which sounds complicated, but if you had to figure out, if you had to explain… Suppose you had to write a paper on how to whistle, you can't do it.

AM So Greenwich Village back in those days. I mean it was sort of the scene and there were so many people who have become extremely famous. Were you part of a community?

BSM No, 'cause I was a little early. I was kind of early for that. Bob Dylan was coming out. Joan Baez was already very well-known, but she was sort of known from Boston and recording. She wasn't, I don't think that she was playing a lot in the Village. So it was very early. Phil Ochs was playing.

I mean, the early sixties was a real creative time, a very unusual time; there's never been a time like that in the U.S. that I've ever heard about. It was a time when students ruled. That's what it was about—it was about students and it was about coffee. And by 1966, in my opinion it was over; it had already been co-opted by big business. Um, and when you see, you know, Woodstock and all these kind of late sixties things being about the sixties, I always say it's a crock. Because to me the sixties was not about the Mamas and the Papas or rock 'n roll players on drugs. It wasn't like that. It was about coffee. There was a little pot around, but it was about individuals having something to say and speaking out one student to another student, and everybody had something to say in those days. And those of us who were saying it with a guitar were just kind of expressing ourselves, and so I was not a part of, like, the manager's scene, you know. By 1966 or so, two or three managers sort of controlled it all and funneled all the money to their, what they called their stable of artists. And I was not a part of that, I was definitely on the outs of that. Another thing that I've always thought was wonderful for me, but terrible for my career, um… when I would do a concert in New York I wouldn't hang around and schmooz and go to parties and do whatever, you know, you were supposed to do as an up and coming star, yeah. I'd take off for the nearest reservation because that's what was interesting to me. And I didn't expect to last anyway. So I did everything wrong. I did not kiss the guys on both cheeks like you were supposed to do when you came from this kind of different cultural background. That I didn't understand. I had never met a lawyer. I had never had a conversation with a businessman. I didn't understand that the New York business scene was also a social scene and you're supposed to schmooz, you know, come over the house.

AM Be bored to tears, I suppose.

BSM I think people probably thought I was a snob, but actually it was very sincere on my part. I didn't expect to last and I didn't know that was what you were supposed to do, and I wanted to use my time to get to know people on the reservations because I was travelling for the first time.

AM Let's have another piece of music now Buffy.

BSM You know, there's a song on my album called *God is Alive, Magic is Afoot*, and my cowriter is Leonard Cohen, and when I'm sitting there doing my digital paintings I'm very often listening to any cut from Leonard's career, but particularly from his record *The Future*. [MUSIC]

AM Were you politically involved in those days, like with the American Indian movement?

BSM Well that came later. But if you're talking about the early sixties, and like the days of protest marches and the civil rights movements, I wasn't. I mean, I wrote *Universal Soldier* and it was kind of the anthem for the peace movement, but for my part I sincerely believed that there was enough people on that bandwagon. You know, there were thousands of people doing that and there was nobody covering the base of native American, native Canadian indigenous rights. Nobody was doing it. Bob Dylan and Joan Baez and Judy Collins were not there, and we really needed to get out the information to people, and I sincerely believed that if the public understood how it is for Indian people then they would respond and things would change. And to some extent that was correct. So that's where I was. It's not that I didn't believe in those other causes, it's just that I thought, shoot, they don't need me. So I went where I felt I could do the most good, and it did do some good.

AM Tell me about the writing of *Universal Soldier*.

BSM Well, uh, I can't remember exactly when it was, but since it's on my first album it was probably in the early sixties. And we were being told that there was no war going on in Vietnam. And a lot of students were saying, there is too, there is too. And then we were being told, those students must be communists or anti-government or something, you know, which was a crock, too. So I had been singing I guess somewhere—probably L.A.—and I had to go through San Francisco anyway. And it was one of those flights where I arrived on the last flight to San Francisco, and then I was supposed to go out in the morning on the first flight to Toronto 'cause I had an engagement at the *Purple Onion* in Yorkville. And here it is, the middle of the night, and these guys are wheeled in on gurneys and stretchers and wheelchairs. And these are soldiers in uniform; man, they're just all bandaged, you know, the entire head a bandage, or they're bandaged from head to foot. These are people who are on the verge of death, being wheeled in by their friends. And I got to talking to their friends, who were my age, right. I mean, here I am, you know, I'm in my twenties and there's a bunch of soldiers. We got to talking and they told me yeah, there's a war. They were coming back from Vietnam. And I got to thinking how absolutely horrifying this is, and who's responsible for war. I mean, you know, where do I complain, you know what I mean. And who's responsible?—these guys who are lying laid out here, and their friends who are bringing them home. And in a way I suppose, yeah, they are responsible. But it has to go farther than that. I mean, what about career military officers who do this as well as they can, who make war with every bit of intelligence the Lord has given them. Of course they are responsible as well. And by the time I was up in the air and on the way to Toronto, I was saying well, yeah, who is it who aims the army? Who is it who gives the word? Well it's the politicians; and I thought I had it. But by the time I got to this little folk club where I was going to appear, I said, well wait a minute, who is it who votes for the politicians?—oh my God, it's us. So it's about the individual responsibility for wars, and you know there's a line in it, it says: *He's the universal soldier and he really is to blame, but his orders come from far away no more. You know, they come from him and you and me, and brothers can't you see, this is not the way we put an end to war.* So that was a very bold thing for an Indian girl from Saskatchewan to be shooting her mouth off about, and it wasn't too much longer before, without my knowledge—I didn't find out for ten years—that Lyndon Johnson was sending letters from the White House on White House stationery to radio broadcasters, making sure that my music was no longer played. And within a couple of years, when I would be asked to come on to the *Tonight Show*, you know, I'd be asked not to talk about Indian people or anything, except you know just giggle and bubble like the other girls do. And, um, things were made very rough for me. When I would do a concert in Toronto, the records would all be in the stores, but when I would do a concert in Philadelphia, you know, there'd be thousands of people at the concert but there weren't any records in the store. And the record company couldn't explain it so, you know, somewhere along the line all those records were just…

AM The word had come down not to distribute it.

BSM It disappeared.

AM How did you find out about the letters from Johnson?

BSM Ten years later… I mean, I had continued to have a career in Asia, Europe, Canada, um, Australia. But in the U.S. I just figured well, you know, they're fickle, you know, they don't like me anymore, you know, it's over for me there. But no, ten years later broadcasters came forward with that information. The first one was in Toronto, then in Chicago, and after that other places. You know, people would say, well you know, at the time we believed that we should suppress you, and I'm ashamed to say that we were wrong and I'm very glad to tell you that I'm sorry that we did that. But you know, it was over by that time in the U.S.

AM But your music had spread out so far then that so many other people were doing your music.

BSM Yes, right.

AM How does that feel?

BSM It feels great.

AM Do you listen to other people doing your music?

BSM Well, when I get to hear it, but it's not as though I have somebody who keeps tab on who's recording it. But at one point, um, I asked somebody to find out how many people had recorded *Until It's Time for You to Go*, just for the fun of it, and it was somebody who had that kind of information at his fingertips, and he found out about fifteen years ago that *Until It's Time for You to Go*, which is just a love song, had been recorded by over 200 artists in sixteen different languages. And it continues to be recorded, so I just don't know how many different artists have recorded it. But it's so flattering, you know, that another artist would care for the song that much to, make it a part of their lives. For Elvis Presley and Priscilla, his wife, it was their love song, and lots of very famous artists recorded that song—Barbara Streisand and Johnny Mathis, Roberta Flack, and Sonny and Cher, and Neil Diamond.

AM Your art work has also been well received?

BSM My paintings have been very well received at the Glenbow in Calgary and as part of the Pixel Pushers Exhibit, which was done by Lori Sheeba, who is living in Calgary. But she heads the Pixel Pushers Group, and she was the first person—she did it in Vancouver at the Emily Carr College of Fine Arts—to initiate the combination of digital art as frameable art on the walls. At the Emily Carr College and also on-line at the same time. And my paintings have since been in several museums, lots of galleries, and I have my second big exhibit in Toronto. And if you saw the Juno tribute, which was so kind to me, the paintings that were shown there, those are some of the paintings that are on exhibit across Canada. And digital art is very new, but Canada has responded. You know, I think Canada… You know, people in the States refer to Canada *as our neighbour to the north, that little country up there you know*—and it always ticks me off man, it makes me just open my mouth and shout. And I always think of Canada as pretty hip. You know, our celebrated lack of self-esteem. You know, it's pretty hip. We're not stuck on ourselves and we are under-celebrated by ourselves. And I think the U.S. is so full of self-advertising, you know, just for money, that they kind of missed the boat even on their own multicultural groups. I mean, you'd never hear about native people in the States, and I think that they're behind times in digital technology as well. I think we're ahead… there are a lot of things that we're doing that don't make the huge headlines that the advertisers in the U.S. will sponsor.

AM Now, from the beginning you've always focused your music on Indian rights and environmental issues.

BSM And love songs.

AM And love songs. But those two, the Indian rights and environmental issues, are things, topics that have sort of been popular and then gone out of fashion and then come back again.

BSM Well they don't make anybody a whole lot of money, except every now and then. When they're gonna make somebody a fistful of money, like when *Dances With Wolves*, or you know, 20 years earlier, *Little Big Man*, you know, then they become popular and everybody puts on a turquoise necklace for that week.

AM Do you think about that, I mean saying well, I'm—consciously saying—I'm sticking at it, I don't care what the rest of you are interested in right now, knowing that eventually people will turn around and look again?

BSM Well that's a little strong. It's much sweeter than that actually. The thing is, I spend so much time with indigenous people throughout the world—not only in Canada, but in, you know, Scandinavia and Australia, everywhere—that I'm trying to give the rest of the world the benefit of the experiences that I have, which are wonderful experiences, 'cause I feel as though the genius for government and the thinking of alternative peoples are what is going to save us from just the same old non-answers to the same old very serious problems. Nobody ever consults with indigenous people, you know, until it's too late. I mean now there's some recognition that, gee, maybe those Indians really do know something about how to survive for 50 thousand years and keep the land happening.. Maybe they do know. So it's a matter of being experienced with indigenous cultures and really loving them, and finding out what fun they are that keeps me happy to pass it on to other people. 'Cause I really do believe in the contributions of native people.

AM Let's pause for a piece of music now. What shall we play?

BSM I'd like to play something by Miles Davis on a record that I play over and over again—it's called *Sketches of Spain*.

AM Oh, I love that too. Why do you love it?

BSM I don't know, just the combination of Gil Evans and Miles Davis, it's just… ah, it's just something happened with that incredible music. They're both fantastic, Godly musicians, and the music is just very, very wonderful—it just thrills me. [MUSIC]

AM That was *Sketches of Spain* by Miles Davis and Gil Evans, the choice of my guest today on Mountaintop Music, Buffy St. Marie.

Do you remain optimistic about love?

BSM Oh boy. Yeah, I do. I'm kind of an optimist about almost everything anyway, you know. I mean, if I see a problem I usually… at least I enjoy trying to find a solution and talking to people and finding out what their solutions might be. But when it comes to love and love songs, I have to say that it's not that much different from writing another kind of song, but it feels different. For instance, a song like *Until It's time for You to Go*, it comes from an emotional place and the emotion can stay very pure to what it is, as opposed to something like *Universal Soldier* or *Bury My Heart at Wounded Knee*, which require a lot of work. They require a lot of cleverness and thinking because in order to describe what you're trying to say when it comes to *Bury My Heart at Wounded Knee* or *Universal Soldier*, I have to figure out how to keep someone's attention on something in which they have no interest going in, and I have to make my point in three-and-a-half minutes and entertain them at the same time. So that's a lot of work. When it comes to a love song, since everybody loves to be in love it's a lot easier to write a love song and to reach that place in someone, just by being true to yourself. And I'm very optimistic about love. I have a wonderful sweetheart now; he's a single parent, he's raised his two kids, who are now eight and nine, from the time that they were both in diapers. He's raised them all by himself.

His family fell apart when his little girl was only six months old. So for a man on his own to raise two little kids on a very low income, it's given him qualities that have made me learn an awful lot about not only parenthood, not only fatherhood, but about that possibility in men, which I had never come across before. And there's always something to learn, you know, with our fellow human beings, and I love him and his kids very much.

AM You've said that you don't think marriage is particularly good for women.

BSM Well, not the kind of marriages that I have seen, no.

AM What are your concerns?

BSM Oh, well I don't know. You know that *Men are from Mars and Women are from Venus*—I think that's a very nice metaphor—and I think that men, you know, once they close the deal they sort of stop romancing, and I think an awful lot of women, we need romance and support. We need things that men don't know that we need, you know. We need a certain connection of the heart and respect of the mind and attention to the body, that men think you do once and then that closes the deal so you don't have to do it anymore, right? 'Cause that's the way guys… That's the way it is for guys, you know. They are trying to make the connection and then get on with other things very often. That's at least, you know, the old-fashioned kind of man. So when I say that I don't think marriage is good for women, I think that men and women go into marriage with maybe different expectations and they never really talk about it. I said that quite a long time ago and I think that men are probably learning, because they have to because women insist upon it, you know. And there is the great popularity of that *Men are from Mars, Women are from Venus* kind of thing 'cause it's very well said in that concept. I mean, I think that women do study emotion, and women do study how to make a better marriage. I mean, how often in a men's magazine do you see 'How to Make a Better Marriage', you know, or 'How to Please Your Spouse', or… You don't see any of that stuff, right?

AM No. 'How to Take a Car Apart'.

BSM Yeah, yeah. Or how about, 'How to Put a Woman Together'.

You know, it's not that difficult. You know, it's just that guys don't hear about it, they don't have that information at their fingertips. It's not that they're not willing to learn and it's not that they don't wanna learn, it's just that they don't come across the information. And so women very often wind up pulling the cart all by themselves, and the man does not even recognize that it's going on because he's not set up for it. So it's not so much his fault, he's gonna have an awful lot more fun if he, you know, gets with it and really tries to interact with his wife the way that he interacted with her when she was his sweetheart, you know. Because the sales job is never over honey, I'll tell ya.

AM You were saying that your sweetheart now has been a single parent, and that of course would be an experience that you could share with him—you'd understand what that was like. You raised your little boy all the way up now. He's off at university?

BSM Yes he is. He's 19 and he's in a music college and doing very well.

AM I remember him so well from *Sesame Street*.

BSM Me too.

AM Why did you get involved with *Sesame Street*? Tell me about that.

BSM Well, first *Sesame Street* approached me like they approached Stevie Wonder and everybody else under the sun; you know, come on and be a celebrity and count from 1 to 10 and then get out of here. I said, na, I know who I am and I have something to give. I've been in this show business thing for awhile and, especially in the U.S., I want to reach children with something that's not only very charming, but also very important—and that's one idea. I want to let little kids and their caretakers know that Indians exist because of the way I had grown up, with nothing but dead Indians and no self-identity. That was my one point. I wanted to do some programming—don't forget I'm a teacher—so I wanted little kids and their caretakers to see that native people not only have families, we have fun, we have grandparents, we have neighbourhoods, we have many cultures, we have languages, we have many ways of counting, and I did wind up counting on *Sesame Street*. I taught the Count how to count in Cree, and Navajo. And you know there's a very big subliminal message; in other words, I was teaching little kids and their caretakers that Indian people know how to have fun, that we have toys, that we not only have a history, but we have a present, and a future, and that they can be a part of it. So *Sesame Street* wound up being my buddies for five-and-a-half years. Now, during the first six months of *Sesame Street* I found out that I was gonna have a baby. So I confessed this to them and figured that they'd say, okay, good-bye; but no, they said we've never had a baby on *Sesame Street*, we've never dealt with family, we've never dealt with sibling rivalry. So we got into another whole avenue of topics besides just native programming. And sibling rivalry is really something, and I feel sorry for little children because their parents—especially new parents—they've never dealt with it. And none of us are really trained for parenthood anymore, and everybody tells the little kid, oh, you're going to have a little baby brother and sister, isn't that fun. And it turns out it's not fun at all. Mommy comes back from the hospital and she's wrecked, she's in bed, it's like she's been hit by a truck. The little kid doesn't get any more attention—it's all coo coo and the baby and poor mom, and this poor little kid is left out. And he thought that he was gonna have a little brother and sister and, you know, play with the wagon and the dolls and, you know, play video games. And the kid just lies there, doesn't smell good, makes a lot of noise—it's a drag. And so that's what we did, you know, we told the truth. Big Bird… The way that we set it up, see, I was… Buffy was the only person who, as Big Bird's best friend, could actually take him seriously and actually see Snuffleupagus. I mean the people at Children's Television Workshop who bring us *Sesame Street* are fantastic, and they are wonderful child psychologists, and they understand what children really need—not that old, you know, baby formula kind of stuff, but what children really need. And they set it up so that Big Bird's best friend all of a sudden was going to have a baby. And Big Bird was prepared for it the same way that most little children are prepared for it: in other words, lied to. And Big Bird found out it was no fun at all, and, you know, he did a whole number on… [mimicking Big Bird]..naaaaah, they're watching the baby take a bath—that's no fun, nobody watches me take a bath. You know, he really put it like it is. And ah, eventually you know, we worked it out. It was quite dramatic. But, you know, it took a couple of weeks, and we actually were teaching parents what to do, and kids what to tell their parents and how to be honest with their parents. You know, just giving the kids the reinforcement.

AM And that it's okay to feel that way; you're not a horrible person.

BSM That it's right on, that it's accurate, that this is reality, yes. Because most of us in our lives are not taught to deal with reality or not taught to acknowledge reality.

AM And then we're told we shouldn't feel like that.

BSM That's right. And this is all a little crazy, huh, especially little children. And then the other thing, once all the sibling rivalry was kind of dealt with we got into breast feeding. Now this was my idea right, 'cause I was nursing my baby and, you know, I wasn't about to, you know, be getting up in the middle of the night and sterilizing bottles. Are you kidding me, it's too much work. I mean, you know, here we are all in the bed together; you cuddle the baby and the baby goes back to sleep and we're all happy. So I was a great believer in, you know, just natural breast feeding, and so I wanted to do this on *Sesame Street*. And they talked it over and within a couple of weeks agreed that this would be a very good thing. So you know the way they handled it was so nice. Big Bird walked in like he usually does and said, hi Buffy, what ya doin? I said, I'm feeding the baby. And he looked and he said, that's a funny way to feed a baby. Now mind you it was all very discreet and it was shot over my shoulder and, you know, breast feeding in an airport, you know, nobody even knows what you're doing. It's not as though you're exposed in any way; you're all covered with your clothes. And babies and mothers know how to do this. And so what I said to Big Bird was well, you know, he's getting everything that he needs to eat for now, and I get to cuddle him. And Big Bird looked some more and he said, oh, that's nice, and then he went back to playing, which is usually the reaction of a four-year-old, you know. It's just perfectly within their grasp.

AM   And I remember as your little boy got to be a toddler and was still with you on *Sesame Street* wasn't he.

BSM Yeah, 'til he was five-and-a-half.

AM   And it was nice because he wasn't acting, there was a real 'this is just us and who we are' sense to it. That must have been great to be able to have him with you all the time?

BSM Yes it was, and it was very hard to be doing two television shows a day with a new baby, or with a toddler, or with a four or five-year-old, you know. It was hard. But they do know what they're doing on that program. And the way they do it none of the children are acting. And you know it takes a long time to set up TV shows; there's a lot of lighting and there's miking, and of course with the Muppets there's a lot of technology that goes into getting that right. And what they do is they set it all up and the children are all in a big room alongside the TV studio playing together, having fun, you know, and having a good time. They're not watching TV, they're just playing together. And then, when it's time to do it the kids come in.

AM   So those were obviously really important years to you?

BSM They were. And I think my peers in the music business probably thought, oh poor Buffy, you know, this is the nadir of her career; but it wasn't really. And what they weren't realizing was that not only did these kids grow up year after year, but also *Sesame Street* is the most viewed television show in the world, and three times a day in 72 countries of the world is a lot of good times.

AM   And important work, you know, really, really worthwhile. You were also doing some singing with your little guy when he was a baby and he'd curl up in your guitar case.

BSM You know, I took 16 years off in the middle of my career to be a mommy and to be an artist. And you know, I think probably when you're thinking about your favourite artist, when they have a hit you think, oh boy, are they creative; but that's usually the time that we're not allowed to be creative because we're out selling records. The time when we're creative is when you're not hearing about us and you think, oh, whatever happened to what's his name, you know. He's probably at home writing and experiencing a life that he'll then bring to you in another two years. And that's what I did. I took two years off and it was the most creative time for me. I continued my learning of electronic music, I was scoring movies, I was doing concerts on reserves and in Indian areas, I was doing occasional concerts for UNICEF in foreign countries, and I was learning about digital technology. I was learning about the first music computers. And so when Macintoshes came along in the early eighties I was just right at the head of the line, and I found out the first day that I could make my paintings, I could record my songs and write them, and I could also write my stories all on the same little machine, and within a couple of years I could do it in colour, a couple more years I could make it portable. So that now I can write and record music in a teepee in Saskatchewan, you know, on a little portable power book.

AM   If you were doing a lot of concerts on reserves and reservations in those years as well, connecting in with other people, did you learn new music too during that time?

BSM Oh yeah. As I would travel from reserve to reserve, I would, you know, be hearing new music all the time. Because it's not as though this grassroots power music is all old music; it's not. Like Loreena McKennitt's music, a lot of it, although it's in a traditional form using traditional instruments, it's brand new, it's contemporary. Some of it is funny, a lot of it's love songs—a lot of the round dance songs are love songs. Some of it has a very strong message; it's all different kinds of music. Just like any other kind of music it has many faces. So I'm always learning from my travels, wherever I go, whether it's to the Arctic or New Zealand, Hawaii—wherever I go, I find that people are always making new music and still retaining values from their own cultures. It's a wonderful world.

AM You've been in Hawaii for 30 years now. Now what made Hawaii home?

BSM The fact that it's very rural where I live. I live hundreds of miles on a different island across the ocean from Honolulu; I don't live there, I'm on a different island. And, um, it's totally multicultural, multiethnic—there are people from all over the world. You know, you'll be checking out groceries and the checker is half Dutch and half Tahitian, you know, or she's from Bali or he's from Japan or China, or his family has been in Hawaii for hundreds of years although they're Japanese or Filipino, or you know, they're originally from Europe or… from everywhere. So it makes it a lot of fun. And Hawaii for me is a lot more like Canada than the U.S. It has much more Canadian values in appreciating each other's culture. It's loose; it's not only concerned with the mighty buck, and ah, most of all it's extremely beautiful. I mean it's not just the weather, because we get some severe weather, we get stuff that makes a blizzard look like nothin. We get hurricanes and we get tornadoes; we had a hurricane two years ago that had 14 tornadoes inside it, and it sat on top of our island for hours. And we have tidal waves and we have volcanoes, so don't ever think that Hawaii is, you know, just one day at the beach. And I live in the mountains consequently. But it's beautiful. It's a wonderful place to live because of the people and the values of the people there, just really loving the land.

AM Now we call this Mountaintop Music, and before we send you off to your mountain top we let you take one book with you. What would you take?

BSM I think I would take *Indian Givers* by Jack Weatherford, because no matter how many times I read it, it's always surprising to me all the different ways that people from the western hemisphere have influenced the rest of the world—not only our foods but our genius for government and our medicines and our ways of thinking, our philosophies, our roads, our clothes, our way of travel, and ah, you know, it's just full of surprising information. Like a lot of people don't know that the biggest pyramid in the world is not in Mexico or Egypt or Peru, it's in the United States.

AM Where is it?

BSM It's in Missouri as a matter of fact.

AM Really?

BSM Yup. *Indian Givers* by Jack Weatherford. I usually have a copy with me, and usually at Christmastime I give them away as presents.

AM And you also get to choose where you would spend the rest of your days if you were being cast away. Where would you go?

BSM In Hawaii. I'm already there, I'm already in heaven.

AM And what's your final choice of music Buffy?

BSM Let's see. I would like to play, from the record Balance, *I Can't Stop Loving You* by Van Halen.

AM And why that one?

BSM I love the enthusiasm that these guys continually bring to the stage. I was at their concert last summer in Toronto. Two nights in a row 16,000 people were standing up, and it just felt as though those four guys, only four people, had brought us the most wonderful show, and it just felt as though each of the people on stage was playing specifically for each of the people in the audience. It was such a generous, exciting show. You know, they've been around for a long time but they continue to thrill people and write incredible songs with… there's just so much positivity and good health. I like it.

AM Thanks a lot Buffy. This has been great.

BSM My pleasure.

TIMOTHY FINDLEY
WITH ANDREA MARANTZ, 1999

AM You were born in Toronto; you're a born and bred eastern, well central I suppose—Canadian.

TF But I am not a WASP. What I am is Irish and Scots—mostly Irish, definitely not Presbyterian. That aspect of my life as a child was wonderful to have because, of course, I had an Irish grandmother, and there's no-one more volatile and giving and storytelling than that. I loved my childhood, I had a wonderful childhood. It was a lovely city, totally different from the city it is now. We lived on a tree-lined street and it was as though one were living in a village, and you walked out of the village. And my father would walk out of the village and get on a streetcar and head down for Bay Street. We walked through the village to go to school, feeding all the horses on the way because it was still the time of horse-drawn wagons.

AM You've spoken a lot, reflected on your childhood, on the positive and the difficult things; it wasn't an easy childhood. You loved your parents, but there were troubles.

TF God rest his soul and God bless him, my father was an alcoholic, and that meant that mother had to be one of those people who… Her parents had been divorced and the last thing that was going to happen was that they would separate. But I ultimately discovered, many years later, that there were moments when my brother Michael and I knew that they were in terrible trouble, and that we were in trouble because of his condition. He would rage and rant and roar and kick things over, and so on and so forth. And mother confessed, long after the problem had been solved—he gave up the drinking ultimately—that she always kept a suitcase packed, ready for flight.

AM Was it something that was in your heart, too—the flight, the idea of leaving, ever?

TF It was a childhood full of privilege because the house was full of books. My best friend was a very creative reader type kid, and we had great games of pretense, we lived pretend lives. And when my friend wasn't there, I had a pretend life of my own. My brother was older than me, I was always the nuisance who tagged along behind. I only had the one friend, and there's nothing sad about that, it was just the way we were. And if he wasn't available, then I would try to tag along with my brother, and my brother was always saying, get the hell out of here—who needs you, you know. And if you're the older brother, passing through and heading for puberty and adolescence, who does need a brat following after. So I had all this imaginary life. And there used to be a maid through the 1930's and '40's, and my life was spent coming home from school, sitting in the kitchen with the maid—she tells stories—and she offered the kind of love that can only be offered by the close stranger who is living in your environment. Mother offered all kinds of assurances and comfort, but she could never offer total safety because we were always about to take flight. And then I would leave the maid in the kitchen and head out for the garden, climb over the wall and go down into the park behind the house, and you just went down into this world of magic that was full of trees and grass, and I had an imagined life in that ravine. And that I think is what got me through. I think my brother suffered a bit more because he had more confrontations with my father than I did. I was always offered as the placebo. When father was in bad shape, I had to sleep with him, mother wouldn't. Michael was terrified of him. I don't think I was so much terrified as merely mystified. But he wouldn't go to bed alone. Now there's no sex here—we're not talking that kind of thing—but he couldn't abide being alone in a bed, so it was decided that little Tiffy, being the gentle child so to speak, was a good calming influence. And that worked.

AM A teddy bear, really.

TF I was his teddy bear, yes.

AM I've also read that despite his problems and the difficulty in the relationship, he always encouraged your creativity.

TF Well, he encouraged the creativity in both of us. My brother was way beyond me in reading, and by the time he was eleven he'd put all the poets behind him and could quote them all. He was reading Gibbon when he was eleven years old—*The Decline and Fall of the Roman Empire*. He was something to behold, but he went on to become basically schizophrenic, an alcoholic himself, and nothing happened. That was very sad, but equally he could drive you just crazy. There's nothing worse than a wasted life. But father, in order to keep Michael going, was really more encouraging to him than he was to me. But he did encourage me to read—he'd put books in my hand; he read to us, he quoted poetry to us. Many evenings, instead of a bedtime story, he would simply stand in the doorway with his cigarette in the dark, and quote poetry. And ultimately, when it came time for me to quit high school—I'd been ill for a year-and-a-half and I'd got behind in my lessons and I didn't want to do any of it anyway; I wanted to be a dancer and go on to theatre—and I had a wonderful teacher. This is now in the beginning of my second year of high school. My parents were very worried. The teacher called the parents in and he said, you know, I think the best thing we can do for Tiff is to let him go. He's intelligent and he knows a direction, he has a direction to head into; we really can't offer him what he needs. And my parents said yes.

AM And where did you go?

TF I went and worked at Massey House and took ballet lessons, and that's how I paid for them. To me in memory it's a riotously funny scene. I am a homosexual and I'm sure that some of that showed, particularly in this late adolescence when I'm seventeen years old. But I went to the factory wearing guy clothes, you know, and big clunky boots, and the jacket and the hat and the lunch pail in my hand, and I'd ride home on the streetcar on the bus, and I'd get home and I would take all that off and put on just ordinary jeans or chinos or something, and a shirt and a jacket, and I would pack my leotards and my ballet slippers and get back on the same bus and go to my ballet lesson.

AM You were already an actor in different costumes?

TF Of course. I was already playing roles. Yeah, the dancing thing didn't work out. I had a wonderful teacher and she became one of my lifelong friends. I had talent, there was no question of that. This is God given and not something you make up. And I had a good body for it except for one thing—I had a fused disc. And I would have made a useful dancer, but never a great one, and who needs to be anything but a great one if you're heading out into the mainstream. But luckily it got channeled into acting very quickly.

AM So how did the move to the theatre come about?

TF Amateur productions. I went out looking to see what they were and found some. There was a man in Toronto, whose name was Earl Grey—he was English—and he'd come to Canada and started what was called *The Earl Grey Players*. And they played, every summer, Shakespeare in the quad at Trinity College in Toronto. Ultimately Earl said, now we're going to start touring, and we have to have professionals who are going to be dependable. So he offered us each twenty dollars—Jack and I—twenty dollars a week, and that was when it became professional. Then, again, going back to my parents and their support, it was decided I needed vocal help. There was a glorious, gigantic woman whose name was Clara Baker. Clara Baker taught Franny Highland and Amelia Hall and Kate Reid; she taught at the Royal Conservatory of Music. So there I was at the Royal Conservatory of Music with Clara Baker. Well the first thing she said when you'd walk in—and there was this gigantic, I mean truly gigantic woman, with a glorious voice, pictures of John Barrymore and all these people all over the wall, all signed to her—and she said, okay, hit me in the diaphragm. Hit me in the diaphragm. And you hit a woman?—or hit anybody on invitation. She said, no, I mean it. Hit me. And you hit iron. And that was what she built, she built through the diaphragm.

AM This would probably be a good place to pause for our first piece of music. Was music important to you? I mean obviously, if you were interested in dancing it played a role in your life?

TF Oh, it played an enormous role. I used to embarrass my parents, I think, although they enjoyed it in their way. I would perform ballets in the living room. I'd buy the records, which I was always nearly killed for—spending your money on a silly recording—but I would buy these records and then I would dance, make up the whole ballet in the living room. I always listened to the opera on Saturday afternoons, the Metropolitan Opera, and loved that. I mean I lived for those… There was a symphony concert every Sunday afternoon on the radio—these were all CBC radio things. There's a book now called *The Red Shoes*, which is about Margaret Atwood But she was very disturbed by *The Red Shoes*, as I was; but I was exhilarated by it because it was about a life of dance. And while it was tragic because the woman gives up her life rather than make the choice between dance and love, for Margaret Atwood it was the first indication that if you're an artist you can't have the rest of life, and she did not agree with that. Even as a kid she knew how wrong that was. So that's why the book is called *The Red Shoes*. Well that was seminal, too. So music was everywhere in my life and I loved musical theatre. I talked about the Saturday afternoon at the opera. And this, in it's time, was one of the great popular numbers, and still is for opera buffs; but people used to sing this in the streets the way we now sing whoever, Frank Sinatra or Elvis Presley or whatever, and it is *Muzetta's Waltz* from *La Boheme*, and it is one of the most glorious moments in all of opera. [MUSIC]

AM Tell me about meeting Tyrone Guthrie, who proved to be a significant part of your life.

TF He was the founder of the Stratford, Ontario Shakespearean Festival, as it was then known. He was one of the great, great figures in theatre and opera, as a director. He had been at the Old Vic in London, he had molded the careers of many, many of the greatest actors. He was the one who did the Olivier/Vivien Leigh Hamlet at Elsinore Castle in the late 1930's. And he was a giant in every sense. And he was married to the wondrous Judy, his wonderful wife, and both of them eccentric as hell. Alec Guiness's wife tells a wonderful story about being out on a punt on the Avon river, and there they are, she with their guests, and they're punting along the river, and there are Tony and Judy sitting on the riverside with a picnic basket, stark naked. And he founded our Shakespeare Festival at Stratford, Ontario. Where I used to study dance was in a dance studio above some stores on Yonge Street, where you went for your audition or to be interviewed. It was a long room, and Guthrie had placed his table at the furthest end of the room, and all down either side of the room it's mirrored because of being a dance studio. And you had to make your entrance and walk the entire length of the room before you got to him, so he could see every nuance of how you moved, how you bore yourself. It was brilliant.

AM But intimidating.

TF And oh, there's nothing more horrifying or terrifying than being auditioned or interviewed for a job that you really want, because of course every actor in the country wanted to be in that first season at Stratford. I'll tell you one very quick and lovely thing about Guthrie. We had rehearsed in the big sale barns up where the market is in Stratford, 'cause the theatre of course was being built. When the theatre was finally ready—we'd had a mock-up of the stage and the balcony and all that stuff—we moved in. The seats had not been put in, but all the tiering had been done. It was all cement. Tony used to get up and he'd walk—it's semicircular as you probably know—like do a half-moon walk on one level, step up two levels and do the half-moon again, so he kept rising further and further away as he was watching us and listening to us on the stage. And what he wore to do this, in this steam bath—we all wore bathing suits, there's no other way you could rehearse—Tony had on a pair of those ghastly English woolen bathing suits for men with a belt that didn't work, so they kept sliding down. He was wearing a pair of plimsole shoes, like running shoes with no laces, and so they flapped; there were these descending shorts, he had nothing on the upper part of his body, but he covered his whole body with a transparent plastic raincoat. And so picture this giant doing these walkabouts, you know, getting further… and when he reached the furthest height, which was quite high and quite far away from the stage, Tony always did this: [TF mimicking finger snapping and clapping]. That meant stop. So I heard [finger snapping/clapping]—I was doing one of my scenes in *Richard the Third*—"Findley?" "Yes, Mr. Guthrie." And you always addressed each other formally in the theatre. "You are under the impression I'm in China? With the face no more; stop telling me everything as if I was as far from you as I could get." You just melt, you know. And I'm making faces, I'm broadcasting everything at the top of my voice. So he could be very direct, and sometimes he could be very, very cruel.

AM   He must have thought fairly highly of you; you were with him again in London in the West End in '54.

TF   Twice. Oh yes. And we had an odd relationship. At one point he went through a period when he said to Guiness, "I'm not sure that Findley's really serious about what he's doing." I don't know what prompted that. He obviously meant it and Alec challenged me with it—Alec Guiness challenged me with it—in a horrendous conversation, which I will not describe except to say it was horrendous. And I was just destroyed, because I thought here are these two giants who had encouraged me to come to England, and in fact Guiness had paid for my going to England and sent me to theatre school there, but then I knew I had to work with Guthrie again. Here came this production of *The Matchmaker* by Thornton Wilder, and I thought, what in hell's going to happen. Well, he was a little distant, but I did well in that play. But he remained, not cool, but just distant. It was as though something had been lost. And I couldn't… I didn't know what it was about, I didn't know what any of this was about, because I **was** serious about what I was doing. The next thing I knew I'd been cast in this all star production of *Hamlet*. Because I was under contract they had to use me in the interim between the ending of one play and the beginning of the rehearsals of *Hamlet*, which was a period of about two-and-a-half months. So there was a new play by Thornton Wilder called *Life in the Sun*. I was given a horrendous role, but it was really just nothing. I only had to do one thing: I had to die. But I had to die in a very spectacular way. I had to die of the plague, falling down staircases, and then having to lie there dead, you know, with your back broken. And I did an understudy and I understudied the role of Apollo, and Apollo has to stand on another of these high ridges, in blazing light of course and wearing gold—I never got to wear the costume. And the actor who was playing Apollo had to go away and finish another job for a week. So I had to go on as the understudy and do this. I thought, here's the opportunity—you know, I'll show you kind of attitude. And I have to be perfectly blunt about saying I did it very well. The result of that was absolutely wonderful, and I went away and broke into tears. Guthrie came to me and he took my hand in both his hands and he said, "Findley, I am apologizing because I had you wrong." And it was over. And what a way to leave what had threatened to be a bad memory for life.

AM   Let's have another piece of music.

TF   This is a lovely, lovely song. Last year, Bill and I toured Canada with Veronica Tennant and Joe Sealy, the great jazz pianist, and with Sylvia Tyson, who of course is the great legendary lady herself. She belongs to a group of four women who call themselves Quartette, and they've just released a new CD which is mind blowing. It is glorious; every cut is a gem, and it's called *Directions*. The song that was visibly the most moving, as well as one of the most moving of the evening in the musical sense, is a song which is called *All Things Can Change*. I think it's important to play that now given what we've just been talking about, is that everything that comes at ya isn't gonna be good, but it doesn't mean that the bad things that come at you are there forever. [MUSIC]

AM   *All Things Can Change*, that was Quartette, the choice of my guest on Mountaintop Music, writer Timothy Findley.

Another very important relationship was with Thornton Wilder, the playwright. Tell me about him?

TF   Well this came about through the fact that I was in *The Matchmaker*—this is the first encounter—with Ruth Gordon in mind to play the lead role. And for people who don't know this, *The Matchmaker* ultimately became *Hello Dolly*, so it's Dolly Levi that she's playing. I was cast as a wonderful, arrogant, awful German waiter in a gorgeous scene in a restaurant, where everything gets mixed up. Thornton was there because he had to do rewrites every day, and the great Prunella Scales, if you know who she is—*Fawlty Towers* and all else wonderful. It was a heavenly company. When we went on tour, Ruth and I went together to see an art exhibit, and all the paintings had been painted by people under the age of thirty. This is 1954; the war had not been over ten years. And so the influence on all of these paintings was the dawning of the atomic age and the horrendous burden that put on the generation that had been born, that is to say come of age in the moment of the first two bombs. So they were all very dark and negative. And we came out and Ruth was very upset. She said, "Oh, you people, I don't understand"—I was twenty-three—"why you can't say yes to anything." Wonderful reaction. She was a great survivor herself and had had to say yes to a lot of things. I went away and I had… I wasn't a writer—I thought I'll say something to her by writing it. And I wrote a story and the story was called *About Effie*, and it was my version of saying yes. But of course it was as dark as it could possibly be. And I gave it to Ruth Gordon and Ruth Gordon read it, and two days later she called me into her dressing room and she got up out of her makeup chair—this is after the performance—and she put her arms around my neck; she was very small and she looked up at me and she said to me, "You have to give up acting just as fast as you can." Last thing I wanted to be. I wanted to be Alec Guiness or Laurence Olivier. She said, "You're a born writer," and she said, "I'm going to give this to Thornton whether you like it or not." And she did. And then Thornton Wilder came to me and he said, "You are a born writer; for instance, you write extremely good dialogue and I think you should try to write a play." So I kept on writing and I wrote this play and the play was called, *A Play*. Everything pretentious that a 23, 24-year-old can possibly do, I did. I crammed it all into one play, and it was called *God's Play*—can you imagine?—and God had hired a cast of actors to take one more stab at making humankind work. And of course it didn't, so it was absolutely… Looking back, I don't know… I'm afraid I have kept a copy that's in the archive, just to prove that it was as bad as he said it was. Some months later —I got charming postcards—Thornton went off to France after we opened in *The Play* and he was writing a novel. And I'd get these postcards from Switzerland and France and Germany, from Thornton saying, *am reading play, how is acting going*? You know. *Am almost finished play, will talk on return*. And then the final one said, *have finished play, must see you urgently at Savoy Hotel*, blah blah blah—and it was the most electrifying thing you can imagine, but there was hardly a good word he had to say. And one of the big things he said: you must get rid of all this pretentiousness. Come down from all the high-minded places, no-one down here can hear you. I mean it was just dazzling.

AM   Let's have another piece of music.

TF   I'm going to take the chance of tugging a few heart strings with this glorious rendition by one of the wonders of the singing world, Annie Lennox, and it's a song by Cole Porter called *Every Time We Say Goodbye*. [MUSIC]

AM   In the late fifties you moved to Los Angeles, which wasn't entirely a happy time for you.

TF   Putting it mildly. I'd ended up there because when *The Matchmaker*, which by this time had played in New York and then we went on a tour of

America—it ended in Los Angeles—there was this extraordinary event. Garson Caine and Ruth Gordon's husband had directed the original production on the stage of *Anne Frank's Diary*, and it was being re-staged in Los Angeles. On the opening night of that play, Ruth telephoned to where I was living in a motel. She phoned and she said, I want you to come and have dinner with us on the opening night. And so we went off to this glorious dinner party at Romanoff's, it was the great restaurant to be seen in, and all the movie stars went there and they were all there that night. We all sat at a table and had this glorious meal. Between the first course and the dessert I felt Ruth's hand come over onto my lap and I thought, oh dear God, what's going on here [laughing]. And meanwhile people like Jimmy Stewart had been coming up to the table and saying, tell us who your charming young friends are, Ruth. So you're dazzled. And then this hand on your thigh, you know. But then she said… [TF laughing]—it's just like a scene in a film. So I looked at her and she said, [TF whispering, mimicking RG] "reach down." And I thought, well okay, reach down. And I reached down and in fact, in her hand, was an envelope. And I sneaked it into my inner pocket in my jacket. We went to the play, blah blah blah—it was a raging success and a wonderful evening for everybody—then we all went out to have drinks before the end of the evening. When we got there Ruth said, what you're gonna find in there is five post-dated cheques, each for a hundred dollars, which in those days was major money for an out of work actor. I said, Ruth, I can't… She said, you are going to write and I want that to happen and this is how it can happen; this will give you a bit of time to stop looking for work as an actor and start writing seriously. Then when I said, well of course I'll pay you back, she said, you never pay me back. She said, do not pay me back, pass it on. Isn't that wonderful?

California. Hollywood. It's a truly ghastly place. And what it does to human beings who have real ambitions to do something worthwhile, not just to become a star, in the present sense… you know, if you haven't appeared in People magazine eight times a year you're not worth your… 'Cause that's what it's about now. It isn't about having talent, it's about being beautiful and being able to read lines with some intelligence. And basically you're associating all the time with vile people who use you, have no sense of having any sense of sensibility about what you might be actually going through. And so I finally left and it was the greatest moment of my life, when I'd made that decision.

AM You came back to Toronto and what did you come to?

TF I went back to acting and got quite a few acting jobs and in fact was doing very well. Went back into the theatre, met Bill Whitehead in the theatre, and within a season, a theatrical season of our meeting, we both decided that we really wanted something else. I wanted the writing more, and Bill wanted another kind of writing, documentary writing, more than he wanted to be producing plays, which is what he was then doing. And so we left the theatre holus-bolus, and one night we went to sleep as actors and woke up the next morning as writers, with thirty-five dollars in our pocket.

AM You were brave.

TF You had to be. And it worked.

AM Now, in 1964, another sort of milestone in your life, is when you and Bill bought Stone Orchard, your farm. How did you find it?

TF We found it by getting lost. We had been living in Richmond Hill, which is about thirty miles north of Toronto, maybe not quite that far. We had lived in Toronto but we moved up into Richmond Hill. My parents had a house; they couldn't live in it because of my father's health, so they let us have it in this poor period of our lives for a nominal rent. And then we decided. We'd made those two moves, why don't we go further and see what it's like living in the country, because the privacy, the quietness, etc.—perfect for writers. As long as it was near enough for Bill to drive, and we'd just bought our first car. For a year-and-a-half in Richmond Hill we were using public transport all the time. We went out driving and for three days, poor Bill, all he heard from me was, we'll never find it. We're never going to find the farm that we want. We'd only been looking three days. And on the third day we got lost, and we found a real estate agent whose sign was on a property we thought we liked the look of. It wasn't the one… it wasn't fully suitable, but it had enough of the elements of what we wanted to suggest, so we finally found our way to the town where she had her agency—which was Sunderland—and went in and spoke to her and told her what we wanted. Our experience with agents up to then had been ghastly. I mean you'd say, this is the amount of money we have to spend, we want a century-old house at least, we want it on at least twenty-five acres of land. The agents would inevitably, as if they hadn't heard a word you'd said, take you to a brand new bungalow in the middle of a town that cost four or five times as much as you'd said you could spend. And this woman said, I think I have two places that just might fill the bill. And she took us out to the first one and we drove through the gates—and it had been empty for five years so there was nobody there at all—and there we stood at Stone Orchard, with these gardens that had run riot. It was the time of year when all the peonies and the day lilies are blooming together, and the roses were already in bloom, and this gorgeous old wooden house, 1848, with attached to it a brick extension that had been built in the 1870's, and beautiful little porches and land—to die for, fifty acres. My first reaction was—and I think I can say this for Bill—we knew we'd come home. I mean, you didn't have to even go inside the house to know. But then when you went inside the house you knew it even more, 'cause it was a charming place. Then we had to discover if we could afford to buy this place. And she said, well the man who owns this in fact lives on the other farm I was going to take you to, right next door. He wants to get out of farming; this is where his parents used to live and so forth, so he wants to sell both properties and get out and get a new life. She said, I could take you to meet him now, and so nervously we said yes. She then left us in his hands, his name was Nelson Purvis. To say the salt of the earth is to insult him, because he was way beyond, but he had that quality also. There wasn't a single iota of pretension to this man. He was there in his landscape as if he'd risen from the earth itself. He was a wonderful man. And we hunkered down in his barnyard. He was a dairy farmer and he had cattle. His wife and daughter had been in washing their hair—this is now latish in the afternoon—and they came scurrying out wearing their robes, with their hair all in towels, and sort of stood peering at… here are people who actually want to buy mom and dad's house. And it hadn't sold for five years. Bill said that he told me to shut up because of past experiences where I'd said, I gotta have that, I don't care what it costs. He said, now boys, you have to understand there is one price for this house next door and one only; there can be no bargaining. And our stomachs just turned over and we thought, well that's the end of that. And he was rolling a cigarette in newspaper. Now we ultimately came to understand that Nelson liked the taste of newspaper, it wasn't because he was poor—he wasn't poor—but he rolled this cigarette in newspaper. And he'd lighted his cigarette and he gazed off into the distance, and he said it's nine thousand dollars, take it or leave it. Nine thousand dollars. We had budgeted, and in those days it was fair to budget for between twenty and twenty-five, and so we… I didn't say anything.

AM Just jumped up and down…

TF But then Bill said, made this devastating statement after calmly saying that's very interesting, yes, we can certainly consider this; he said, but I am the driver, Timothy Findley doesn't drive—and I have to go to work in Toronto nearly every day, if not every day. So he said, I have to see what the drive is like. For three days I was left hanging there, tied with all these chains inside, while he drove—and very realistically, of course he had to think of this—and at last he said, yup, I can do this. And we bought it, and of course it changed our lives, virtually forever. We pumped all our water out of the hand pump for over twelve years. We were drinking the water out of the cistern, not knowing. We had some electrical work done, and when the electrician was in the house doing the electrical work—he knew the house, so he saw one of us go to the sink and drink a glass of water out of the tap—he said, I see you're drinking the water out of the tap there. Yeah, that's what it's for, ha ha ha… He said, no, not unless you've cleaned the cistern.

Cistern? Cleaned the cistern? Down we went, and in the cistern a dead skunk, a dead groundhog, dead mice—you know, the whole number. We never drank that water again.

AM Let's have another piece of music. What would you like to hear?

TF Given all the pianos in my life, I find it astonishing to say this, but in my lifetime, you know, through my mother whose father owned a piano factory and therefore visiting musicians would come, and my mother sat at table with a man who had studied with Franz Lizst, which seems to me like five thousand years ago. And in my lifetime, the greatest pianist/composer was Sergei Rachmaninoff, and I lived in his time. I heard him playing himself on the radio. He composed in my lifetime and his preludes for the piano are among… they're side by side with the great preludes of… I would say almost any one of them would be appropriate for me because this is the kind of music I used to listen to when I was alone. [MUSIC]

AM 1964 was also the year that your first novel was published—*The Last of the Crazy People*—and it was published in paperback.

TF No one in Canada would buy it. No Canadian publisher would buy it. It was the story of a little boy who kills his parents and his aunt. They would say things, as one did, pushing the book back across the table: beautifully written Mr. Findley, but we can't publish this; children don't do such things in Canada. So it was ultimately picked up by an American publisher, Bantam Paperback Publishing Company.

AM Did you get discouraged?

TF Oh boy, did I ever.

AM But you were able to keep the belief that you were a novelist, that that was who you were?

TF Absolutely. There was no problem with that. It made you want to scream sometimes. Good things began to happen late in the 1960s. By this time Margaret Laurence had happened, in the mid-sixties when she published *The Stone Angel*, and it became clear that Canadian writing was heading into an era where a great deal more than had ever happened in the past was going to start happening because there were more and more writers arriving on the scene—Marion Engel, Graham Gibson, Margaret Atwood, and early, early Alice Munro. And it was an extraordinary period and I look back on that period, through to the mid-eighties, to being—I think it will remain—the golden age of Canadian writing. You can take a big swatch of those writers' names and hold it in your hand anywhere in the world and they compare absolutely, sometimes above par. And I mean America and England and France—the writing community in Canada now is just dazzling.

AM *The Butterfly Plague* also came out in the sixties, and then into the '70s, your big novel of that time was *The Wars*. Tell me about writing that one?

TF Well, I'd written two novels in this dark period after nothing happened with the first two. I submitted one of them, which ultimately became *Head Hunter*. I submitted it to a publisher, who must remain nameless, and got the word back: We cannot, we do not want to see any more of this novel—you have traumatized our editors. Traumatized their editors. It was pretty gruesome, but at the same time this is not very responsible editorship.

AM Delicate little things.

TF Yes, but this is the thing that was… I was getting reactions like this. There was an opportunity to have *The Last of the Crazy People* presented as a Canadian paperback by another unnamed Canadian publisher, but at any rate, whoever this was who was in charge of this new series of Canadian paperbacks that were going to be done, phoned me up and said, I have to tell you, we're not going to take this book on; I mean, who needs another book by some fag writer. And it happened unfortunately in conjunction with these two novelists that no one wanted to publish.

AM But what do you do with that kind of a thing? With someone saying something like that?

TF Well, I got so lucky with having Bill Whitehead, who just simply said stand up, and we're just going to keep going. I decided I wanted to write a play; if novels weren't working, maybe the theatre would. I was hired to be the playwright in residence at the National Arts Centre, and this is the first time that had ever happened. Bill's ex-partners, Jean Roberts and Marigold Charlesworth; Jean was the director of English theatre at the National Arts Centre, and Jean said, I want you to come here and I want you to consider writing a play. So I did, and I wrote a play called *Can't You See Me Yet?* I gave it to Jean, Jean and Marigold read it, they were then making up their season for the next year. About three or four days after I gave it to them Jeannie was up, she was ill and they were up in their cottage up at Black Bernard. She had my script in her hand and she said, I want to do this, and she put it down on the floor with the other plays. Marigold directed it and it was a great, great production of a play that had some problems—all first plays do. But it was good. Well, it was torn to shreds. This is the kind of critical reaction you can get. You have to at least suffer it once, if not many times, but at least once. Things were being said about the play that were outright lies. It was as though they wanted, and I think what their agenda was, they wanted to destroy Jean's mandate at the centre. And they were a very mean minded bunch of critics in those days down there. The last one was a guy who used to broadcast on the radio. He just died. And I didn't smile or chortle or anything, but I said, well that wraps that up. And he was the most devastating of all, and unfortunately I heard him. And I was, we were in the National Arts Centre in the office section and I walked through the office section raging, went into an office and slammed the door—a very childish reaction but I think somewhat understandable. At that moment Bill Whitehead came in to me and he said, okay, I have something to tell you. We had a dear old friend who lived in Cannington, a wonderful woman called Isla Lambert. And we had bought her a beautiful dress for her to wear to the opening night of the play, and she was so excited about coming. On the morning of the dress rehearsal, the day before we opened, a telephone had rung in our apartment at six in the morning and I thought, well… Bill answered the phone and he came in and he said it was nothing, it was just someone in the costume department saying you have to remember to bring something I was supposed to bring to the theatre. On this day when I walked in and slammed the door in the office and this guy had given this foul review, and Bill said I have something to tell you, and I looked at him and I said Isla died. And he said, yes. And he said I was waiting to tell you because I knew this broadcast was coming, and he said, I hope it gives all of these reviews the perspective they deserve. And it was over. That's what I mean about being lucky. If I hadn't had Bill in my life, God knows whether one really would survive moments like that, that is to say intact. And we're just going straight down the road to the next thing. Well the next thing it so happened was me sitting in the maid's room in this huge apartment that he had in Ottawa. And I'd taken it as mine. And one night I sat there during rehearsals of *Can You See Me Yet*, and a blazing image had come into my mind and I wrote it all down on about four sheets of paper. The whole book. And the next morning I went out into the hall and Bill's room was down the hall in the other direction. I said, you gotta come and hear this. I said, I have found the next novel and it's not like the dark ones, it's positive and it's full of light and it's going to be the most wonderfully positive thing I've ever done. And Bill said, oh, what's it about? And I said, well, it's about this young Canadian in 1915 who goes off to the first world war, performs an act of absolute madness in the trenches at the front lines—tries to save all these horses, they're all burnt in a barn, he's horribly burnt, and he dies.

AM And he thought, what are you talking about.

TF But as he says now, and I believe this myself, too—I was right. It is a positive piece of work. It's life-affirming, not death-affirming. That was the breakthrough. And it won the Governor General's award and then people went back to the first two published novels and started paying attention to everything thereafter. It's been terrific.

AM Let's have another piece of music.

TF I think one that's sort of lovely, it's a song I very often play. I have a videotape of Stephen Sondheim's *Sunday in the Park With George*, which is about the French painter Georges Seurat, who was a pointillist, and literally everything is little dots and it's the creation of a single painting, but it tells the story of lives as he does this, makes the painting.

Everybody comes alive and it's wonderful. In it Seurat is nearly going crazy trying to get it right, as all artists do whatever your discipline is—there's always that moment when you think you'll never get it right. They had a beautiful technique whereby they had a gigantic scrim and you could see him through the scrim painting the painting with this… Well it looks frantic, all these little dots going on this scrim, and he sings a song called *Finishing the Hat*. It's—well, it will speak for itself, but when I'm really locked in a corner and can't get out, this is what I play. [MUSIC]

AM From Sondheim's *Sunday in the Park With George*, that was *Finishing the Hat*, the choice of my guest on Mountaintop Music, writer Timothy Findley.

AM Well, we've come to the part in the program where we have to send you off to your mythical mountain peak, but before you go you can take one book with you. If you were going to have to go away and spend the rest of your days, what book would you take?

TF Well, it's corny to say this, but it has to be the only book you could take, and that is the collected works of Shakespeare. That is to say, if English is your language and what you do is write, you will never tire of the language, the wonder of his characters. There's always more to discover about the people in his plays. And I was an actor and I never got to play Hamlet.

AM So you could play Hamlet all you wanted when you're cast away.

TF I can play it all I like at the top of a mountain. Very interesting idea, Hamlet on the mountain top. No, it's gotta be Shakespeare because it's the only book that makes any sense.

AM And if you could pick any spot on earth to be cast away to?

TF Well, there too, Stone Orchard would have to be… There is a little island there, it's not a mountain top island, but a little tiny island sitting in the middle of a farm, and there's a gazebo where I could live by the pond under the willow trees.

AM And for a final choice of music, what should we play?

TF I love film music. If one is imagining, you know, packing the bag and getting ready to go and going, I wouldn't mind departing to the music from a beautiful Italian film called *Cinema Paradiso* It's written by Ennio Morricone It's ravishingly beautiful music in every sense, but it's also, it has very joyful moments; so I would want it at both ends of the journey. I'd want it as I'd leave wherever I'm being exiled from, and I'd love it to be being played just as I stepped ashore, either on the island or on the mountain top.

AM Thank you so much. This has been a real pleasure.

TF You're very welcome Andrea. Thank you very much.

AM Well, of all the honours that you've received—and we'll talk about those a little bit later—tell me about having a street named after you in your home town.

TH Wasn't that great? I was just thrilled. I got a phone call one day and there had been some talk about it and they invited me down to city hall, and I wasn't sure why I was going to go there. And they invited my mother, who is in a retirement home.

AM There, in London?

TH In London, Ontario. Two or three of my friends were there, and the mayor got up and mentioned that they were going to name a street after me in my honour. And I thought that was very gratifying. And what I like about it, it was in the area that I grew up, I played in... There's a little park down there and I played in that park and I went swimming and I caught fish down there. And I still drive by there once in awhile and drive along all the streets. There's about six streets that flow into it, so every one of these streets that's got your name up there; it's gonna be nice when my grandchildren, when they get old enough to realize. I really am looking forward to that day when I can take them down in the car and say, Tyler, Carly, look up there. That's grandpa's name.

AM So take me back to those early days of fishing and everything around London, Ontario. Your dad was a railway worker.

TH He worked for the Canadian National Railway, and my mother (my father got really upset when I said it one time in an interview) but she was... she had several jobs. She worked for a catering company and she also went out and scrubbed floors. And my mother said to me, don't tell people that. And I said, Ma, I'm proud of that; you worked hard and there's nothing the matter with hard work. And they were just very simple folk. Why, we still have the same house in London that we grew up in, and it was a wonderful, wonderful family thing you know, with my aunts and uncles, and my grandma was very close to us and I would hop over the back fence and run over and see grandma—she used to live the next street over.

AM And your mum was an amateur pianist.

TOMMY HUNTER
WITH ANDREA MARANTZ, 1999

TH Yes, yes she played a little bit. Her two other sisters had taken some lessons. My mother was a very hard worker and she used to watch them playing the piano and my mother would watch where they were puttin' their fingers and everything, and she learned to really play by ear. I had her on stage a couple of times playing the piano.

AM Are you more like your mum or your dad?

TH Hmmm... I think I have a lot of my mother's temperament. My mother at times had a short fuse and there's times when I do, too, I must admit. I have certain characteristics of my dad, but I think my mother, ah, my mother was feisty. She still is.

AM In everything that I've read about you, people mention your tenacity and your hard work. It's remarkable. By the time you were 19 years old you had practically 10 years experience. You saw... A big turning point was when you saw Roy Acuff when you were nine years old.

TH I have no idea why I wanted to go to the show. I don't remember listening to anything on the *Grand Old Opry* or any place where I could have heard Roy Acuff, he was not a major recording artist I bugged my dad to take me to this show. And I went there and the minute that curtain went up there was this acoustic music. Remember, there were no drums, there was no big monitor system and no big PA system and intricate lighting. It was well lit, I could see it, it was plain, simple sound and I could hear the stringed instruments playing and I could hear the excitement in Acuff's voice. I could hear him, when he pushed you could hear the resonance coming out of his throat, and Acuff was a good performer. He didn't hog the stage, he shared it with his friends. And I guess when I think about it, it was almost (to some kid in London, Ontario) it was like a comic strip out of the 'Lil Abner. Acuff made it to me. I perceived that he had nothing to do and they all got in their car in Tennessee, and he called somebody who worked over at the farm and somebody who had a farm up the road a bit, and some guy who worked at the General Store, and they said, come on, let's go up to London, Ontario and take our country music and go and do a show for the folks. And that's exactly the way it came across. Now, I mean after… I wasn't always that naïve, I found out that they did tour and they were travelling, but that sound that I heard, that…you know, the old stand-up bass. Remember that?

AM Absolutely.

TH And you could hear his hand hitting the side of the string, and [TH imitating the sound]—the good sound and they would… they blended their voices in harmony.

AM And was that the first time you'd heard country music?

TH That's the first time I'd ever heard it that I recall.

AM And it just went right inside you.

TH Oh it sure did. I mean it was a wonderful, wonderful sound.

AM And the fascinating thing, one of the fascinating things that I've read about you is that from seeing that show at nine years of age, that's what you ended up basing your television show on.

TH That's right, yeah, that whole format. Do you know, Acuff did a strange thing that… I mean, I can remember this. I grew up with, you know, going to church and my mom and dad taking me to church and everything, and I remember on the stage they would all gather round and they would, would… Acuff did what they called the Jug Band, and so they would get an old jug that obviously had been used one time for some moonshine whiskey, and a guy would play the harmonica and they would just… to create a little different sound. And then all of a sudden they would all put away the comedy things and Acuff would say, you know, back home on Sunday we all gather around and we love to go to church and sing some of our gospel songs. And here's a typical gospel song that we sing down in Tennessee, and we hope you folks enjoy it. The minute he said that, the guys who had hats on they'd all take their hats off and they'd all gather 'round the microphone, and one guy would play the guitar. Their enthusiasm, their love of the gospel music was so sincere. And that's what came across. That was so important. But it was a little thing about taking the hat off. And I remember one time we had a bass player. He was brand new in our band and he had a cowboy hat on. And I did a gospel song and boy, at the end of the show I come over and I said, I'm gonna' teach you something: when the minute I introduce that gospel song, you take that hat off. And he says, why? I said, just take it off, it's disrespectful.

And it's a little small point, but that was… I said it and it was. That's the things I remember when I was nine years of age. It's just little things.

AM It's fascinating how it's those little tiny details that make all the difference.

TH That's right. And see, Acuff and I… He did my television show and it was just so rewarding. As a matter of fact I cried, 'cause it was all of a sudden full circle for me. Here was all the entertainers that I knew, and when he did the show I was waiting just to go out after he finished, and it was all that sound and I went right back from standing here right back to when I was nine years of age. And it was a wonderful, very emotional moment, and I started to cry. And I wiped it all away; I can't go out looking like a boob on TV so I wiped it all away…

AM   With all the pancakes streaming down…

TH   …and walked out. But it was very emotional for me because it had all gone full circle. And Acuff was such a wonderful man. We had a picture taken together—this is a little side story—we had a picture taken together and I got the negative, and I made two copies out of it and then I destroyed the negative. I never wanted it to be used for any promotion picture or nothing. And I told Roy what I did. I said you have one copy and I have the other copy and the negative is destroyed. This is strictly for you and I. I had it framed and I wrote on the back, thanks for giving me the format that was the groundwork for our television show for 27 years. And Roy knew that, long before I wrote that. He often said he watched that television show the first time and he said, that boy saw my show.

AM   And he recognized it right away?

TH   Oh sure, he recognized every little bit of it. See it's the little things. It's like doing a television show. We would have Glen Campbell on the show. Everybody'd say, that's really wonderful—Glen's a nice guy, he's a good singer and we like each other. The whole secret to that was when Glen would come over and I'd come walkin' in, and Glen would put his hand over on my shoulder and he'd say, "thanks Tommy, boy I've enjoyed doing the show". And I would touch him, I'd say, Glen, a pleasure to have you on the show. And none of that stuff was rehearsed. It was sincere and warm, and that's what makes it. You can write certain things, but when it happens naturally and people enjoy doing the show and I enjoy having them on the show, that's what comes across. It's like doing the readings when we did the show. My producer Les Pouliot came over one time and he said—we'd finished—and he said, we're gonna' be doin' this again; Tommy, can I see you for a minute. And he pulled me into the dressing room and he said, well, now that we know that you can read a story, let's go out now and do it for the old country boy that just finished plowing up a field somewhere in the middle of Saskatchewan. He's worked hard and I'll go out and talk to him. Big, big difference.

AM   Let's have your first piece of music. What would you like us to play?

TH   Well, one night I was sittin' in a hotel room listening to a song that—I was astounded how many people had heard it—but McDermott, John McDermott had recorded a song, *Sonny's Dream*. Great, great song.

AM   Now, what is it about this one that gets to you?

TH   It's just a simple, nice song, and I think McDermott is a great performer and a fine singer and I think he does a great rendition of it. [MUSIC]

AM   So you basically grew up performing. Were your parents supportive of this?

TH   Oh, very much so, very much so. My mom and dad were the biggest fans that I ever had. My dad would invite me over to the railway shop at Christmas time to go and to perform there. They were great. They would come to our shows and once they were there I would introduce them to the audience, you know, and they learned to bow and wave pretty good. No, they were wonderful, wonderful. They gave me a lot of good advice; my dad always wanted me to stay in school, and he used to shake his head sometimes. He was great, he was a very simple man. I remember one time coming back on a train. I was at… we had just played in a bar, and if you could've seen this bar. I was probably 17, and ah, I used to shave my hair so I could have a receding hairline. Then I'd put the cowboy hat on and wear it way back to make me look older and so, ah, boy I tell ya, I got to know every crook and gangster and lady of the evenin'—I'm tellin' ya, they were all in there. And my dad came in. There was three of us, there was a bass player and a fiddle player and myself. And ah, so we started at eight and worked 'til two in the morning. And none of the other guys were singers, so I had to know everybody's favourite songs. And back then I had a good repertoire, a cross-section of music. But my dad came in on a Saturday night and that place was just jumpin', and I swear my dad's hair turned white overnight. He looked at this bar and looked at his son and just said, what has happened? So that night

I got paid and we were going back home on the late train back to London. And my dad and I we went into the middle of the train, just to sit and talk, and he says, saw that place you played at tonight. And I said, yeah. He says, are you sure you wanna do this for a living? And I said, yeah, I sure do dad. I said, dad, look how much money they gave me. And I showed him the money. And that was more money—my dad never made that in a month—and it wasn't a lot, but my dad was making I think 25 bucks a week and worked six days a week, too. I mean Saturday was a work day. And he said, that's good son, that's a lot of money, but will you be making it next week and the week after and the week after that.? I said, that's a good, good point, you know, and which is so typical of a lot of entertainers or musicians. You hear the story, you know. So they're making a lot of money one month and they starve for three; so you have to average it out, you know.

AM Then you got this singing part of a hillbilly in a theatre production.

TH Yeah, it was a play called *Dark of the Moon* and it was at the Grand Theatre and they wanted a hillbilly singer. So I went down there with the best Bill Monroe, Lester Flatt, Earl Scruggs songs that I could find, you know, because my hillbilly was like bluegrass—real bluegrass hillbilly music. So I went in there and here's a group of actors, amateur actors, but they were a doctor of philosophy (worked at the university) and somebody else who was a businessman. And these were all people who were very well connected, but bluegrass music they didn't know anything about and they wanted to do this play. So I walked in they said… I'm auditioning and I start, I just went into this real bluegrass thing, played all the bluegrass runs and sang as high as I could. So at the end of it they were doubled up in laughter. And I was really offended. I left and thought I had failed miserably and was just terribly upset at the ignorance of these people laughing and everything else. And I was 14 years of age. And the next day the guy, the announcer called me and he says, boy, they loved you. I says, loved me?—they laughed at me. And he says, no, you've got the part, they want you in the play. And would you go back

tonight to start the rehearsals. And I says, they laughed at me. And I couldn't get that out of my craw. It just bothered me. And Mary Ashwell got the group together. Anyway, she walked over and she says, I want to apologize, I'm very sorry. You know. I said, well I thought you wanted bluegrass music and I gave you the best rendition I have and you're sittin' there laughing at me. Anyway, we healed everything. And all those people… We entered the play into the Western Ontario Drama Festival and we won that, then the Ontario Drama Festival and we won that. And then we competed in the Dominion Drama Festival which was held in Victoria, British Columbia. And I remember riding out on the train, and I think it was a five-day trip from Toronto on out to Victoria. So every night they would say, Tom, get your guitar out, you know. And we had people coming in from every car forward and backwards, and we had all the train crew in there, and I'd sit around and sing all these songs. But I picked songs that they would know and, remember, this is not my audience style. But I remember on three or four nights—now as I said I was, now let me see, I was 15 now—and I remember saying, do you remember the first time we met and you laughed at the stuff I did, and now I've got you tapping your foot and clapping your hands and singin' on the choruses to all the songs? That taught me a lot. Here was a group of people that were from every walk of life, had no more interest in country music than fly to the moon. That wasn't their… But if it was presented right and you said, help me on the chorus here.. And I went *y'all come,* you answer me. Okay, *y'all come, y'all come.* And I got them participating and involving them in the music, and suddenly they all became fans of country music, or became fans of mine.

AM Let's have another piece of music.

TH I'm not sure whether a lot of your audiences have seen… There was a show that I had watched with a beautiful blind singer who was so very talented—Andrea Boccelli—and I remember watching that show and thought he was absolutely wonderful. And he had a special guest on one time, Sarah Brightman, who I had never seen before, but I thought that she was just great and I ran out and bought their CDs and have now become a big, big fan. I just think their singing and their music is wonderful and terribly relaxing. The song is called *Time to Say Good-Bye*. [MUSIC]

AM Tell me about your first television show *Country Hoedown*?

TH King Ganam had come to London. King was playing fiddle and he was on a television show called *Holiday Ranch*. And I guess he had a dispute with and he left the show—he was very, very popular—and he left the show and Ganam was travelling and touring all over the place, and he was looking for a lead singer for his band. And somebody had told him about me in Toronto and he'd forgotten my name. And when he came to London to do a show he said, there's a… mentioned to the manager, there's a fella that sings country music in this town. And the manager said, are you thinking of Tommy Hunter? He said, that's the guy. Yeah, he said, what's he like. He says, well why don't I call him up and get him to come on down here. He says, great, I'd like to hear him. So I went down there and auditioned for Ganam and he said, what are you doing in London? I said, well you know, I travel around and do some shows here. And he says, well, nothing's gonna' happen to your career here, you're gonna' have to move down to Toronto and I can probably help ya' if you come there. So I said, let me think about it and we'll see what we can do. So the next day he called me again and he said, I really want you to come down to Toronto. Can you get on a train and come on down and I want to talk to you. So I got ready and went down there and he said, I can't promise you any work, but I've got some jobs that I'll use you. So I said, okay, so I moved to Toronto.

AM And you were 19 at this time.

TH I was about 18 when I first got there. And we worked on a Thursday and then he didn't have anything for the next two-and-a-half weeks. Well, my dad gave me 25 bucks and that was running low, so I went out and got a job at Eatons selling paint. And I was selling paint and I'll tell ya' there's some barns around that area of Toronto that have got enamel on the side of the walls. I had no more idea of what's the difference between flat and semi-gloss and barn paint, but at any rate we had a

wonderful time. And we continued to go out and do some shows and worked at Eatons and sold the paint, and then finally, Ganam called me one day. He says, we're gonna' do an audition for a summer replacement show. The show was *Holiday Ranch* and we were gonna' do a summer replacement. And they brought in Gordie Tap and Marjorie, Norma and Jean (the Hame Sisters), Tommy Common, a girl by the name of Lorraine Foreman, and King Ganam and his Sons of the West. And I was part of the band and I sat in the back and played rhythm guitar. And they were gonna' let me sing a song, but I couldn't get off that bandstand because if I did, they had to pay me five dollars. And the budget was mighty tight. And they wouldn't even let me put on makeup 'cause if you put on makeup you got paid extra again.

AM So you were the pale guy in the back.

TH I was the pale skinny, hungry looking kid in the back. So they were originally gonna' call it the King Ganam Show. But Gordie was brought in to emcee the thing, and of course it was a lot like the Don Messer thing. Don Messer stayed in the background. Don Tremaine, who was the announcer, he was really the host of the show, which was very confusing. So Ganam, he wanted to stay in the background and so they said, no, it's gonna' be very confusing like the Don Messer thing, so let's call it *Country Hoedown*. So the show started and it was supposed to be a 13-week show, and after about six or eight weeks that show had really taken off. Boy, it was really very, very popular. And the show lasted nine years. And it was a producer by the name of Len Casey who came in and, Len said, what's that kid doin' back… why do we keep pushin' cameras down there for him to sing a song. He's part of the show, make him part of the show—bring him out, let him come out here and be part and let him sing his songs.

AM Let's have another piece of music, Tommy. What would you like to hear?

TH There was a young performer that did our show when he was first getting started. I think at the time he was still living in California, and then he came back after he was very successful. And I've always been a big fan of his—I know how good he is talent wise. But very few people know how generous he is with his time. He's a good businessman, he's good for country music, he sings good and country and boy is he talented. His name is Vince Gill and this is *The Key to Life*. [MUSIC]

AM I want to talk a little about those very early days of televison, what comes to mind?

TH People think of television today in colour. You have to remember, I look at it, when we were getting started, in terms of black, white, grey. We didn't have the colours to work with. So when we created a scene that we were, say, gonna sing a song around a campfire, we would have a campfire, but we had to make it late at night and we had to, you know, there's the moon and there's the stars. And you had to do all this kind of thing. You learned to do depth of field, you know, to make something that really wasn't any more than 10 feet long look as if it's running for miles. And Nicoletti was our first set designer, and I watched old Nicoletti and watched him create something on a, just a plain set and he would paint things in it. And I'd look and watch that and then I'd look at the camera and I'd look at what it is, and it was amazing.

AM The difference. What the camera saw from what you saw?

TH Yeah. It was fascinating. When we were on breaks, I would take the camera and move it around and look and see what I could create and how things worked. I was really fascinated with television, and I think that helped me an awful lot in later years. It got me into some tough arguments, but at least I had a chance of knowing back then what good writers were and what good producers were, and I learned to tell the difference between good and bad. And I guess I was always trying to push the show to make it even better. I was never happy to accept just an average television show; I wanted the best of everything. I wanted the best writers and the best producers, and I guess I did that for our audience.

AM So you spent nine years on *Country Hoedown*, which was one of those kind of barn type country shows. It wasn't really what you wanted.

TH No. It wasn't. When the show started, to me the success of what *Country Hoedown* was, was a group of people that liked each other—that came through. We were all brand new to television, we hadn't learned the little tricks and the little things, so we were wide-eyed and we were innocent. And that came across—the camaraderie and the communication—we had nothing else, no other gimics, so you looked straight at that camera and in so doing you communicated with the viewer. And that was to me the success of it. Where we ran into trouble with *Country Hoedown* was when the producers wanted to change it. And I was good as long as I was singin' "*don't let the stars get in your eyes*" or something. Tommy Common was good as long as he sang, like, some of those great Marty Robbins things he used to do. Then the minute you put him into another area and put me into area, I felt awkward, and the audience sensed that awkwardness. And we were all starting to suffer from it, and the show eventually. The ratings just started plummeting.

AM But your star had sort of been rising through that whole thing because you ended up with *The Tommy Hunter Show*.

TH Well, thank you. I guess I was stubborn. There wasn't a lot they could do with me. A choreographer… I could drive a choreographer crazy 'cause I was tall, I was gangly, I was awkward. So he'd say, can you not pay attention?—start with the left foot, every time you're startin' with the right foot. And then he'd say, alright, we'll bend, we'll start with the right foot. The tape would come on and I'd start with my left foot, you know. So he said, we can't teach you anything,. They never really concentrated on giving me choreography. And I really felt… I was so embarrassed tryin' to dance or do choreography, so they just said, leave him alone. So, whenever I got in trouble I always sang a song called, *Won't You Ride in My Little Red Wagon*. And the producers always remember that. I ran into one guy and he said, if I ever heard *Little Red Wagon* one more time, because when they would present a song I'd say, no, no, I can't sing that, are you crazy?—some Perry Como song. They'd say, well what are we gonna' do? I'd say, *The Little Red Wagon*. We had a lot of fun and it was wonderful. And I remember when the CBC came to me and said, you know, we want to talk to you about the possibility of doing your own show. And they said, is there anything you want, or what you'd like to see? And I said, I don't know what I want, I can't tell you. I mean, this is scary stuff now, because I don't have all the cast, my buddies from *Country Hoedown*. I'm going out on my own now. But I said to them, the only thing I can tell you I don't want is a barn. Let's get away from that hayseed image. I think our music has moved up the ladder in its acceptance, so let's try to get it out of the barn.

AM   Well, let's talk about some of the people that you had on the *Tommy Hunter Show*. Johnny Cash.

TH   Johnny was wonderful. Johnny and I go back so many years. We used to have the same manager.

AM   Talk about two guys with very different public images, though. You're the country gentleman and he's the gangster, "The Outlaw," isn't that what they called him?

TH   Well, yeah, they called 'em outlaws, but really, Johnny wasn't all that bad.

AM   But the image certainly.

TH   Oh sure, he was tall, the man in black, he looked rough, you know—come on, ride this train, you know. He looked scary. Johnny wasn't scary at all, he was one of the nicest guys around. There's many guys in our business who have done far worse things than Johnny ever thought of doing. He got into some drugs, but really, he wasn't as bad. But Johnny knew how to take advantage of a thing. He looked rough. But Johnny's a good marketing man. He turned it around, he said, all right, I look rough; so he always took the part of a convict. Well, that became successful. He'd recorded an old Lester Flat and Earl Scruggs song (I think it was called *Folsom Prison Blues* and that became successful, so he says, let's take the show to Folsom Prison, right. So now, what side are you gonna stand on?—so Johnny got on the side of the criminals. Johnny was a… to this day, is a nice, nice… He's a very gentle man, he really is. A wonderful guy.

AM   You had Garth Brooks on the show before he was "Garth Brooks."

TH   Well, no, actually he had had a couple of hits, but you know, he wasn't swinging on ropes and smashing guitars at this stage. But no, he came up and did our show and, I remember the very first time he did the show, our producer, Les Pouliot walked over to me while I was out in the back and he said, we could be having problems with this Garth Brooks. And I said, oh, really? And he came in not knowing the show. He flew in, he had worked probably every bad club, been in every worse situation he could come into. Now all of a sudden he's up in Canada and he's doing a television show. And when he first started he was, I don't want those monitors there, pull them over here… can you put that… where's this camera?—you know, he was like, very much protecting himself. And once we played him the track, all of a sudden he realized, oh, this is a very professionally operated show. And then he settled right back down. Nobody was out to hurt him and to harm him. So he relaxed. And he became a wonderful guest, just absolutely great, and a big fan. Then, when our show eventually got sold to the U.S. network and started being seen down there, then a lot of the artists… everybody was calling to do the show, they wanted to do the show. I mean, Reba McEntire, when she was first getting started. Fine singer. She was living in Oklahoma then and she had had a couple of albums out and met with some good success, but not to the super, super stardom that she has reached today.

AM   And Shania, when she was Eileen?

TH   Yeah, Elly Twain. I remember her coming on the show, and she was great, just wonderful. And you could see that look, that sparkle, and that something that's a little different. You know the nice thing about it is that Shania Twain, as successful as she has become—I mean, millions and millions and millions of records—we were sitting at home one night and she was being interviewed on one of the top American networks, and she had mentioned that the very first television show that she had done was *The Tommy Hunter Show*. And I thought that was very nice, because they're in the U.S. and not a lot of people would be familiar with the show, but she looked back as a very memorable experience and something that gave her, you know, something she could talk about or it maybe opened up another door for her or got her going somewhere. But anyway, that was nice. A lot of people forget where they got their early starts.

AM Well, you surrounded yourself with really, really top people.

TH I was very fortunate, yes. I didn't always have a producer like Les Pouliot who was really the best. I had some very good producers and I had some not so good producers. Les Pouliot joined our show, and I was so thrilled to have him on because, first of all, he experienced the same thing as I experienced. He knew the public. He loved country music. When somebody would play a steel guitar or a fiddle lick and I'd look at Les and I'd go, oh, isn't that… you know. But the same… that little lick rung his bell, too.

AM And then, when it was cancelled after 27 years, there was a lot of anger across this country.

TH Yeah, there really was a lot of. People were very upset, very very upset about it. I remember, I was down in Florida at the time. And finally, when I came into Canada, I came in with my tail between my legs. I felt that I was… I had failed, that I was the worst, and oh, I felt dreadful, just terrible. I was really in a down, down mode for a long, long time. And it was actually a friend of mine, and he says, don't feel bad about it. He says, do you know how many people that I know, that are patients of mine. One day they're top CEO of a major company, and the next day they went to work and they had their personal stuff—here's your cheque, good-night and good-bye and that's it. And they come in here, they didn't know what in the world had happened to them. So he said, don't you worry about it. And it was funny; many doors have opened up, I'm now touring and doing things. You know, I tour 60 or 70 days a year, and I didn't have that kind of time before to do it.

AM And I mean, it's small comfort, but when you look at how most TV shows are a flash in the pan, literally—I mean, they're cancelled after weeks. It can be a cruel medium in a lot of ways.

TH Well see, I could never say anything. Like when I would do an interview or talk to the press, somebody would say, well, you know, what do you feel? Well, I really couldn't say an awful lot because, no matter what I would say, people would say, well, how could you talk about being cancelled? Good heavens, you were there for a total of 36 years, 27 on your own show—what are you complaining about? And that wasn't good, so I had to remain very, very quiet about it.

AM But at the same time it was your job, and that's tough…

TH That's right..Sure, it was a shock at the time. But I think that a lot of people that come to see our show to this day, see… Television shows and personalities such as myself, people having invited me into their living rooms for so many years that they'll come to our show and they'll say, I remember when our daughter was born and we brought her home the first night, and your show was on and you sat there and I can remember a song that you performed that night, and it was so appropriate for the situation of having a new daughter here, you know. And these are all the associations, all the memories. And remember, for 27 years, it was a long time. I love those memories.

AM Let's have another piece of music.

TH Well, alright. We had talked about bluegrass music before and, , I guess Acuff played such a part of my life… I don't know whether you have a copy of the *Wabash Cannonball*…

AM Oh yeah.

TH …but why don't we get Mr. Acuff and all of his Smoky Mountain boys and girls to gather 'round the microphone and we'll have Oz kick it off…
[MUSIC]

AM I want to ask you about some of the other aspects of your life. You're passionate about short-wave radio?

TH Yes, I love short-wave radio. I've always been a big fan of radio, I guess going back to the old days when you could scan across the dial and pick up some far away station. I guess in my search to find country music. And everybody forgets those days, when, you know, today you drive across the country and you can just tune the dial and every community has a 24-hour country music station. Back when I was growing up, there was the odd community that would play maybe an hour or two hours of country music, that was it. There were some stations, WJJD down in Chicago played the *Suppertime Frolic*. There was a station, WWVA in Wheeling, West Virginia, that played country music starting about eleven o'clock at night to the wee hours of the morning. And they would sell everything, from baby chicks… And this is serious, dead serious. They would sell… you would get a box of 50 chicks sent through the mail—I think they were $1.98 or something—get 50 chicks. The old story goes about the guy, he says… he said, every week, he said, I've been sending away for those baby chicks. And he said, well, you must have a lot of chickens by now? He says, no, I don't have any. So, well what happened? He says, I don't know, I'm either plantin' 'em too deep or too far apart. Anyway… They would sell you a pure white bible, and then you could get—at Easter time—they would sell you a pure vinyl (100 percent pure vinyl) plastic table cover with The Last Supper. It's unbelievable what they sold. But that was my interest, that got me tuned in. I was always fascinated that I could pick up some station in Texas. And then later in life I started… when we first started travelling overseas to go and do some tours with our servicemen, I started tuning into the short-wave radio. And I was fascinated that I could pick up a lot of very, very interesting stations. And then when we would travel more, I found out that I could pick up CBC, and I would listen to CBC radio and get all the news from home and know what was going on. And they did just tremendous. And I told you before we started what a big fan I am of CBC Radio—I think it is absolutely healthy, it's doing so well, and no matter where I travel across Canada I am a big, big fan. And I make those viewpoints known when I'm at any radio station, private or otherwise, that I'm a big fan of CBC radio.

AM Well you mentioned the other big hobby and interest in your life, your boat?

TH I've always been interested in boating. I guess also I love doing amateur photography, and once the television show was gone, my wife Shirley said, you know, you've always wanted to get back into boating again and now is a perfect opportunity. We're at that point in our life, the children are all busy working and they're setting up their own careers, and you don't have the pressures of a television show any more, and so we decided to get into the boating business. We cruise in an area called Georgian Bay, which is probably the best fresh water boating in the world. I And so we bring the grandchildren on, they spend a couple of days, and after a couple of days you have to…

AM Give them back to their mum and dad.

TH Yeah, that's right. So they come up and they enjoy that, and it gives me a chance… we have a little dinghy that we tow behind, and so I hop on the dinghy and disappear off to some uncharted waters with my camera, and leave very early in the morning and sit up there where the birds are just starting to sing and the sun's coming up, and I love taking pictures of things like that.

AM You have an Order of Canada, Order of Ontario, all kinds of music awards, and you're an Honorary Citizen of Tennessee and a Kentucky Colonel. What's a Kentucky Colonel?

TH Well, I don't know. I think you can go to the Derby and they give you a free mint julep or something. But no, a Kentucky Colonel, I don't know. They give these honours out and, I was very flattered…

AM Did they make you wear a little white beard or something?

TH No, they were very nice. I can't remember how or why I got it. Somebody, they sent it through. I think when our television show was on the U.S. network. I know that Ned McWerther was the Governor of the State of Tennessee, and he was a fan of our show, so he bestowed that honour upon me. When I was growing up… With the kids around, it's kind of tough for kids when your father is in the limelight so to speak. And what I did, I made sure any award that I got, I had everything in the office and my office was at the furthest little corner of the house down in the basement. And at our house you'd never see a guitar when you walked in, you'd have no idea what I did for a living. And the kids didn't grow up in that musical, you know, my dad's a celebrity and I can banter his name around and get everything I want, you know. They never grew up in that kind of environment.

AM Let's have another piece of music.

TH All right. There's a group—and I'm not sure whether you're going to be able to find this record or not—but ah, a group called the Osborne Brothers and they've done many, many recordings over the years. I've heard everything they've ever done, and they have (in my estimation) three songs that are pure caviar. They recorded a song called *Rockytop* a number of years ago, which was… it's a legendary, just good, get up every day go-get-em country song. They have another one called *Rank Strangers* and I didn't realize it, but the one called *Kentucky* has now been adopted as the official Kentucky song. And the reason I like this is I love the way they do the three-way harmonies. If you listen real closely, you'll hear the notes changing and bending, and listen real close, they have wonderful, wonderful harmony. Incidentally, it also happens to be Roy Acuff's favourite song. [MUSIC]

AM Now, before we send you off to your mythical mountain top, we let you take one book with you. So if you were going to go away in seclusion and you could only take one book, what would you take.?

TH Well, there's a lot of obvious things that I could say. I could come at it from many points of view: I could probably say the bible because it would give me a tremendous amount of guidelines and guidance and comfort. You may have some listeners that just want a very simple book—and particularly kids if they just want a real simple book to read some time—there was a book that I enjoyed and somebody gave me a copy, it was called *The Old Man and the Sea*. And I thought it was a very simple story, but if you really read that, there's a lot of thought—just the struggle between a man and something that he had caught, that he didn't know what he really had and… And I remember there was one part of that story where it talked about a jetliner that was flying over and he felt so alone, and the parallel between him out in this little dinghy with his hands bleeding and struggling to hold on to this great fish that he had caught, and then to see… he was looking up watching this jetliner going as they were pulling out the linen and people were about to partake in some nice food at 30,000 feet… it was kind of a nice little book…

And I was given that book to read… I actually went back in to try to elevate my education a little bit, well even while I was doing *Country Hoedown*. And the teacher said, your reading skills are very limited and he said here's a book I want you to have. And read it. And he says, if you like that book I can find many more like it. So that was a good introduction to me. So just in the off chance that there's some kids that are listening that are, you know, wanting maybe to get interested in reading a little bit, that's a good book.

AM We also let you choose a location—it could be anywhere on the earth—but, if you were going to be cast away, where would you want to spend the rest of your days?

TH Boy, that's tough. That is really tough. Frankly, I guess I would have to say I find the best seclusion for me is when I'm anchored in a very quiet bay. Last year my wife and I, you could see this—what's the satellite, you know?—the Mir, Mir Spaceship. And they had mentioned that if you were at a particular place at a certain time of night, and we were up at a very quiet bay all by ourselves—there was nobody around, there's no cottages, nothing—and it was the most gorgeous night. And Shirley and I went out on the bow and stretched out on the bow at eleven o'clock at night and just looked up at all the billions and—I sound like, you know, Carl Sagan—but the billions and billions of stars, and we finally spotted the Mir space station going over. And to think of the technology that was involved to put that there, and here we are up in some small little insignificant bay in this part of the world, looking at this thing that we have created and put up in space. And I think that's intriguing, to be just out in the blackness of night and just to feel, to hear some birds or some animals crawling around at night, is good. So I would have to pick a little quiet bay up on Georgian Bay.

AM And for your final choice of music?

TH I am a big, big fan of a young lady who I think has a tremendous amount of talent, by the name of

Cindy Church. And I saw Cindy do the country awards. She was without a doubt the best thing on the awards show. She was brilliant. And I think she has enormous talent. Why they haven't discovered her bigtime in the United States is beyond me. I'd love to take her one time down to the *Grand Ol' Opry* and put her right on that stage, just her and her guitar, 'cause I think those are probably the toughest country audiences that you'll ever find because they've seen everything. And I think she would just make them open up their eyes. She's very, very good. So I'm a big fan of Cindy.

AM Tommy, thank you so much for coming in today. It's just been such a pleasure.

TH Thank you very much, thank you. I have really enjoyed it. I was saying to my manager this morning that I have... out of all the interviews I've done over the years, I can probably remember three that I've really relaxed and just talked and had a good time. I'm now proud to say I can make it a fourth.

AM Thank you.

TH You're more than welcome. Enjoyed it.

ERNIE COOMBS
WITH ANDREA MARANTZ, 1998

AM Now, I have to call you Ernie, but I want to call you Mr. Dressup.

EC Well okay, you call me Mr. Dressup and I'll call you Ms. Marantz. How's that? We can be very, very formal.

AM Very formal. Yes, very formal indeed. Well you grew up in Maine—I've read this in all kinds of places—but I don't know where in Maine.

EC Well, in a few different places in Maine. I was born in central Maine in Lewiston, and shortly after that my folks moved to a place called Waterville, Maine, a little town not too far from Lewiston where my dad taught school. And I stayed there until I was I think 15, and then we moved to a coastal town—a little village actually, of Yarmouth—and I went to high school there, and then I was drafted into the army, went to art school and just came back to Maine in the summertime and vacations after that.

AM What kinds of things were you interested in as a little boy?

EC As a little boy I liked art, I loved to draw. I used to get into trouble in school because I was always doodling, and every once in awhile the teacher would say, [EC mimicking teacher] "Ernest, would you like to share your picture with the rest of the students here?" And so it was just assumed that I was going to be an artist, so I did go to art school after high school and after the army, but I never quite got to be a commercial artist. I got into theatre and scene design, and then into acting and so forth.

AM Now how did you make that leap from the set design, which of course would be a natural progression from the interest in art. How did you become an entertainer?

EC Well, I was always a big ham and also I was a bit of a geek when I was in school. And I'd keep doing stupid things and people would laugh at me, so I would pretend that I did them on purpose just to be funny, and I developed, I guess, the fine art of make believe. So I worked in a lot of theatres, especially summer theatres where they never have quite enough actors on the staff. So for the little roles they would say, Ernie, why don't you be the butler in this, or some walk-on, and most of those parts were very funny—there were only three lines, you didn't even have to rehearse, but you'd get a lot of laughs. So that sort of got me interested into going on stage where you just got makeup on your face, instead of paint and glue all over your whole body. So I sort of evolved into that and also started working for a touring children's theatre in Pittsburgh, Pennsylvania, where I both did the scenery and the props and acted, and got some sort of major roles, if you can call them major roles in children's theatre.

AM Now was that a deliberate choice? Were you interested in children's theatre or did it just sort of come up?

EC No. Actually, to tell the truth I've never made a deliberate choice in my life. Things have fallen into my lap, I've been extraordinarily lucky. And so just when I would be thinking, well I need some money, I wouldn't know what to do about it, somebody would call up and say, we need somebody to do this, could you do it? And I'd say yup, and I'd be on my way again. So my career was actually carved for me. I didn't… You know, they say knock on the door of opportunity, well I just went down the hall and there were all these doors open and I'd stumble from one to another.

AM How did you meet Fred Rogers?

EC Oh, well that was through the children's theatre as I say in Pittsburgh. Fred was doing a very successful show on public television called *The Children's Corner*. He didn't appear on camera, but he played piano backstage and accompanied the woman who was in front of the cameras, and he did all the puppets. And every show that we did in the children's theatre we would take down to WQED studios and perform one scene from it as guests on *The Children's Corner*. So I got to know Fred from that, and then later on he and I started doing a 15-minute, almost ad lib little children's program at noon-time.

AM What kind of a program was that?

EC Well, it was called *The Prince*, and Fred was the prince and he made his entrance on camera coming down a children's slide, with his bow-tie on of course, and a crown. And I played Parmazelle the Turtle, and this was from one of our children's shows in which there was this wonderful turtle costume, and Fred really liked it.

AM So you were dressed up as a turtle?

EC As a turtle with green paint on my face, and we used to sing songs—Fred would make them up two minutes before air time. He had a piano in his office and he'd say, Ernie, how about… [humming a tune] and I'd say, okay, let's do it. We had nothing to lose because we had a very small audience, and I used to draw pictures; it's kind of hard to hold a marker in your flipper, but we managed it. And so we got to be very good friends and I got to know his family and he got to know mine, and he was the best man at my wedding and has remained a very strong friend ever since, and a very great influence on what I know about children's television.

AM Now was he sort of focused right at that time on the children's entertainment field?

EC Yes, yeah. He was a very dedicated man, very knowledgeable. He's actually a Presbyterian minister. And he hated standing up and giving sermons so they said, alright Fred, your ministry will be toward children and the betterment of children's lives in general. So his program is basically dedicated to that proposition, and everything he does he puts all of himself into it and all of his education and all of his feelings toward children, whereas I came into it as an actor in sort of a happy-go-lucky way.

AM I think just in case there's anybody who doesn't know who Fred Rogers is, I guess we should make clear that he's Mr. Rogers, which most little kids say as one word—all one word—Mr. Rogers. Now then, how did you end up in Canada?

EC Oh, well it was through Fred. He had been approached by CBC to develop a program where he actually appeared on camera, and he was a little shy of it but they persuaded him to do it. And one year he came up here weekends and would do two or three shows which are just shown on Saturday mornings—to CBC; and I came up here once with him and met some of the people in the children's department here. And then the next year they really worked on him and said, you've got to come up and stay here and do a daily show, at least to prove to yourself that it can be done and that you are an on-camera personality. So he said, okay I'll do it, and at that point I'd been… I was out of work, I just had a brand new baby, I was just supporting myself by freelancing and any way that I possibly could, and Fred said, I need a spare puppeteer, can you come to Canada? And I said, oh yes. And I came up here and we did Mr. Rogers for a year, for a season, and he went back to Pittsburgh and I was asked to stay at the CBC to work on a new program called *Butternut Square*.

AM I remember *Butternut Square*.

EC Yeah, well that was my first, well no, my second show here counting Mr. Rogers.

AM Now tell us about that show. What were some of the elements in *Butternut Square*?

EC The set was a large… the whole studio, and it was a little village square with a tree, a butternut tree in the centre and a little park bench, and then scattered all around the square were little sets and various characters. There was Mr. Music Man, who was Don Hymes, who was our musician, our piano player; and Mr. Dressup, that was me, and I had a little place where there were lots of costumes and where I would do crafts. Um, let's see… we had a little set the first year which was Mrs. Trapeze's Variety Store, and Mrs. Trapeze was a not too likable little puppet woman, or woman puppet, who owned a dog named Finnigan. And that's where Finnigan first appeared.

AM   And that was the same Finnigan that we all came to know so well?

EC   The very same—Judith Lawrence's wonderful Finnigan. And I think by the end of the season even Judith decided she didn't care much for Mrs. Trapeze, even though it was her creation.

AM   Well, what was so… what was unlikable about her?

EC   I don't remember. I just remember that she seemed sort of snippish, you know, and really old maidish in the worst sense of the word, and at that time anyway it was decided…

AM   To teach children to be tolerant of their neighbours I suppose?

EC   I'd love to see one of the old films of that just to see what she was really like, but uh, anyway, Casey came along the next season because we needed somebody who reflected the point of view of the little preschoolers. And of course everybody loved Casey, and from then on we never looked back.

AM   Well, so did you create the character of Mr. Dressup or was he sort of given to you?

EC   Uh, no, I don't think I did. It's awfully hard for me to remember exactly, but Bruce Attridge and Fred Raynsbury were in charge of the children's department then—they created the concept of the show—and I remember meeting, before we actually started, in Bruce Attridge's office, talking over what kind of a character I would be. And they knew that I could draw and that I liked to do pantomime and crafts and sort of generally do this and that, and I'm sure it was Bruce's idea that kids love to dress up, so why not have a character who dressed up all the time for… I didn't even have to have a reason—I just appeared in a different kind of a costume every time I was on camera. I'm sure it probably was Bruce that said, why don't we call you Mr. Dressup.

AM   Well, let's pause for your first piece of music now. Has music been part of your life?

EC   I love music and I'm a big radio fan. And this is kind of surprising, considering that I love music, that I got my first hi-fi player… I still call it hi-fi; what do you call it—stereo set, yeah, with those flat things, the CD's. Just got one last November. Up until then I just listened to little dinky radios and I did have a disc player, 33-1/3 rpm disc thing, but uh, anyway, uh… and I've come over the years to get very fond of classical music and opera, and at an early age I played clarinet very badly, and I still toot away on it and a saxophone now and then. But I never had what it took to be a professional musician. But more and more I've come to just love music, and carry it with me all the time; I have a Walkman and tapes and I can't go anywhere without it.

AM   What would you like to hear first?

EC   Well, this is something that just knocked me out the first time I heard it. I was in the car and listening, had just turned on the radio, and I heard this chorus from *Nabucco* by Verdi, and it's the chorus of the Hebrew slaves—it's called *Va Pensiero*. I don't know what it means, but I sort of think it means go figure, I don't know. But there's a little story about this. Apparently, when they were rehearsing *Nabucco* there were workmen repairing the roof of the opera house, , I'm not sure what opera house it was, but of course it was in Italy, and they tried to get the workmen to stop. They said, but we've got an opera here that we're rehearsing, and the workmen said, ah, you know, we gotta work, we gotta work, and they kept pounding away—until they started singing *Va Pensiero*. And at that point all the workmen apparently put down their tools and just listened, mesmerized. And that's the same way that I heard it for the first time, I just thought this is beautiful. So that's it, it's called *Va Pensiero* from *Nabucco*. [MUSIC]

AM   So tell me about the early shows of Mr. Dressup. How did you launch from Butternut Square into Mr. Dressup?

EC Well what happened, we were forced into it. Like I said, I've never made any decisions, I just wait for somebody else to make the decisions. It was in 1967, Expo '67 was coming up and CBC needed facilities and budget and equipment and personnel to go to Expo in Montreal. And they had to take them away from some program, and everybody said well, it was an accountant's decision—they probably looked down the line and said, hey look, we're spending a lot of money on a kids' show; let's get rid of that one.

AM This sounds frighteningly familiar doesn't it?

EC I'm not sure that's exactly what happened, but at any rate they said they were going to cut it at the end of the summer and would not be resuming that fall, but would go back into production eventually. And as soon as it was announced there was a huge outcry; we never realized how much of an audience we had developed already. And that was just two years, at the end of the second season. So there was enough of an outcry, so they said, well alright, we'll carry it until Christmas of 1966 and then we have to pull the plug. So we went through until Christmas, actually I think it was a little after that; but in the meantime Stu Gilchrist, who was our producer at the time, said, uh… found out that they were going to replace that time slot, which was just twenty minutes, with imported animations, cartoons—of good quality of course. But he went to the powers that be and said, I know how much those things cost, what would happen if we just got Ernie and Judith—so it would be Casey and Finnigan and Mr. Dressup—didn't have any more live music, we'll tape three shows a day so it won't cost much, we'll write them ourselves, um… We'll just need one little corner, the old Dressup corner set, we don't need the whole studio. He talked them into it. So it was decided it would be a new program; we couldn't call it Butternut Square anymore 'cause the square was demolished, gone. So it was just going to be called Mr. Dressup. And that's what happened.

AM So you were taping three days a week and then writing furiously the other two?

EC Three shows a day. Twenty-minute shows, that's only an hour a day. And in between shows we'd decide what we'd do for the next show. I mean it was almost literally on the back of an envelope kind of thing.

AM So was it kind of part-time then—you only had a few months contract?

EC Well, I used to take the summers off when we were in production, but actually I was doing quite a lot of freelance around here as well. I did some shows for TV Ontario, and I remember one summer I was working and commuting to Maine for a couple of days, and then I'd be back up here. So it was never part-time, it was always pretty full-time.

And also, when we were doing Butternut Square, I think the first year we did a hundred and forty shows. And that's a mess of shows.

AM What kind of creative input did you have to Mr. Dressup in the beginning?

EC Well, some. We were a kind of a group; we'd talk to the writers and we'd all sort of get together and throw in ideas. We were allowed to create and to ad lib. We had to ad lib 'cause I could never remember dialogue and neither could Judith, so we always figured we could say something better than anybody could write it anyway.

AM You'd know where it was going, but not how it was going to get there?

EC Exactly. And the writers found it easier to write out full dialogue—I guess it made their ideas flow better. We said, just do an outline and we can do it. So we would paraphrase, but we would have enough input into the show so that if there was something we absolutely didn't think we ought to do, we wouldn't do it. Sometimes nobody knew that we weren't going to do it until we were taping the show, and then they'd say, oh, they're not doing this page. But it was really a group affair. The writers, you know, they all came from different directions, different backgrounds, so they all had different kinds of ideas. So it was just wonderful that the results that we got, you know, they weren't just a single track.

AM You had your own little kids by that point. What did they think of their work?

EC Well then, of course, they were raised up to see daddy on television every day, so they didn't think it was at all odd. They were quite proud of it, really. There came a point—always does in school—when they were I guess around 10 or 12 years old, maybe 12, where kids can be kind of cruel and mean. So they'd come to school and they'd say, he dresses up in women's clothes, nya nya nya… you know. And they actually got through it pretty well. You know, they'd come home and they'd be upset, and I'd say, well look, everybody's father has a job doing something, and mine just happens to be on television and a lot of people know me from television, and sometimes that makes people uneasy and they'll say things.

AM But you know, it's interesting because Mr. Dressup, I would have thought, would be away from most of that, because people think so fondly of that character.

EC It gets me. I'm still surprised by it, and one of the things I do now—in fact, I was out in Calgary, doing sort of lectures to college kids, telling what it was like to be Mr. Dressup. And a lot of the funny things that happened along the way and on tour and in the studio. And after I did the first one—I think the first one was in Winnipeg—I was really not prepared; they were coming up and hugging me. You know, I was just kind of choked up.

AM And these are 19 and 20-year-olds.

EC Nineteen, 20, 21-year-olds you know. Great big strapping guys would say, I used to watch you all the time when I was a kid and, in fact, I watched the other day and uh, can I hug you?

AM What was it like being on television in the early sixties?

EC My recollection is that it was a lot of fun. In fact it's been a lot of fun all of these years. Then we were live, we didn't even have tape. It was recorded on 16 mm film right off the studio monitors, and those films—that's how they syndicated it because they couldn't go on microwave—they mailed the films across the country to different centres and they would, I don't know how long it took, but anyway they would play this film. So there was no editing. Whatever we did was captured on the film and, warts and all, there it was. So we learned to improvise very well and to cover our mistakes as gracefully as possible.

AM Now there must be some stories from the live television.

EC Oh, there are tons of them. Some I can't relate. But there were always things happening, like, well with myself; if I was doing a craft and I would get some tape stuck to my fingers, and normally you'd say, okay cut, we'll start over again. And there I'd be with my fingers stuck together with tape and then trying to get it off and it would just stick to my other fingers, and of course you can always say to the kids at home, hey, this happens to you a lot doesn't it? Don't you hate it when your fingers get all stuck with tape. And oh, another thing that was constantly happening, and we do have this on film in black and white. I always had trouble with any kind of fasteners on my clothes, buttons, zippers, snaps, Velcro—they tried everything and I always botched it. And there's one memorable bit where I kept trying to do up the zipper on a jacket—tried and tried, turned my back and tried, changed the subject, closed my tickle trunk, tried again, then said, well, it's time to go outdoors, let's go over here; oh, I think I'd better pick this up, tried again, tried again. It seemed to me, I can remember, it seemed to me it took ten minutes, but it was probably a matter of seconds.

AM Seemed like a lifetime I'll bet.

EC Yeah. But that's the kind of thing that happened. And of course forgetting the words of songs and having to make them up in meter and in rhyme; we got to be pretty good at that.

AM Let's have another piece of music now. What would you like to hear?

EC Okay, well I really like Beethoven. I know we can't play an entire symphony, so one of my favourites is the *Sixth Symphony*, it's the Pastoral Symphony. I think we'll try for part of the fifth movement from that—that's the ending one, you know, when the storm has passed and…

Beethoven wrote this right after he'd come out of a real series of being very despondent and down; he almost took his own life. He knew he was going deaf, even though he was just in his late twenties, and I think it's a wonderful, beautiful tribute to a man to reflect all the beautiful sounds of nature when he could no longer hear them. [MUSIC]

AM   The *Fifth Movement* from *Beethoven's Sixth Symphony*, the choice of my guest on Mountaintop Music, Ernie Coombs.

AM   So what was the biggest challenge of performing with puppets?

EC   [laughing] Not to break up when Casey said something outrageous.

AM   Did he do that a lot?

EC   Oh, I wish we had a tape of every one of our rehearsals. Judith Lawrence is such a clever ad libber, and she's so intelligent that she can just come out with some things that would just knock my socks off—of course during rehearsal. But she'd put in some zingers sometimes while we were actually taping the show, that only she and I would know were outrageously funny things. Another thing, working with puppeteers, the physical part is that you mustn't step on them, because in our situation they were right behind the counter with me, or in the early days it was just Judith. And she'd have maybe three puppets laid out and I had to be careful I didn't step on them, and she usually sort of leaned on one hand. And many's the time I'd take a little side step and I'd feel this crunch, and Casey or whoever would go, aahhmm. Very early in life… I think I naturally relate to puppets because one of the things that we would do when we were trying out for *Butternut Square* was to just do a little scene with the puppets, just to see whether you would look at the puppet's eyes or look down at the puppeteer. And I always found it very easy just to look at the puppets and forget the puppeteer was there.

AM   Did you separate the puppet from the puppeteer?

EC   Hmm, yeah.

AM   I mean, you knew you weren't talking to Judith when you were talking to Casey?

EC   That's right; because there have actually been times after a rehearsal, we'd go back to the meeting room—or the green room—and I'd say to Judith, did you hear what Casey said?

AM   Oh, really?

EC   Honestly. It would be so funny and sometimes she'd say, no, I wasn't listening.

AM   You know, Casey was kind of an interesting character in that sometimes he'd be a sulky little boy.

EC   Hmhm, just like real kids. It would have been terrible if he'd been sunny natured all the time and syrupy, but he wasn't; he was the product purely of Judith. And maybe also, while I'm talking about Casey, a lot of the things that the college students ask is: is Casey a boy or a girl?

AM   And?

EC   And he was purposely made… He is a "he." We always referred to him as "he." But Judith made it androgynous in looks and also in the name so that it could be either one, so that the little girls could relate to him as well as little boys.

AM   And the voice too was, you know, you couldn't really tell.

EC   At that age, you know, boys' voices/girls' voices are pretty much the same.

AM   So were there many Caseys and Finnigans?—many puppets? Did they wear out?

EC   Only one Casey.

AM   Oh good, I'm relieved.

EC   He was lucky, he got a paint job every season and come back looking the same as he did the season before. I was surprised, looking at some old, old pictures, that Casey didn't always have those rosy little cheeks when he first started out. And sometimes his freckles would be in different places, whereas Finnigan, being made of fur, actually wore and was getting kind of bald around the chin just from rubbing on things. So she made a new Finnigan and she only had enough material, the original material, to make one more puppet. So the new Finnigan appeared—he was fluffy and new and didn't look like Finnigan at all to me, and I couldn't relate to him.

AM   Oh oh.

EC   He just looked like a strange little animal. And it took, oh, a couple of weeks of Judith's hand inside him to, you know, change him into that kind of little lopsided look that the real Finnigan had.

AM   Did you have a favourite, a favourite puppet?

EC   I think Finnigan was. He has this little raffish, mischievous quality, and of course he didn't talk. I could hear him. Casey could hear him and I could hear him; well a lot of people could hear him, but he didn't talk aloud so he wasn't a noisy little thing, but he was humorous and he was the kind of little fellow that you could have fun with.

AM   Let's have another piece of music.

EC   Okay, where are we here. I've got a list; these are not coming out of the top of my head. Oh, this is another beautiful… it's a beautiful duet and that I first heard while riding in the car, and I almost pulled over to the side of the road to cry because it was so just utterly beautiful. I'm not too sure that I can pronounce this correctly: it's *Au Fonds du Temple Saint*, from *The Pearl Fishers*, and it's by Bizet, and the two men have this just knockout duet. [MUSIC]

AM   Outside of Mr. Dressup, when you weren't in the studio, what kinds of things were you involved with in your life?

EC   Oh… Well, I've always enjoyed old cars and there was one point where I had five cars. And since 1952 I'd had a 1932 Auburn convertible sedan, which just now I'm able to drive again. It was put away for a number of years, but it was the second car that I ever bought; it's a real classic car and I drove it summer and winter all over the place for six years.

AM   What does it look like? What are those like?

EC   Well, it's got four doors and a convertible top, a vertical grill, huge headlights. You know, the '32s they were kind of squared off. A long hood and a hundred horsepower engine, which was quite a lot for those days. I drove it because it was the only car around that I found that I could buy for five hundred dollars. And I'd hate to tell you what it's worth now, but I intend to drive it everywhere again as I did then, because that's what cars are made for. But then I got into, when I should have been restoring the Auburn years ago, I got into a lot of sports cars, English sports cars—MGs and Sunbeams and uh…

AM   So you must be a mechanic.

EC   No I'm not. Yeah, I can pull an engine or a transmission, but I don't know what I'm doing.

AM   Everyone that I know that's had an MG has had to play with it constantly to keep it going.

EC   Oh yes, they're the most wonderful and awful cars in the world. Especially the TDs, they were just… I don't know, they're just a lot of fun, and it's a typical British sports car you know. Well, the Morgans are another beautiful sports car that haven't changed for years, and they say that Mr. Morgan, the second Mr. Morgan who's still making them by hand now, somebody complained about something on the car that kept happening over—like a door flying open—and Morgan said, oh yes, it happens in my car all the time; annoying isn't it. Never think of changing it, you know, just go along with it.

AM   No, no. Has to be eccentric.

EC   So anyway, cars and the house that I still live in we bought about, oh, over twenty-five years ago. We did a lot of remodeling and did it ourselves 'cause I like to do woodwork and, you know, tear down walls and put up other ones, and plumbing and electrical stuff. So I like to do that and I still do, and in the summertime we'd go to Maine and I'd do a lot of water colour painting until I took up golf. So I play a lot of golf and—badly I should say—and I like bird watching and listening to music and, uh, what else do I like…

AM   Do you paint? Did you continue to paint?

EC   Yeah. I'm not painting nearly as much now as I did. As I say, it's because I go down to the cottage and I'm faced with all this beautiful scenery, and then my brother calls and says do you feel like playing nine holes, and boom… I keep swearing I'm going to, and I've got a lot of friends who have paintings that I've done. And this is maybe, the last one was fifteen years ago, and they say, if you come back from Maine without a painting I'm going to pound your head in. So I think I'd better get back to doing that.

AM   But I guess there's a connection between that sort of painting and set building and the renovation stuff that you're interested in.

EC   Well yeah, it's all manual work. I love to work with my hands and express myself that way, and I don't know what I would do if I weren't able to do things with my hands. You know, even working on cars, doing body work and pulling the head on an engine, you're still using your hands.

AM Yeah, that creative, making things kind of endeavor.

EC And gardening, too. I enjoy gardening.

AM What kind of things did you do with your own kids?

EC Oh, one thing that I did… Well, my daughter, being a girl, was enamored of horses, and so we actually got her a pony 'cause we have a huge field out back of the house and we fenced it off and made it into a pasture, and I made a storage shed into a stable. And so for awhile she had a pony, and then she had a beautiful quarter horse named Red. And I'd like to say that we used to go riding together, but we didn't because I'm a lousy rider. My wife is terrified of horses, and so what we did, we'd go… When Cathy was showing her horse, we'd go to quarter horse races and shows and that sort of thing. Enjoyed that a lot. And then when Chris, my son, who was three years younger than Cathy, got into freestyle skiing, we were part of the support for the southern Ontario team. And I would do the on the hill announcing—you know, next, uh, so and so coming up, degree of difficulty "5", and he'll do a triple spread—that sort of thing. Freezing to death standing there with a microphone frozen to your mittens. And Lynn would help; she would be down at the bottom of the hill with some of the other moms, doing the scoring and that sort of thing. And it was great because it got us out. Lynn was sort of an anti-winter person at first; she thought winter is when you go inside and hibernate. And having the kids skiing got us out. There was a ski hill right down in the valley beside the house, so we took up skiing and enjoyed it. So we would go out every weekend with the freestyle team and sort of chaperone them and have a lot of fun with the other people, and do a little bit of skiing ourselves.

AM Boy, it must have been exciting to watch your kid doing those freestyles.

EC Exciting, and wondering when he was gonna break his neck. But he won the Shell Cup one year and he hasn't skied for years since. He enjoyed being with the guys.

AM Ernie, what kind of relationship did you develop with your young audience as Mr. Dressup?

EC Probably in the beginning I think I was sort of an eccentric uncle. Now I'm a grandpa, and still eccentric. It's a very close thing. You know, you probably find it yourself; even watching somebody read the news every night or somebody you see frequently on television, you begin to think you know very well and they're a very close friend of yours. And that's the way the kids react to me. A lot of little kids that I've never seen before, they'll say, this is Mr. Dressup, and they'll give me a nice hug around the knees and not be too shy either. And I think it's just because they've seen me so much it's like, uh, I'm one of the family that comes and visits.

Also, kids are very personal about their relationship to people they see on TV and their TV, 'cause they usually say, I watch you on my TV, as if they have the idea that they've got this TV and it only gets the neat stuff that they want to watch, and probably nobody else can watch it.

AM I remember Fred Penner telling me one time that one of his little viewers said to him: Do you like our new rug?—thinking that he could look out of the TV and see his new rug.

EC Oh, that reminds me of something, I'd forgotten this thing. Somebody wrote and told me… Well, they were playing… they'd recorded my show and they were playing it in the afternoon for their son who was in morning nursery school, and I opened the show I guess by saying, boy, I'm really thirsty. And the little kid had some orange juice and he took and he poured it into the tape player.

AM He was being helpful.

EC Yeah. And they said, well it ruined the VCR, but it was worth it just to have the kid appreciate the television that much.

AM Did you get lots of letters from the kids?

EC Not an overwhelming amount, because I've always answered all the mail myself and read it all, so it was never more than I could handle. Sometimes it would pile up, but since most kids our age, or the age of our audience, can't write, we didn't get as many letters as you would get from an older group. A lot of them were just pictures, you know, that were sent in. And a lot of them also were written by the parent on the dictation of a child.

AM Did you keep any of them?

EC Not nearly enough because that's one of the big things when I'm going around the college circuit, is reading some of these letters, and some of them were quite wonderful and I wish that I'd saved all the wonderful ones now. But you know, when you're answering a whole bunch of them you think, well I can't let these pile up, but, uh… I'll just give you an example. This was from an older child, who wrote it herself, and one of her questions was: Does Casey know that he's a puppet?

AM Oh, that's a great one?

EC Think of that. How are you gonna answer that. Well, we thought about it for a long time; we passed the letter around and so on. And finally I think we did write back and say yes, Casey knows that he's a puppet, but he doesn't mind.

AM So after, what was it, about 4000 shows in 31 years when you retired?

EC Yeah, we figure… yeah, a little over 4000.

AM Now why did you retire?

EC Well, I felt that it was time. More and more interviewers were saying, any plans for retirement? And I'd think well, are they trying to tell me something. And we were just at the point where things were going well and I think our ratings were still good; but I realized that I wasn't getting any younger and, you know, you can't tell what's going to happen when you get to a certain age. And there were things that I wanted to do—more travelling. Not touring and travelling, but travelling on my own, and also to have a little more time and not have those dark, dark mornings in the winter when you had to haul yourself out of bed and get to the studio whether you felt like it or not. And so I said, well I think I'll retire next year. And we gave everybody plenty of warning so that everybody concerned with the show would be able to expect to, you know, find other means of employment, or deployment. And I just thought I'd free myself up and have more time available.

AM Was it difficult though? To walk away from…

EC Well, it never… it doesn't seem to have stopped, that's the funny thing. We're not taping any more; it's hard for me to think that it was over two years ago when we taped our last show because I'm still doing my touring show, and I'm still Mr. Dressup—I can't avoid that if I tried because we're still on the air and I still look like Mr. Dressup and sound like Mr. Dressup, and I still do personal appearances and telethons and I'm spokesperson for Save the Children Canada, as Mr. Dressup. So my time seems to be filled up pretty well so I don't seem to be sitting around saying, gee, I'd like to go back in the studio.

AM Getting nostalgic.

EC And then, I come down to the CBC often to pick up my mail and I'll crash other shows and go into the studio, so I get to see all the technicians and writers and musicians and costume props people, and camera people that I liked so much. You know, it's like have a big family and just having a reunion every once in awhile.

AM Let's have another piece of music.

EC Okay. I think I mentioned I used to play clarinet when I was a kid and when I was an older kid, and I used to love Dixieland jazz—that was the first kind of music I really, really liked. And when I was going to school in Boston we used to hang out at a local jazz club, and since I was a clever artist I managed to forge my driver's license so it said that I was 21 when I was really only 18. That was the only way I could get into this club to listen to all these wonderful jazz artists playing live. I'll confess it now because this club is closed and the statute of limitations has run out and I am over 18 now anyway. So I really like the really old, old-time jazz, and I was tempted to bring in an album that was recorded in somebody's living room in New Orleans—a very very crude recording—but it was on 78 rpm and I don't think anybody can play those records anymore. So instead I brought in a record by one of my favourite local jazz bands, the Climax Jazz Band, and they play at a place here called The Chicken Deli, which has great wings and it's just wonderful on a Saturday afternoon to go in there and eat some suicide wings and listen to the guys in the jazz band play. And you can bring your kids and have a wonderful time. And the piece I've picked by them, it was written by Sidney Bechet, who was a very very famous soprano clarinetist… saxophonist rather, which uh, looks like a funny looking clarinet. But Sidney Bechet was an outstanding figure in the jazz world and they do a wonderful job on their record, and the number is called *Elastic*, by Sidney Bechet and the Climax Jazz Band. [MUSIC]

AM Do you watch kids' shows, do you take sort of a professional interest in what's going on in the field?

EC No, I don't watch many. Awhile ago I thought I'd… I took about a week I guess and started watching things, particularly in the morning because I felt I should because people are always asking me what I think of other children's shows and I'd hate to say, what other children's shows? So uh, but I don't do it on a regular basis because it seems once I get up in the morning and, I don't know… Watching television during the daytime is sort of sinful to me because I was brought up without television at all, and then it was only something you watched after your work was done at the end of the day. So having it on in the daytime doesn't seem right, you know; you can't watch television and write letters or do work, so… I'm just not used to watching it very much.

AM So, but what do you think of the sort of state of that field right now? What do you like about…

EC Well, when I'm asked that I think I'm supposed to say, oh it's terrible and we need to clean it up and so forth, and there are some really terrible shows, there are some very very dull shows as well; but there are a lot more children's shows now than there were—especially when we started. When we started of course we were the only shows on television because there was just CBC in a lot of areas. And now, you know, there's satellite and there's cable, so there's a huge range of children's shows to choose from; and I think if anybody's at all any kind of a parent at all, they can be selective and just look at the shows that are available and say to the kids, well you can watch this, this and this, but not this and this. And if you can—if the child asks—you can tell them why you don't want them to watch such and such a show. And there's plenty out there to choose from so that the child can get pretty good nourishment, which is what they need out of television.

AM Now it's interesting though, isn't it, that the shows that I think of from my childhood were, you know, Mr. Dressup and Chez Helene, and Friendly Giant, and then along came Sesame Street, which was such a completely different kind of a program.

EC Yeah. I can remember when it first started, and of course it was written up a lot to begin with. And we were kind of aghast because ours has always been a very easygoing show, and a real time show. And when we heard that they were going to do this thing that was based on the way commercials are shot, then we said oh, this is horrible and, uh, this won't last, will it. Wrong. But it was a complete antithesis of everything that we liked to do on television, and yet it had its very very good points. They were addressing things that we didn't address I think.

AM Let's have another piece of music.

EC Now where are we here now… oh, yeah, Mozart. Mozart has never written anything that I didn't like, so I was thinking what in the world can I choose from Mozart because I probably play more Mozart than anything else, and I have yet to—I've heard everything he does. But I don't know whether this will be too long or not; we can play just an excerpt from it, it's *Concerto 21 in C Major*, which is actually the *Elvira Madigan* theme, you know… [humming]

Well there's more to it than that, but it's one of his lovelier melodies, and also I'd like to add that it's a great thing if you're going to have a child to play Mozart to the child before it's born. And my son and daughter-in-law just had a beautiful little—our first granddaughter—a few weeks ago, and they were playing Mozart and the child responds, in the womb; you can feel it moving around and appreciating the music. And then you can continue playing music to them, you know, as they grow, and it's wonderful for their cognitive powers. And Mozart seems to be the best; I don't know whether it's the rhythms, the melodies or the harmonies, but anyway it's a good idea. So this is a good one to start your future child out on, *Concerto 21 in C Major*. [MUSIC]

AM Mozart's *Concerto No. 21 in C Major*, the choice of my guest on Mountaintop Music, Ernie Coombs.

AM Well, we're about to send you off to your mythical mountain peak, but you get to take one book with you.

EC You know, this has been very very hard, taking one book…

AM Oh I know, it's a terrible one.

EC Well, I chose… I'm partial to Charles Dickens and I find I reread Dickens every summer. So I was going to choose *David Copperfield*. And then I went to my library at home and I don't have *David Copperfield*—I've taken it to the cottage—so I called our local lending library and said, I need *David Copperfield* in two hours, and they were all out. So I chose… I said, well well well, *Pickwick Papers*. And they said, yeah, we've got that. So I grabbed the *Pickwick Papers* from them, and here it is fresh from the library and would you like me to read something from it?

AM Sure, that would be great.

EC Okay, this is chapter XXXI. Now I haven't read this book for at least fifteen years, so I just opened it and started at the beginning of a chapter because the thing that I like about Dickens is his sense of describing things, and he's so wonderful you can actually feel and smell the scenes that he describes. So here we go, Chapter 31, which is all about the law and sundry great authorities learned therein.

Scattered about, in various holes and corners of the temple, are certain dark and dirty chambers in and out of which, all the morning and vacation, and half the evening too in term time, there may be seen constantly hurrying with bundles of papers under their arms… etc.

AM Perfect.

EC Isn't that a mouthful? His sentences go on and on and on, but I just adore it.

AM And you can see them, you know the type.

EC I was in London just a few weeks ago when my little granddaughter was born, and I went past the Olde Curiosity Shoppe, which of course is mentioned in Dickens, and I thought Charles Dickens actually walked on this very sidewalk I'm walking on. Whoa!

AM Now, if you were going to go somewhere to spend the rest of your days, to be cast away anywhere in the world—and it doesn't have to be a mountain top—where would you go?

EC Well, it wouldn't be the studio. You know, I would probably go to Maine because that's where I've grown up. Or Nova Scotia, Newfoundland—any place where I could be in touch with the ocean.

AM Is your cottage on the water?

EC Oh yes. It's getting closer to the water all the time. We get these huge storms and these great waves come in and bite away a little bit of the land. But I just love the ocean; the ocean has millions of different moods and it's beautiful to look on, and it's wonderful to see the sunset. My cottage looks west and out over the ocean and the islands, and I can see the sun go down every night. And summer or winter it's gorgeous.

AM So we'll cast you away to your cottage in Maine, and what's the final piece of music you'd take with you?

EC Another lovely piece by Schubert, another piece that makes me choke up when I've heard it, and I don't possess it yet. I've just heard it a few times and I haven't been able to track down a CD with it on it; but it's called a *Nocturne in E flat major for violin, cello and piano*, by Schubert, and the one I heard the best, it's by the Katherine Wilson Trio—I heard it right here on CBC, too.

AM Thank you so much for coming in today. I've really enjoyed this.

EC It's been a real treat, Andrea. I've liked it.

JH Your autobiography, Karen, *Movement Never Lies* is a very personal book. You really have been generous in sharing your life and your thoughts, your personal thoughts, with the world in doing so. Now I guess it must have been a bit difficult, too, because you write about all of your colleagues in dance, and many of them of course are still around on the arts scene. So, was there a little bit of a tug there?—how much should I say or not?

KK Oh, it was I tell you a lot of sleepless nights, because I'm sure that there are some people whose feelings have been hurt or who don't remember things quite the same way I did. But so far they haven't told me about it. I'm sure I'll hear. You know, I was always disappointed when I read autobiographies where I didn't get to know anything real about the person or I felt it was a superficial kind of thing, or felt that they just presented me with what they wanted me to know about them. And I decided that people had all these ideas about who I was and what I was all these years, I might as well set the record straight and tell it the way I saw it, which is what I tried to do. And also to let people know who I am and what's important to me and what I've learned, and what it really is like to have the kind of career I've had and to be a celebrity in Canada—all those things.

JH I do want to go back to your family history. Your mum and dad were quite a couple—I understand your mum was a bit of a tomboy actually?

KK Well, she grew up on a farm outside of Winnipeg, so yeah, she was herding the cows, riding to school on horseback, and she would get up early in the morning and milk cows, and…

JH Who do you think you're most like, your father or your mother?

KK Um… I think I'm most like my mother and I try to be more like my father. I find my mother is very energetic and intuitive, and my father very calm and logical. So I always admire my dad. My mum's the sort of bright light, go go go all the time, and my dad's the one who thinks things through.

JH But they both love to dance, don't they?

KAREN KAIN
WITH ANDREA MARANTZ, 1995

KK Oh yes, and still you can't get them off the dance floor. They're quite amazing if we have a fundraising party or something for the National Ballet. They'll be up on the dance floor and, yeah, they were sort of champion square dancers in their day, which is, you know, in some way it should come back—it's so much fun.

JH I gather that you had decided at a fairly early age what you were going to be when you grew up?

KK I was taken, as a birthday present by my parents, to see a *Giselle* in Hamilton. And I'd never seen ballet before; it wasn't on television in those days. It just, you know, swept me away. It was so dramatic and wonderful and it was Sue La Franca dancing the title role, and I still can—in my mind's eye I can picture her—you know, this sort of full dramatic effect of what she did. And that was it, I just thought, well, this is what I want to do. Now of course I had absolutely no idea what that meant, what that entailed, and I didn't find that out until much later. But it didn't matter because it was fine with me, although there were many days that I was incredibly discouraged and I'd call home, very homesick…

JH   At the National Ballet school?

KK   Yes. And we lived just too far away for me to commute, so I was in residence, which was another tricky, difficult situation. And my mum, who was not a stage mother at all, was always happy to, okay, forget the whole deal, we'll just bring you home, you'll go back to regular school and, you know, don't worry about it any more and… I would never—as much as I was homesick and unhappy or whatever—I would never leave the school, I wanted to be a dancer so badly. I don't think it's a very usual thing for a child to know so early on and to be so focused on what they want to do, but I was.

JH   It's often unusual though that a child retains that drive, that strong desire, and you did. How would you attribute that?

KK   I don't know what I felt so strongly even though I wasn't always encouraged to continue, but certainly I guess that that way of expressing myself became very important to me. And I realize that even before I had seen the ballet and everything, I used… I mean, music for me was the motivation. I would go off by myself and put on the record player and dance by myself or imagine dancing to things, you know. So it was always there, it was always sort of my way of expressing whatever I wanted to express, and I guess that didn't leave me no matter how tough things got or how much I felt maybe I wasn't really cut out for the life or whatever. Deep down I wasn't going to give it up.

JH   So you began your dancing at the age of six, and one of your first teachers was Betty Carey-Love. She was one of the first to notice your raw talent?

KK   Betty Carey was at my final *Swan Lake,* and she still has a ballet school and she's still teaching. And she is a very attractive lady and she wore, in those days she wore fish-net stockings and a rather sexy leotard, and so all the fathers were quite happy to bring their kids to the ballet lessons. But she's the one who took me aside with my mum and said that she really felt that I was talented—this was after about a year of working with her—and that we ought to consider auditioning for the National Ballet School. Now, in those days the National Ballet School did not go across the country looking for students, and we'd never heard of the National Ballet School. And my mother sort of questioned me about this, you know, did I really want to do this. Now, by this time I was almost 10 years old and of course I thought, wow, you know, this is the way you really can become a dancer (if you go here) because you get your academic training and your dance training all together in one place, and this is the only way to really become a top-notch classical dancer, and if that's what I wanted to do, which is I thought I wanted to do that. So I was taken into Toronto to an audition. And in those days, again, it wasn't kind of these official auditions the way they do now where everyone has their number and all that. I was just put into a class with much more advanced students, and I just tried to keep up. I only did the beginning exercises, but I tried to keep up as much as I could, which wasn't very much. Betty Oliphant, who took the audition, could see just by looking at me what I was capable of. And then, after the last one was over, she made me do some little exercises where I had to pretend I was a princess and I was greeting my subjects and then greeting the king and the queen, and of course, well, for any little girl, you know, with an imagination, this—okay, I could do this.

JH   Done that before.

KK   So, my mother burst into tears 'cause she said she didn't even recognize this person who came in, you know, and I guess on the strength of that I was accepted into the school. And so I actually left home when I was 11 because I moved into residence. And that's pretty hard. And it was pretty hard for my family and for my mum especially.

JH   And a huge expense.

KK   A huge expense.

JH   At that time as it still is, I guess, for some people whose children have to board.

KK   Yes. And I got partial scholarship some of the time because it was just too much for my parents to do with three other children and everything, and my mum said, I *can't believe I forgot to teach you how to do your own bun*. But my mum had always done my hair for me in the morning, you know, like mothers do—it's kind of normal—so, I realized the first day of school that I just could not get my hair into a bun. You know, I was having the worst time even doing a ponytail. So I looked pretty bedraggled for a few weeks 'til I got the hang of it.

JH There was one experience you had at an early age involving, I think, rehearsals to a certain song by Patti Page? Would you tell us that story? That could have discouraged you.

KK Yeah, well that was actually my very first dance teacher, which my mum picked because it was close enough to the house where we were living; we had moved to Ancaster from Hamilton, which is outside, a little suburb. And I could walk, so she didn't have to worry about getting me there. She gave us ballet lessons in the basement. I have this very strong memory of the kitty litter, the smell of kitty litter in the corner, a big old couch that we flung ourselves whenever we got tired, and the fact that the whole lesson was done to only one record, and that was Patti Page singing *The Tennessee Waltz*. And the whole lesson. Now maybe the lesson was only half an hour long, but it was a lot of time to listen to that song, and it sort of spoiled it for me because I could never hear that record again without thinking of those lessons, and I mean really, I was a little girl so it really stuck.

JH So I guess this first piece of music, which I'd like you to choose now, will not be *The Tennessee Waltz*?

KK No, it'll never be *The Tennessee Waltz*. I'd have to be pretty desperate to pick *The Tennessee Waltz*. No, I picked this piece of music by Beethoven because I danced in a ballet made to this music, and I just adore it. I could have picked any section of it, it is the most glorious, wonderful music. Some people might remember it from—it was used in *Fantasia*, I think. James Kudelka who is our choreographer at the National Ballet of Canada, he did a ballet called *Pastorelle* to it, and it's one of my favorite roles and a ballet that I love to watch; it looks like a painting, it's quite glorious. So this is the allegro movement of Beethoven's *Pastoral Symphony No. 6*. [MUSIC]

JH Your parents, who you say are—your mother at any rate—not a stage mother, but they were dedicated to your wish to become a dancer, and with three other children that wasn't easy I'm sure.

KK They were always, you know, questioning me to make sure that this is what I wanted to do because they realized how tough it was, and I was always absolutely determined that this is what I wanted to do. You know, I thank them in my book, I actually dedicate my book to them, because they never stopped me from following my dreams, and then those dreams came true for me. And you know, they could easily have just said, no way we're letting you do this, you'll never make a decent living, it's a short career, who knows if you'll succeed. It's not just talent, determination is a huge factor in it—determination, discipline, all of those things. I've seen people with much more physical talent than I had not make it because they just weren't motivated. They were also the ones that had all the clippings in the basement and all my souvenirs, so that when I went to do this book I had references. Because I didn't keep any of that stuff. If I was on the road and I got a nice review somewhere I'd, you know, I knew it would make my mum happy. I really wasn't that interested in keeping it. I'd clip it out and send it home, you know. So she kept everything. So it was very helpful to me to have all that. And actually my parents spent weeks two years ago sorting through them all and cataloguing them and putting them in the right years so that I would have, you know, it would save me time in going through them.

JH And your decision at the age of 11 going to boarding school and choosing this course for the foreseeable future. It means missing out on other things that other 11-year-olds and teenagers have as a normal childhood, doesn't it?

KK Well, it does. But I don't regret any of it; I want that to be really clear. I didn't learn how to drive until a few years ago, you know. And I did eventually, but I think it's a little easier to do that when you're a teenager than it is when you're 40 years old. I would have learned if I'd been at home and there'd been a family car. I mean, all my siblings learned how to drive, you know. But there wasn't a time or a place for me to do that in the life that I chose. I didn't learn how to play tennis, I didn't learn how to play a lot of sort of popular games that people know. I wasn't aware of some of the top television shows of the period, you know, things like that. Certainly I saw Ed Sullivan on Sunday nights, but I never saw any other television really during my growing up years. Certainly we did have, the pop culture was still part of the National Ballet School. I mean, we sure knew who The Beatles were and all of that. I actually, in a lot of ways, I thought it was easier being a teenager there. First of all we wore uniforms, which I think was very helpful because we were not focused on clothes and hair and all that stuff, and who I was going to impress. I mean, you got up in the morning, you just put on your uniform and you knew everybody else was going to have their uniform on and I think that's a really helpful thing as a teenager, you know. I think there's just far too much attention spent on 'the look', you know, and being with it and cool and all that stuff. So I didn't have any of that, but I did miss my family, and you know I didn't really get to know my brothers and sisters until I was, you know, in my 20s. And we are extremely close now, but we missed sort of the teenage years together.

JH   I want to ask you about some of your hairier moments on stage. There's a couple of incidences that happened on stage. Your first performance with the National Ballet and that leotard. Would you tell us that story?

KK   Well, it was a unitard, which now I guess we call cat suits. Now they're sort of in fashion and you wear them under things, but as dancers we often have to wear them as costumes. This was a white unitard and I was going into a role that—it wasn't a new ballet and I was taking over someone else's part who had left, and it was my first performance with the National Ballet of Canada. I was very nervous, very shy, never spoke up for myself in those days. And I went to my fitting, I tried on this white unitard and I could tell that the legs were really too short for me, it was really pulling, you know, and the crotch just didn't, like, come up where it should. And I kind of very shyly mentioned that I thought maybe the legs were a little too short. Obviously the person before me had been smaller. And I was told very sort of brusquely, oh, it's fine, you know. And in those days we had a wardrobe master who was really tough. I mean, it was the style, you know—really tough. And so, you know, I just shut my mouth and did what I was told and got to the performance, and the first thing we did was a very modern piece, very avant garde. And a group of women ran forward and sort of went into the splits in the second position, like straight out to the side. As I did that I could hear the stitches just popping, and of course the whole unitard had split. Now, we do wear something under the unitard, so it wasn't pornographic or anything, but it was really—I felt this really cold breeze all of a sudden and I was so embarrassed, you know. But I learned a lesson. I learned that, you know, when I know something's right I have to, you know, be insistent and not let someone talk me out of it.

JH   How about the time that you and Frank Augustyn crashed into each other? This was I think your first performance together in *Romeo and Juliet*?

KK   Well, Frank had had to learn the ballet very quickly because I was going to dance it with a much more experienced partner and he was injured; so if, you know, Miss Franca had decided—Celia Franca had decided—that Frank would be a perfect Romeo. He was a little young, sort of (as I describe him, a bit like an Afghan puppy), but he looked right and he was very strong and everything. So we rehearsed it, got to the performance and we were a little underpolished to say the least. But it was kind of going okay until we got to the very passionate bedroom scene where Romeo is saying good-bye to Juliet and, you know, the next time she sees him is when she wakes up in the tomb and he's already dead because he thought she was dead; you know, it's the greatest tragedy of all time. At one point, Juliet, in desperation before he leaves, runs across the stage and sort of… does this sort of suicidal leap, and he runs and catches her at the last minute. It's a very exciting piece of choreographer. Well, I took off and I was really in the spirit of the thing and really passionately involved, and he took off with me. And somehow our lines of direction on the stage, they kind of crossed instead of going parallel. And our feet just caught up, but we had so much momentum going forward that the two of us literally skidded… like, you know, rolling and skidding across the stage, and it didn't quite look like the right choreography. So… and there was such a nasty review.

JH   Was there?

KK   Oh, there was a lady who wrote a nasty review and it just devastated Frank 'cause he was a year younger than me, and they said I was too much of a woman for him. Like, can you be crueler to a young man than that?

JH   I don't think so. Well, speaking of reviews—and I hope you got this in the spirit it was probably intended—Fotheringham's review. Of you and Frank again?.

KK   I saved that review because it made me laugh so much. It was the finale of the whole ballet after three hours of all this dancing. And our particular part had gone really well and the crowd really loved us and it was great. And then there was the little bit where I have to run across the stage and jump up onto his shoulder. But I was so kind of enthusiastic about the reception I was getting, and I jumped so hard and fast, that I actually flew past his shoulder and he caught me by the ankles. And there was this huge kind of gasp from the audience 'cause I wanted it to look like it was supposed to be like that. And then Alan Fotheringham wrote it up in his article and it just, you know—of course, he's a writer so it was very well put and very amusing. So I saved that 'cause I enjoyed that article.

JH   Aside from those very infrequent mishaps, do you know when it's going to be a great performance? When you're in the wings ready to go on do you feel it?

KK   You want every performance to be a great performance. I mean, that's what we're aiming for, that's what we rehearse all those hours for, are those performances that are really special and take off. It happens so rarely. And sometimes the more you want them to happen the less frequently they happen, at least in my experience. I must say, though, that I wanted my last *Swan Lake* in Toronto to be a special performance, and in many ways it

was. I mean, there were some little things that go wrong—there are always little things that go wrong in every performance because what you're attempting is so difficult. But that's also what keeps you working. I wouldn't have been interested in working on *Swan Lake* for 23 years if it hadn't been so difficult and so challenging to me. But I ended up with a performance that I felt was special and I was proud of it, and… but it happens so rarely, and it especially happens rarely when you want it to badly.

JH   And you say of thousands of performances a dozen, or a few more than that, were really to your satisfaction.

KK   I think a dozen would be pushing it.

JH   Really?

KK   Yeah, but that's alright. That's alright, because as hard as I try I don't always do the best that I'm capable of. And that's really what I want to do and that's what I work for, but it doesn't always happen.

JH   I'd like to hear another piece of music now, Karen. What would you like to play?

KK   I've selected some music from the final scenes of *Swan Lake*, which I think are the most heart wrenching and most wonderful bits of *Swan Lake*, and the music that sends shivers up and down my spine. So I hope you'll enjoy it. [MUSIC]

JH   You reached your full height, 5'7" isn't it?—at a relatively early age.

KK   By the time I was 12.

JH   Yeah. So there you were. And certainly how you look (your physical appearance, your physical attributes, are so central to dancers) is… Would you say when you're thrown into such intensive training and there you are going through growth spurts and all of that, is it a breeding ground for insecurity? Are you so focused on your body that you, sort of, I hate my body or I love my body?

KK   When your body is your major instrument for the career that you want so badly, you're competing at a very high level, constantly wish you had better this or better that and compare yourself with others constantly. So you have to have a very strong sense of yourself. And everyone thinks that, oh, you know, I look like the ideal ballerina so I must have it all, and of course nobody has it all. The performing artists that I most admire, none of them have it all when you look really closely at their… what they were born with. We look in the mirror and we're very sort of pragmatic and realistic and we see ourselves and we see what we aren't accomplishing, so, yes it is a world that can breed a lot of insecurity and a lot of problems. People were always on me about my weight, and in those days there wasn't a lot of nutritional counseling. So of course if, you know, if the choice was cold slaw or a peanut butter and jam sandwich, I was going for the peanut butter and jam sandwich—you know, like any kid would.

JH You describe yourself, certainly in your early years, as being very shy and insecure. And yet that magical ability you had even at the audition to transform yourself, on demand—go out of the room, come back in and be the fairy princess—do you understand how it is you can do that?

KK Well, you have to remember that by the time I did that little transformation, I was doing that for my mother and Betty Oliphant—those two people; it was a little easier for me to do that than it was to stand up in front of thousands of people and try the same transformation. I was kind of excruciatingly shy as a young child, really even one on one. Now, I'm not shy at all one on one. Having to go out in front of three thousand people and attempt steps that 50 percent of the time I fall down on, and knowing that I'm really trying to do these as well as I can with that kind of pressure. I'm not a born performer, I'm not the person at the party who stands up and tells jokes and has everybody in stitches. I'm the one who is enjoying the one who's performing, and that's still the way I am. So I'm sort of introverted really.

JH So is it really like actors often describe, that they are normally socially not extroverts, but they lose themselves in the role and they can do anything, whatever the role requires?

KK Yes, absolutely. That's what I feel. I feel when I get into a role and I'm totally believing that I'm for this period of time living the life of this character, and often disguised in the costume in a wig and makeup and everything, then I lose that fear. And I'm still afraid of some of the steps I have to do, but I'm not—it's not Karen the person out there, it's Karen the actress—I'm not so frightened. And for me it's fun. It's fun, it's creative, and it's an adventure then. But just to be myself and stand up in front of people is still excruciating for me.

JH Let's have another piece of music, Karen. What would you like to hear now?

KK Well, one of the pieces I picked was from *Les Mis*, and believe it or not I enjoy pop stuff as much as anybody else. Right. And *Les Mis*, of all those big shows, I have to say *Les Mis* was the one that made me cry, you know. Really, I loved the show, and there's one particular song in it called, *I Dream a Dream*, and it just breaks my heart, I think it's such as beautiful song. And this version has Debbie Burns singing it. [MUSIC]

JH Karen, I want to give you a few names, colleagues and so on that you've worked with, danced with, and just tell me what thoughts come to mind. First of all, Rudolph Nureyev, a man who practised always and warmed up in a wool toque.

KK He was, well, what is it they say—40 percent of your body heat is lost through your head—well he always believed that and he was always in wool and he loved to cover his head, too. 'Cause he wanted to be really, really warm. I mean dancers understand that. Your muscles work better, everything works better, you're looser, you're more flexible when you're really, really warm. So yes, he always wore a toque.

JH And was he as fantastic to work with as his legend leads us to believe?

KK Yes he was, he was. Certainly he was temperamental and certainly there were episodes where he was less than stellar. For the most part—and I worked with him for more than a decade—he was the most loving, generous man/artist. Quite an amazing capacity for work. Something… I mean, most dancers have a capacity to work hard; this man would just amaze us with the kind of power and strength he would continue to do. I mean, as people who were sort of much younger than him, we would be exhausted and he would show us that we could go on and work harder and do more, and so he was such an inspiration like that. And to me personally he just took me under his wing, and he was my mentor. He decided that I was talented and that he was going to help me have a career, and he took me all over the world. He gave me advice, he sought me out as a partner and, you know, he took me to places where I never would have danced—Vienna, London. I mean, I did dance in London with The National Ballet, but with other companies in London, Australia. He just insisted that I put myself out there on the international stage and get myself well-known, you know. So he was really my friend and my mentor and the streak of generosity in him was quite astounding to all of us, because we'd worked with some other superstars who were not like that. It was all about them, it was never about anyone else. I mean, he was a legend. He is a legend.

JH   Frank Augustyn, your little Afghan puppy that grew up.

KK   Oh, he's a long way from an Afghan puppy now. Frank's my dear friend. You know, you build bonds with people when you go through a lot of really difficult times and rough experiences together, and we did and we sort of supported each other, and we were a team. We had a wonderful partnership. It was a very special, magical partnership. I think I appreciate it more now in retrospect, remembering what it was like, than I actually did at the time. At the time I think we were both surprised at all the attention we were getting, and sort of didn't really feel that we deserved it.

JH   You were "it" overnight, the two of you.

KK   Yeah, it was sort of overnight because of Moscow and all of that. And, you know, it was also again timing, that the country was ready to believe in its own and to be delighted that there were some dancers doing well in the country, and it was the beginning of the sort of major dance boon in the eighties that was felt all over North America. So we were very lucky in that respect that we were sort of riding this wave of the dance boom.

JH   And you'd hold hands apparently in the wings before you would walk on stage and dance.

KK   Well, we'd try to give each other courage, and we did. And, you know, the fact that we rehearsed together endlessly and did so much work on each role, I think that it was evident the kind of time and energy that had gone into the preparation for our performances over the years. You know, that we knew each other so well and our timing was down so perfectly together—our coordination.

JH   Another Canadian ballet dancer who I think preceded you to the National Ballet School, Veronica Tennant?

KK   Well, Veronica was another mentor for me, not because she chose to be, but just because of her behaviour. She was already the ballerina in the company when I joined in 1969-70, and from day one she was extremely generous to me and encouraging, and she was one of those rare people that is not threatened by other people's talent around them, that they have a good sense of what their talent is and that they know that other people's talent doesn't mean that they're not talented, you know. And so she encouraged me and she stepped aside on occasion to let me go ahead of her, without any kind of rancor or anything, and we've remained friends—we're very good friends.

JH   I want to switch gears a bit and talk about the ballet shoe. And you devote quite a lot of space in the book to—I mean, it is of course the central tool of the ballet dancer—but you say that it takes literally a lifetime to find the perfect shoe. Have you found the perfect shoe?

KK   No. I'm still experimenting and trying and, you know, also quite honestly your feet change over the years. But if you get Evelyn Hart and I together, all we talk about is how awful our shoes are and, you know, try and give each other pointers, and it's always, you know, the ballerina's problem. They are handmade. Each pair is a little bit different because they're not machine mass produced. In order to find two pairs of shoes for my last Swan Lake, I spent weeks sewing and breaking them in and trying to feel exactly how they supported my foot, exactly how the block was—so how I could stand on them. And people ask me if they really are wood, you know. And they're not wood, but people always think they are because you can hear them, you know, sometimes when they're too hard.

JH You know what was fascinating was how you literally rated ballets—individual ballets—according to how many shoes they required, how many shoes you'd wear out during the performance.

KK Yeah, and what kind of shoes you need. I mean a ballet with a lot of jumping in it, perhaps *Giselle*, a ballet where you have to appear that you're sort of sailing through the air, you would never wear really new shoes that aren't broken in. You wear them almost without any block at all, without any hardness in them, because you don't want the audience to hear you running or jumping, you know, and hear that, you know, tapping of the shoe, because that would break the illusion that you in fact are an airborne creature—you know, lighter than air.

JH You learned a lot too about dancing through injury, and a lot of your male counterparts too, who have some of the most grueling leaps and jumps as well. Things are a lot better now, but did you have a lot of luck, I guess that we would call it, in not having serious injuries throughout your career?

KK Yes, I've been lucky in many ways, and probably genetically lucky, too, because I have had lots of aches and pains and kind of aggravating injuries, but I've never had any major injuries—and I'm touching wood here; I'm not a really superstitious person, but that's one thing I'm not going to fool around with. Part of that is just the way I'm put together, you know. I'm strong. But part of it is also the fact that I train very hard and I get my body very used to the kind of workload that it's going to have to take. And I think that that's a very important part of what we do, is the training. But some people, no matter how hard they train, their bodies just don't adapt as well to the workload and they get a lot of injuries. And also, you know, we used to work just on the hard surfaces of the stages, the way they're built. And they're built for, you know, automobile shows and things, they're not built for ballet dancers.

JH Concrete floors some of them?

KK Yes, concrete—wood laid on concrete—that's the way most modern theatres are built, and we would jump on that and, you know, we don't have the benefit of shock absorbing running shoes the way a jogger would, or anyone else. We just have these little canvas shoes or leather shoes, or the point shoes which are satin and canvas.

JH So does a dancer's feet become very misshapen or very injured over the years, not having all that protection of a proper shoe?

KK Well no, they don't have to be. You see, we are trained so that our actual feet become the shock absorbers. I mean, we are… they are so strong, they're so strengthened from the dancing. So, you know, we have feet I would like to think more like cats, so that we can land without making a lot of noise, and that there's a lot of muscle control and balance and technique involved in that. I often wear orthotics in my walking shoes because I had some problems with my feet a couple of years ago, and again I had to learn completely different strengthening exercises, and I started wearing orthotics when I could. And all of that really helped my feet. You learn a lot about yourself when you are in a career this long.

JH Just a final note on feet, and something a little more aesthetic actually. I really was interested in the comments you made that some dancers try to make their feet as expressive as their hands, and I'd never really given the expression of the feet their due. But that really opened my eyes to it. And do you believe that?—that feet are such an integral part of the expression?

KK I do. Yeah, I think if you watch a really high calibre ballerina you will see that the feet have to speak as much as the hands. And that is something that we all try to do.

JH And your feet are good because they have such a good arch, so they are expressive, is that so?

KK Well, just having a good arch isn't enough. I mean, it's the way you use your feet. I've seen people that don't have particularly good arches, but they have feet that are extremely expressive and interesting to watch. You know, if you're a dancer your whole body is your instrument, every square inch has got to be expressive. And the feet are very important, they're often accentuated in dance.

JH The exclamation points at times. Well, how about another piece of music. What would you like to hear now, Karen?

KK Well, there's a song for two men that I've heard many times, written by Bizet, and I... It's quite a popular piece, but it's very beautiful. It's called *Au Font du Templessant* and it's from *The Pearl Fishers*. I t's for the tenor and the baritone. [MUSIC]

JH I'm thinking of the title of your book, Karen, *Movement Never Lies* and how you say you can tell a dancer's character and what they're really like by how they move on stage. Can you explain a little bit more about what you mean when you say movement never lies?

KK Well, it occurred to me after all these years of dancing myself and watching other people dance, that the inner life of a performing artist becomes very visible in their performances. When they get on the stage, no matter how good an actress or actor they are, if they are having problems, if they are somebody who's going through a difficult time in their life for whatever reason, it comes through, either in a kind of energy or in the choices they make in their characterizations. For whatever reason, the person is extremely transparent on stage. Because for me it's very evident when I look back on my career that my inner life was reflected on the stage all the way through, even though I didn't really realize that, and how I couldn't hide even if I thought I could.

JH And even if you feel completely transported into the role, into the character that you're dancing, nevertheless the real person will show through?

KK Yes. And in my experience, I mean, all I have to work with are my thoughts and feelings when I'm creating a character. That material exposes, you know, what I choose to use and what I have there exposes parts of me that I might not even know about, and that's the really interesting thing about acting, is sometimes you do get to investigate parts of your personality that are sort of dormant in your real life, you know. But then you have to dig really deep if you're going to create a believable character, and so some of those characters are far from what you're like in everyday life, but they're still part of you, and the choices you make do reflect who you are. And I find that a fascinating thing, you know, to watch people and to see… and to know them in real life and then to see how rich their imagination is, or how deep their character is. And people who are not very complex and not very deep, do not usually end up creating characters that are that either.

JH So you're comfortable on stage, would you say that much?

KK I can become comfortable on stage, I'm not always comfortable on stage. Once I've done a role many times and it feels like a second skin to me and I feel confident that I really have gone in the right direction and that it works for people and they believe it, and I believe it, you know, right through and through—then I can feel comfortable to a degree, as comfortable as anyone could feel. I try to pretend that the audience isn't there, I try to put that out of my mind. If I were to keep telling myself there are 3000 people watching you right now and they want their money's worth; well, if I focused on that I would never take a step on the stage because I'd be too terrified.

JH So you're in whatever the magic world is of the story of the ballet?

KK I love that magic, I believe in that magic and I try to create that magic when I'm given the opportunity to do that. And it is, when I step out of the wings onto the stage, for me it is a magic world, it is a sort of sacred place, and I can really transport myself and hopefully other people if I can get myself into that state of mind. As an audience member, and I believe this about most audience members, I have a gut reaction to what I am seeing and I either believe it and be moved by it or touched by it or amused by it, or I'm not and it leaves me cold. But, you know, people are always apologizing to me, oh, I don't know anything about dance—who interview me—and I... you really don't need to. I mean, it may enhance your enjoyment, but on a basic level I think it's something that cuts through anything. You don't need to be educated. You either see the beauty of it and understand how much goes into it, or you don't.

JH Considering that you are a Canadian superstar and would have had opportunities to dance in companies in other countries, permanently, were you not tempted? Did you never consider leaving Canada to dance elsewhere?

KK I was tempted many times, and I did on many occasions—not for good—but I did go and work with wonderful choreographers, work with wonderful companies, and I had a lot of opportunity to investigate and to challenge myself in other areas. I think one of the reasons that I stayed with The National Ballet of Canada—I mean there are a lot of them—but one of them was that they gave me the freedom to accept a lot of the opportunities I was presented with. I mean, they also refused some of them because they needed me at home for various reasons. But, I went off to New York to work with Elliott Fell, then I went to France very frequently to work. So all of this really expanded my horizons and gave me insight, and I could bring it all home and apply things to roles I had in Canada. So I got the best of both worlds; I was with The National Ballet of Canada, which I still believe is one of the top companies in the world, with one of the most varied, wonderful repertoires anywhere, with incredible dancers all the time, that kept me challenged. But I could go off to France and have, you know, brand new ballets made around me and be a star in Paris, which was so incredibly exciting, and of course eventually I made the choice that Canada was where I wanted to be and where I wanted to stay, and that I had lived out of a suitcase for long enough and that that world of being a guest artist, travelling and being lonely—certainly professionally very exciting, but privately not so fun—I decided that wasn't for me.

JH So no regrets?

KK No regrets at all. I had the opportunity, I explored it, and I made my choice.

JH At 43 Karen, with a wonderful long career of 25 years, with ballet being the domain of the young dancer for the most part, are you optimistic that you can continue to dance, that there will be roles for older (I guess we have to call ourselves older) women on stage that will be satisfying too for you?

KK Again, I'm incredibly fortunate because already in the last two years there have been two wonderful ballets created for the dancer I am now. One was *The Actress* by James Kudelka, which was an amazing piece of work which I can hardly wait to do again, done to Chopin's *Preludes*, 24 Preludes, and I had 24 partners almost. Sort of the life of a ballerina, on stage, in the studio and in her dressing room—I had three areas of the stage—I mean, a really beautiful, beautiful piece. In May I have the pleasure of doing a ballet that I've loved ever since I first saw it, and it's called *A Month in the Country*, choreographed by Sir Frederick Ashton, who is no longer alive, but it's never been done outside the Royal Ballet in London. It's never been given to any other company. And Anthony Dowell, the artistic director, who was a famous director himself, has agreed to allow The National Ballet of Canada to do it, especially for me as a 25th anniversary present. Again, it's Chopin music, which I adore. You know, but it's not just me. I saw recently a company in Toronto for the first time called A Netherlands Dance Theatre III. I don't know if you've heard about this company, but it's so hot in Europe. It is a company for dancers over 40. Now the pickings are pretty slim over 40, there are only five people in this company, but it is in such demand. And it went to New York recently, and I saw one review that said that this was the most interesting work to watch, was with the more mature dancers. So I'm hoping that the North American attitude of… in—well maybe in everything, but in dance specifically, that dance is just for the young and it's only about virtuoso tricks. I'm hoping that the public is beginning to realize that. That there's so much more to the art form than that. I'm not saying that that isn't a good part of it, that's an exciting part of it. But the other emotional ways that you can go with dance, the deeper things and the richer things you can say, can't really be said by teenagers.

JH So, offsetting perhaps some loss of physical ability or strength or endurance or whatever you lose gradually with age, are you a better dancer for the traits that you're describing? For your understanding?

KK I think so. I think the audience, when they see a more mature artist—now, you know, I shouldn't generalize…

JH But for you though, Karen, would you say you're better?

KK   But for me, I think my performances are richer than they used to be, and I don't think that there— at this point anyway—there is enough noticeable decline in the physical side of it that it should be something that people would be losing out something in the performance. And I think the same when I see Evelyn Hart dance. I think that her dancing is better now than it was 10 years ago. And I hope that the audiences see that, too.

JH   Are there a lot of good dancers coming up through The National Ballet school? Do you see a tremendous future ahead for Canadian ballet?

KK   I see, in The National Ballet itself now, extraordinary talent coming along, and in The National Ballet school. The young ones, the training is evolving, it's getting better, they're improving. I think it's very exciting.

JH   And young people are going for it still, are they?—are interested in career ballet?

KK   Oh yes. It's very hard to get a place in The National Ballet school. It only takes a hundred students, so it's difficult, it's hard to get in. And you know, they have to pick only the ones that they feel have everything going for them in order to make it. But, the talent is extraordinary, the training is getting better. You know, in every way in that area it looks bright. What doesn't look bright is the funding and the support for these organizations. You know, if there's one thing this country should do, it is that it should support excellence, it should not support mediocrity and spread everything thin and make everybody happy. When we already have proven that we have institutions that are excellent, let's keep them there. I mean, I'm not saying we should never criticize them and that we should never take long hard looks at them, but financially we should support them and we should let these talented children have a place where they can become artists of world calibre.

JH   Let's have another piece of music, Karen.

KK   Shostakovich, *Piano Concerto No. 1*, by Dmitri Shostakovich. It is just a piece of music that I love deeply. [MUSIC]

JH   Now Karen all of the Mountaintop Music guests are allowed to take one book with them to their mountain top. What would you choose?

KK   I chose *Love in the time of Cholera* by Gabriel Marquez, a South American writer. It is an extraordinary book. I read this book, and his use of language is so rich I could smell the things he was describing, I could taste the things he was describing, I could see it all like a film in my eye. I mean, I also admire writers who can say things with a minimal number of words and, you know, it gets straight to the point. This writer has a descriptive vocabular that is so extraordinary, plus the story is bizarre and wonderful. I could read this book over and over—I love it.

JH   You also, Karen, get to choose where exactly you would like to spend the rest of your days. It could be lake Winnipeg, it could be cottage country in Ontario—where do you think you'd like to go?

KK   Well, it wouldn't be Lake Winnipeg because of those mosquitoes. I remember them well. I think if I had a cottage in the Muskokas, and I could live there with my husband and some dogs and some cats and lots of visiting friends and relatives, I could be very happy there.

JH   The cats being the ones that you tried to collect as a child and couldn't keep and had to constantly give away.

KK   Yeah. Well, I keep them at a minimum. I mean, I have two now, I think that's a good number.

JH   Well, I wish you lots of magic and enjoyment on your lakeside retreat with your choice of book. And I want to ask you for a final choice of music before you go.

KK   Well, the final choice is a ballet choice, but it's a beautiful piece of music. It's by Tchaikovsky and it's the *Pas de Deux* from *The Sleeping Beauty*.

JH   Thank you very much for joining me on Mountaintop Music. Bye-bye.

KK   Bye-bye.

IAN TYSON
WITH JUDY HAMILL, 1994

JH   You haven't done a lot of media interviews as a rule over the years, so I'm really glad for this book tour and the chance to talk with you.

IT   Well, I sure evened up the odds this week I tell ya. It's been more fun than I thought it would be. It's hard work, it really is. I didn't know they started at 7:30 in the morning—it's just like gettin' me on a ranch, they don't end until six o'clock at night. I'm not crazy about the signings. People for some reason want you to… they come with entire quotations and things that they want you to write. They dictate things, and of course you can't do that. If you sign, you know, "happy trails – Ian Tyson"—that's about as good as you can do. I think they're somewhat disappointed when you don't write the cryptic message.

JH   Your autobiography, *I Never Sold My Saddle*, starts with your parents. Your father, George, leaves Liverpool at the turn of the century and works briefly on a ranch in Bowden. Did he have cowboy in his blood? Did he have this dream of being a cowboy?

IT   I think so. He got here in 1906 and I guess saw just about the last year-and-a-half or two years of open range before… it was still pretty open, they hadn't fenced it all up and you could still ride, you know, all the way down across the line to Montana without hitting a fence. So he saw that and he cowboyed around Innisfail for awhile, I understand, and up around Yankee Valley here. And he told me stories about Yankee Valley. And then he drifted on out to Vancouver Island, where he was when he joined up in the great… you know, when they all joined up in the cavalry in the Great War. He was the one that should have had the biography actually, 'cause he led a pretty astounding kind of life, you know. He survived so many different things.

JH   Did he tell you stories when you were a kid?

IT   Yes he did, you know. And it's curious because I know a lot about my dad. My sister and I, who have, you know, we have become close over the years as often you will… You know, we fought like cats and dogs when we were kids, you know, and we've become close; and I've told her the stories and she said, you know, I never… I had no idea that all these stories—he never told me any of them. He just told his son, you know. Remembrance Day is always a day full of ghosts for me.

JH   And so many of the pictures in the early part of your autobiography are Ian as a kid on a horse wearing the cowboy gear.

IT   That's right, yeah.

JH   Was this it for you?

IT   The die was cast pretty early, yeah. He led a wonderful, colourful kind of life, and you know, he had one foot in the 19th century and the other foot in the 20th. I've always thought the turn of the century must have been… that's the actual, the time I'd like to have seen, is right around 1900, 'cause you know, it's such a collision of the industrial thing coming to the open west. You know, it was the last days of the bad guys and the train robbers—everything was still going on and they had airplanes, you know.

JH   You went to art college, the Vancouver School of Art, and graduated there. Were you thinking of becoming an artist seriously at that time?

IT   Yes, I wanted to be a designer, an illustrator. Never became one. That school was a very French impressionist, post impressionist school; I mean, it was their way or the highway, you know, as far as painting was concerned. But I wanted to do the more… you know, more realistic, literal kind of stuff, but you couldn't do that in those days at the Vancouver School of Art. So it wasn't until later that I learned a little bit how to draw and illustrate.

JH   Well, yes, you're famous for that bottle of Resdan Shampoo!

IT   I don't know why that sticks in people's minds.

JH   You designed the logo. It's great trivia. That's amazing.

IT   Yeah, I guess it is, because it sure won't die, it won't go away.

JH   I was amazed to learn that you only started to learn to play guitar when you were 23 years old.

IT   Twenty-two I think. Yeah, huh-huh, it's true. See, the guitar in the popular sense was very uncommon in those days. And it's hard to believe that now that everybody can play three chords, you know. Your maiden aunt can play three chords and mine—if I had one—she could probably play two or three, but in those days nobody played guitar except very, very scarce professionals.

JH   Where did you get your first guitar?

IT   It was second hand, it was a hock-shop guitar. It was a German made Honer or Hoffner or something like that. I remember it very well, it had a rectangular sound hole and it was a pretty tough old guitar, but I don't know where it ended up.

JH   We talked about you first learning guitar back in the fifties. The next year you played with a rockabilly band, The Sensational Stripes—remember that?—shared a stage with Buddy Holly, Eddie Cochrane, Laverne Baker and Paul Anka. Not bad. Not bad for a rookie.

IT   Yeah, well it's just one of those union… those things. The package shows used to come to town, and big jazz shows and later on those rockabilly shows. I think there was a union regulation or something because they had to have a local band on or whatever; but we got to be the local band that night and I got to hear Buddy Holly and the Crickets—blew me away, completely. Those were the loudest amps I had ever heard. And I'm sure by today's standards they weren't that loud. But they were sizzlin' and crackin' and poppin'—one of those old Fender amps, you know. It was great. Waylon Jennings played bass for Buddy Holly during that era, and I was just thinking I don't know if he was the bass player that night or not. He's the one that survived… he didn't get on the plane, you know.

JH   When you decided to move to Toronto, 1959, that's a… you know, that's a major shift. That must have been culture shock for you going from west to east like that?

IT   Well, yes, I think it was, but you know that oft' told story of me standing at the crossroads on highway 97 goin' south to Seattle and the other one goes towards Spokane—that's true I think. Because that's the reason I went east, was the first car that stopped was goin' east. So we ended up in Chicago and then many days later this old fella, he took his time, it was like a tour of the western states. It was kind of fun actually. Toronto was a very small place then, a quiet little, funny little upper Canada city. And nothing was open after… you know, the bars closed at twelve, and Sunday was like, it was like a morgue, you know. And all these immigrants—English primarily, English and German and Italian immigrants—started the counter culture there. And that's what happened. The counter culture started with coffee houses and the coffee houses were a big deal.

JH   I saw you at the River Boat, though.

IT   Yeah, you would have. Oh yeah, we played there. There was actually a period of time there, maybe six or eight months, when the folk music thing hit there were more coffee houses than there were folksingers to fill them… to sing in them. The demand was greater than the supply. And I remember I had two, I was singing in two of them and I'd go back and forth, and I made thirty bucks a night instead of fifteen. It was a real grassroots, beatnik coffee house, folky thing. And it was very exciting 'cause a lot of energy. For me it was always the Scots-Irish cowboy songs, but Sylvia was… she was into a lot of those eclectic, the Appalachian ballads. And there were hundreds of them and they were just there. If you could, you know, if you could read music they were in the sharp collections. But I couldn't read it, so it didn't do me any good 'cause I couldn't read a lick. Still can't.

JH   How did you get to Greenwich Village? I mean, what an exciting scene for you two.

IT   Yeah, it was. We were accepted very quickly in Greenwich Village as part of the 'in' inside circle, you know. And there were all of us, and Peter, Paul and Mary were being formed, and Bobby Zimmerman from Minnesota, was there, and soon to become Bob Dylan… and Tom Paxton, and Ian and Sylvia, the Tarriers, and the Journeyman, Carolyn Hester and Judy Collins—we were all there, so it was an exciting time. There were two or three hangouts: A Kettle of Fish and Gertie's Folk City and places like that. And the McDougall Street scene—it was a small scene but there was a lot going on.

JH   You've got a pretty good memory of the sixties—it's sort of a blur for a lot of people, often for musicians.

IT   Some of it is a blur for me, too.

JH   I'd love to hear the story about how you wrote your first, and I still think your best—one of your best—*Four Strong Winds*—in an apartment in Greenwich Village.

IT   In my manager's apartment, Albert Grossman.

JH   'The' Albert Grossman.

IT   The late Albert Grossman, and he's been gone now for about 12 years, and I really miss… I miss him. He was a great innovator and entrepreneur in those important days, I think, and I just borrowed his apartment one afternoon, one rainy afternoon, to see… I figured it couldn't be that difficult to write one of these things, and it didn't take very long (maybe an hour or so) because those early tunes are… they're the easy ones to write because you've got that whole storehouse of information there which you haven't tapped, you haven't used it, you know. But after 50 or whatever, then they get tougher. But the first few are pretty simple, pretty easy to write. That's how I remember it anyway.

JH   And that song, *Four Strong Winds*, I mean it's practically public domain. Of course it's not, but I'm saying.

IT   It will be soon.

JH   I mean, it's the western anthem. Does it still amaze you how this… it's almost not your property anymore. As you say, it may soon be public domain, but how many ways, how many times it's been covered?

IT   I think that's very flattering for a writer, you know. And you don't get many of those tunes, and a lot of tunes—unless you're a Bob Dylan—the standards are wonderful, and I've got two of them, so I'm happy with that.

JH   And another song, *Some Day Soon*.

IT   Judy Collins had the first great version. She and Stephen Stills were running around together in those days—Stephen Stills of Crosby, Stills, Nash and Young—and he liked the song very much and he talked her into doing it. She didn't want to cut it and he talked her into recording it and, ah, it became her biggest…

JH   Why wasn't she keen?

IT   I don't know. The song was… it didn't go anywhere for a long time, it just kind of laid there. And I don't know if people, you know, I don't know if they couldn't hear it or what. And it was just one of those magic cuts 'cause it was a live cut, it was right off the floor, I don't think there was an overdub or anything on it. They just did it.

JH   Are you generally happy with how over people cover your songs?

IT   Most of the time, yeah, most of the time. I like to see them change it a little bit. I don't like to see lyric changes too much, which occasionally happens.

JH   Well, let's get onto your list of music, Ian. Now, what's the first piece of music you'd like to hear?

IT   How about *Brothers in Arms*, by Mark Knopfler and Dire Straits. I think that's a wonderful song, revolutionary kind of song. I think it's one of Mark Knopfler's great, great compositions in which that beautiful, lyrical guitar style that he plays seems to be shown off at its very best. I think it's just a terrific tune. [MUSIC]

JH   I want to talk a bit about the change in your sound going from mainly, of course, a duo with

Sylvia, to Great Speckled Bird, getting a band together and going more from a folk sound to more of a synthesized rock and country sound. Bob Dylan was doing a bit of this, too, at the time.

IT   There were two or three…

JH   Was it a forced choice sort of?

IT   Yeah, I wanted to do it. There were three or four bands at the time that were pioneering with that, The Byrds, and Great Speckled Bird, etc. And it was ahead of its time. We didn't really know what we were doing technically and we had a lot of… We were kind of a pretty divisive group, too. It was a very volatile group and looking back on it now I can see that it couldn't possibly have held together any longer than it did, which was about, I don't know, 10 months or something. That album has been all remastered on and it's out on a CD. It's all DAT and, man, they've cleaned it up. It's really quite remarkable how they've cleaned up the sound. I don't know how they do that.

And some of the cuts, there's a couple of cuts that are pretty good. And there's some cuts that are pretty bad, but it was ahead of its time. You know, but we've always said that and music critics have said, you know, for years that it was ahead of its day. So now we'll see. I mean, maybe it'll sell just as few copies now on its reissue as it sold back then, or maybe it'll sell. It'll be interesting, but I have no intention of playing those songs, or… I don't want to play with those guys and I don't want to play those songs, and it's just a different chapter. But I don't remember writing them and I don't really remember what the motivation was. I mean the theme, there seems to be kind of a strange theme in there, but I'm not sure what it was. Everybody kind of contributed their own ideas; it was a very democratic group, the way groups were in those days, you know. And that was, I guess, it's strength, and the weaknesses of it, too, because you had to have a consensus on everything, which doesn't work, you know, and it just eventually blows up.

JH   Let's talk a bit about the TV years. You spent five years hosting *National North: The Ian Tyson Show*, for CTV. Do you have any good memories of television?

IT   Oh yeah, I loved it. I learned how to sing on television.

JH   You learned how to sing.

IT   I learned how to be a solo singer on television, I really did. See, because my years—my bigtime years—I learned how to be a duo singer, and that's a very… that's a whole different thing, you know. I mean, it's as different from driving a bus and driving a tractor, you know.

JH   Even though you sang lead and Sylvia was really harmonies?

IT   No, it's still a duo thing—you're still kind of projecting your voice and laying your voice against some harmony. And we had a pretty unique style that sometimes had no vibrato, and other times had too much. But when I… I had to learn how to learn solo when I started that television show, and the demands were such that I think I did, you know, like 12 songs a week when we were taping, so I'd be required to learn 12 or 15 songs a week. And I learned in a hurry, it was great. Yeah, you know, there weren't monitors, or if there were, they didn't work, and it was live TV basically. It was live to tape. I don't know why they bothered to tape because whatever went down on that tape stayed, so it was essentially live TV. And I learned how to sing ballads on that show.

JH   Yeah. The glitz didn't bother you, the whole technology of doing television didn't bug you?

IT   Well, the money was good, you know. Money was great. I didn't want to wait around to have happen to me what happened to Tommy.

JH   Tommy Hunter.

IT   Tommy Hunter and Ronnie Hawkins and all those people that had those shows, you know. And Robbie Lane; I mean they all waited around 'til they got canned, you know. And I thought, heck, I'll beat 'em to it. So I walked after five years. But I wanted to train cuttin' horses anyway, I wanted to go to Texas or Alberta and train cuttin' horses. You know, I'm very very fortunate it turned out to be Alberta, 'cause see the land boom was goin' on in Fort Worth, and you could buy… you know, people bought ranches—$200 an acre ranches in those days—that became, you know, 15 years later were worth millions and millions of dollars. So that's fine, but I discovered after that that wasn't where it was at, you know. I'd rather now have the ranchland stay ranchland. You know, we can't develop… we'll develop ourselves into… we'll become like the east if we keep on developing.

JH   Heaven forbid.

IT   I've often said it and it is true. I mean, television in Canada… music hasn't always been good to me in Canada, but television always has. And I don't know why that is. I don't watch TV anymore.

JH   I was wondering if you would go back and do some television if you were invited to guest or host?

IT   No, I don't believe. That's another era.

JH   Let's have some more music. What would you like to hear now?

IT   *Sketches of Spain*, the great interpretation of that by Miles Davis. I think that one of the, you know, all time superb innovations in jazz is his version of *Sketches in Spain*.

JH   Do you listen to jazz a lot?

IT   Hmhm. Yeah, I do.

JH   Is it a late night thing for you, or?

IT   We don't have late nights anymore, Judy—there ain't no such thing. Nine o'clock, that's it. Twyla usually turns on the CBC FM in the morning and just leaves it, we listen to classical music mostly. And then around suppertime, well, we'll play a bunch of jazz and maybe have a big hit of… a big shot of Merle or George Jones. No line dancing, none of the hat stuff.

JH   None of that Cyrus kid.

IT   The hat stuff has gotten pretty abysmal. [MUSIC]

JH   In 1980 you released the first of your cowboy albums , *Old Corrals and Sagebrush*, what a landmark album that was.

IT   That was the first one.

JH   In terms of bringing the cowboy music back.

IT   Yeah, it was the first one. But, you know, *Old Corrals and Sagebrush* wouldn't have happened without Elko. Yeah, Elko was a cowboy poetry gathering that was conceived by two people, Hal Canon, who's a state folklorist in Utah, and Waddy Mitchell, who's a buckaroo in Nevada out of Elko. And they originated and conceived the Elko poetry gathering. And they thought there was going to be 40 people there, and it became a phenomena. You know, it's one of these things that comes out of nowhere and nobody can figure out why or how, but it happened the same time that *Old Corrals* came out as an album. They wanted to have Ian Tyson down there singing because they knew about me. I don't think, I don't know that there would be a *Cowboyography* without Elko. I mean, Elko was so much a part of that. And when *Cowboyography* came along, this whole new brand new thing, the first new cowboy music that had been written in 50 years, there was a pipeline, there was a conduit. And it was Elko.

JH   It must have felt great for you getting that music down, recording these albums and seeing how people were just eating them up.

IT   Yeah, it was wonderful, you know. How many people get a second chance like that, you know. It was a whole new career. And those guys, those buckaroos down in Nevada, they didn't know anything about Ian and Sylvia, they'd never heard of Ian and Sylvia. So, there was no… I had no problem with, you know, like I'd have in Toronto, you know. You know, you gotta keep walkin' 'em through it, walkin' 'em through it, you know— that's not what I do anymore.

JH   I'm not a folkie anymore.

IT   Well, I am. You know, I think this stuff is folk music, but it's not… Those people, the people in the east, they're in 1964 and that's where you are for them and they won't allow you to ever change. So, Nevada was wide open. They didn't know about my past and they didn't care. I mean, they knew the story; they heard the songs and the stories and they loved them and it was like, you know, they said it was like Charlie Russell coming back. It was pretty weird, pretty strange.

JH   There's a great story about your surprise at how successful *Cowboyography* was, how people just adored this album at the gig that you did in Kelowna.

IT Well, that was the first indication I had. It was a rodeo dance and it was in a big bowling alley over there, and it was jammed by eight-thirty that night. And the people that were dancing by the stage were singing all the words to *Cowboyography,* which had just come out, and it blew me away because I was amazed that all these couples could come out… I could see they knew all the words to the songs. I realized that there was something really going on here.

JH I know you feel really strong about the west and the changes to the west that you vehemently disagree with, and of course you were very front and centre at the Oldman dam protest and so on. Are things… are people starting to appreciate your point of view and all of your fellow conservationists, you know, that are trying to preserve the west. Are things starting to move a bit in that direction?

IT I think things are changing and I think there's some genuine reasons for optimism. I think the Whaleback thing was a great, great decision, a great moment in this province. I think it was a wonderful thing that happened, and at the same time that that happened they stopped Disney World in Virginia, which was amazing. I don't think anybody dreamed that would ever happen. There've been some remarkable decisions that have gone with the environmental movement. And when I say environmental movement, I don't mean the eco nuts—I mean, I don't mean the crazies—and there really is a coalition between the responsible environmentalists and the responsible ranchers. And there really is a coalition starting, I see signs of it. The crazies on both ends of the spectrum—the rednecks and the eco freaks, are… you know, they may be as vocal, but people aren't listening to them. People are figuring it out, you know. I mean, people aren't stupid and people are figuring it out. But I think it's an exciting time and I think it's a fairly optimistic time for the west and its open spaces.

JH I'm glad you can say you're optimistic, too. Would you consider taking a turn as a politician to fight for some of these goals?

IT No.

JH There was a bit of talk about that.

IT Yeah, I can be more effective outside the beltway than being inside it.

JH Do you still do any competition in cutting horse? You're still breeding them, of course, and training them. You still compete?

IT Yeah, I still compete, not very successfully anymore. Cutting teaches you patience, which is probably one of the great things about cutting. You know, really the true joy of it all is riding a promising colt and he's making those first great moves, and that's where the real joy is, you know. If you can go on and take that colt to town and be a champion, that's great, too, but that doesn't happen to me much anymore.

JH I read that you stopped the chewing tobacco habit. Are you still okay with that?

IT Yeah, have you got any on you?

JH No, I certainly don't.

IT Yeah, it's gone. I sure enjoyed it while I did it, though. Yeah, it was great.

JH Well Ian, we're at the point in our mountain top fantasy where you get to choose a book that you're going to take with you to your mountain top, or wherever you choose to go. What book would you bring along?

IT Oh, that's easy. *Lonesome Dove* by Larry McMurtry. No contest. The greatest western ever written.

JH So you would be happy to read and re-read that book?

IT Yeah, I've read it about three times.

JH You also of course have the choice of where you are going to spend the rest of your days. I have a feeling I'm not going to be surprised by your choice.

IT Well, it would be on the eastern slope of the Rockies in southern Alberta, definitely. And there's a ridge down towards the Whaleback that I've climbed many, many times. It's not on the Whaleback, but it's down towards that country, and I've written a lot of songs up that ridge, climbing up that ridge.

JH You can sit out in the wind with a notebook and write a song there?

IT I don't use a notebook, I take along a little Sony—you know, a little Sony recorder or whatever.

But I… you know, I only get maybe two lines or three lines at a time, per hike you know. And so when I get back you've only got, you know, there's only two or three or four lines that you're gonna' have to… And you just scribble them down and put them on a tape. Tapes are… you know, cassette tapes are wonderful because it's just, you know, total instant recall.

JH You say you're still writing songs, and I think it must have been in your biography, *I Never Sold My Saddle*, that you say you'd really be interested in recording some old standards, releasing some old jazz standards. Like what?

IT Oh, um… I'd love to do some of the old Harold Arlen songs—*Over the Rainbow* would be great. We do that as an encore in the concerts and people seem to love it. But also, some of the rarer ones, some of the old Peggy Lee, Jerry Southern tunes. You know, there's some pretty rare… there's some off the beaten track… Cole Porter tunes and Harold Arlen tunes, and they're wonderful. But I can't figure out how you'd make any money doing it because, ah, you don't have the copyrights, you know, and that's the tough part. I have a theory—I don't know if it's true, but I think that's why Canada's produced a bunch of singer/songwriters all the way… You know, Joni Mitchell and Gordon Lightfoot and these people, 'cause it's an economic necessity for you to write your own songs because that's how you make your money. And people don't understand that in Canada. They don't understand that if Judy Hamill records an Ian Tyson song, all the royalties from radio play will go to Ian Tyson, they won't go to Judy. So, you'll get the glory maybe, but it won't pay your bills. So that's what produced, I think, such a plethora of singer-songwriters in Canada. And it's a good thing.

JH What do you want to listen to as you head off to the eastern slopes in that ridge?

IT Well, I think we should… the finale should be Vivaldi—and almost anything by Vivaldi—but perhaps *The Four Seasons* would be appropriate as the finale piece.

JH What season would you like to hear?

IT Oh… Autumn.

JH Ian, it's been a great pleasure to meet you, finally, from my days in Toronto as a kid and having you here as my guest on Mountaintop music. Thank you very much.

IT Well, thank you for having me Judy, it's been a real pleasure.

AM So what are you smoking, a cigarillo? Cigar?

MR Yes.

AM Are those your favourites?

MR Yes. I can't afford to buy them in Canada—they're outrageously expensive—but people bring them to me from London and New York, where they're a third of the price.

AM You prefer that to cigarettes, or are you still a cigarette smoker?

MR Cigarettes are very bad for you.

AM But cigars are just virtuous?

MR That's right.

AM I want to talk, start I guess, with your growing up in Montreal in the St. Urbain Street neighbourhood. What kind of a kid were you?

MR We were mischievous, but not by today's standards I guess, 'cause when you think what we thought was mischievous would be very tame. But I was brought up in a very orthodox Jewish family and I went to a Jewish parochial school for the first seven years, then on to Baron Bing High School. And it was a working class neighbourhood, but I wouldn't exaggerate the difficulties. I mean, we ate well and we never went hungry and it was very self-contained—it was both warm and suffocating because everybody knew where you were and what you were doing. And it was a pleasure to go to Paris where nobody knew me or what I was doing.

AM It was a Jewish neighbourhood, but was it a mixed neighbourhood as well?

MR Well, it was… I mean, for the most part it was Jewish. There would be a few Ukrainian families possibly, and a couple of Chinese families, but I mean it was just about ninety-nine percent Jewish.

AM You've been able to tap into that neighbourhood and the characters who live there throughout your career. Is it memory? Do you go back? How do you keep that alive?

MR Well, I send a book down the memory well from time to time. It's now largely a Portuguese and Greek neighbourhood. It hasn't changed physically that much, except there are now television aerials and aluminum storm windows, and the signs are often—with corner shops—are Greek and

MORDECAI RICHLER
WITH ANDREA MARANTZ, 1997

Portuguese. What is amusing is that St. Lawrence Boulevard, or The Main as we used to call it—which is where we used to go to buy our clothes and our food—has now become a very trendy street full of trendy restaurants and discos and clubs. And that's very new.

AM That's Montreal though, too, isn't it?

MR Yes, yeah.

AM Montreal, a city of food.

MR Yes it is, yeah. But, it's, you know, a diminished city. I mean, there are empty shops everywhere and houses for sale, and…

AM Is it like that in the neighbourhood that you grew up in?

MR No, because the poor have no choice, and if you're tied to a corner candy store or if your father drives a taxi or if he's a carpenter or working in a factory, he can't leave. So it's largely the middle class that has left, the English speaking middle class, Jews and anglophones and the young. So the average age of Montrealers, I think—English speaking Montrealers—is climbing all the time, because the young graduate from McGill or wherever and off they go to Vancouver, or Toronto or Calgary or the United States.

AM   Were you interested in books when you were a kid?

MR   Yes. I began really by reading nonfiction. I thought fiction was very frivolous, I was probably right. And then someone gave me—I guess I was twelve or thirteen—*All Quiet on the Western Front* to read. That was the first novel I read, and I was just enchanted and began to read novels. But it wasn't until I got to what was then Sir George Williams College—it is now Concordia—that I really realized how little I knew or how little I'd read, and I really began to play catch-up. And it was a time, in 1949, there were a lot of war veterans there, much older than I was, and I fell in with a group of veterans who really educated me I guess. So I began to read e.e. cummings and Elliot, and God knows what

AM   And you didn't stay at university.

MR   No, I got very bored there, I found it very boring. I left when I was nineteen to go to Paris, which was not a very original thing to do. I mean, we were, or I had by then read Hemingway and Fitzgerald and thought we could repeat the experience. And that was true of most of us there at the time. I went over in 1950, the same time as Mavis Gallant, and Mavis and I met shortly before I went over. And so Mavis and I used to see each other in Paris occasionally, and of course we still see each other.

AM   You write a lot now about Quebec's long history of anti-Semitism and those kinds of issues. Was that something that confronted you when you were young, when you were growing up there?

MR   Yes, it did confront us, yes, 'cause, you know, there were signs on the highway to Laurentians… there were street fights and all kinds of things. So, and you know, there was that march down The Main where they all were screaming death to the Jews, and so on.

AM   You remember that?

MR   Yeah, I remember, and I remember the conscription riots and, uh, a gang of French Canadians attacked the YMHA. Little did they know that we were—not me, I was too young—but older brothers and cousins were waiting for them and then just poured out and chased them away. But, um, you know, there was anti-Semitism… And the English speaking community was culpable as well. I mean, there were quotas at McGill and there were hotels in the Laurentians which were restricted, and so on. But I think the basic resentment of French Canadians against the Jews was that we identified with the English speaking community in Montreal. But of course English was the language of mobility in North America, not French. And Quebec was a political backwater, it was very corrupt. And also we weren't welcome in the French school system—not that we would have gone had we been welcome, to be honest. But it's a confessional school system, it was very church dominated at the time. The church was notoriously anti-Semitic—I mean one of them—and the pantheon of nationalist or sovereigntist heroes is the Abbey Groulx, who was an admirer of Hitler and led a campaign not to buy from Jewish shopkeepers. You know, he was really a vile little man.

AM   And yet he was considered one of the leading lights.

MR   Yes. And now we have a huge metro station named after him and, I mean, as late as 1954, Groulx wrote to a friend how the Jews were behind every swindle in the land, and so it was a bad time. It's not so now, it's not really so now, you know. It has changed.

AM   You had sort of rejected the religious part of being Jewish by the time you were at university?

MR   Oh, earlier. But I was very grateful for that upbringing. You know, it was full of great legends and richness and so on, but I found it stultifying and I broke away when I was about thirteen or fourteen and became a labour Zionist for awhile, and I thought…

AM   Did you have a Bar Mitzvah?

MR   Oh yes. Oh, I had a very religious Bar Mitzvah, yes—I did the whole works—oh yes, you know.

But, uh, then I became a labour Zionist and I went to Paris instead. It was a good choice.

AM Tell me about arriving in Paris that first time. You must have had a whole picture in your head.

MR Yes, well, you know, it was just so exhilarating. I remember arriving in Paris and I had a truck, and I found a hotel on the rue de Crujasse off the Blvd. St. Michele, and, ah, it had been a Bordello during the Second World War I discovered later.

AM Oh, just where young writers want to go.

MR Yeah, and I fortunately had the address of a Canadian painter, Joe Plaska. That was the first friend I made in Paris, and Joe introduced me to a number of other people. And then I fell in with—well I knew Mavis of course—but then I fell in with Terry Southam and Mason Hoffenberg and the whole new story crowd. But to begin with I really only knew Joe, and he was very welcoming and I would go to his huge one-room flat on the Blvd. St. Germain very often and meet other people.

AM And was it Paris that was an inspiration, or just being away?

MR Oh, it was just so beautiful, and I mean, coming from Canada, which then had a population of about thirteen or fourteen million, I was very provincial. The beauty of Paris was just astonishing, you could walk for hours; I'd never seen anything like it.

AM Let's pause now for your first piece of music. What would you like to hear?

MR I think I asked for the *Queen of the Night* aria from *The Magic Flute*.

AM Why this one?

MR Oh, I've just always enjoyed it… You know, it's terrifying and wonderful, and anything of Mozart's will do fine. [MUSIC]

AM Well you have to know what you're doing to sing that one. That was the *Queen of the Night* aria from Mozart's *Magic Flute*, Roger Norrington conducting The London Classical Players, Beverly Hoch as the Queen of the Night—the choice of my guest on Mountaintop Music, Mordecai Richler.

AM Did you speak any French while you were in Paris in the 50's?

MR Yeah, I spoke some French.

AM And did you get involved with the Parisian community?

MR I knew several French writers, but not… You know, it was a curious thing… ah, we went there to meet each other. There were Americans, Canadians and a lot of painters—Sam Francis and Larry Rivers and Norman Blume—and we formed our own community, but it was joined by a number of French painters and writers and so on, yes.

AM How were you keeping body and soul together?

MR Well, I had some money I'd saved, and I cashed in an insurance policy. In those old neighbourhoods the parents would buy policies from Prudential. And the insurance agent would come around once a week with his big ledger and you'd give him fifty cents. And I had a policy which would have come due when I was twenty-one for a thousand dollars, and I was nineteen and I found out I could cash it in for eight hundred and something dollars, so I grabbed it. And I had some money I had saved from working, and you could live then on eighty or ninety dollars a month. I mean, you couldn't live well, but I ate one meal a day and for the rest bought a loaf of bread or something. But, uh, you could get by on very little, and it was just so wonderful to be there I didn't feel I was suffering.

AM And all you wanted really was to be a writer. You didn't do anything else?

MR No, I didn't. With hindsight… you know, I published very early—a novel when I was twenty-three which I've kept out of print ever since. With hindsight, I think I published far too early, and other writers I know—peers—had to do jobs they didn't like for a number of early years, and they can now draw on that office life or factory life or whatever it was. I never did anything but write, so with hindsight I wish I'd been obliged to do other things.

AM The book you mentioned, that was *The Acrobat*.

MR Yes.

AM You're not very kind in your recollection of that book.

MR No.

AM What don't you like about it?

MR Well, it was very derivative and I was writing about things I really didn't know about, and…

AM Well, you were twenty-three.

MR Yeah, I was trying to write like Hemingway, and it wasn't awfully good.

AM But it must have been, in your group there—in your peer group—a great accomplishment just to get published.

MR Oh, it was absolutely wonderful at the time. You could pass by a bookshop in London and there was someone foolish enough to have bought your book, and so you felt, well, now I can really say I'm a writer—although you knew better—but you could say that. And so, sure, it was exciting, yes. Nothing is quite as exciting as publishing the first book, however bad.

AM And what else did you write in those days? Did you start writing essays right away?

MR No. When I was in London later on, I began writing for The Spectator and The New Statesman and Encounter and The Observer, and so on, none of which paid very well at all. And then around 1958 or 59 I was asked to rewrite the film of *Room at the Top*—a friend of mine was directing it—and I didn't get a credit, although later it was acknowledged, but that was my introduction to the film world. And in those years, as I couldn't support myself with my fiction or my essays, I would just about every eighteen months sign to do a film, which would take about three months and would pay sufficiently for me to have enough money for two years.

AM Did you enjoy film writing?

MR Well, they were street corner deals; you know, you were a hired hand and you did what you were asked and you got out as quickly as you could. And like, see in America it was a totally different proposition in that if you're going to write films you have to move to Hollywood. In England you could live in the same dingy flat and carry on the same life, and you were just working on a film, so it was a lot easier. The British are not nearly as rigid about this one's a novelist and that one's a screenwriter. Writers tend to do a lot of things.

AM Let's have another piece of music. What would you like to hear this time?

MR Well, I've always been… I'm a great fan of the Threepenny Opera, especially if Kurt Weill's, and I think the *Pirate Jenny* song is the most stirring revenge song I've ever heard, and I adore it.

AM When did you first see the Threepenny Opera?

MR I think I first saw it in London. I think it was a production of Sam's, of Sam Wanamaker's. Really I owe my theatrical education to my wife, 'cause I'm not much of a theatre goer, but I think that's when I first saw it… yes, in London at Swiss Cottage. I even think Georgia Brown sang that song, yes. She's dead now, Georgia. [MUSIC]

AM Tell my about *Duddy Kravitz*.

MR Well, that was really a breakthrough for me because it was the first time I really found my very own voice, and I wrote most of that in the south of France. And I had a Canada Council grant of twenty-five hundred dollars, which was very important and saw me through writing the novel. I wrote it rather quickly as a matter of fact. I'd never written a novel as quickly as this, but I guess I was 28 or 29.

AM And you were involved with the screenplay for that one as well?

MR Yes, I did the screenplay 'cause of my old friend, Ted Kotchuf, with whom I had already done a film in London, and we were sharing a flat in London for a long time. I managed to put it together… there was a screenplay and it was no good, so I was brought in and then rewrote it, rewrote the screenplay, and the film turned out to be very successful. I mean, I was very pleased with it.

AM I remember I had just read the book, and then I saw the film really soon after I had read the book, and I recognized everybody as they walked onto the screen.

MR Well we were very lucky with Richard Dreyfus. Ted had gone down to Hollywood to audition people, and Florence and I and the children were… I was taking them for a drive through the Maritimes, and Ted phoned me—found me in some hotel—and said he'd found an actor who didn't look like the boy as he was described in the book, but he thought he was the best one for the part, what should he do. I said, grab him. And so Richard came up to Montreal in a Greyhound bus and I met him at the bus station. We put him up for a few days before he was accommodated somewhere else. But then we got Jack Warden and all kinds of people, and they all worked for very little, as we all did. In fact, that film was made for nine hundred and forty thousand Canadian dollars.

AM You're kidding.

MR From beginning to end. And then only later was it sold to Paramount. So we made it for nothing.

AM And did you make good money on that film.

MR No, no.

AM That's sort of all down the road.

MR Yeah. None of us made… I mean, Richard was hired for twenty-five thousand dollars.

AM Launched his career though.

MR Yeah. Well, he'd already done *American Graffiti*—it hadn't been released yet—but it wasn't a very showy role. And we've remained friends and we see each other.

AM What was your family's reaction to this success of the book and then the film? This kind of… set you really on your way.

MR Oh, you mean Florence?

AM Yeah… and your kids. How many did you have at that point?

MR I guess just two; they were just infants. But, oh no, one minute… we were in Canada then when the film was being made, and then we had five… you know, 'cause Jake was a little tot, yeah. Well, what was amusing about the film is that when the novel came out it was notorious in the Jewish community in Montreal, mostly by people who never read it. But when we were making the film they all wanted to be extras, and lined up for hours, and little did they know how punishing a day that is to be an extra. So I was pretty amused by it.

AM Change your life, that book?

MR You know, when it first came out it didn't do that well. I don't think it sold more than a thousand copies in Canada, maybe twelve hundred in the States and similarly in translation. It was only later it began to grow in terms of sales, and now it still sells, you know, I don't know—fifteen or twenty thousand a year I guess.

AM The Jewish community was up in arms over *Duddy Kravitz*, right from the beginning, and through your career you've received a lot of criticism from that quarter. What's that all about?

MR Well, it's local gossip. I mean, I've won the Jewish book prize twice in London, my books do very well in Israel. But in Montreal, in some areas of the Jewish community I'm still notorious. But they've never read any of these things, really. They just know that, oh, they're terrible. But *Duddy Kravitz* was never supposed to be a metaphor for the Jewish people; he was typical of the boys I grew up with and I thought he was very endearing, too. So I don't understand.

AM Now, were there other authors at that time that were writing about the Jewish community in Montreal.

MR Well, there were two poets. There was Irving Layton and Leonard Cohen, and I think Leonard published his first novel around that time. I could be wrong, or maybe it was earlier or maybe a year later, or… but, uh, he's only written two novels I think, and he's primarily a songwriter now and a poet. And Irving was somewhat older than we were—is somewhat older than we are—and he was a well-known poet. And before that there was the Jewish poet, A.M. Klein in Montreal.

AM Let's have another piece of music. What would you like to hear this time?

MR Well I was a bit stumped, so I suggested something which I find appealing, and that's Handel's *Watermusik*.

AM Do you like Handel, generally, or this particular…

MR I like this particular one, yes. [MUSIC]

AM I want to ask a little bit about how you work. Do you have a daily routine?

MR Well yeah, I'm very much a creature of habit. I get up very early and I work for about three hours in the morning, and, uh, I've always worked at home. Then I have lunch and a nap and I might do an hour's work in the afternoon and that's it. So I work for three or four hours a day. But I work every day except when I'm on one of these mad, febrile…

AM You don't take weekends?

MR Well, there's no sense in weekends in a writer's life because one day is much the same as another. It was baffling for our children because, they thought every father works at home, which was not the case. But then they complained that their friends were taken out for all these big treats on the weekends 'cause that's the only time they saw their father, whereas I was always at home and I didn't feel very strongly about weekends.

AM On the other hand, they probably had more access and knew you better than a lot of their friends.

MR Yes, yeah. Because by the time they came home from school I was done, yes.

AM Do you work on a computer?

MR No, no.

AM How do you write?

AM Well I've always worked on a manual typewriter. I'm very hard on them, and four or five years ago it became pretty difficult to acquire a new manual, and then even if you did or if you had one serviced, then the problem was finding ribbons. Then if you found the ribbon it had been in the shop for so long it looked like you'd been using it for two years when you first put it in the machine. So I went as far as an electric typewriter and that's what I've been using for the last seven or eight or ten years, I don't know.

AM And you write in an office at home?

MR Well, a room, yeah. I guess you could call it an office if you like.

AM Does your environment change how you write?

MR Well, whatever houses we've acquired, Florence, being very loyal, the first thing she does is goes and looks to see if there's a decent room for me to work in. In London, and for awhile Montreal, and where we now live in the eastern townships, I just work upstairs in very pleasant conditions. I work in London—we spend the winters in London, it's a much smaller flat—but the only thing I miss there is my library, 'cause I have a huge library in our house in the eastern townships. And you never know which books you're gonna need or what to take, so I do miss the library, but that's all.

AM So what's the library for now? For research? For inspiration? For…

MR Well, I mean, the books are… I read for pleasure in the library, but also I have all kinds of reference books or I might have a biography of John Foster Dellas and I need to know the name of the law firm he worked in during the fifties 'cause I have some character whose father worked there. So I mean it's just things that you need. You don't know what you're gonna need, and I have some memorable newspapers and magazines as well.

AM So are you tempted to learn the computer and get on the Internet for your research.

MR No I'm not.

AM It doesn't appeal to you at all?

MR No, no—it's all a mystery to me. I intend to keep it that way.

AM Did you read much to your kids?

MR No. I did from time to time, but the good reader in the family is Florence, so she read to them for the most part when they were very young, 'cause she's a very good reader. When uh… I got into children's books because when Noah was about eight or nine he wandered up to my office, or work room, and said he would like to read a novel I'd written called *Cocksure*, and I said he was far too young. And he said, well, why don't you write something we can read, and that seemed a very reasonable request. So I wrote this children's book and I gave it to Florence and I asked Florence would she please read it to the children at the dining room table and see if they're offended or whether they're amused or whether they're… and I'll go by whatever they say. So they enjoyed it a lot and so I sent it off to a publisher.

AM And they were all in it?

MR Yes. That's why I said see if they object or, if they did, I said we'll just keep it as a family joke. But no, they were all for it and that's how all that happened. And I did two more since and I'm supposed to… I'm doing one more.

AM Did the kids ever… did they know that when Dad's in his room writing you don't go running in?

MR Oh, they were very good. Yeah, no no, they were very good. And then of course, once they were at school, by the time they were out, I was out. But, uh, they knew I was up on the top floor and to leave me alone, yes.

AM How often do you rewrite scripts? Your books, your manuscripts?

MR Well, there's no rule. I mean, sometimes I can rewrite eight or ten times, and sometimes just twice. When I wrote a novel called *Solomon Gursky Was Here*, which was very intricate and dealt with a span of about a hundred and fifty years—and in that case I tried all kinds of constructions; I once put it in chronological order and it seemed to die in my hands, so I did an awful lot of rewriting there. Also, I was writing about things I really didn't know firsthand, about nineteenth century London, about an English mining town in the nineteenth century, about men on the Franklin expedition and so on. And that, for the first time involving a lot of research and a lot of insecurities as a writer because how did these people talk, and so on. Not voices I'd heard.

AM Your wife Florence has a role as your unofficial editor. Does she read all your stuff?

MR Florence is the first person I trust with my work and I take what she has to say very seriously. She is a highly intelligent reader and she worked as an editor for a brief period in London for Widenfeld & Nicholson. But she has read voraciously over the years and she has very good taste, and I take what she has to say very seriously, yes.

AM Do you get into arguments about it at all?

MR Disagreements from time to time. I mean, if she's displeased by what I've done I'm obviously very upset and can be quite disagreeable, so it's a heavy responsibility for her. It's not very pleasant because, of course, she'd like to say everything I've done is wonderful, but if it isn't she has to tell me, and that's not something she enjoys doing. So it's asking a lot of her really.

AM How about your relationship with your official editor or editors?

MR Well, the one I've been with longest is Bob Gotlieb. Bob was at Simon and Shuster and he did a novel of mine, a satirical novel called *The Incomparable Atuk*. That was many years ago and then Bob moved to Knopf and has been president of Knopf, and then he was editor of The New Yorker; I did a couple of pieces for him. And now he's left The New Yorker and he edits about five or six writers still among them. He edits my work. And the last two books here was with Louise Dennis, who is also very astute and very helpful.

AM Is it a difficult relationship though, with an editor?

MR I've never had any problems with Louise. Bob and I have a great rapport—we're very old friends—and it's never a question of line editing or anything like that. We talk on the phone, he says you've gone on too long here, or something else is a bit of a cheat or doesn't quite work, and then I will do what I think is right. And sometimes I'll say, no no, I'm not touching that, or whatever, you know. But again, he's a very sympathetic reader, he wants it all to be splendid, so there's never any quarrels or anything.

AM Let's pause for a piece of music. What would you like to hear now?

MR Well, we couldn't do better than the choral last section of Beethoven's *Ninth Symphony*.

AM What is it about this one?

MR Well, it's so joyous and exhilarating and there's nothing wrong with it at all. [MUSIC]

AM From Beethoven's *Symphony No. 9*, that was the Monteverdi Choir conducted by John Elliott Gardiner. That was the choice of my guest on Mountaintop Music, Canadian writer Mordecai Richler.

AM I want to bring up the famous New Yorker article on Quebec's language policies. You were somewhat surprised by the level of fury from Quebec.

MR Well, you know, the Parti Quebecois' strong suit is not humor, and they tend to overreact to everything and so they were seething. And they credit me with having enormous influence in the United States, which is nonsense, and so they were very upset and people got up in parliament and denounced me as a racist and asked that my book be banned, and it was all so embarrassing and kind of silly.

AM Was it embarrassing? Or is there some part of you that thinks that's kind of fun?

MR I thought some part of it was fun when the articles appeared in the New Yorker. But once the book appeared I thought everyone knew what was in it, so what were they all so excited about. So then it became tedious and then there was a lot of unpleasant mail and threats and menacing phone calls, which I didn't take too seriously, but if Florence answered the phone, or one of the children happened to be home, it was very ugly. But that died down.

AM You had a little run-in with P.Q. Minister Bernard Landry.

MR Yes I did.

AM Tell me what happened.

MR Well, I'd never met Landry, he's not a man I particularly care for. And I'd been to lunch—a long lunch—and I'd gone into the Ritz to the tobacconist to buy some cigarillos, and Landry was coming out from checking his coat. And we'd never met. And he turned red in the face and he said, "I hate you, I hate you, you're a racist." And the best I could come up with was, "Well you're just a little provincial bumpkin, Landry." And he said, "I have a university degree," which totally startled me, you know.

AM Brilliant comeback.

MR I had no idea, you know, sort of proving my point, but I had no comeback to that. I should have said, have you got it with you, or…

AM Then, of course, there was the famous Parizeau statement about why they lost the referendum, which inspired you to establish a prize.

MR Yes. So what happened is… You see, Parizeau and Landry thought they had won the referendum—their private polling showed them that they were winning—but of course they always do better in the polls than they do in the actual ballot box because a lot of people have second thoughts before they vote. So they were deeply disappointed. I think Parizeau was a bit smashed, and he blamed the ethnics and the money and talked about revenge, or promised revenge. And so I established a Prix Parizeau prize with a purse of $3000 for the best work of fiction by an ethnic or impure wool. Then one of the separatists charged me before the Human Rights Commission in Quebec. And unfortunately I finally got a letter from the Human Rights Commission, an official letter saying they were not going to prosecute, because I would have enjoyed that enormously. Yeah. I mean there are prizes for Jewish writers, there are prizes for French writers—it's all nonsense. But we're awarding it again this year in Montreal.

AM Mordecai, what would you have done if they'd won that referendum?

MR Well, you know, had they won by one point it would have been chaos in this country; I don't know what would have happened, because obviously Parizeau had plans afoot to make a unilateral declaration of independence. And I don't know what would have… I mean, the Canadian dollar would have gone down to what—sixty cents or fifty cents? And there would have been an acrimonious situation. Well, if the Crees didn't want to go with Quebec in the north what would happen? Would Ottawa send in troops? I don't know, it would have been a total disaster. And I think Bouchard would not have welcomed it either unless it was a decisive 60-40 or something. But I mean, so we were all saved very deep trouble I think. And it was, you know, they never… I don't know whether we're gonna have a third referendum. I doubt it because it doesn't look too good for the Parti Quebecois right now. But if we do then we'll be asked the direct question—Ottawa will insist on it—and I don't think they can win on a direct question because it turned out, 25 or 30 percent of the people who voted yes thought they could vote yes and still be a province in Canada, and it was a total muddle—a very murky question.

AM You haven't given up on Quebec, though, have you?

MR No, it's my home—Montreal's my home. And look, I enjoy living in Quebec, and I think the two cultures have enriched each other enormously.

And I like hearing French in the street and I like the whole mix, and I just wish we could get over this wasting disease.

AM Let's have another piece of music.

MR Now I'm a Gilbert & Sullivan fan, and one of my favourite Gilbert & Sullivan numbers is the executioner, the lord high executioner's, *I've Got a Little List*, from The Mikado.

AM Did you ever act?

MR Oh no.

AM This is one of the ones that's done at schools so often. I was wondering…

MR Oh really. No, no. I never did, no. I saw that Brian MacDonald did a lovely production of it some years ago, and I went to see that.

AM In Montreal?

MR I think I saw it at Stratford, and then it did go to New York. [MUSIC]

AM That was *I've Got a Little List* from Gilbert & Sullivan's The Mikado, the choice of my guest on Mountaintop Music, Mordecai Richler.

AM Do you still visit the old neighbourhood in Montreal? You're living out in the Eastern Townships now.

MR Well, we retain an apartment in Montreal, in downtown Montreal. We go in once a week and spend the night in Montreal. Not really. I mean once or twice; but I mean I'm not falsely sentimental about it. I don't get down there very often. Nobody I know lives there any longer.

AM Do you still keep up with the people you grew up with?

MR Not with the kids I went to school with because one of the things about going away, as I did for twenty years, is there's a fracture or separation in your lives, and so many people have had different experiences over the years. So I haven't really got any friends that I had in high school; I haven't retained any of those friendships.

AM What's the strongest thing about the split between the two countries—the way you live your life, half in England and half in Canada?

MR Well, it renders each one of them more pleasurable because you see them freshly. And so to go to London for five months and not read every day about today's crisis in Quebec is kind of a relief. But then after five months I kind of yearn for Montreal, and it enhances both places for me. It seems to me it's the best of both worlds.

AM Well, before we send you off to your mountain top, you can choose one book, only one—it's a terrible thing to say to a writer.

MR Well, the best short story collection is still the Bible, so I'd take that with me.

AM Just Old Testament?

MR Oh, both.

AM Both? For the short story value.

MR Well, for the language and for the stories, yes.

AM If you were going to take another one, we'll just… Because you're a writer we'll give you another choice. Is there something?

MR Well, I'd do the obvious thing. I'd take a collection of English poetry or plays of Shakespeare, you know. So it's not very original.

AM Things that you can keep mining, though.

MR Yes.

AM You can also choose a location. I know this is another terrible question to ask of someone that lives in two places, but if it could be anywhere in the world—with politics and climate and everything else aside—where would you spend the rest of your days?

MR Well, I'd spend them the way I'm spending them now. I'm quite content with the arrangement I have.

AM But if you had to pick one, if there was one spot.

MR Well, maybe I'd one day retire to Provence; I don't know, that might have a lot of appeal.

AM Is that a place you holiday?

MR No, I lived there many years ago and we have friends there and it seems like a wonderful place to be, so that wouldn't be insufferable.

AM And a final choice of music. What should we go out on today.

MR Well, how about something—anything—from Jellyroll Morton; that would be very pleasing.

AM What do you like about him?

AM Oh, he's just such a graceful jazz player, musician, pianist.

Do you remember when you first became aware of his work?

MR Gee, I guess in Paris, because we used to go to listen to a lot of jazz. Sydney Bechet was there, and a number of my friends in the hotels had records, jazz records, and so I began to listen to jazz quite seriously then, although I'm far from being an expert.

AM Do you listen to a lot of jazz at home?

MR Yeah, from time to time. I like opera a lot and we go to the opera, but I'll play jazz… I play it in the car, you know, when we're driving to the city.

AM Thank you very much. It's been a real pleasure.

MURRAY McLAUCHLAN
WITH ANDREA MARANTZ, 1999

AM You know, I think we're cousins. Somewhere back we're related because my name, the name I was born with, is Lauchlan, and spelled exactly the same way as your McLauchlan.

MM It's more than likely, yeah, that we are distant cousins.

AM And you were born in Scotland, but you didn't go back for 40 years.

MM No. I went everywhere else pretty well, I mean with regards to the kind of travelling I've always done. If it was for leisure or for adventure I tended to want to go some place warm. My memories of Scotland were small, industrial, damp—you know. I didn't have the Sir Walter Scott romantic image of the brave highlander marching across the moors.

AM What sort of things do you remember from those early years of your childhood? You were five, six when you left?

MM I was five. I mean, I remember quite a lot of stuff. Your memories when you're a little kid, they're vivid, but they're all jumbled up and, ah, they're German expressionist memories—they don't make any sense. I mean, one of the most vivid recollections I have of when I finally did go back was to go back to the house that I was born in and walk upstairs to the room that I was born in, this council house in Paisley, and realize that my shoulders were rubbing the stairwell walls on the way up the second floor. I'm not huge, I mean I'm a six-footer; this house was so tiny, and yet my memories of it are big. And a lot of people lived there, and everybody had their own little space. But, you know, you'd put several people in a room, in a day bed and this and that, and that's more or less how we lived. We lived like people used to live before there was North American wealth I guess.

AM Well, there's a great story at the beginning of your book about your return to kind of a rough neighbourhood.

MM Well, it wasn't that rough when we lived there in the late 1940's and early 1950's, but it sure is now. I mean, parts of Fergus Lee Park look quite nice—I mean, they're well-kept and there's flowers in the window boxes and the kids are clean and such. But there's a whole area of flats that were condemned because of a flood from the Clyde River not too long ago, and they were taken over by squatters and junkies and gangs and stuff, so there's almost a demarcation line along Drums Avenue where my childhood house was, and on the one side of it it looks a bit like West Beirut. I mean, literally you see like, a couch pushed out onto the sidewalk, and half-naked children playing and, you know, a huge, enormous, large woman with two backsides (one in front and one in the back) sittin' with a can of Newcastle on a sofa with springs sticking out of it on the sidewalk. You know, it's like that.

AM Did you feel connected to that place?

MM Oh, very much, yeah. I mean, yeah, I was born there. I mean it's still very, very much a part of me, and it's very much a part of my nature insomuch as there's a big part of the core being of Scottish which is this tendency to tilt at windmills and you know, want to die in defense of lost causes. You know, it's a kind of… there's a romanticism attached to it. As they say still waters run deep. I mean, Scottish people aren't overtly terribly, terribly, terribly emotional, necessarily, although they can be quite passionate. But in terms of the deeper feelings, I mean they're very passionate people.

AM Why did your parents move to Toronto?

MM They actually met and married originally in Canada. My mother had emigrated first to Windsor, Ontario with her mother. My father had gone separately and was living in Detroit. He was a machinist and he was working in the car plants over in Detroit. It was the boom. It was also prohibition in the United States, so there were dances and such in Windsor, and my father would come over and cut a rug, and he was quite a dancer as a matter of fact, and singer. There was an acquaintance between the two families. He was staying with a family in Detroit that were distantly related by marriage to my mother's family. So there was an introduction and, actually, as the story would have it, one night my father came over to Windsor and ended up—he got a snootful of some home concoction that someone had made, and the net effect was that it paralysed him, he could barely move. You know, he was lucid and everything, but he couldn't get up. So he stayed, and he ended up chatting all night to my mother. And they became an item, and eventually push came to shove and they got married. So he moved over the river. Then along came the crash, and there were a lot of very, very, very hard years. My mother didn't like the UK. I mean, she didn't like it because of the class system, because your accent could mark you because you could be held down just by however you're born. I mean, everyone knows that about… if you have a north country accent in England you're doomed. Well, if you have a Fergus Lee Park accent and you're Scottish to boot, you're doubly doomed. You'll never get, you know, above your station in life. At least certainly not at that time. I don't know how… things have changed a bit, I'm sure. Now you can be in the film industry. You know, they had terribly hard times, escalating slowly downward. I mean, I don't think anyone really understands what was going on in the 1930's in Canada. I mean, it was… I don't think anybody now has any real idea how desperate that was. I mean, people who really wanted to find work just couldn't, and there was no… nothing to fall back on. I mean, there was no social safety net, no welfare system per se—it wasn't there. I mean, it was literally be hungry. It got to the point where my father's spirit was getting so broken by it that when he had an offer from relatives back in Scotland that there might be something there, that things were turning around a little bit, he decided to go back. And my mother didn't want to. They got back there just in time for the war. There was plenty of work. My father was an air raid warden, he was machining a lot of parts and bits in factories. One of his jobs was to rifle the barrels for the battleship King George, which was actually sunk during the war. But he basically did that.

AM Your dad was interested in music. He played the organ, is that right?

MM Yeah. He was principally a singer. He was a really fine baritone and sang church music. He belonged to a Gilbert & Sullivan singing society, operatic society, and actually was offered a chance to go down to London and audition to take a career with a company, with a recital company down there as a professional singer. He talked it over with my mother and she said, anything you want to do, I'll stand by you and we'll pack up and we'll go. But he decided that he shouldn't do that. The cover story was essentially that, a) show business isn't fit work for a man. You have to have a solid position of some kind, you have to be, you know, working to support your family. It's too chancy. I had an intimation that maybe that was a kind of code for, he was a bit frightened that he might not succeed at it. My mother more or less alluded to the fact that that was possibly true, later on in life after he died.

AM Now, when you arrived in Toronto as a little boy, dressed in your kilts?

MM Yeah.

AM What did the neighbourhood kids think of that?

MM It was a source of great amusement—that and the fact that the accent that I showed up with when

I arrived in Canada was nearly unintelligible to a Canadian kid. It was all full of, ah, you know, slang. And the accent itself was thick and impenetrable to anyone that wasn't really, that wasn't from that area of Scotland as a matter of fact. So, you know, as it works out among children, half went over to them and half came back to me. As I got Canadianized they got a little bit Scottishized, and some of the neighbourhood kids wound up picking up expressions and saying things in the the way of a kid from Fergus Lee Park. The kilt went pretty quickly once I was over here, you know. No kids wore kilts and, you know, you're not going to be a pariah among children. [MM imitating Scottish brogue] They're young adults, put them in twos.

AM Was your mother musical at all?

MM Oh, quite the contrary. Bless her heart, God bless her heart, she tried very, very earnestly to play the violin and that, too, was a source of great amusement. She had a bit of a tin ear as far as being a vocalist was concerned. It did not run in her side of the family.

AM Can you remember when you first started to love music?

MM Hmmm. I don't recollect having a love affair with it. I mean, I remember when I started to love words.

AM What was that about?

MM You know, making music or goofing around with it, was just something… it was an adjunct, it was just something nice—playing harmonica or trying to learn *Dashing Away* on the keyboard, and that sort of thing. But I think I was more interested in songs. And I was always more interested in songs because, yeah, I liked dance music and I liked, you know, I liked the emotion of songs; but I always was more attached to what they were about, and I was more bookish really, book oriented. The things that first blew me away were works of literature, and also I was oriented towards the visual arts. I drew, painted incessantly. I mean, I ran around and sang all the time, just like my kid does, but you know, there was not any particular… you know, I wasn't a young Mozart or anything like that. But you know, I didn't even really bash away at any instruments with any real major seriousness until I was almost into my teens.

AM Painting, as you mentioned, was also an early and enduring passion, it's something that you still love. One of your early teachers was Doris McCarthy. How much of an influence did she have on you?

MM Well, Doris was a very influential teacher, for me and a lot of other people. She was already a well-established water colourist when I encountered her, which was in my early days at art school. But more, Doris particularly had a way of shaping a kind of philosophical overview that I had toward creative work in general, that's still a very major part of my thinking, even to this day. And I see Doris now. I mean, she's kind of back.

AM And part of I think what draws a lot of young people to the idea of an artist's life, is the idea of something that will be your whole life—you know, as if being an artist will define all those areas.

MM Well, oddly enough, you start out thinking that it might be a great job, that it's really cool and you get to wear neat clothes and the hours are great, and you might get laid a lot because you're just so cool. Later on you find out that it's not a job, it's an avocation, and that's something that eats your life. I mean, even brain surgeons get a chance to go the party once in awhile and not have somebody, you know, wanting him to bore holes in their skull.

AM Let's have your first piece of music. What should we play first?

MM You know, I'm a very nonstandard music listener and, and it's an impossible thing to pick out music that you… I mean, I think I'd have to take a dumptruck to wherever I was going. But there are certain touchstones, certain songs, certain sensibilities of things that I like, and again, there are a lot of them; but these are just sort of the first ones that coughed themselves up. I love great singers and that's one of the reasons that I picked the first guy. I've always found that there's an incredible sweetness and a purity, reassurance, warmth, sophistication and intelligence, and musicality to the voice of Nat King Cole. Just as a singer I've always just adored him. And I also particularly like this type of song 'cause it's pure romance. And damn it, there just is not enough romance in a cynical world. So when I want to sit down and actually have a glass of wine and listen to something, I like romantic music. Let's listen to *Unforgettable*. [MUSIC]

AM   When did you begin to think you could make a life as an artist?

MM   What started to really change me a great deal in the mid-period of art school, was an exposure to books. I mean, they were a pretty interesting collection I think, you know, for a 15-year-old kid basically. You know, there were the big ones that started me looking at stuff hard, like you know, the classic Steinbeck *Grapes of Wrath* ilk, Faulkner—things that started to form what in me were… I mean it's almost a bad word now, but kind of social democratic sentiments. My father was a lefty, he was a union organizer who'd lost his teeth for that and got beat up badly for it from time to time. You know, it was the beginning of a period where I started to question things pretty hard. And along with that came a sudden exposure to folk music as well, but the really good stuff. I mean, the works of Woody Guthrie, and also the history of what that meant, how that tied into the literature and the social democracy and the leftism, and all of that.

AM   Well, that's the thing folk music has always had, such a close relationship to story-telling, to literature.

MM   Well, I mean, at its best it was always a type of music that sustained people through their trials, or told their stories, you know, and love affairs. Or they were tutorials in a way, or sometimes just downright funny.

AM   And when you were 17 years old there you were in Yorkville coffee houses with your guitar.

MM   It started to escalate. I was beginning to realize that slinging a guitar over your shoulder and looking cool was a really great way to get girls. It was like, you know, the bo-ho dance—the sort of sullen, romantic, troubled young man. You know, it works like a charm on a certain type of girl.

AM   So, when you were 17, were you doing your own songs?

MM   No, I didn't really start to try and write with any degree of seriousness until after art school was finished. And I think it really began when I was hanging out at The Village corner club on Avenue road, Pears. That was a place that became a sort of a… like a home away from home for me. That was the time when I first started going there that I got the idea that maybe I could do this. I mean, I'd certainly been inspired to do it by hearing the first of the New York school of singer/songwriters that were emerging, obviously the leader of which was Dylan. But this wasn't just folk music. This was, you know, for me—the way it impacted on me—was this was something really radically different, something new. This was like taking the poems of Ezra Pound or T.S. Eliot or Dylan Thomas—all the power of lyric that those poems had, all that power to evoke really profound emotion—and adding to them this sub-intellectual quality of music. And the total being something bigger than it's parts, or something more moving. It was like, essentially, not just a hybrid art form, but it was something that was quite new.

AM   And the power of that kind of music, the idea that it was really going to change the world.

MM   Oh, it had a tremendous impact on me. I mean, as soon as I started hearing "that"—it's a really ill-defined thing, what "that" is—but I think probably, there were very few people who did it really, really well. And I think I just use the example of Dylan because I think he's the example that people would really most readily understand, but there were a lot of really good writers around that were making wonderful songs in this new idiom.

AM   The root was still coming from the written word more than from the tune of the music?

MM   Yeah. It still is with me. Principally, my focus… Only arguably am I a musician. I mean, I can play a fairly decent piano and a fairly decent guitar, but I've always looked upon the instrument as a tool of accompaniment. I find that songs move me in a different way than pure music does. That's changing mind you. I mean, I sat down and got a couple of really good 16-year-old Scotch's in my gullet, and relistened to Leonard Bernstein's whole recording of *Rhapsody in Blue*, by Gershwin, and went, Jesus Mary and Joseph, this is so good. I mean, it's so provocative.

AM   It tells a story.

MM   Well, it's, you know, it's like… I mean, when I listen to the opening of *Rhapsody in Blue*, it's like I see, you know, the three angels sitting up on top of a building in Manhattan, watching the whole scene go down as the sun comes up, you know.

AM   And as a young man you went to New York.

MM   I should have put *Rhapsody in Blue* on your list I guess, I never thought of that.

AM   Well, we don't have 15 minutes to play it. You went to New York and, ah, I guess…

MM   Eventually, yeah.

AM   What was New York like at that point when you arrived?

MM   Well, I mean the first time I went there I was pretty well fresh out of art school and I was all full of, you know: Wow!—The Village Wow! Gurty's Folk City. Wow!

AM   And it was this attraction to Dylan and that kind of work that got you there?

MM   Well, it was like, you know, if you were a painter it was like going to Paris. It was like, here are all these clubs where all this stuff had happened, all these people had been, and you just knew it 'cause you'd read about it. I was like, you know, it was like going to New York and being a fan, and it was intensely exciting. And damn, you know, you're only there for a couple of days and just wandering around going, oh wow, oh wow, oh wow—like a tourist. The second time I went to New York I was already married and I'd essentially, I'd hit the end of my tether in Canada. I was starving to death. Bernie Finklestein, who by this point I knew, the guy who founded True North records. And Bernie just finally took one look at me and said, you know, look, the best advice I can give to you is get out of here. You know, go down and live in New York or something and see if you can actually get something together doing what you want to do, because at the very least, just because you're here, nothing will happen. And he was quite right about that. You know, at that time you hit the ceiling pretty fast in Canada, but like, the next young group from the United States that came through the town got all the press. That was just the way it was. And before you relax, that's the way it still is. Myself and my wife, well we packed up what was left of our belongings in, you know, in a suitcase with a rope in it basically, and got on a bus and went down there. And, you know, within a few short days I had made a publishing deal with the Albert Grossman office. Albert was at that time managing, you know, Janis Joplin, still managing Dylan, managing The Band. It was, you know, it was the hottest managing office in New York.

I sold them my publishing catalogue, for money. Because I was starving. I mean, so I think I sold all my publishing for about $1400 bucks U.S., or something like that—everything. And that was everything I'd written, things like *Honky Red, Farmer's Song*, you know, would apply to that. Like, there was a term to the deal, so like all the stuff that I eventually would require for the first two albums was all subject to this deal.

AM   Yikes.

MM   I put that money in a New York bank account and stuck it so that I could only take a little bit out every week, and then we moved into the Albert Hotel and we lived in New York for almost a year. I was basically not doing all that great down there, but the interesting thing was that while I was doing that, up here people are going, oh yeah, Murray, he's living in New York, you know, he's with the Grossman office, you know Tom Rush recorded his stuff. I mean, all this rumour mill got going, so when I came back to town it was like I'd been, you know, touring the United States, playing Carnegie Hill.

AM   But it does, it sounds great. The guy that's handling all these, you know, biggest stars in the world at that point, is… I'm, you know, working in his office every day and we're hanging out.

MM   Well, it had an important role in changing the way I was perceived when I got back to Canada. And certainly the fact that Tom Rush had recorded my songs. And he had a well earned reputation for discovering young writers—James Taylor, Jackson Brown, Joni—quite a number of people, although there's no timeline there. He was just known for discovering those people.

AM   Let's have another piece of music.

MM I picked one that I thought would be interesting because, you know, in some respects it's not thought of as being the best song this guy ever wrote necessarily. I think it's one of the best, but it's not that thing for which he was best known, meaning the great anthemic civil rights things, or iconoclastic folk rockers, or things like that. This was a real, kind of almost adolescent boy love song, pulling your collar up against the wind, leaving your girl 'cause ya got to be free—you know, it had that sort of spirit about it. But it was the song that probably, more than anything else the sound of it set me off one night when I heard it. It just sort of tweaked something in me and it answered some longing that I didn't even know that I had, just the way it sounded. And it probably had as much to do with setting me on the course that, you know, I'm on, as anything did, although for a variety of different reasons. And the song I picked is, *Don't Think Twice, It's Alright* from Bob Dylan's Free Wheelin' album. [MUSIC]

AM You'd already paid your dues—the folksinger dues as you perceived them in those days. You'd done the hopping the freight trains across Canada and living in the little garrets, and…

MM Yeah. Well, I mean, that was a romantic version of a no option situation again because, I mean, I had that 'come to Jesus' meeting finally with my father where there wasn't really any option. And, you know, again I wasn't mad about that, I understood that completely. But I mean it was like, okay, yeah, you live here you do this; you're not willing to do that, you get out. So, I got out. I had thirty-five cents.

AM But was it good? I mean, did it end up being grist for the mill?—did you learn things on those kind of trips ?

MM I learned a tremendous amount and I also, I think, have an understanding of what pure freedom is that very few people likely would ever experience, based on that time. You know, you can just wet your finger and stick it up in the breeze and go, I'll go that way. I also learned an awful lot over that period of time about how to survive. I think that's a very good lesson, too. I mean, I think I learned some of the same lessons that my daddy did. 'Cause life on the road can be extremely dangerous, and I had no idea just how dangerous it could be. On some occasions we had some very good luck on our side.

AM What's the scariest thing that happened to you while you were hopping freights?

MM Well, on the first one we ever caught my friend Nick nearly lost his legs. I chickened. I wouldn't go for it, the train was going too fast. He caught the wrong end of a boxcar and wound up bouncing along the tracks with his legs underneath the train, hanging on for dear life and trying to pull himself up. So, if he'd lost his grip then he would have been under the wheels. His legs were bouncing along about a foot in front of the following set of wheels. But he got away with it somehow. But he lost all his stuff, too, because he'd thrown it all in the boxcar and couldn't get on the train.

AM Had total commitment, right?

MM It was, you know, it was a fairly precipitous event. But there were a lot of, you know, a lot of… we spent much time living like rats.

AM And singing Johnny Cash songs.

MM I had guys pull knives on me who would try and rob us or things like that, you know, that would happen. You know, it's not all bad, those were very sporadic things. A lot of time, I mean, we had… people were really wonderful. There were like, good Samaritans, or they were generous, and there were a lot of characters, and we had like, just good adventures that were interesting. People got us jobs and, you know, it was a different time because people's attitudes hadn't hardened towards weird looking guys wandering around with guitars or something. It was really before that summer happened in San Francisco where all the kids hit the road. So the only people that were on the road then were really… I mean, that's what we were, we were migrant labourers. We were looking for work, we were just looking for anything to do to survive. We stuck that out for quite a long time until I realized for myself, I really don't want to spend the rest of my life being a hobo.

AM Let's have another piece of music.

MM I've always really been a big on many levels— first of all, overcoming adversity, sheer musicianship, fire, versatility, and exotic qualities—I've always really, really liked Django Reinhardt's playing. The favourite stuff I've always liked of Django Reinhardt is when he was playing with Stephane Grapelli in that Paris Hot Club Band. And the thing I loved about that stuff the most was… The other two guys, other than Stephane, the other two guys in the band were like, they're almost square in their playing—so, when Django gets up an solos, you know, he's playing all this wonderful solo with his very limited number of fingers, like it cooks along really neat and it's fun. There's like, lots of humour in his playing, but the underpinnings of the band fall out and the groove gets really square. But when Stephane Grapelli is playing his solos Django's playing rhythm, the band just smokes. Like it's unbelievable how good he is at both ends of the spectrum. It's gypsy, sexy music—I like it. [MUSIC]

AM The Mariposa Folk Festival, first time was in 1966. What was that experience like?

MM Yeah. Just to get invited was a pretty major pinnacle of achievement. I mean, from a practical standpoint it put you in a different league from punting around coffee houses. Mariposa I had a great deal of difficulty with as a festival, where folk music as it was understood before had changed, from a more traditional base to embracing this new urban singer/songwriter phenomena. But, you know, it wasn't all like, New York guys. It was also people like Joni Mitchell, who was getting big, even though she hadn't recorded yet then. So, it was embracing this, and that was in turn becoming pop music. That music was becoming pop music and folk festivals were very uneasy bedfellows at that point in time because there were a lot of idealogues that were kind of, you know, running them. I mean, they weren't bad people, but they just, they had a view of the world that when something became popular it was per force naturally tainted in some way. I don't hold that necessarily to be true. It really depends. I mean, if something just becomes popular among people.

AM I'm going to toss some names at you and you tell me a story about these people, okay?

MM Gosh.

AM Joni Mitchell.

MM Well, I mean Joni always referred to me, like the seven dwarfs she called me Grumpy because principally, I mean, I was… Light her up a Vantage and give her a half bottle of wine and she's like a monologist and raconteur; she's interested in all kinds of, you know, occult, woo-woo, theoretical metaphysical whatever stuff—she has very strong opinions about stuff. And initially when I first met Joni, I mean, I was kind of overawed by her. Anyways I was sometimes just so sour about some of that stuff, I think that's how I earned my nickname. I was in love with Joni or, like, I was infatuated with Joni, like just about 25 million other guys I suppose at one point. I confessed to her, you know, from the bottom of my heart that I thought I was in love to her, and her response, her reaction was, well is it hanging you up? I think she was probably the first, you know, what would now be defined as an empowered woman, you know, that I ever ran into in. It was like, you know, my experience at the time, and probably everybody else's, was, you know, you say something like, I love you, and the other person is supposed to go, I love you too.

Well, no, that's not how it works. It's actually like, I love you. Well, that's terribly nice. For you. Is it a problem for you?

AM Not exactly a big ego boost.

MM Oh well, yeah. It's like, you know, take a slap on the side of the head kid and get over it. But, you know, I really, yeah, I still love Joni I think, but it's a different kind of thing now. I mean, I think I really appreciate her in spite of the fact that occasionally, I believe, I have pissed her off once or twice.

AM So, what comes to mind if I say Bob Dylan.

MM I only met Dylan once, at Gordon Lightfoot's house, and I didn't really expect any great thing to happen. I mean, because I dug his work so much and I'd already had enough experience myself with people coming up and saying stupid things, that I was more or less content to like, sit on the couch in the corner and go, you know, I'm glad you're over there, I'm just glad you're here in the world, you know, I love the songs. I didn't want to walk up and go like, man, what did you really mean when you wrote, you known. I just think that's the dorkiest thing in the world to do. He's a real sourpuss, you know, but that's understandable. Or at least he was then, he seemed like a real sourpuss.

AM How about Gordon Lightfoot then? You knew him quite well.

MM He's probably one of the most down-home guys I ever met, who had his psyche and his life enormously complicated by getting incredibly big and incredibly famous and having people put incredible demands on him. And it made him rather more paranoid than he might have turned out had he remained a simple man from Orillia.

AM You have an interesting little passage in your book about when he was living with Cathy Smith?

MM Yeah, she lived with him for some time.

AM That she would come to visit when his demons were becoming overwhelming, which I guess is something that's sort of peripherally known about him, too.

MM Yeah, yeah. But Gordon went through a period of time where he had quite a lot of problems—I think it's fairly well-documented—and ah, he could be a really difficult person to be around. You know, that's not uncommon. I mean, they've all been through it. Jerry Jeff Walker's been through it and Kris Kristofferson's been through it and Johnny Cash has been through it and Waylon Jennings has been through it and I've been through it. And everybody has.

But you go through that period where you just, you know, like you just rail out and lash out at the slightest provocation when, you know, you're hurtin' for one reason or another or your life is out of control in one way or another. You know, he was having a fair bit of trouble in that respect.

AM Cathy Smith is kind of a sad character in that she became more notorious than famous.

She was the woman, of course, that was there when John Belushi died.

MM Well, she put the needle in him, yeah.

AM And went to jail for it.

MM Yeah, she did. And she was a really smart, really, really beautiful lady and a pretty good singer. I don't know for what reason people do, but she just chose like a different path and became, you know, I don't know—I don't exactly know how to characterize her. I mean, she wasn't exactly like a groupie.

AM I was going to say, it's a cruel word, but…

MM I mean it's not exactly the word that sums her up either. I mean, I think she wanted to be around people who had a certain level of fame and a certain level of power and a certain level of access, and she was willing to accommodate that by doing whatever it was that she had to do. And at the end of the day it came down to basically being involved in the supply and demand end of the industry. And certainly when she was living with Keith Richards and Anita Pallenberg that was the big deal, and she became like the go-getter for a lot of people. You know, she was singing with Hoyt Axton, she sang on one of my albums as a back-up singer. Oddly enough, the real head shaker in the matter is that the song that she sang on of mine was a song called, *Do You Dream of Being Somebody*. And ah, there's more than a little irony there.

AM How about Neil Young?

MM Again, I mean, like Neil isn't somebody that comes up to my house and has dinner with me every other week, but I first encountered Neil fairly early on in the game. I mean, when the Buffalo Springfield had broken up, Neil was doing a solo guitar kind of folk tour. It was before the *After The Goldrush* album. So he was touring; he came up and played the River Boat, he was broke 'cause you know, they just got ripped off from the Buffalo Springfield—nobody had any money. So, he was like scuffling and he was around, he was like, a funny guy. I mean, I knew his dad, you know, probably more than him, just from reading scrubs on skates and stuff like that. His dad was more famous than…

AM Scott Young's Sport Stories.

MM Exactly, yeah. When I first started to get sort of hot, to the point where like, I could put 800 bums in seats in a college theatre or something, Neil happened to be on tour at the time doing the beginnings of this really weird tour called, it was the *Tonight's the Night* tour. And there was an album associated with it with a whole bunch of really dark songs that he had written about this guy he knew who'd overdosed on heroine. He was just obsessed on doing this particular collection of songs and the smaller venue tour. Well, you know, smaller venues for Neil by that time meant 6,000 seat halls or 8,000 seat halls. I got sort of hauled out to do a, just a guest opening thing really for Neil, at one of the universities out west of Toronto, and, you know, I got quite a reaction. Neil just said, you know, why don't you come on the rest of the thing, man. And I said, sure, okay, and we stayed with the *Tonight's the Night* tour, which was a real—it was quite an experience 'cause, first of all, it was very dark. It had been largely abandoned by management. I mean, Neil's manager was not in favour of doing this at all, he did not see it as a career enhancing move. It was the era where, you know, American university students had discovered quaaludes and cheap wine at the same time and, ah, they were also a rock 'n roll crowd. They were rock 'n roll fans of songs like *Cinnamon Girl* and stuff like that. For them, you know, Neil young was like *Cinnamon Girl* or Buffalo Springfield or whatever. I mean, they were really abusive—cat calls, a sea of, just a rolling sea of abuse and shit would come pouring off the crowd. You know, for me, I'm out there with a bass player going, you know, good-bye mama, good-bye to you, too—and they're screaming, get off the stage you dummies. You know, all of that. And of course, universally, they were all yelling, you know, "NEIL YOUNG-G-G-G" all the time. Then I got up and was like the human folk sacrifice and they'd scream and yell at me, and I ended up just swearing at them off the stage—you idiot mother… you know. And of course that got a big reaction, they loved that I swore at them.

And then Neil would come out. But the weird thing was that he'd be singing all these, you know, [MM singing like Neil Young] … *he was a working man, he liked…* and all you could hear over this music he was playing was, [MM mimicing crowd shouting] "NEIL YOUNG-G-G-G." They thought, you know, they don't recognize the song, they didn't even know it

was him. They were so stoned they thought he was somebody else, so they were yelling for Neil Young.

AM Isn't a performer's life wonderful, eh?

MM Well, it was a real eye opener, that whole tour.

AM You've never loved that, though. That wasn't the thing for you, the performing part of it.

MM I don't have any great attachment to performing. It's never been the raison d'etre you know, for what I do, and it really evolved out of having the capacity to write songs and realizing that nobody's gonna hear them if I don't get out and sing them. I'm ill-suited for the profession. It sounds kind of like a negative thing to say, but I mean, I don't require the feedback from people.

AM The applause?

MM Like, for reinforcement of my personhood, that makes you want desperately to get out onto a stage and get it. And, you know, I'm not 'dissin it, but like, a lot of performers are like that, you know. It's a Celine Dion or a k.d.lang kind of mentality, where you really come alive on the stage. Not me. I mean, I just get out there and go, well I'll do the best I can, but I hope it's over.

You know. And just try and sing the songs and relax and have as much fun as I can with people. But fundamentally, all appearances to the contrary, I'm happier not in the spotlight than I am in the spotlight. So I picked a dumb profession I guess.

AM Let's have another piece of music.

MM Initially I said take any cut from the Sinatra album that was *Live at The Sands* with Count Bassie and his Orchestra. Or, if you haven't got that one in stock, then there's a really wonderful version I always loved of that great Harold Arlin song, which is… You know, it used to be a cliché in the bars until you like, get old enough to understand the irony in it. *One For My Baby* is the song, but it was a particular one that was done with an arrangement conducted by Nelson Riddle, which is just gorgeous. Harold Arlen's version just stinks, but never trust a songwriter's opinion. [MUSIC]

AM Peter Gzowski was a guest on this show and one of his choices of music was your song, *The Farmer's Song*, and he was telling a story about being way up north and being serenaded by a group of Inuit kids. That song, more, maybe more than any other of your songs, really has a life of its own.

MM Probably another reason that Inuit kids and people would relate to that song—I mean, a lot of people in southern Canada don't really know this—but one of the biggest things in Inuit culture is fiddle music. It's huge. And like, we're talking traditional east coast fiddle music. And the reason is that for years and years and years and years and years, the only darn thing they ever heard on the radio was Don Messer. And that was music. So, everybody, you know, started playing the fiddle and learning the traditional tunes and harmonics, so there's a whole Inuit Don Messer's school of fiddling up there that's alive and well. My song, curiously enough it's in that tradition, musically. I mean, I know it sounds a strange thing to say, but the sensibility of it, the way its structured, the way the choruses and chords are inverted—they're not logical, they have a sort of a, like a British flare to them, it's not American country music. There's a different way of structuring it so it's much more traditional than Nashville.

AM It's interesting when we were talking earlier about you being a painter. A lot of your songs are like portraits—they're portraits of people and portraits of, you know, pieces of time. And that song particularly I think is such a strong little portrait.

MM I have this great memory of doing the Ralph Emery show in Nashville the first time, and I sang that song 'cause people knew it. The songs of mine that are known in the States, people know are… they were recorded by other people or sung by other artists—for instance on their road tours—and quite a number of… George Hamilton IV recorded *Farmer's Song* and *Child's Song*, and David Bromberg cut songs of mine. You know, Kristofferson actually did *Honky Red* on the road, so did Waylon Jennings. But, you know, it gets around. And, ah, I remember this way Ralph Emery looked at me and went, [MM mimicing Ralph Emery]—*What's that, what's that line?—moppin' a face like what?* And I said, mopping a face like a shoe—it's a simile. [MM mimicing RE]—*It's a what?* [MM in exaggerated tone, explaining]—Well, what I'm meaning to assert by this Ralph, is that the farmer, the farmer person sitting upon the tractor, exposed to the elements for his life, develops a toughened facial skin due to UV exposure, which makes it something like shoe leather. Thus, mopping his face, straw hat, old dirty hankie—mopping the sweat from his brow, from his toughened, leathery skin; thus mopping a face like a shoe. [MM mimicing RE]—*Oh. Thank God I didn't use a metaphor.*

AM Oh, no kidding, he'd be lost for hours. Another serious passion of yours is flying. How did you take that up?

MM An airplane's more than a machine to me, and I think that's when it started, this idea that they're not only physical objects, but they're objects of art. No matter for what purpose they were created, whether evil or good, they still have this grace about them, the same as a clipper ship does or any finely wrought beautiful thing that has to cooperate with the laws of physics in order to accomplish what it does. There's a natural fluidity to them and grace, even brutish when it occurs. And they're all different, that's something I came to realize later as well. They have a personality, every bit as much as a ship does because they're made by all kinds of people, they're fabricated by all kinds of people. And each one of those people invests a little bit of themselves into it. And the collective personality of the end result has a personality of its own. Six airplanes sitting on a line and every single one of them will be different. One of them will be a rogue and one of them will be a sweetheart. One will try and kill ya, the other will take you wherever you want to go forever, and never break. And I don't know why that is, but I know it's true 'cause I've experienced it. So airplanes became magic, they became sculpture, they became objects of art, they eventually became symbols of freedom. And eventually when I decided, as an adult, to learn how to fly, and I had got to the point where I had… I doubted in my mind whether I was really capable of learning to do anything new anymore 'cause I'd been out of school for awhile. And there was another element of it, too, which is, all of flying is really about fear management. My simplified version of what life is all about is to figure out how to eliminate fear, how not to be afraid of something. 'Cause fear is the real enemy. That's what turns you into somebody that you don't like when you make those little decisions because you can't stand up and take the shot, or you're afraid to stand up and take the shot. So airplanes brought that into my life, the act of learning how to fly. You're sitting on a runway and you're going to solo for the first time, and you're looking down the runway and you have sweat dripping off your upper lip and off the end of your nose and you're really scared, because you don't know what you're doing. And you're gonna go way up in the air all by yourself in the airplane and you're absolutely convinced you don't know what you're doing and that, you know, like if you screw up you're gonna kill yourself or ruin a perfectly good airplane or embarrass yourself to death, which is worse. And there's that moment where you actually have to decide whether you're gonna do it or you're gonna taxi off the runway and not do it. And that's a moment that every single person who's ever learned to fly an airplane shares. And it's one of the big moments in your life because it's gonna shape forever how the rest of your life goes.

AM Let's have another piece of music.

MM I really love Thelonius Monk, and pretty well everything he does—[MM humming…] they're really good pieces. They're all like, really nicely written. They're things he wrote and worked on with other people. And it's got all that wonderful, like, you know, he hits a dissonant note and you think like, geez, the guy hit a clam. Then you realize he didn't. Like, it's just a, a voicing that—he's laughing—it's like a little Thelonius joke. And he's a really eccentric player; I mean, there's a lot of humour in his playing and, ah, I think he's smoked a lot of dope. [MUSIC]

AM You have two kids, a daughter who's now adult I guess.

MM Officially.

AM Legally and officially.

MM She's a political adult.

AM And a six-year-old son? Is it a different experience with the little guy? Parenthood?

MM Well, yes, it's a different experience because I'm sharing it, and I didn't really have that opportunity with my daughter for a variety of reasons. You know, it wasn't possible. I think probably, the lessons I might have learned the first time around have been taught to me the second time around—all the really important ones. And, you know, for me the really important ones are, what a refreshing idea to no longer have the luxury of being at the centre of your own life, you know. It's been visited as clearly upon me as it could ever be that I'm not the important person here. That's been visited on me with such ferocity. I mean, I know as clearly as I can know anything, that I would go and sell my ass on Yonge Street to make sure that kid was alright; I just don't care about anything other than that.

AM Murray, are you still as uncomfortable, uneasy with the music industry as you were 10 years ago?

MM I don't feel like I'm a part of it. And I put myself there. I don't feel like, hurt or rejected or anything like that. But, you know, I sort of exist I guess, in some respects in it, insomuch as I have an easier peripheral alliance. I have many songs out there and they're still being cut by other artists currently. As far as my life as being an active performer, video making, oscar winning rabbit, that's… you know, I don't really see that as reigniting. I mean, never say never 'cause I'll probably make more music and do stuff, but I don't really see that I would be part of that. I'm more disappointed with the music business, I think, than anything else. Simply because when I started out doing it, the last thing in the world anybody had in mind was making it a business. It was, you know, idea driven, counter culture, gypsy lunacy, and somewhere along the line it sort of devolved, in my opinion, into being pretty much all about being a fashion statement and being niche marketed. More than ever, using up its young and never allowing them the grace to grow old or get better. I mean, there's still a variety of wonderful music being made and some of it still finds its way into the mainstream, but largely it's not a business about making human beings better or making them feel things that they otherwise wouldn't feel, it's a business that, like the rest of the world, is all— unrelentingly, forever, completely—about money. And I'm sick of money. I don't mean like, I'm sick of paying my bills.

AM But it's not the raison d'etre.

MM Yeah. I mean, if one more weenie does a talk show about like, your RRSP, on the television, I'm gonna throw up. I'm sick of hearing about it. I'm sick of looking at the *Globe and Mail* and seeing that the business section is five inches thick and the entertainment arts section is like, four pages thick. I mean, I just think our priorities are really screwed. I mean, I'm not a curmudgeon, but I'm just, I'm sort of disappointed in that. I just think that it's… I think like, the rest of the world has a better take on all of that than North Americans do. I just think we've just gotten really stupid.

AM Well, before we send you off to your mythical mountain top, we'll let you take one book with you. If you could only have—this is a terrible thing to somebody who loves books like you do—but if you only had one, what would it be?

MM I really thought about that really hard before I realized that what you'd really asked me to do was get the computer of my mind to find the square root of three. And it's sort of like still operating in there like a virus, and the fact is, like, I don't think I could make that choice. The joke name that some of my friends—Lorraine Segato for instance—coined for me is, my tribal name is Murray Manyheads. The reason is 'cause I just have, I mean I have a… I'd enjoy reading a manual from ICS about like, how to do trigonometry, because suddenly it dawns on me that you can measure the height of the mountain if you know the distance and the angle. Or, you know, I mean I like poetry, or I love biographies—many, many books. I mean *Tracy & Hepburn,* Bill Lear, the guy who founded Motorola and designed the lear jet and such. I mean, millions and millions of books— big ones, little ones, Nicholas Monseurat *Master Mariner Triology*, *The Cruel Sea*, those great maritime books; Ernie Gann, the aviation books. I mean, you know, where do you stop? So I figured that, not only that, but I've been travelling around the world for a long time and there's a zillion places that I really like, and my ideal… You know, you say the mythical mountain top, where you would want to roost. I mean, I would like to just keep moving and, you know, sort of move from one place to another in season— like a migratory bird—so I figure that the end result would be, what I'd really like to have, would be a hot air balloon and the encyclopedia Britannica.

AM Well done.

MM That was as close as I could get.

AM And for a final choice of music?

MM Gee, I'm a big band nut. I know, you could touch it all off… Okay, here, here's the choice. I just made it now. Ah, find a really good record, a good version of *In the Mood*.

You know, I love the intro. It's got all the same stuff that I liked about, you know, *Rhapsody in Blue*. It's evocative. And you can jitterbug to it.

AM Murray, thanks a lot, this has been great.

MM My pleasure.

AM You were born in a small town in New Brunswick, Shampers Bluff?

FP Well, it's much smaller than a small town. Actually, I was born… I lived there but I was born down the road four or five k's from there in a place called Grey's Mills. I mean it was essentially a small farming community.

AM There's just poetry in both those names, isn't there?—Grey's Mills and Shamper's Bluff. What's the landscape like?

FP Well, if you can sort of imagine wooded foothills with the St. John River floating through them, that's rather what it's like. I was born and grew up right on the banks of the St. John River, and where I live now it's one of the most beautiful, beautiful sights in the lower St. John. The water at one point stretches about five k's—well, from the foot of the property to the far side.

AM You wrote quite lovingly in your book *Shadow Light* about your mother. What kind of influence did she have on your life?

FP I think she had a lot of influence in a couple of ways. She was the fairest person I've ever met, and thank heaven I told her that well before she died. I said, mum, you've been a real role model to me in a number of ways, and one of them is this—and it meant a great deal to her. But I think the influence that she had on me which I didn't recognize for years and years and years, was that—and it really enabled me to have the kind of life, the kind of career that I've had—is that she had a strong but relatively unexpressed aesthetic sense. She was the sort of person who, because she was, —I hate to say the word—farm wife, and worked very hard; she didn't even have time for a flower garden, she loved flowers. So she grew geraniums on her kitchen window sill and on her dining room window sill and things like that. Once a year of course she trimmed the tree, and I thought it was Santa Claus when I was very young. And she could trim a tree as no one I have ever seen to this day can trim a tree. We had those wonderful old lead icicles, and she would… After she got the ornaments on—they were quite beautiful ornaments and they were all just hung very particularly—she would put the

FREEMAN PATTERSON
WITH ANDREA MARANTZ, 1999

icicles on, not just out on the tips of the branches, but way back in so the tree shimmered from its very core. And of course in those days there were just lamp lights and no electricity, so it was very, very special to go into the living room at night or early on Christmas morning. The tree always got trimmed on Christmas Eve, none of this putting it up on the first of December business. And she also noticed things. She noticed and would comment on the way a flock of birds would change its hue as it turned, and she would comment on the sound of dried grasses rustling in a ditch. And of course she loved wildflowers. She made it possible for me to acknowledge the value of these things because she acknowledged the value of them. She really married into a household which was entirely left brain, and I remember one day—oh gosh, she was in her eighties and my father was in his eighties—my sister's youngest son, who was at that time about seven, he was having lunch with his grandfather in sort of the apartment to the old farmhouse where they lived. My mother for some reason was away that day and my sister happened to walk in without them knowing she was there, and my father was giving his grandson advice on life and what was important and what wasn't. And he was pointing to my mother's geraniums above the table and he said, now you see them things—and Stephen sort of nodded his head—well they're completely useless. And my sister just went right through the roof—I'm surprised she's still not hanging from the ceiling. I mean there was that conflict.

AM   But that's really the way he saw the world, wasn't it utilitarian.

FP   Very utilitarian. If you could eat it or wear it, it was good, that's where its value came from. I didn't realize until I was at least in my forties what a basically insecure person he was. He was a controller, and like most people who try to control others, terribly insecure.

AM   When did you first pick up a camera?

FP   Well, I did have a little one when I was a little… somewhere in I don't know, grade eight or nine—but that didn't get very far, we didn't have any money—and really picked one up when I went to Europe for the very first time in the late fifties, 1958, and like everyone else I bought a camera to take with me. Now right away I realized I enjoyed this a lot. I also did not know the camera was defective, and when I came home all the photographs that I had made in England and Yugoslavia primarily, and throughout Europe, I didn't have one. When I found that out it was one of the great downers of my life up to that point.

AM   How about music? Was there music in your house when you were growing up?

FP   No. There was no one in the house that played music. My sister was able to go and take piano lessons from a woman up the road—that was acceptable for a girl. But I was supposed to do other things.

AM   Weed the turnips.

FP   Weed the turnips. However, because we often had four men helping around the farm and because my mother was so overworked, I was often seconded as it were on Saturday afternoons, especially in the winter months, to help her clean. And I'd scrub floors and then I'd wash floors and then I'd polish floors. And of course, what was on the radio?—just one thing, CBC and *Saturday Afternoon at the Opera*. And so here I am not knowing a darn thing about music, but listening to Carmen and to Madame Butterfly and all of this kind of thing.

AM   Did you like it?

FP   Well, I've never become a great fan of opera and I guess perhaps that's my left brain. You know, later when I could see opera, when I was living in New York and so on and used to go down to the Metropolitan Opera and go and get standby seats, and I thought, this is so wooden. You know. By which time… you know, before that I'd done some acting in university and really enjoyed theatre, but I found opera very wooden by comparison.

AM   You've had a very interesting career path. You took your masters degree in Divinity. What drew you to that spiritual pursuit?

FP   Well, it was partly accidental in the sense that I was nominated for a Rockefeller scholarship, which for most people who don't know about them, they're sort of the equivalent of Woodrow Wilson fellowships, which are much better known. The only stipulation if you receive one is that you attend a seminary, that you seriously think about the possibility of entering the parish ministry. And I at that point thought, well, why not?

AM   Were you religious at that point as you were growing up as a young man?

FP   Well, yes and no. Earlier on, in a little country church which is essentially an evangelical baptist type, I had a brief stint with that. To me, the terms religion and spirituality are tossed around a bit loosely. I think when we speak about our, a person's spiritual centre, what we're really talking about is a sense of wholeness, a sense of personal wholeness, which involves of course our relationship with our environment, our relationship with other people. It involves probing our unconscious and allowing that to bubble to the surface. Religion perhaps can be best defined as ultimate concern about ultimate things. The problem has been that it has in the pursuit of that, religion—all religions—have developed dogma. And dogma always is… it destroys creativity, it's putting the cap on it, it's saying everything that needs to be thought about in this regard has been thought about, so you can close, just accept that and… So this is why in the end I… I don't know, the term spiritual has far more meaning for me than the term religion.

AM   Let's get to your music, what's your first choice?

FP   Well, first of all I should say because of my lack of musical training there's a benefit in a way in that… in that I've allowed myself to come to music very much from an emotional point of view. So it reflects how I may feel about things at any particular point. I don't know, to start with a piece that I love now or ah… . Well, one of the pieces that when I first heard it I just—and it was Loreena McKennitt's *Dante's Prayer* from her album *The Book of Secrets*—and frequently at night, very late at night, I'll put that and other music on. In my house I have little pools of light, I have no overhead lights; so I'll make myself a big pot of tea or take a glass of wine or something and listen to music from, say midnight to four a.m., and that's one piece that really affects me very profoundly. [MUSIC]

AM   Tell me about moving from rural New Brunswick to the Big Apple. Do you remember your first impressions of New York?

FP   Oh heavens yes. I mean physically my room overlooked Broadway, if you can imagine my dorm room. And it overlooked a stop light. And here I'd come from this sort of amazing quiet of the forest to this. I mean it took me about three weeks before I could get over this constant starting and stopping of vehicles and blowing of horns and ta da ta da—it was a crash course in the twentieth century urban living anyway. But then, I mean I began to realize the richness of a place like New York City. Right across the street was the Jewish theological seminary and they had very close ties with the Union theological seminary, which was a highly ecumenical institution and with students from all over the world. And typically, being in the United States, I was classified as being from overseas… [laughing] But anyway, the thing about Union that I remember and I will **never** forget, it had a very profound affect on me, was that while it was extremely high-powered academically—I mean they just floored us with the work that we were expected to do—it also was a place where both the students and the profs gave one the private space, the solitude that you needed, and on the other hand there was always that caring support. A person never really felt alone there. And only, I think, within the last maybe three years, have I stopped having an occasional dream about Union. I'm always going back.

AM   At this time were you seriously into photography?

FP   I became serious about it when I was there. I'd been continuing at Acadia where I did my undergraduate work, shooting around the campus, and then when I was in New York I needed extra money and I taught two afternoons a week at a Quaker school, a very good school in Brooklyn, New York. And two of the teachers there were very keen amateur photographers and they introduced me to their teacher, Dr. Helen Manzer, and she gave night courses. And I went to the first of these and I'll never forget, I mean she really opened my eyes in so many ways, but the thing that she did was insist on discipline; she believed in the importance of knowing craft. And it was not so much photography as it was the craft of visual design which she felt was essential to visual expression and good visual communication. Ever since then, and more and more and in the workshops I now teach myself, I've made the parallel comparison between the importance of visual design and the importance of linguistic design. By the time we get to school we're certainly talking in sentences and we're taught there that different parts of sentences, whether they're spoken or written, are the building blocks of speech. And then we also learn that by rearranging, say an adverb, within the context of a sentence, we can alter the nuance of that sentence or in fact its entire meaning. Well, it's exactly the same thing with visual design, where you take building blocks like line, shape, texture, and by altering say the orientation of a line, moving it off the vertical into the oblique, it becomes a far more dynamic line.

And I have to see, I have to know that when I do that I'm going to change the meaning of it. People who compose music are doing precisely the same thing. I mean we might speak here of the design of language, the design of visuals (they don't have to be photographs) and musical composition, or you can say the design of music. A few years ago when Betty Oliphant was still the head of the National Ballet School, she invited me to go down there one day and give a course or a workshop to the students in photography. And I just about died, but I took it on. I love that kind of challenge.

So anyway, after the first session, three or four of the younger students came running up to me and they said, oh, we were so worried about this, we don't know a thing about photography .But they said, you talk our language. And I said, like what? And they said, well you talk about balance, you talk about rhythm, you talk about all of these things. And of course those terms apply to music, to dance, to design, to writing.

AM And very interestingly, you brought some of those ideas into the masters thesis you did while you were at the seminary: *Still Photography as a Medium of Religious Expression.*

FP Right. Looking back… Now I haven't reread that for quite a long time [laughing]. But it's there. On the bookshelf. It was a pretty left brain exercise. I mean I was, as academic theses usually are, but I was at that point comparing the secular and the sacred so to speak, in visuals. I was pointing out that some photographs are essentially secular in content; in other words there's no religious symbolism involved whatever. And the approach has, the style has, no sacred content so to speak— it's not symbolic either. And then I went up to where you have religious content, but a say documentary treatment of it; there was no commitment to the meaning of that symbol. And then I took what you might call secular content, such as a car or a tree or something like that, but it was treated in a way that was symbolic, that went beyond that to deal somehow with some question of who we are as human beings and what our relationship to our world…

AM Do you remember a particular photograph that you felt that way about?

FP The sort of final category I had, and I don't want to put it above say the previous one, is taking a religious symbol and treating it in a religious so to speak way, and there was a photograph I came across made by a man by the name of Willoughby, and it was actually of a crucifix—a black and white image—but he hadn't photographed the crucifix and the body of Christ straight on in a documentary way. He had gone around to sort of one arm of the cross, and he'd restricted the focus so the focus fell on the nail in one hand, and then the figure of Christ was there by implication. I mean it was. And so the symbol to begin with was a cross, which is a religious symbol, a crucifix, and then… but he had focused in on, made it clearly about suffering, about human suffering, which was of course represented also by Christ. So that for me was where they really came together.

AM You went to Edmonton, '62 to '65, you were the Dean of Religious Education at Alberta College. So the seminary did something for you definitely.

FP Got me a job at Alberta College.

AM Set you on that career path.

FP Well actually, when I was here in Alberta I did more photography than I'd ever done in my life. I mean I… Fortunately I was able to arrange my classes so I had a four-day week, so I was photographing everything from animals in the mountains to the river as it ran through Edmonton, the hoarfrost in the morning to the badlands, to rodeos to bike rallys to… I mean I just went wild. And because I have never had, what shall we say, a security hang-up—I was quite willing to spend money on what really mattered to me—and here I was for the first time in my life I had some money to spend, not a lot, but enough to indulge something that mattered to me tremendously.

AM Had you started thinking of photography as a potential career?

FP I did while I was there. I used to haunt Mike's News Stand on Jasper Avenue, and the library, looking at magazines and thinking, I wonder if I can sell a photograph to any of these. And eventually I did begin. And the first picture I ever sold, the first picture I had published was of rush hour traffic on Bellamy Hill in Edmonton. And then the second thing… that was in the old *Weekend Magazine*, and then there was the second thing I sold, and this is where my sort of writing skills came in handy even early on, was an article on wildlife in the Rockies and getting very close to them. And here I drew on the psychology I'd learned in dealing with domestic animals. I mean how do you get close to a herd of cattle that don't really want you around. You gotta get them home on time, you know, and things like that. And so I simply applied these in the wild and got a lot of good photographs and then developed this story, based on the psychology, for what was the old *Star Weekly*. And to my great chagrin, when it came out it was under the title: *How to Win Wild Friends and Influence Animals*—right out of Dale Carnegie, who was not my philosophical soul mate.

AM   No, I guess not. It must have been a big thrill to have your first photographs published though.?

FP   Oh gosh, I remember that first picture that came out. I think I must have bought every copy of the paper that weekend at Mike's News Stand. I still have a pile of these things somewhere.

AM   Let's have another piece of music. What would you like to hear next?

FP   Well, one that is in a way related; it's literal but it's just the sheer love that's in the music, and it comes from a woman who obviously is singing about what matters to her. And it's by Rose Vaughan and it's called *Sand and Sea and Stone and Sky*. [MUSIC]

AM   So during this time when you were working at Alberta College teaching, were you developing some of your theories, your ideas about photography as art?

FP   I think not at that point too much. What I was really doing was trying to become good at the craft, well at the medium. The real craft is the visual design. So I was really working at that and I also began giving some workshops, evening classes—if you can imagine the gall of me—at the Y in Edmonton. And I remember I had four students the first time I did it, and then the next time I had 16 students, and the next time I had 32 students and we had to cut it off at that point. But one of the things I found out because I've been teaching ever since, is nothing beats teaching for learning yourself. Every workshop I teach, whether it's in Canada or elsewhere, I come away feeling, whoo! you know. There's been some comment or some insight made by a student, or some question asked, that's started me thinking or feeling in a different way. And there have been workshops that I've done where I've felt I should just give the students back all their money and pay them, you know, because of what they brought to it.

AM   A major breakthrough in your life came from the National Film Board, the project for Canada's centennial: *Canada: A Year of the Land*. What did you take away from that?

FP   When I was getting into photography, I mean prior to that time, there was a perception about that the only thing of really significant value photographically was photographs of the human condition, which was a concept that I, just in my soul so to speak, I just rejected. Because I believe that we are one species among millions of species, that the planet was no more created for us than it was for prairie grasses and bison and for quail and fish. So that book focused on the natural beauty of Canada, and for the first time as it were there was a big, bold statement that said, look, this is good, this is worth looking at, it has value. And the value is an aesthetic one, it's a spiritual one. And that book sold. Like I mean it sold in centennial year, it was phenomenal…

AM   It was huge.

FP   …well over a million copies.

AM   Do you think that because it was Canada's centennial that that gave the opportunity for making that shift, that maybe without a celebration it might have taken longer.

FP   Oh absolutely. I agree. I think it struck a chord that a lot of people were afraid to admit they had ever heard struck, you know what I mean.

AM   How did your life change after that assignment?

FP Well, the next year no one had any money so I didn't get any work [laughing]. But it was a big break. I continued to get work from the stills division of the Film Board.

AM Let's have another piece of music now Freeman. What should we play?

FP Well, why not the fourth of the *Brandenburg Concertos* by J. S. Bach.

I first heard these when I was studying actually for university. I guess at that point it was the composition of the music, the pattern that I detected in it—I was very attuned to that. But the lovely thing about the pattern of the Brandenburgs are that, as they should, you lose the pattern, the pattern gives rise to the emotional response. And I've always responded very emotionally to his music. [MUSIC]

AM Tell me about moving to Toronto?

FP I moved to Toronto and worked for a year with the United Church of Canada studio.

AM What kind of work was that?

FP Well, it was kind of boring. It was back to documenting, you know, churches and functions and… Although I did have some nice assignments in the west. Like this was in the days when there weren't many homes for senior citizens and they were all privately funded, the church fit into them. And it was really the work that was done, in many cases, like in western Canada by the United Church, that made the government realize the need that existed. And I relate well to old people because I grew up in a house that had four of them, you know—my grandparents plus a great uncle and a great aunt.

AM All lived with you?

FP All lived with me, yeah. So I found it very easy to do that. But anyway, and then I went to Africa in centennial year. I went to Expo first, then I went to Africa. And because my sister, who's younger than I, she and her husband had been in Ireland studying and then they decided they would take a year to volunteer in Botswana as teachers, and I thought what better opportunity to go over than while they're there. So I spent three weeks with them and then made enough contacts that I spent another, gosh, three months travelling through the bushfeldt as they call it—the bush country—which is very different from anything around here.

AM From what we would know as bush country.

FP Yeah. And sandy, sandy soil. And you know, you go through these vehicle tracks that heaven knows when the last vehicle was over them, and one carried all one's petrol and all one's water and all one's food. And you might go for three days and then you'd come across this little tiny village in the woods. The trip I remember most was with a Peace Corps volunteer who had been commissioned to go out and pay pensions to veterans from one of the wars—five dollars a year is what they got. And I remember this one village I came to and here's this old, old, old lady sitting beside the road. She'd been there waiting for three weeks for us to come, because she didn't know when we'd be coming. She was waiting for five dollars. And she couldn't read or write, and of course I was signing the name and I would put my name beside the X. But do you know, speaking of music, one of the most magnificent things that happened was, one afternoon I was wandering through this village, it was a little bigger, and all of a sudden this incredible choral music—I could hear it coming through the bush. And so I walked toward it and it was a… .it was the little one-room school and the kids were singing. And I just sat down and there were windows but no glass in them, and I just leaned against the wall of the building and listened for half an hour. And I mean, I don't know what it is about Africa, but it is born in their bones this ability to sing and to harmonize, and it was just utterly magnificent. So here I am in the wilderness, the total wilderness, listening to some of the loveliest choral music I've ever heard.

AM Your relationship with the continent of Africa has been very important to you. What is it about Africa that sort of soaked into your imagination?

FP Well, the part of Africa where I spend the most time is the southwestern coast, which borders on the Atlantic, and it's an area that's very dry, a northern part of South Africa, all of Namibia even up into Angola. Namibia for example is desert, of one sort or another—great vast rocky canyons, dunes up to 450 metres. I mean, that's phenomenal. And then great stretches of undulating plain just lying flat with big rocks a metre across—I mean like fieldstone with springs of grass coming up through them. But especially in the dune country, I have this feeling… You see, here in Alberta and in fact in virtually all of Canada and much of the world, the basic bones of the earth as it were, have a quilt over them of vegetation which protects them. But there that quilt doesn't exist and you see that structure, you see almost the cheekbones and, you know, the chin bone And I just have this feeling of just seeing it the way it is underneath. And I guess the only comparable experience I've had at all is in certain parts of the very high arctic in Canada. Why I like it, why I respond to it, I don't know. It's at a very deeply emotional level.

AM   A lot of the work that you have done there has focused on Namaqualand? What took you there in the first place?

FP   Wildflowers. [laughing] I love wildflowers and I had heard about this place, but everyone who told me about it had never been there. And so when I was in Africa, I don't know if it was my fourth visit, it was 1980; anyway, I was determined to go.

AM   Sort of the Holy Grail of wildflowers.

FP   It is. It's that place in the world which has <u>the</u> most spectacular annual display of spring wildflowers. A place with the second most, well equally spectacular but not so many species, is western Australia, which I got to this year. And it was the best year they'd had in living memory so I was really lucky. Anyway, I was a little late. Spring comes there in late July, August, or early September, and August is the big month. And I didn't get there 'til the middle of September. Anyway, I loved what I saw but I knew I was late. And then that one night, this one particular night, I stumbled into this little nine-room hotel in this little remote village, and got the only room that was available. And the woman who managed the hotel—owned and managed it—for the only time, the very first time in her life, had decided to put on a slide show in the dining room after dinner because there were six or seven people there from Capetown who'd come up to see flowers, and for some reason they had to turn around and go back. I think one of them had become ill. So she didn't want them to be disappointed. So anyway, I look at these slides, they were utterly God awful—there's no other way of describing them—but the subject matter blew my mind. And I just said, oh, I cannot believe that such beauty exists. So afterward I spoke to her. I didn't tell her that I was a photographer, I just gave her one of my books. And I didn't tell her I'd written it, because I knew what some of her problems were and I knew the book would help her. So anyway, she went to bed and the next morning I was eating breakfast and she came storming in and her Afrikaans, which is her first language and she was hardly speaking any English the night before. Well, she was now speaking fluent English and she said, you're a professional photographer and you sat through my slide show last night and I am moritified.

FP   And I said, now look, just hold on, no harm's been done. But look, she said, can you stay a couple more days? And I said, yeah, I can stay two more days. And she said, I'm just gonna' cancel everything. And she was teaching English actually in the local school and she was supervising the building of a couple of apartments for senior citizens in the village, and she managed, if you can believe it, a home for 150 neglected black kids. So she got everything in place and she said, well the best flowers left this year are up on the mountain. So up we tore in the mountain, and she raced me around all over the place and I was just beside myself. And so the next day I said, Carla, I just want two places, one for the morning and one for the afternoon. And I photographed those and so then we promised, you know how you do, we'll write, etc. And the following year I was sitting at home minding my p's and q's one day and there was a telegram came, in the days when you still got telegrams, and the message was: Flowers excellent. Come at once. Carla Swatt. Well, it took me nine days to get there. But they were. It was just a fabulous year and, ah, I've gone back every year since. I don't always go in the flower season any more because it's like the colour of the autumn in eastern Canada you know, with all the reds and the oranges and everything. I mean, you go expecting leaves and this mass of colour, but the country's beautiful even when they're not there. So I've learned not always to go at the same time.

AM   And completely different to the other landscape that you're obviously attached to, you've moved back to the area you were born and raised in.

FP   Yeah, I love water, too.

AM   What drew you back?

FP   Well, what draws anyone back? There's a sense of rootedness and it's very hard to give up those things. And we do them, I think it's safe to say… I mean, we all can't go back to where we came from as it were, but we can never leave it completely either. It's always in us. And I think if one has the opportunity as I have had, to go back after having been away for 17 years, I go back on my terms and I participate in this now not as a child or as a young person, but as an adult. So that things have changed in me and I guess it helps me to appreciate a lot of things there more. For example, my right arm, my very, very dear friend and right arm, advisor, consultant, office manager and everything, Linda Titus, whom I've worked with for 14 years, died of cancer about six days ago. And we had discussed the possibility of this—I don't mean with her, but with her sister—of my being away. I saw her just the night before I left and she really couldn't walk any more at that point, and here is a woman who was utterly unafraid of dying, but who was terrified of not living because she had so much to live for—a husband that she loved profoundly, and he her. You know, grandkids that she's not going to see in school, let alone graduate, let alone get married. And yet, she had a support system in that community that was phenomenal, and the day she died I called a neighbour of mine and he said, this community is having a hard time today. That's a shared experience. And those experiences are very difficult to come by in large urban areas. And that's something I think we lose; it's a great loss to us as human beings. And her sister, who is my new secretary, very like Lin in many ways, she and her three daughters (the oldest is in high school) just moved in. She was Linda's principal caregiver, and those three girls saw their mother look after their aunt and support her and cheer her up and keep her going, and the two of them fought together, I mean for life. And those girls will be deeply shaped by what they've seen in these last few months, what they've experienced.

AM   Let's have another piece of music. What would you like to hear, Freeman?

FP   Well, speaking of Linda I think maybe one of Albinoni's *Adagios* would be quite, quite fitting.
[MUSIC]

AM   Another important part of the work that you're doing in Africa are those abandoned desert mining towns on the southern coast of Namibia. Those houses of sand are just absolutely amazing. Can you describe the towns. What do you see when you walk up to these places?

FP   Well, first of all I should say that the reason they exist is that they were built by diamond mining interests, German interests, about 1910, in the desert where there were diamonds. They were occupied for approximately… well up to about 1940, when the technology for extracting diamonds from the desert changed and it was more economical to move people out and just send the workers in, rather than keep their families and so on in there. Because getting water in was a heck of a problem. So they said, you're leaving, you can take whatever you want, you can leave behind whatever you want, and then once they moved them they sealed it, because there were still diamonds in there. And with the exception of one town the other three have been off limits ever since. So to get permission to go in is to go where very few people have been during the last 50 years. And so here are these towns, quite beautiful homes in many cases—clubs, hospital, quite ornate, often in German styles (you know, the managers' homes at any rate)—but they've been blasted by the hot desert air which is just driving the sand against them, and by the salty mists of the Atlantic, often coming in on very strong winds as well, so that window panes have been broken and doors have blown open and the sand has just moved through the buildings. The dunes will literally go… a dune will go in one door and snake through a whole series of rooms and out another. And then because in many cases roofs are partly off, but maybe the lath structure is there, you get this alternating black white black white black white, and that pattern moves across these dunes inside the buildings and because the sun is moving they're moving all the time—they're changing. And so you can't just sort of polk your head in the building and take a picture and think you've got it. I mean you could be there all day, and in one building on two occasions I've spent literally six hours in this one building without leaving it, because the light was just changing the patterns constantly. I found it a very deeply emotional experience because there are no footprints. The one town that the public is allowed into, people go traipse traipse traipse traipse through, and they leave footprints right away and they destroy the beauty of the dunes, which they don't see, and in so doing they destroy the sense of time as well. Time passing. And then 15 or 20 or 45 minutes later they're gone. Fortunately, they just go to certain buildings which seem to be the ones they should see. Meanwhile there's two-thirds of the town they don't bother to visit, which is where I spend my time in that town.

AM   How did you hear about these places?

FP   Well, from the contacts I made over there. And the reason I got into these three that are off limits is that the manager for *De Beers*, for one of these regions, is also a photographer and took a workshop from me over there. But you know what's so beautiful about those towns for me is that there's no restoration. And in that sense, I think part of what we do when we restore things, what we're doing of course is restoring human history and we're not letting ourselves go back to the dirt that we all came from. We don't want to face that almost. And there it's happening; nature is completely taking over these samples of European culture that were stitched on the African desert. The going down is beautiful, the aging is beautiful. It's so natural. I can imagine what I haven't seen. I can imagine when they were new. So now as these towns go down, for me they're at the zenith of their symbolic power.

AM   Another recurrent image in your work, an area that you're interested in photographing—and you're wearing the *Harley Davidson* sweatshirt right now is motorcycles. How does that jive with your interest in the natural world Freeman?

FP   I should start off by saying it's kind of an escape machine for me. The place I live is beautiful, I'm surrounded by nature and so on. It's also my place of business. So the phone rings and there's computers and there's email and there's this, that and the other thing. So there are times when, certainly during the last few years, I've just needed a quick escape. So I'll hop on the bike, ride maybe just 25 kilometres up to a farmer's market and buy a great big bag of grapes to take home with me, and then order a frozen yogurt and just relax and bliss out for a few minutes and go home again. And I feel so much clearer, because there's something about riding a motorcycle—I call it relaxed attentiveness. You know, you obviously have to pay attention, you must always be paying attention; but at the same time you relax into the ride once you've got the craft down.

From a natural standpoint I think motorcycles are essential, I mean at least the ones that stay on the roads are ecologically neutral because, I mean, I use half the gas that I would in my truck, I use almost no parking space even with a good-sized motorcycle like a Harley; I don't feel—maybe I'm wrong, maybe I'm fooling myself—but I don't feel like I've violated my basic principles.

AM   Let's have another piece of music. What would you like to hear?

FP   Well, a couple of years I was doing workshops in Israel, and one of the things that I like to do is to say to people, look, the best place to photograph is wherever you are. If you're in Israel, Canada looks exotic; if you're in Canada, Israel looks exotic, or something like that. Just photograph where you are. And so I stood outside the classroom every morning (in an area about 10 metres) and from where we were on the Dead Sea, sort of halfway up a mountainside, we looked down on the Dead Sea across at the mountains of Jordan. And I made a lot of good photographs from there with the students, especially with the coming of the light in the morning and these great lines of light in the blackness of the Dead Sea, and then they'd become gold and they'd become silver and then finally you'd get bursts of light emanating through clouds. It was wonderful. And I made up an audio-visual for that, and that music that I chose to go with it was music from *Officium* with the *Hilliard Street Ensemble.* [MUSIC]

AM   Well, it's about time to send you off to your mythical mountain top now, but we'll let you take one book with you. Now, if you were to be cast away and could only take one book, what would you take?

FP   I'd take Carl Jung's *Man and His Symbols.*

AM   Why that?

FP   Because as many times as I've read it, and I have read it many times, I do not think that one can ever have too much encouragement in getting the conscious part of our lives in touch with the unconscious part of our lives. I mean, I think every human being is like an iceberg, you know. A tenth of us is above water and nine-tenths, which is a very important part of the iceberg, is below water. It's the unconscious. And many of the messages that come to us through our unconscious come in the form of dreams, which again our culture has dismissed as being, oh, it's only a dream. Well, it's not only a dream. Every dream comes, I think you can say safely, in support of healing and creativity. And all dreams have meaning, some much more significant than others. So I have a lot of good books now on dreams; I don't mean these dream dictionaries you buy… you know, these quickie things you know. One that I've read recently two or three times, is *Where People Fly and Water Runs Uphill* which is by Jeremy Taylor, who's a leading Jungian psychotherapist and dream analyst and a person who lectures a great deal on the nature of creativity. And that's one thing I might come back to is, we refer to ourselves as creatures. Creature, creativity, creation: those words, they are linked, and ah, for me, one of the most important things is, whatever a person believes about the nature of God or doesn't believe, we still are part of a creation, a universe which is vast beyond our comprehension and understanding. Powerful beyond… And yet, here we are functioning with a degree of awareness of that. For me, the way to say yes to whatever created me, or to the creation, is to be creative, to honour

and to delve into those parts of myself which will help me be more creative than I have been. So that's why Jung and dreams and things have become so significant a part of what I'm reading.

AM   And if you were to pick one place in the world, if you could just be one place for the rest of your days, where would you go?

FP   Well, that's very difficult. I mean, it's very tempting to say right where I am now. And I would be perfectly satisfied with that answer. But I'm willing to limit it even more than that and say that about two minutes from my house there's a cedar glen, a small cedar glen, and the cedars are big and there are no lower branches so you can walk easily, and there's this wonderful mat of brown twigs. And in the centre of this glen is a rock, which is very nice to sit and lean against or sit on. If you're speaking about my very last day or two, I'd be quite happy just to be taken to that glen. In fact, one of the things that I want to do—I've been in overdrive from a professional sense for the last three years (I'm going to be taking a year off)—but one of the things I'm most looking forward to is going down early in the morning with a couple of bottles of water and some fruit, with no camera, and just spending the whole day until it gets dark sitting in that glen, and feeling it and listening to it and getting in touch with it again, because I feel that while what I've had to do I suppose professionally, obviously it's important, I'm beginning to realize now that I'm losing… I've been pulled away from these experiences. So, where do I want to spend my final days? I guess at home.

AM   And for a final choice of music?

FP   Healy Willan has at least three CDs out, and the one I think that's my favourite is *Apostrophe to the Heavenly Hosts*. I didn't deliberately save this 'til the last, but since we're talking about my last days, and I think just about anything on that I love. And that's a disc that I often put on late at night and I'll let it run through for however long it goes, 76 minutes, by which time I'll make some more tea and play it again.

AM   Freeman, thank you so much for coming in.

FP   It's been a pleasure. Thank you.

Michael O'Halloran has been a CBC Radio producer for 18 years. He has produced *The Homestretch, Saturday Side Up, Sunday Arts* and was a producer on the network show *Prime Time*. He also produced the nationally syndicated program *That's a Good Question ?*. He created *Mountaintop Music* in 1991 and produced it for 9 years. He currently is the producer of *The Calgary Eyeopener*.